MEDIA ANALYSIS
UNDERSTANDING AND APPLYING MEDIA THEORY
Year 12 ATAR MEDIA
Australian Tertiary Admission Rank

Lisa Merante

Media and English Publishing
mediaandenglishliteracy.com

COPYRIGHT

© Lisa Merante 2024

All rights reserved.

No part of this publication may be reproduced, stored in a retrieval system, or transmitted in any form or by any means, electronic, mechanical, photocopying, recording or other means, now known or hereafter invented without the prior permission of the author and publisher.

Trademark notice: the use of product or corporate names has been done so for identification purposes only, with no intent to infringe.

Every effort has been made to acknowledge and attribute authorship of copyrighted material. Should any errors have occurred the publisher would welcome information to assist in ensuring accuracy with information in any future editions.

Photocopying beyond that set out by fair dealing requires written permission from the publisher.
info@mediaandenglishliteracy.com

Publisher: Media and English Literacy Publishing

For secondary senior school age.
Mass Media—textbooks.

Disclaimer:
QR Codes and URLs were accurate at the time of publishing. Neither the author nor publisher is responsible for URLS changing or expiring.

ISBN: 978-0-6453498-4-9
(paperback)

First Edition 2024

Lisa Merante is a Media teacher with more than 30 years of experience in her field. Her commitment to Media Studies has seen her involved in exam writing for the Australian Teachers of Media Western Australia (ATOMWA) and exam marking for School Curriculum and Standards Authority (SCSA). She has taught in Australia and internationally. *Media Analysis: Understanding and Applying Media Theory Year 12* is her fourth book. She lives in Perth, Western Australia, and has decided not to include a relatable anecdote about her dog because she doesn't have one, and no one reads the author bio anyway.

Thank you
ACKNOWLEDGEMENTS

Thank you to my students who motivated me to write, and write, and write, and eventually complete this book. I am just as surprised as you are: many years of dawdling, delaying, dillying and dallying, and finally it is done. You're welcome.

Table of Contents

Chapter One — 10
Film History
- The Beginning 11
- Patents War 12
- The Lumière Brothers 13
- First Feature Length Film 14
- The Coming of Sound 15
- Technicolor 16
- Arrival of Television 17
- Social Media Impact 18
- Streaming Services 18
- The Arrival of Artificial Intelligence 19
- Film Trends 22
- Review and Sample Questions 23

Chapter Two — 24
Auteur theory
- Auteur Theory 25
- Francois Truffaut 25
- Andre Bazin 26
- Andrew Sarris 27
- Pauline Kael 29
- Auteur Theory Pros and Cons 30
- Auteur Theory: Where To Now? 31
- Personal Expression 32
- Auteur: a curated selection 33
- Auteur: a signature style 35
- Signature Style: Tom Tykwer 36
- Review and Sample Questions 38

Chapter Three — 40
Film Movements
- Film Movement Timeline 41
- Film Movements 42
- Surrealism 44
- French Impressionism 45
- Classical Hollywood 46
- German Expressionism 47
- Soviet Montage 48
- Film Noir 49
- Italian Neo-Realism 50
- Bollywood 51
- French New Wave 52
- British New Wave 53
- Japanese New Wave 54
- Hong Kong New Wave 55
- New Hollywood 56
- Australian New Wave 57
- New Mexican Cinema 58
- Dogme '95 59
- Art Films 60
- Review and Sample Questions 63

Chapter Four — 64
Film Aesthetics
- Film Aesthetics 65
- What is Film Art? 66
- Art Film Techniques 68
- Film Aesthetics in *Run Lola Run* 70
- Innovative Visual Aesthetic 70
- Case Study: *Run Lola Run* 70
- Innovative Aural Aesthetic: *Run Lola Run* 76
- Film Aesthetics: Narrative *Run Lola Run* 78
- Manipulation of Narrative Structure 78
- Video Game Aesthetic: *Run Lola Run* 86
- Review and Sample Questions 91

Chapter Five — 92
How Narrative Functions in a Text
- Narrative Defined 93
- Narrative Elements: *Everything, Everywhere All at Once* ... 94
- Narrative: Story Elements 96
- Genre 97
- Point of View 98
- Theme 100
- Montage 101
- Propp's Theory 102
- Applied to *Harry Potter and the Philosopher's Stone* ... 103
- Hero's Journey 104
- Applied to *The Lego Movie* 105
- Todorov's Theory 106
- Applied to *Run Lola Run* 107
- Binary Oppositions 108
- Applied to *Run Lola Run* 109
- Syd Field Paradigm 110
- Applied to *Everything, Everywhere, All at Once* 111
- Review and Sample Questions 113

Chapter Six — 114
Codes, Conventions & Techniques
- Codes & Conventions 115
- Symbolic Codes: Applied to *Memento* 116
- Written Codes: Applied to *Monsters, Inc.* 118
- Audio Codes: Applied to *Boy* 120
- Technical Codes: Applied to *Three Billboards Outside* ..122
- Conventions 126
- Conventions: Applied to Horror Genre 128
- Conventional use of Codes in Horror Genres 129
- Manipulation of Time 130
- Manipulation of Space 131
- Selection and Omission 132
- Review and Sample Questions 135

Chapter Seven — 136
How Context Affects Content
- Context Defined 137
- Context Shapes Content 138
- Context Analysis: *Run Lola Run* 140
- Context Analysis: *The Bicycle Thieves* 144
- Context Analysis: *The True Cost* 146
- Review and Sample Questions 154

Chapter Eight — 156
Stereotypes & Representations
- Representations Defined 157
- Stuart Hall: Representation Theory 158
- Dominant, Emerging, Oppositional 159
- Representation Analysis: *Run Lola Run* 162
- David Gauntlett: Representation 168
- Media as a Tool to Challenge Stereotypes 173
- Timeline: Women's Rights 174
- Problems with Stereotyping 180
- Review and Sample Questions 181

Chapter Nine — 182
Values, Attitudes & Ideologies
- Values, Attitudes & Ideologies Defined 183
- Key Terms 184
- Dominant, Emerging, Oppositional: Values 185
- Ideologies 186
- Dominant, Emerging, Oppositional: Ideologies 187
- How a Text Disseminates Values & Ideologies 188
  - Applied to Short Film: *Hair Love* 189
  - Applied to *The Bicycle Thieves* 193
- Review and Sample Questions 194

Chapter Ten — 196
Audience and Communication Theories
- Audience Defined 197
- Audience Demographics 198
- Audience Reception vs. Production 200
- Communication Theories 201
- Hypodermic Needle Theory 202
- Reinforcement Theory 203
- Diffusion of Innovation 203
- Agenda Setting Theory 204
- Uses and Gratifications Theory 204
- Spiral of Silence 205
- Semiotic Theory 205
- Cultivation Theory 206
- Reception Theory 206
- Fandom Theory 207
- End of Audience 207
- Uses and Gratifications: Applied to *The True Cost* ..208
- Agenda Setting Theory: Applied to *The True Cost* ..212
- Reception Theory: Applied to *The True Cost* 217
- Review and Sample Questions 221

Chapter Eleven — 222
Documentary Techniques
- Documentary Defined 223
- Documentary Techniques 224
- Documentary Conventions 226
- Persuasive Techniques 227
- The Documentary Dilemma 229
- The Documentary's Claim to Truth 230
- Bill Nichols: Poetic Mode 232
- Bill Nichols: Expository Mode 233
- Bill Nichols: Observational Mode 234
- Bill Nichols: Participatory Mode 235
- Bill Nichols: Reflexive Mode 236
- Bill Nichols: Performative Mode 237
- Documentary Analysis: *The True Cost* 238
- Suggested Documentary Films 248
- Review and Sample Questions 250

Chapter Twelve — 252
Propaganda
- Propaganda Defined 253
- Where can Propaganda be Found? 254
- How does Propaganda Work? 255
- Propaganda Techniques Used to Persuade 256
- Agenda Setting & Propaganda 258
- Propaganda and Trump 266
- Propaganda, Trump and Agenda Setting 266
- How Trump used Propaganda 270
- Propaganda: Trend of Social Media Use 274
- Propaganda: Germany vs. America 276
- Triumph of the Will: Propaganda Techniques 278
- Review and Sample Questions 282
- Index 284
- Media works 287

The Year 12 textbook builds on the foundation established in the Year 11 textbook. For instance, the Year 11 textbook provides detailed content on communication theories, whereas this book succinctly summarises them. Some narrative theories are covered in the previous book, while others are addressed here. For a comprehensive understanding, it is advisable to use both books together.

The following **four books** work in conjunction with one another to assist in building critical thinking skills by introducing essential concepts, theories, and frameworks for examining media texts. Media Production and Analysis, English, and Drama students could all benefit from the content and deconstruction techniques provided to scaffold the analysis of a text.

1. Media Analysis: Understanding and Applying Media Theory Year 11
2. Media Analysis: Understanding and Applying Media Theory Year 12
3. Media Production Journal
4. Media Analysis Study Compendium

mediaandenglishliteracy.com

Things you should know about this book ...

Focus on key theories **applicable to texts you have studied** in class, including:
- selected communication theories
- a few narrative theories
- auteur theory
- representation theory
- genre theory

Ensure all theories apply to your chosen texts and can effectively support potential assessment questions.

Some texts are analysed more than once. Textual examples from the same film will appear several times across the book. This is done intentionally to showcase how a text can be used as evidence to support numerous essential content items.

Texts analysed

- Hair Love (2019).
- Harry Potter and the Philosopher's Stone (2001).
- The Bicycle Thieves (1948).
- Monsters Inc. (2001).
- Everything Everywhere All at Once (2022).
- The Lego Movie (2014).
- Three Billboards Outside Ebbing, Missouri (2022).
- The True Cost (2015).
- Memento (2000).
- Triumph of the Will (1935).
- Epilog (1992).
- Run Lola Run (1998).
- Boy (2010).
- Selected tweets from Donald Trump.

... it encourages critical media literacy.

Chapter One
Film History

- Persistence of vision
- Celluloid film
- The kinetoscope
- Kinetograph
- Patents war
- The Lumière brothers
- First feature length film
- D.W. Griffith
- Coming of sound
- Technicolor
- Arrival of television
- Analogue to digital
- Social media impact
- Streaming services
- Artificial intelligence
- Film trends
- Sample questions
- Review

Film History & Film Art

Film History

1. Persistence of Vision

1872 Eadweard Muybridge, settling a bet for Governor Stanford, experimented with the concept of persistence of vision by placing twelve cameras attached to trip wires to capture a running horse to determine if all four hooves were off the ground at one time during its trot. The resultant still images, when viewed together like a flip book, showed that a horse does lift all four feet during its gait.

Why is this important? **Persistence of vision** is the phenomenon stating that the brain retains an image momentarily after it is seen, and if still images are seen in quick succession the result is the appearance of continuous movement. Muybridge's experiment, showing a sequence of a horse's running movement, laid the foundation for moving pictures.

The initial application of this type of 'moving image' came in the form of novelty devices such as Muybridge's zoopraxiscope and William Horner's earlier zoetrope. These pre-film devices used a spinning disc containing sequential still images, and when spun fast enough the still images appeared to move. The concept of twenty four still frames per second is used today to create the illusion of fluid movement.

2. Celluloid Film

Flexible celluloid film replaced glass plates and allowed for lengthier stories to be told. Glass plates, which were mounted to a spinning disc such as a zoetrope, were limited to showing a small sequence of movement.

1884 George Eastman invented film on a roll rather than on slides. This photographic film was flexible and durable. One year later Eastman refined his invention with the advent of transparent celluloid roll film.

Many people experimented with celluloid film in its embryonic stage. These pioneers include Louis Le Prince, Etienne-Jules Marey and Friese Greene, who all experimented with different camera and film configurations. However, it was George Eastman's company that perfected **transparent, flexible film** creating a cornerstone for the development of cinematography.

3. The Kinetoscope

1891 Credited to Thomas Edison and William Dickson this large device was the precursor to the modern film projector. Just shorter than an average adult, this large box allowed for one person to peer through an opening at the top to view a short film.

The kinetoscope, or early film projector, although only allowing for one person to view the film at a time, set the technological groundwork for the modern projector. It used a strip of film that continuously moved between a light bulb and a magnifying lens. The rapid continuous motion created the **illusion of movement.**

FILM HISTORY
in brief

The **kinetograph** was a motor driven camera that captured movement using 35mm film with **sprocket holes** that grabbed and advanced the film at regular intervals. This **perforated film system** was devised by William Dickson and was to prove crucial in how the film industry landscape developed.

4. Kinetograph

1897 Thomas Edison patents the kinetograph, the earliest known movie camera which he, along with Dickson, had developed in the early 1890s.

William Dickson worked as a laboratory assistant for Thomas Edison. His contribution to cinematography was significant. He is credited with the innovations of the **kinetoscope** and the **kinetograph**. Dickson left Edison's employment in 1895 and set up on his own, founding **Biograph.** To avoid conflict with Edison he developed a 70mm wide film camera that took on the Biograph name. In 1896 Edison, along with three partners formed the first **motion picture movie studio** where they produced and distributed films. In 1898 Edison sued **Biograph pictures.** His lawsuit claimed that Dickson had infringed the patent for the kinetograph. The U.S. Court of Appeals ruled that **Edison owned the rights to the perforated film sprocket system** but not the rights to the movie camera concept.

5. Patents War

1897-1917 Edison secured the patent for sprocket holes in film; specifically how it was clawed through the camera. Anyone wanting to use film with sprocket holes had to pay. Edison held over a thousand patents for numerous inventions, notably the phonograph, the incandescent light bulb, the kinetograph and the kinetoscope. Due to his strong-hold over the technology needed to make, and exhibit films he was able to bring together other patent holders such as Vitagraph, Eastman Kodak, Pathé (to name a few) and eventually Biograph to form a consortium known as the **Motion Picture Patent Company**. This group created a strong-hold **monopoly over production, exhibition, and distribution of film**. Any smaller independent companies wanting to work in the industry had to be prepared to pay for the right to do so, or face serious legal

Film production at this point was mostly on the **east** coast of America. Independent filmmakers, those who were not a part of the MPPC, were furious at having to pay Edison and his cronies in the **Motion Picture Patents Company** to make films that were controlled in terms of length, content, and equipment used. To escape prosecution for working outside of the strict guidelines many independent film companies headed **west** to Los Angeles, where low taxation rates, warm weather and judges who were less enthralled with Edison's hold over the film industry, were appealing. One of these independent filmmakers was Carl Laemmle, who by 1915 opened Universal Studios. By the end of this year the MPPC found itself in court fighting charges of **illegal restraint of trade** due to its **monopoly** stranglehold on the industry. The court found against the MPPC, and Edison and his consortium dissolved the company by 1917. This set the stage for the emergence of the **Hollywood studio system.**

FILM HISTORY

in brief

6. The Lumière Brothers

1895 Meanwhile in France, Claude-Antoine **Lumière**, father to Louis and Auguste, described Dickson and Edison's **Kinetoscope** to his sons, explaining what he had viewed whilst on a trip to Paris. The main problem with it, that he saw, was that only one person at a time could view a short film, and the device was cumbersome. The brothers experimented with the problems surrounding the kinetoscope, specifically its bulky size, the jerky action of grabbing and advancing the film, and their desire to have many people view the film at once rather than being limited to one person at a time. By 1895 they had developed the **cinématographe**, an apparatus that could record, develop, and project images. The jerky film action was solved when the **Lumière brothers** noticed that a sewing machine worked using intermittent movement; they adapted the technology to make use of the grab and pull process that left a frame stationary for only the briefest of moments, thus creating a fluid movement. The cinématographe was revolutionary in that it was quieter, lighter, and afforded a shared viewing experience. The significantly reduced weight of approximately nine kilograms, in comparison to the nearly five hundred kilogram kinetograph meant that short film content moved away from events staged in front of an immobile camera to location filming. The content was, at this stage, still filmed as one continuous long shot.

On December 28th, 1895, the Lumière brothers showed "La Sortie des ouvriers de l'usine Lumière" (Workers Leaving the Lumière Factory) in a cafe in Paris, becoming **the world's first publicly screened short film.** The brothers used the cinématographe to capture short moments in time, approximately forty five seconds to a minute in length, known as **actualities.** One of the most famous of these "L'Arrivée d'un train en gare de La Ciotat" (The Arrival of a Train at La Ciotat Station), shown in 1896, depicts a train speeding towards the screen. The realism had audiences believing that the train would lurch out of the screen, and head straight for them. Folklore tells of audiences screaming and ducking, as if on a roller coaster ride to avoid the train.

The success of these short films saw the **Lumière brothers** dispatch projectionists to all corners of the globe showing more than forty of their films, which not only **preserved history**, but opened new worlds to many who had never travelled far from their homes.

At this point in history **film is seen as a novelty**, something fun, a mere entertaining diversion.

Film History

7. First Feature Length Film

1906 The first feature length film was shot in **Melbourne, Australia. Charles Tait** directed **The Story of the Kelly Gang** which ran for over an hour, used about thirty actors, and took approximately six months to produce; a significant feat for the time.

The screening of the film was done by the Biograph company. The cinematography used only one camera with its perspective staying at a wide shot for all but two brief shots for the entirety of the film. Most of the film has been lost, thought to have decomposed, with only seventeen minutes of the original having been preserved and digitised.

Early films were short in duration, lasting approximately ten minutes. Their content often depicted a snapshot in time rather than a complete narrative. In 1903, *The Great Train Robbery*, a short ten minute film did use the **conventional story arc** of beginning, middle, and end, to great audience reception. The idea of a complete narrative appealed to the Tait brothers, who lived in Australia, worked in show business, and had begun to include films into their program at the Melbourne Athenaeum play theatre. They had seen *The Great Train Robbery* and decided to make a film drawing inspiration from its **narrative structure**. Their film's content capitalised on the popularity of Ned Kelly and his gang of outlaws. It was as controversial as it was sympathetic to the bushrangers, and some towns attempted to ban its screening. Charles Tait, the older of the Tait brothers, is credited with directing the world's first feature length narrative film *The Story of the Kelly Gang*.

8. D.W. Griffith

1908 -1916 Griffith's prolific period of film production begins in 1908 where he worked for the **Biograph company** as a film director. Before turning his hand to directing films D.W Griffith acted for both Thomas Edison's Movie company and Dickson's Biograph company. He is however, best known for his **innovation in filming techniques**, in particular his use of:
- close ups
- cross cutting
- using the shot rather than entire scenes
- revolutionising the practice of editing by cutting using rhythm and tempo
- using different angles, perspectives, and shot sizes
  - continuity of visual information
  - eyeline match
  - and shot composition.

Between 1908 and 1913, whilst working for Biograph, Griffith made over four hundred short twelve minute films. It was these films that gave Griffith the time and space to experiment with **embryonic film language.**

Griffith is known as the **father of film language.** His first feature length film *Birth of a Nation* was made in 1915 whilst working for Mutual films. Although producing a canon of film techniques, the film is condemned for its racist content. D.W Griffith's legacy is instrumental in laying the **foundation for film grammar** as we know it today. It was through his experimental techniques that David Wark Griffith is seen as a major contributor to filming techniques used by all filmmakers today.

Film History

Introduction of sound

9. The Coming of Sound

1927 Films were **never 'silent'** they were accompanied by a **live orchestra** who played the appropriate mood music. Some films had people making **sound effects** or a person **narrating** the action behind the screen. According to the National Film and Sound Archive of Australia Charles Tait's *The Story of the Kelly Gang* was enhanced by sounds coming from behind the screen, including dynamic elements to **create realism** such as gun shots and hoof beats. The experimentation with **synchronising sound** with film occurred over many years. In the late 1890s Thomas Edison and William Dickson had attempted to achieve this goal but could not get the synchronisation correct and so they abandoned their attempts, instead focusing on images.

The Jazz Singer, 1927, directed by Alan Crosland, although not the first film to have sound, is the first feature length film, running for eighty eight minutes to contain **synchronised recorded music**. Al Jolson sings numerous songs and lip synchs speech, notably Jolson's ad-libbed "Wait a minute! Wait a minute! You ain't heard nothin' yet!" The **dialogue** only lasted for a few minutes of the entire film with most of the narrative still using **title cards.**

The technology used to achieve this was **Vitaphone**, a sound on disk system developed by Western Electric and Bell Telephone laboratory. It was purchased by the **Warner Brothers** to save their failing studio. Audiences were delighted with the Vitaphone musical sequences and Al Jolson's ad-libbed dialogue, so much so that people were turned away from screenings, thus saving the Warner Brothers from financial ruin. The Vitagraph system was flawed, it used **sound on disc** that had to be manually synchronised to the film, therefore human error could occur when trying to project the image on one device in concert with the sound on a second device. **Synchronisation** was always an issue, which is why Vitaphone technology was short lived, replaced by **optical sound** on film by 1931. Optical sound technology stored the information directly onto the transparent film thereby eradicating synchronisation issues. Optical sound remained the norm for many years until the advent of digital sound in the 90s including Dolby surround sound and Dolby Atmos.

How sound transformed the industry:
- 'Silent' films could attract an international audience as language was not a barrier, with the **coming of sound** this was no longer the case.
- Actors now had to learn lines and consider their **accent and intonation** rather than just body language.
- **Scriptwriters** were needed to create realistic dialogue (among them were writers such as Aldous Huxley and William Faulkner).
- **Heavy** omni directional sound **equipment limited** the movement of the actors and therefore **constrained the plot.**
- Cameras were **bulky and mechanical**, their noise being an issue for the fledgling sound industry.
- **Cost and availability** of sound equipment meant the industry had a slow uptake with converting to talkies.
- Small **independent filmmakers** struggled with the cost associated with talking pictures, and many fell by the wayside.
- Cinema theatres needed to be **equipped** to play the new films with sound.
- 'Silent' cinema musicians whose job it was to sit in the pits and play the score for the film **lost their jobs.**
- Jobs such as the **inter-title card writer** became redundant.

FILM HISTORY
in brief

10. Technicolor

1930s As with the transition from 'silent' to talking films, the transition from black and white to colour film took time due to economic and technological issues. Moreover, like sound, **colour in film** has existed in various formats since its **inception** using techniques such as **hand painting, tinting, and toning.** Setting the groundwork for experimenting with colour film is a British man, Edward Turner; a decade before Technicolor he experimented with mixing red, green, and blue filters superimposed on film. Unfortunately, the result was blurry, and Turner died before he could complete his work.

Technicolor film was birthed in 1916 by Herbert Kalmus, an American scientist who used a **two colour process** that involved two pieces of thin film negative; one piece was dyed red, the second blue, these were then sandwiched together to create a final film roll. The issue was the solvent used to adhere the two together, it frequently failed which propelled Kalmus to move to the **dye transfer process**. This involved a large camera, that did not record in colour, instead **recording on three strips of film** simultaneously, each piece of film used **red, green, and blue filters**. Each negative was then transferred using a massive machine that pressed cyan, yellow and magenta, one at a time, onto a carrier film using a two hundred and forty feet pin-belt loop to hold it in place. The process was slow and expensive. **Technicolor held the rights** to the process and if a studio wanted to film in colour they had to **rent the required equipment**.

The first to use the three strip colour process was Walt Disney in his Silly Symphonies short film *Flowers and Trees* (1932). *Becky Sharp* (1935) is often **cited as the first feature to use colour.** The more well-known and commercially successful mainstream features of *The Wizard of Oz and Gone with the Wind* (1939) are amongst the **first to use colour to audience acclaim.**

The **tri-colour film process** remained the industry norm until the 50s when other companies such as **Eastman Kodak** stepped in with colour contained to one film strip known as a monopack rather than using Technicolor's tri-film system. The Eastman colour negative film allowed companies to use their own equipment rather than rent, as Technicolor had insisted, and this simplification and economic necessity pushed Technicolor aside. Additionally, an **antitrust suit** was filed against Technicolor in 1947 forcing it to break up its monopoly hold on the colour film industry.

The **rise of television** in the 1950s saw the film industry's pressing need to create a point of difference, making **colour films essential to attract audiences** away from the new black and white television phenomenon.

FILM HISTORY

in brief

11. Arrival of Television

1950s Although **John Logie Baird** transmitted the first mechanical television signal in 1925, affordable television did not become accessible until the 1950s, **replacing radio** as the mainstay of family entertainment. **Popular culture** entertainment such as *Leave it to Beaver* engaged the audience. Equally, the News brought a visual dose of reality into people's living rooms, shaping society by privileging certain content over others. For instance, male dominated sports signalled their perceived importance, and advertisements representing women attending to domestic chores whilst their husbands relaxed, assisted to **mould gender expectations.**

Although the technology to transmit **colour television** had existed since the mid 1940s the reduction in cost only made it commercially viable by the 1970s. Prior to this black and white television was the norm, with people attending the cinema to see movies in colour.

Cable television has its roots in the 1940s when CATV (Cable Antenna Television) experimented with erecting cable antennas to improve the quality and reach of television reception in remote areas of America. In the 1970s America's HBO (Home Box Office) used satellite technology to create an effective, stable network that delivered **video-on-demand** content for a subscription fee. **Pay TV** was born. In Australia pay TV saw a slow uptake with Foxtel arriving in 1995. It took another twenty years before **Netflix** entered the Australian market in 2015, bringing with it original programmes such as *Stranger Things* (2016), which saw a significant uptake in demand for subscription TV. The **subscription TV market** now includes numerous players including Stan, Disney+, Amazon Prime, Kayo, Binge and many more.

12. Analogue to Digital

2013 By the end of 2013 analogue transmissions had been phased out in Australia and replaced with digital signals. **Digital TV** came with higher definition pictures and sound, as well as the ability to access more channels. The conversion to digital signals was necessitated by the need to have **more broadband width** for the copious amount of content entering the airwaves. Analogue broadcasting used significant amounts of the broadband spectrum space. The digital spectrum allows for more information to be carried using less space, thus freeing up the broadcast spectrum for essential services such as the police and fire-fighters. The remaining space gave room for emerging technologies such as social media, gaming, and subscription video on demand to flourish.

Due to the digital delivery of hundreds of programs across multiple channels audience members now have **more variety,** and a **greater quantity** of content, than ever before. **Niche audience** groups arose due to fragmentation occurring from audiences being spread across a smorgasbord of offerings that broke the audience into smaller groups. Potentially niche audiences offer advertisers **targeted marketing opportunities.** However, consideration needs to be given to audience **use and gratification** extracted from consumption of media content. The fluidity of the use or gratification gained from specific content means that audience members can move from **niche to mainstream** in order to **gratify differing needs or uses** depending on context. The introduction of the **digital broadcast spectrum** has shifted the television landscape, creating a significant change in content delivery, and audience construction.

Film History

13. Social Media Impact

2000s Cultural, technological, and social shifts have seen an unprecedented change in movies in the past decade. **Social media platforms** such as Twitter (now X), YouTube, and Meta are used as a venue for **immediate audience feedback** on content. The fact that audience members can **influence film content prior** to its release is a significant shift in the film industry landscape. Real time interactions with directors on social media channels has allowed for fans to express their satisfaction or dissatisfaction towards aspects of the filmmaking process such as casting choices. For instance, the 2019 *Hellboy* reboot was initially meant to have British actor Ed Skrein play the role of Major Ben Aimio, who is a character of Asian heritage. **Audience backlash** at the casting decision saw Skrein voluntarily step aside to be replaced with Daniel Dae Kim, an actor of South Korean heritage. **Social media has given a voice** to the previously powerless to champion inclusivity and authenticity in film character representations.

YouTube, a video sharing platform, can be used to **distribute the work of independent filmmakers**. Social media platforms have created a more democratic system that has given public access to a previously closed field. New filmmakers can **showcase their work** and garner interest via social media, using it as a stepping stone to propel their career. **Marketing campaigns** are integral to the success of a production via a fan base as social media drives interest in films, be they blockbusters or independent films.

Covid greatly impacted attendance at movie theatres, as a consequence social media channels and streaming services have **transformed the distribution and consumption** of films, allowing access to individual creatives rather than institutions.

14. Streaming Services

2000s Streaming media allows the user to watch content using the internet without having to download it. Content is **continuously streamed** onto a device for **instant consumption**.

Streaming allowed for instant access to media content and **instant gratification**. **Binge watching culture** arose from the view-on-demand nature of online easily accessible media content. For instance, Netflix's concept of binge watching arrived when the company uploaded *House of Cards* all at once, every episode could be consumed at the pace of the consumer's choosing rather than being doled out episode by episode over a period of days or weeks, thus changing the media landscape forever.

 Streaming impacted the film industry as it **altered viewing habits** and allowed filmmakers to **bypass the traditional distribution model** of showing films at a cinema, then having a television and DVD release. Instead, filmmakers could distribute their content directly to a streaming platform like Netflix. This **alternate distribution** channel allowed smaller film companies with **niche content** to reach a niche audience, thus creating a broader landscape of film content.

Streaming services work on a **different financial compensation model** to legacy television and film, hence why the Writer's Guild of America went on an extended strike in 2023. Their aim was to secure fair compensation from streaming services who reaped significant financial reward without having provided fair remuneration to the creative writers who had initially propelled the shows to fame.

Streaming has significantly impacted distribution, viewing habits, and the creative writing process.

Film History

Impact of artificial intelligence

15. The Arrival of Artificial Intelligence

2000s Artificial intelligence's arrival has created a shift in the film industry. Like any technology it has its pros and cons:

Pros:
- Can assist with **repetitive tasks** such as colour grading, or administrative work such as scheduling.
- Can come up with **ideas** about character arcs, locations, obstacles, goals, climactic story points, and resolutions that the writer had not initially entertained, thus pushing the creative boundaries.
- Can r**educe production costs** and streamline the filmmaking process.
- Potentially reduce costs associated with **copyright**. For instance, using AI to create a soundtrack rather than paying royalties or a human creative.
- Produce stunning visual effects, **compressing work flow** that would usually take months or weeks into days or hours.
- Huge amount of **creative potential** can be realised by leveraging the capabilities of AI tools.
- Allows small, independent filmmakers to access powerful tools to assist in the production process.
- AI allows for dubbed films to look realistic as mouth movements are changed to suit the language.

Cons:
- As artificial intelligence has been trained using the vast database of information found on the internet there is the significant **potential for copyright to be infringed** when AI scrapes internet data to create media assets such as film scripts, music scores, lyrics, titles and so on. In 2023 Hollywood writers in the *Writers' Guild of America* went on strike for just over five months, in part due to the impact artificial intelligence was having on their jobs. The major Hollywood studios had threatened to outsource writing to AI without recompense to the original writers whose content was used to train the AI. The fear is that AI will replace human creatives as it learns more about the nuances of genre, audience preference, emotional scriptwriting, and realistic dialogue.
- **Ethical and legal use of AI** needs to be established now, right at the embryonic stages of AI use. After five months of striking the *Writers' Guild of America* came to an agreement with the Hollywood studios. The agreement, which will last until May of 2026, allows for AI to complement, but not replace humans. When the agreement terminates we will need to look at the technological landscape to see how far AI has progressed, how much AI has benefitted or detracted from the filmmaking process, whether audiences engaged with AI infused films, and whether human creatives are valued or side-lined.
- Potential to abuse AI, particularly around **deep fakes** constructing AI versions of people to say and do things that never occurred.
- **Intellectual property ownership** - will the original human creatives be recognised for their work, benefitting financially from their content or will AI take over?
- **Job loss** - ultimately some jobs will be lost by AI automation, but will others be created in their place?

Artificial Intelligence

How is artificial intelligence reshaping the film industry?

Pre-production
- Assist with idea generation and character development.
- Scriptwriting: AI natural language algorithms can assist in generating dialogue.
- Storyboarding: AI powered storyboard generators.
- Casting: AI can be used to search databases for suitable actors or it can be used to create virtual actors.
- Assist with administration - scheduling, planning permits, location sourcing, budgeting and research.

A.I. tools
- Storyboard generator and vision board: cuebric.com
- Scriptwriting: squibler.io, scripthop.com
- Shooting schedules: celtx.com
- GPT4 - can assist to write songs, screenplays or shape writing to a given style.
- Casting: castingdroid.com
- Text to image: Sora
- Plotdot.AI

Production
- Assist with set design ideas.
- Continuity: AI used to monitor prop continuity.
- Actor performance analysis: continuity of emotional portrayal.
- Cinematography: AI powered cameras.
- Lighting: used to create complex lighting effects.

A.I. tools
- AI powered cameras: ARRI and RED
- Continuity: Filmustage
- Actor performance: Morphcast and Affectiva

- Ability to analyse significant amounts of film footage in a short time frame. AI's role in film restoration is useful because it is faster than humans and therefore could potentially save films from deteriorating in a time sensitive manner.
- Potential issues are that AI is trained in common film deterioration issues such as scratches, colour fading and dirt marks, these formulaic algorithms do not take into account the creative context and requirements surrounding the film's aesthetic. Human intervention may be necessary to ensure the integrity of the film is not compromised.

Artificial Intelligence

How A.I is re-shaping the media supply chain

POST PRODUCTION

Post-production
- Post-production: AI can assist with visual effects, voice effects, colour grading.
- Audio: create royalty free music, sound effects and voiceovers.
- AI can create visual effects, special effects, edit films, subtitle films, produce graphic designs and work on mundane tasks such as background removal.

A.I. tools
- Runway ML: video editing with AI assistance
- Adobe Firefly
- Beatoven creates royalty free music based on prompts
- Dall-E-2
- Blackmagic DaVinci Resolve
- Colour grading: Colorlab Ai, Filmora
- Audio: Cruo Mix, Roex
- VFX: Weta FX, Digital Domain
- Subtitles and translations: Unbabel, Wavel AI, Papercup
- Synthetic voice dubbing: Flawless AI, Respeecher
- AI. presenter: D-ID
- AI voiceover: Amazon Polly
- Music generation: Aiva.ai, Soundful.com, Boomy.com, Loudly.com
- Editingtools.io

DISTRIBUTION & MARKETING

Distribution & marketing
- Marketing: AI can use machine learning of best practice regarding a film's genre to create trailers and other marketing materials for films.
- Assist with distribution.
- Audience engagement: data analysis of audience preferences, behaviours, values, beliefs and tastes to tailor content allowing for precise insights.

A.I. tools
- Solutions to automate aspect ratios for distribution to different platforms e.g., Deluxe Media
- Movio, Pilotly, Cinelytic (used by Warner Bros and others to predict a film's box office receipts)
- HeyGen
- Blanc
- Adobe podcast

21

Film Trends

Film trends reflect a shifting landscape where filmmakers innovate and experiment with new technologies and film grammar, whilst leveraging issues pertinent to their era to engage their intended audience and offer unique insights. Film trends include, but are not limited to:

- **Increased commentary on societal issues:** the current trend is to focus on race, sexual orientation, gender, and diversity.
- **Embedding of AI into all facets of film production** to streamline and automate the filmmaking process. For instance, the current trend is to use AI to write and supplement script writing, character development, and idea generation.
- Concern over the **data-drive curation of content** by AI whose formula is about economic gain not about diversity in content, or stretching the boundaries in order to encourage critical thinking.
- **Issues with disinformation and deep fakes:** concern over AI use in the non-fiction realm; who is checking the accuracy of the information?
- **Erosion of trust** associated with genres historically associated with truth, accountability, and integrity, e.g., news, documentaries.
- **Virtual reality and augmented reality** allow for an immersive storytelling experience and offer new ways to engage the audience.
- Trend in showing **diversity in representation** for both cast and crew.
- Social media trend: more presence and weight given to **short films on social media platforms**.
- **Dominance of streaming platforms**: film distribution has changed forever due to Covid. The historical concept of privileging a film's release to cinema has ended, the trend of distributing to a streaming platform like Amazon Prime, or Netflix is now an audience expectation.
- **Rise of independent filmmakers**: trend to distribute straight to content hungry streaming platforms such as Amazon Prime, Netflix, YouTube and so on, has provided a more accessible platform for independent filmmakers to find an audience.

What is the relationship between technology and storytelling?

Where is creativity in this process? What are the concerns around copyright? And, more importantly, what happens to people's jobs? What happens to content selection, does it narrow, will we find ourselves in a small echo chamber, or is technology going to open up a significantly larger playing field for experimentation, manipulation, and innovation?

- Example of AI made movie: *Zone Out* (2018), made for the Sci-Fi London 48 hour Challenge by the AI program Benjamin with Ross Goodwin and Oscar Sharpe as directors. Many issues with dialogue and faces in this early AI version; however, compare this to SORA AI in 2024 that uses a text-to-video model thus highlighting the rapid advancement in technology. Many pros and cons surround the use of AI, certainly it has streamlined the filmmaking process and seen a massive growth in VFX, however, as AI is data driven, the creative and emotional side of the film experience still remains in the hands of humans.
- Issue: AI being used to determine content for humans - what safety mechanisms are in place to ensure that humans are not being feed a small echo chamber of content, so slowly we don't notice our ignorance growing.

Film History

Review & sample questions

Sample questions containing film history:

1. Analyse the impact changing technology has had on genre.
2. Discuss technology's influence on a filmmaker's personal expression.
3. Discuss how technology has shaped the process of production, distribution, and exhibition.
4. Analyse how independent films make use of changing technologies.
5. Analyse media trends in relation to technology's impact on audience expectations.

 **HISTORY - main essential content to discuss:**

01 • **Technological and theoretical groundwork** - persistence of vision, flexible celluloid film and the means to project to a large audience all needed to come together to lay the groundwork for a commercially successful film industry.

02 • **The patent war over film sprocket holes** - independent filmmakers wanting to be free of the tax imposed by Edison's sprockets, started the move west, founding Hollywood's film dream factory.

03 • **D.W. Griffith's influence on film grammar** - his contributions to filming techniques, ranging from camera movements to shot sizes, are the basis for cinematic language as we know it today.

04 • **The arrival of sound, colour, and television** - these technologies shaped the production, content, and employment prospects of film crew and changed audience engagement with the media landscape.

05 • **Streaming** altered viewing habits by creating an instant gratification, binge watching culture. **Social media** has allowed for immediate audience feedback on content, and has created a platform for independent filmmakers to distribute and exhibit their work.

06 • The impact of **artificial intelligence** on the technical and creative elements of filmmaking include pros such as reducing repetitive tasks, cutting costs, and compressing work flow; cons are concerns associated with copyright infringement and the loss of jobs for humans.

Chapter Two

Auteur theory

- François Truffaut
- Andre Bazin
- Andrew Sarris
- Pauline Kael
- Pros and cons
- Where to now
- Curated selection of auteurs
- Tom Tykwer as an auteur
- Sample questions
- Review

Auteur Theory

Francois Truffaut

 **François Truffaut**, writing for the film journal *Cahier du Cinema* in 1954, wrote an essay entitled *Une certaine tendance du cinéma Français* (A Certain Tendency of the French Cinema). The central thesis was a move away from defining the director as a person who simply stages the scene, *a metteur en scene,* basically someone with technical ability, to reclassifying the director as **an auteur, or author, someone who takes the creative lead in the creation of the film.**

In coining the term **auteur** Truffaut drew from **Alexandre Astruc's** 1948 essay, *Birth of a New Avant-Garde*. Astruc posited that the film director used the camera like a writer uses a pen. He argued that film is a form of artistic expression, and that directors use their camera like an artist paints, or a novelist uses a pen. The filmmaker, like any artist uses film to express challenging ideas. He stated that film was no longer a 'fairground amusement' but rather a serious mode of expression.

Astruc used this comparison to highlight the ability of the filmmaker to express new ideas through the lens of the camera, not to simply record what was occurring but to create new ideas. Just like traditional art forms, film is creative, thought-provoking and original. It can stimulate critical thinking by encouraging its audience to actively engage with its message. Film is capable of leaving an artistic and intellectual impact on its audience and demonstrates that it should be held in the same high regard as established art forms.

French film critics were inundated with American films following the removal of the embargo at the end of World War Two. As France had been occupied by Germany, film imports had been curtailed to minimise any form of resistance. The *Cahier du Cinema* film critics viewed Hollywood films from directors such as Hitchcock, Howard Hawks, and Nicholas Ray, en masse. The Cahier critics were aware that these films emanated from within the confines of the studio system. **Auteur status** was attributed to these directors, as despite studio restrictions, their films **displayed personal expression,** recurring motifs, and control of their craft **across a body of work.**

Andre Bazin

Auteur theory origins

 Seen as an early proponent of the **auteur theory Andre Bazin,** one of the co-founders of the *Cahier Du Cinema* and a role model to Truffaut took a slightly different stand on the concept of **authorial directorship.** Bazin responded to his young colleagues in his 1957 essay, *On the politiques des auteurs*, although agreeing with his young film critics that film should hold the same status as art, he was critical of some aspects of **auteurism.** He did not reject auteurism, rather he **questioned the lauding of established Hollywood directors as the sole source of creative meaning in the production process.** He wrote that a film was a construct of many aspects; it is made within a social and historical context that influences its content, the camera should capture the mise-en-scène, not manipulate it, and that films (especially American films) were **made within the confines of studio institutions.** The studio system, including its churning out of **genre based films**, has a creative authorship, which Bazin argued should be attributed to the studio institutions. He suggested that genre structures arise from the studio and that the director simply used these structures. Although directors manipulate and at times subvert genre conventions, Bazin pointed out that the **original creative structure arose from the institution,** and therefore credit should be given where credit is due.

Bazin argued that the **auteur theory had a halo effect** that attributed status to films simply because of the name of the director and the success of their previous works, and therefore did not allow for clear and objective analysis of these films. He felt that some films were attributed a higher status, not based on technical or artistic merit but rather on the assumed creative ability of the director's previous films. Bazin was trying to point out a **flaw in the auteur concept**, that it did, by its very nature contribute to a halo effect, and did not allow for total objective analysis of a film made by a known auteur. As Bazin points out when discussing the proponents of the director as auteur, "for, rightly or wrongly, they always see in their favourite directors the manifestation of the same specific qualities. So it is that Alfred Hitchcock, Jean Renoir, Roberto Rossellini, Fritz Lang, Howard Hawks or Nicholas Ray, to judge from the pages of Cahiers, appear as almost infallible directors who could never make a bad film" (Bazin, 1957).

 **Andrew Sarris,** an American film critic, spent time in France and was acquainted with the critics of the *Cahier du Cinema*. Sarris' seminal essay, *Notes on the Auteur Theory in 1962* **privileges the primacy of the director**, highlighting his authorial control to an American audience. This notion had been circulating in France and Europe since Truffaut's 1954 essay however Sarris **pushed the idea to the foreground with American film critics and audiences.** The intent of Sarris' essay was to highlight the value of Hollywood films as being a serious contributor to the Arts, a vehicle for critiquing and reflecting society, and not a fairground sideline to be dismissed as insignificant. Additionally, Sarris wanted to make people aware of the extent of **creative input required by a director** in order for a film to achieve success, as previously the actors, the story, and the genre were prefaced over the director.

Andrew Sarris

Andrew Sarris' essay added to the *Cahier du Cinema* film critics by making three major points about what constituted an auteur:

1. **Technical competence:** The first premise of the **auteur theory** emphasises a director's **technical skill as a key measure of quality**. A poorly directed film lacks significance in critical assessment, but discussions can focus on various elements like the subject, script, acting, colour, photography, editing, music, costumes, and set design. Sarris' argument centred around the fact that to be considered a great director, you at least had to be technically good at what you did.

2. **Personal signature:** The second premise of the **auteur theory** states that a director's **distinguishable personality** is a key measure of their artistic value. Directors must demonstrate **consistent stylistic traits across their body of work**, forming their unique signature. The look, feel and style of the film should be clearly attributable to the director.

3. **Interior meaning:** The third key aspect of the **auteur theory** focuses on the **interior meaning** derived from the interplay between a director's personality and their material, highlighting the cinema's artistic pinnacle. Sarris describes this as the soul, the expressive difference that is more than just mise-en-scène, it is the ability of the director to imbue passion, life and soul into his or her material. It is the **film's theme** or message.

Sarris later went on to write *The American Cinema: Directors and Directions, 1929-68.* He compiled categories of directors from the 'Pantheon Directors' to the 'Less Than Meets the Eye' directors. His pantheon directors included Fritz Lang, Orson Welles, Hitchcock, Buster Keaton, D.W Griffith, and John Ford to name but a few. His directors relegated to the 'less' list had amongst them Billy Wilder and John Huston. Additionally, Sarris had a 'Strained Seriousness' list onto which he placed Stanley Kubrick. In later years Sarris did revise some of his lists.

Notwithstanding, Sarris' work caused significant debate and divide within the film world. His greatest known rival was **Pauline Kael** who responded with her 1963 essay *Circles and Squares.* She critically questioned the **auteur theory** by claiming that it was overly simplistic and did not offer film critics free range to discuss originality in new works. She believed that Sarris' three components for defining an auteur were too **formulaic** and did not consider the totality of cast and crew contributions to the flavour of the film. Her **criticism of auteur theory** allowed for a counterargument to flourish and established the **recognition for the collaborative nature** and multi-talented contributions made by all on a film production.

AUTEUR THEORY
— a signature style

In rebutting Sarris' three points of what constitutes an auteur Kael argues:

1. "... the first premise of the auteur theory is the **technical competence** of a director as a criterion of value" (Sarris, 1962). To this Kael suggests that technical competence, for the most part, is based on the judgement of the audience and critic, but she points out that to stretch boundaries, to be creative and experimental it is important to step aside from the standard template of what already exists, and not allow a narrow definition of technical competence to limit the playbook of artistic expression. She argues that directors should be judged on the quality of their films, and if they can create outstanding work without relying on conventional practices, then this shows a distinctive style. She claims that a work of lesser quality can be redeemed, to a slight extent, with a show of technical competence however, craftsmanship is needed to do so.

2. "... the second premise of the auteur theory is the **distinguishable personality** of the director as a criterion of value" (Sarris, 1962). Kael struggles to contain her angst at the suggestion that a distinguishable personality can be deemed a criterion of value. Kael principally argued against the main tenet of the auteur theory which stated that an auteur has a signature trait throughout a body of work. To this she argues "Traditionally, in any art, the personalities of all those involved in a production have been a factor in judgment, but that the distinguishability of personality should in itself be a criterion of value completely confuses normal judgment. The smell of a skunk is more distinguishable than the perfume of a rose; does that make it better?" (Kael, 1963). Her argument is why should a director be congratulated for having a distinctive style, particularly when that style is simply different. She argued that directors do have a style seen across a body of work, this doesn't necessarily mark them as a good director. In fact, she proposes that the repetition of stylistic elements can become formulaic. She claims that the director has learnt how to manipulate the audience and simply delves into the same basket of tricks to repeat the performance in his next film. She suggests that when a well-known director produces a good film we focus on the movie and not the director, however, if the movie is terrible we focus on the signature style of the director as there is little else to grab hold of for redemption. Her worry is that famous directors can be attributed with achievements based on who they are rather than what they achieve in a particular film. Her argument is that a film should be judged on merit, not obscured through the lens of a director's 'distinguishable' personality.

3. "The third and ultimate premise of the auteur theory is concerned with **interior meaning,** the ultimate glory of the cinema as an art. Interior meaning is extrapolated from the tension between a director's personality and his material" (Sarris, 1962). To this Kael argues that a work of art arises out of the unity of the artist expressing himself through his chosen form, she does not see style having to arise out of tension to ensure a great work. She disagrees with Sarris who suggests that the ideal auteur is someone who signs a long term contract, infuses elements of their personal style into any work, and if this style happens to clash with the story or theme it has the potential to enhance tension. Kael questions why substance in films is ignored and stylistic consistency is praised.

Pauline Kael

Kael **argued against the auteur theory**, preferring to see each film analysed in isolation, without referencing the director's previous work. Additionally, she saw film as a **collaborative process**, one in which many people should be attributed with artistic input and expression. Her essay *Circles and Squares* does articulate some good points against auteur theory however it is reductive, and at times tends towards emotion rather than reason. Kael continued her attack against the director as auteur when in 1971 she wrote an essay entitled *Raising Kane,* in it she attacked Orson Welles as not being responsible for the overall narrative construction and direction of *Citizen Kane.* Kael described the film as a 'shallow masterpiece' and she attributed the true genius of its origin to Howard Mankiewicz whom she claimed is the original screenplay writer, not Welles. Much controversy surrounds the reliability of Kael's argument against Welles. Despite this, or because of it, a historical tension surrounds the supporters and detractors of the auteur theory. Given that more than half a century has passed since Sarris introduced the auteur theory into American film culture, the fact that it is still in use, and debated, highlights the importance, or more accurately, the application of the concept. The **auteur theory has clearly morphed and changed to reflect its context.** Today the term is inclusive of all who contribute to a film, including: actors, screenwriters, set designers, sound engineers and anyone who contributes creatively and can show **a distinctive style across a body of work** when shaping a film. Knowing this, it is interesting to note that the auteur theory is **perpetuated by marketers** who use the bones of the theory to link audience identification to the director above and beyond anyone else who contributed to the film's construction. How often do you see a film marketed as *By the Cinematographer of* or *The Award Winning Screenwriter of*. You are more likely to see *From the Director of*, thus perpetuating the **myth of the primacy of the director** and continuing the Sarris and Kael debate.

"The three premises of the auteur theory may be visualised as three concentric circles, the outer circle as technique, the middle circle as personal style and the inner circle as interior meaning" (Sarris, 1962). The three elements, when used consistently and in unison, define a director as an auteur.

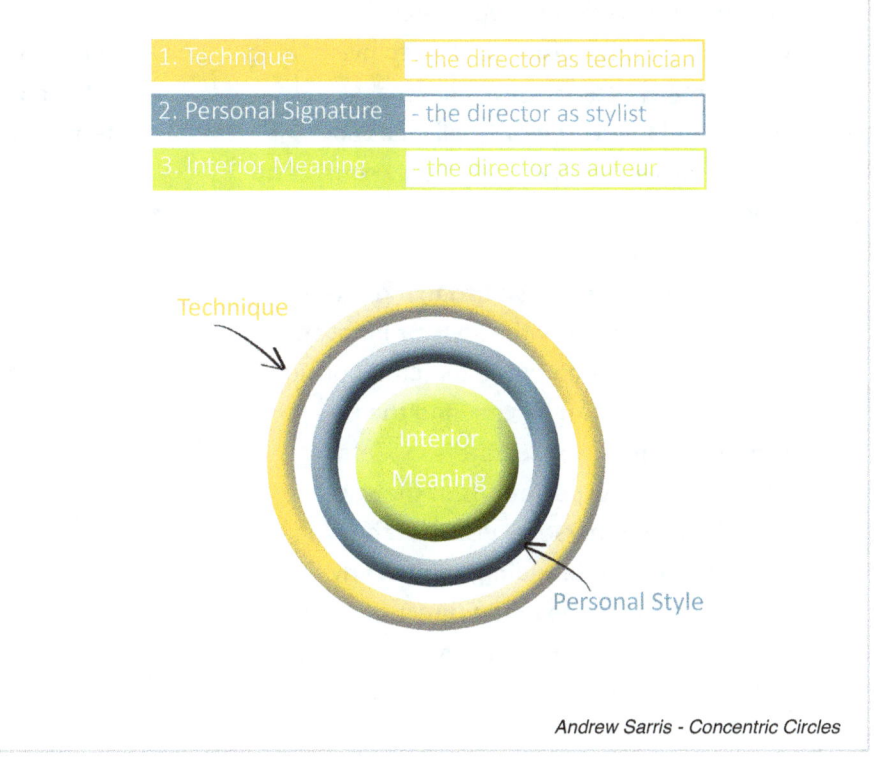

Andrew Sarris - Concentric Circles

Auteur Theory

Pros and cons

AUTEUR THEORY PROS

- Acknowledges the consistent, **distinctive, personal style of the filmmaker.**

- Recognises the significant contribution of the director, often working within the **confines of an institution.**

- Identifies **repetition** in use of **motifs** and **themes** across a body of work.

- Recognises a filmmaker's **personal vision** and interior meaning.

- Recognises **control over craft**, specifically a heightened technical competence to show an innovative approach.

- The director is credited with having the **principal creative vision**; although overseeing many creative contributors, he/she is recognised for synthesising all ideas and output into a cohesive, stylistically consistent whole.

- A known director is **easier to market** as the audience can identify the style or innovative approach attributed to the director. Consider Wes Anderson, Tim Burton, and the Coen Brothers — how do marketers tap into the audience's expectations of the style, technique, and personal vision of the director? **Auteur branding,** particularly trading on the name of the director, cultivates a fan base and creates recognition that assists with marketing.

AUTEUR THEORY CONS

- Film is built on a foundation of teamwork; it is a **collaborative process**. By looking at the end credits of any film you will be able to see the investment made by numerous skilled artists and technicians. Consider the Academy Awards given for artistic and technical contributions in film: these include Best Director, Best Actor in a Leading Role, Best Costume Designer, Best Cinematography, Best Film Editing, Best Original Score, Best Visual Effects, Best Original Screenplay and so on. John Williams has been nominated 51 times for his musical compositions for films such as *Star Wars, Jaws, Jurassic Park,* and the *Harry Potter* films to name a few. His significant contribution to these films would be largely ignored under the original design of the auteur theory. To ignore the contribution of all film personnel and only credit the director is antithetical to the filmmaking process.

- Too much emphasis is placed on the director's singular vision in order to determine the worth of a film.

- Attributes worth to a director based on previous films rather than looking at each film in isolation.

Auteur Theory - Where To Now?

 Commodification of the auteur

Is the **auteur theory** just as viable as when it was introduced in the 50s by Andrew Sarris, or is it redundant? Its original intent was to credit directors working inside a constrained studio system, yet still managing to show artistic expression and merit despite the boundaries placed on them. This revering of the director has some benefits:

- The **auteur can be used as a commodity platform** due to their recognisable aesthetic style. The repetition of the style leads to **audience familiarity**, connection, and potential audience return. Once the audience is familiar with, for instance, Tim Burton films, they are more likely to engage with his next production if they appreciate and recognise his style.
- The commodification of an auteur can occur through their 'celebrity' status which can be used as a **marketing vehicle** for merchandise associated with their films. For instance, Steven Spielberg's *E.T - the Extra Terrestrial* made millions in merchandise.
- Marketing continues through avenues such as the Director's Cut. By **branding the director** and placing him/her on a pedestal allows for repeat viewing or selling of extended version DVDs to a cult audience.
- **Possessory credits or vanity credits** arose in the 50s in line with the introduction of the auteur theory. They are used to credit the director and signal him/her as having sole creative vision. Will we reach a point where *A Film by* will simply list all contributors in alphabetical order rather than elevate the director as auteur?

Large studio blockbuster films do have competition in the form of streaming services such as **Netflix** who produce and distribute their own feature length productions. What impact will this have on Hollywood auteurs? Television, and the rise of video-on-demand services means that **proven directors are migrating from film,** lured by the available budgets, and a desire to leave their distinctive creative stamp on a work using their **directorial prominence**. Consider:

- Yorgos Lanthimos: *On Becoming a God in Central Florida.* Developed for AMC.
- Nicolas Winding Refn: *Too Old to Die Young*. Developed for Amazon Prime.
- Guillermo del Toro: *Trollhunters*. Developed for Netflix.
- Jane Campion and Gerard Lee: *Top of The Lake.* Developed for BBC UKTV.
- Alfonso Cuarón: Roma. Developed for Netflix.

A potential **shift in the auteur landscape** is the continued growth of YouTube and TikTok. As a distribution medium available to the masses, it has seen the rise of numerous content creators. The medium dominates in terms of gaining exposure and giving opportunities to emerging filmmakers. Does this medium **exclude attributing auteur status** to a filmmaker? Or, if the filmmaker shows a unified, consistent, artistic style and vision, does this **elevate them to auteur despite their choice of medium**? Steven Spielberg has commented that Netflix films are made for television and therefore should not be in the same category as cinema release films. Does the medium limit a filmmaker's ability to showcase innovative, artistic, technical and expressive capabilities?

It goes without saying that YouTube is scattered with dubious content, so is television, and so are some cinema theatres, the cream rises to the top - the best are recognised, sometimes despite, and sometimes because of their choice of medium. **The future of the auteur in a changing, increasingly on-line world,** where films can be self-produced, directed, edited, written, and filmed may see the theory return to its roots where a true auteur will be a person who completes most of the production roles, stamping their personal aesthetic throughout the film.

Personal Expression

An auteur is someone whose films show a **signature style**, technically and thematically **across a body of work**. An auteur can be a director, screenwriter, producer, cinematographer, editor, music composer, costume designer, actor, production designer, or even a studio - the defining characteristic is that their **filmography shows a clear and recognisable stylistic or thematic signature.** The move away from the director as the sole source of creative vision to include actors, studios and so on is in stark contrast to the original intent of auteurism, where the director was seen as having sole creative direction of the film.

The **auteur theory is no longer framed around the director as the sole creative contributor to a film**, rather, the collaborative nature is acknowledged and celebrated. The following is not a definitive list, rather a starting point to assist with discovering talented auteurs who have displayed consistent artistic innovation and personal expression across a body of work.

Ken Adam
Art Direction
- The Madness of King George
- The Spy Who Loved Me
- Goldfinger
- Barry Lyndon

Emmanuel Lubezki
Cinematography
- The Revenant
- Birdman
- Gravity
- Children of Men
- Sleepy Hollow

Katharine Hepburn
Actress
- On Golden Pond
- The Lion in Winter
- Guess Who's Coming to Dinner
- The African Queen

Robert De Niro
Actor
- Raging Bull
- The Godfather Part 2
- Taxi Driver
- The Deer Hunter
- Cape Fear

Saul Bass
Title Designer
- The Man with the Golden Arm
- North by Northwest
- Psycho
- Vertigo

John Williams
Music Composer
- Jaws
- Star Wars
- Schindler's List
- E.T. the Extra-Terrestrial
- Harry Potter Series

Roger Deakins
Cinematography
- Blade Runner 2049
- Skyfall
- No Country for Old Men
- Fargo
- Barton Fink

Bernard Herrmann
Music Composer
- Taxi Driver
- Citizen Kane
- Obsession
- Cape Fear
- All That Money Can Buy

Edith Head
Costume Designer
- The Sting
- Butch Cassidy and the Sundance Kid
- The Facts of Life
- Sabrina

Michael Kahn
Editing
- Raiders of the Lost Ark
- Schindler's List
- Saving Private Ryan
- Fatal Attraction
- The Post

Gregg Toland
Cinematography
- Citizen Kane
- The Long Voyage Home
- Wuthering Heights
- Grapes of Wrath
- Les Miserables

Meryl Streep
Actress
- Sophie's Choice
- The Iron Lady
- Kramer vs. Kramer
- The Devil Wears Prada
- Julie & Julia

Jack Nicholson
Actor
- One Flew Over the Cuckoo's Nest
- As Good As It Gets
- Terms of Endearment
- The Shining

Thelma Schoonmaker
Editing
- Raging Bull
- The Aviator
- The Departed
- Hugo
- Cape Fear

Auteur

A curated selection

A curated selection of directors as auteurs: some of the individuals are additionally known for their acting, screenplay writing, and cinematography skills; however, the focus is on their directing skills. The selection does not preference, or order directors in any particular way, nor is it definitive.

Howard Hawks
- Bringing Up Baby
- Rio Bravo
- Gentlemen Prefer Blondes
- The Big Sleep
- His Girl Friday

Roman Polanski
- Chinatown
- Rosemary's Baby
- The Pianist
- Carnage
- The Tenant
- The Ghost Writer

Danny Boyle
- 127 Hours
- Slumdog Millionaire
- 28 Days Later
- Trainspotting
- Steve Jobs
- Shallow Grave

John Huston
- Prizzi's Honor
- The African Queen
- The Asphalt Jungle
- Key Largo
- The Treasure of the Sierra Madre

Orson Welles
- Citizen Kane
- Touch of Evil
- Mr Arkadin
- The Magnificent Ambersons
- F for Fake

Francis Ford Coppola
- The Godfather Part 1, Part 2, and Part 3
- Apocalypse Now
- The Outsiders
- Bram Stroker's Dracula
- The Rainmaker

Wes Anderson
- The Grand Budapest Hotel
- Moonrise Kingdom
- The Royal Tenenbaums
- Fantastic Mr Fox
- Rushmore

Quentin Tarantino
- Pulp Fiction
- Inglourious Basterds
- Reservoir Dogs
- Kill Bill
- Django Unchained
- The Hateful Eight

Ingmar Bergman
- The Seventh Seal
- Wild Strawberries
- Monika
- The Virgin Spring
- Cries and Whispers
- Fanny and Alexander

Steven Spielberg
- Jaws
- E.T. the Extra-Terrestrial
- Jurassic Park
- Schindler's List
- Close Encounters of the Third Kind

Kathryn Bigelow
- The Hurt Locker
- Point Break
- Strange Days
- Near Dark
- Zero Dark Thirty
- K-19: The Widowmaker

Steven Soderbergh
- Sex, Lies & Videotape
- Ocean's 11
- Erin Brokovitch
- Magic Mike
- Traffic
- Behind the Candelabra

Billy Wilder
- Sunset Boulevard
- Some Like It Hot
- The Apartment
- Double Indemnity
- Ace in the Hole
- The Lost Weekend

Aki Kaurismäki
- Shadows in Paradise
- I Hired a Contract Killer
- Drifting Clouds
- The Man Without a Past
- Juha
- The Other Side of Hope

James Cameron
- Avatar
- Titanic
- The Terminator
- The Abyss
- True Lies
- Aliens

Alfonso Cuarón
- Children of Men
- Gravity
- Harry Potter and the Prisoner of Azkaban
- A Little Princess
- Roma

Clint Eastwood
- Gran Torino
- Unforgiven
- Million Dollar Baby
- Invictus
- Mystic River
- American Sniper

Pedro Almodóvar
- Broken Embraces
- Volver
- Women on the Verge of a Nervous Breakdown
- Talk to her
- Julieta

Sergio Leone
- A Fistful of Dollars
- The Good, the Bad and the Ugly
- Once Upon a Time in the West
- For a Few Dollars More

Peter Jackson
- The Lord of the Rings: The Return of the King
- The Hobbit: The Desolation of Smaug
- King Kong
- Forgotten Silver

John Ford
- The Quiet Man
- Grapes of Wrath
- Stagecoach
- How Green Was My Valley
- The Searchers

Miloš Forman
- One Flew Over the Cuckoo's Nest
- The People vs. Larry Flint
- Amadeus
- Man on the Moon
- Taking Off

David Lean
- Lawrence of Arabia
- Doctor Zhivago
- A Passage to India
- The Bridge on the River Kwai
- Ryan's Daughter

Paul Thomas Anderson
- There will be Blood
- Inherent Vice
- Magnolia
- The Master
- Punch Drunk Love

Alejandro González Iñárritu
- The Revenant
- Biutiful
- Birdman
- Babel
- 21 Grams

Charlie Kauffman
(Director &/or writer)
- Synecdoche, New York
- Eternal Sunshine of the Spotless Mind
- Being John Malkovitch
- Adaptation

Stanley Kubrick
- Dr. Strangelove
- A Clockwork Orange
- 2001: A Space Odyssey
- The Shining
- Paths of Glory

Coen Brothers
- Fargo
- The Big Lebowski
- Barton Fink
- No Country for Old Men
- O Brother Where Art Thou?

Christopher Nolan
- Memento
- The Prestige
- Batman Begins
- Inception
- The Dark Knight Rises
- Dunkirk

François Truffaut
- Jules et Jim
- The 400 Blows
- Breathless
- Shoot the Piano Player
- Day for Night
- The Wild Child

Hayao Miyazaki
- Spirited Away
- Princess Mononoke
- Howl's Moving Castle
- My Neighbour Totoro
- Castle in the Sky
- The Wind Rises

Alfred Hitchcock
- Psycho
- Rear Window
- Vertigo
- The Birds
- Spellbound
- Notorious

Andrei Tarkovsky
- Solaris
- The Mirror
- Stalker
- Andrei Rublev
- The Sacrifice
- Nostalgia

Martin Scorsese
- Taxi Driver
- Raging Bull
- Goodfellas
- The Departed
- The Last Waltz
- Casino

Woody Allen
- Annie Hall
- Hannah and her Sisters
- Manhattan
- Zelig
- Crimes & Misdemeanors
- Radio Days

Ridley Scott
- Blade Runner
- Alien
- Thelma and Louise
- Gladiator
- The Martian
- American Gangster

Tim Burton
- Edward Scissorhands
- Corpse Bride
- Charlie and the Chocolate Factory
- Batman Returns
- Frankenweenie

David Lynch
- Eraserhead
- Blue Velvet
- Mulholland Drive
- Inland Empire
- Lost Highway
- The Elephant Man

Sofia Coppola
- The Virgin Suicides
- Lost in Translation
- Marie Antoninette
- The Beguiled
- Somewhere

Frank Capra
- It's a Wonderful Life
- It Happened One Night
- American Madness
- Mr Deeds Goes to Town
- Meet John Doe

Jane Campion
- The Piano
- An Angel at My Table
- Sweetie
- The Portrait of a Lady
- In the Cut

Peter Weir
- Picnic at Hanging Rock
- The Truman Show
- Gallipoli
- Dead Poet's Society
- The Last Wave

Auteur Theory

A signature style

Tom Tykwer, a German film director with a lengthy filmography has a **recognisable signature style** across many of his earlier films. The following deconstruction of Tykwer's personal expression used to establish him as an auteur will focus on:

- **Run Lola Run** (1998), an eighty four minute feature film whose premise centres around the protagonist, Lola, having twenty minutes to come up with one hundred thousand Deutsch Marks to save the life of her boyfriend Manni. The narrative premise plays out three times with altered outcomes in each.
- **Epilog** (1992), is a short twelve minute film that sees the major characters in an endless loop of a relationship breakdown focusing on infidelity and the loss of connection and communication between them. The film focuses on the epilogue, or the final dying moments of the relationship.

Tom Tykwer as an auteur

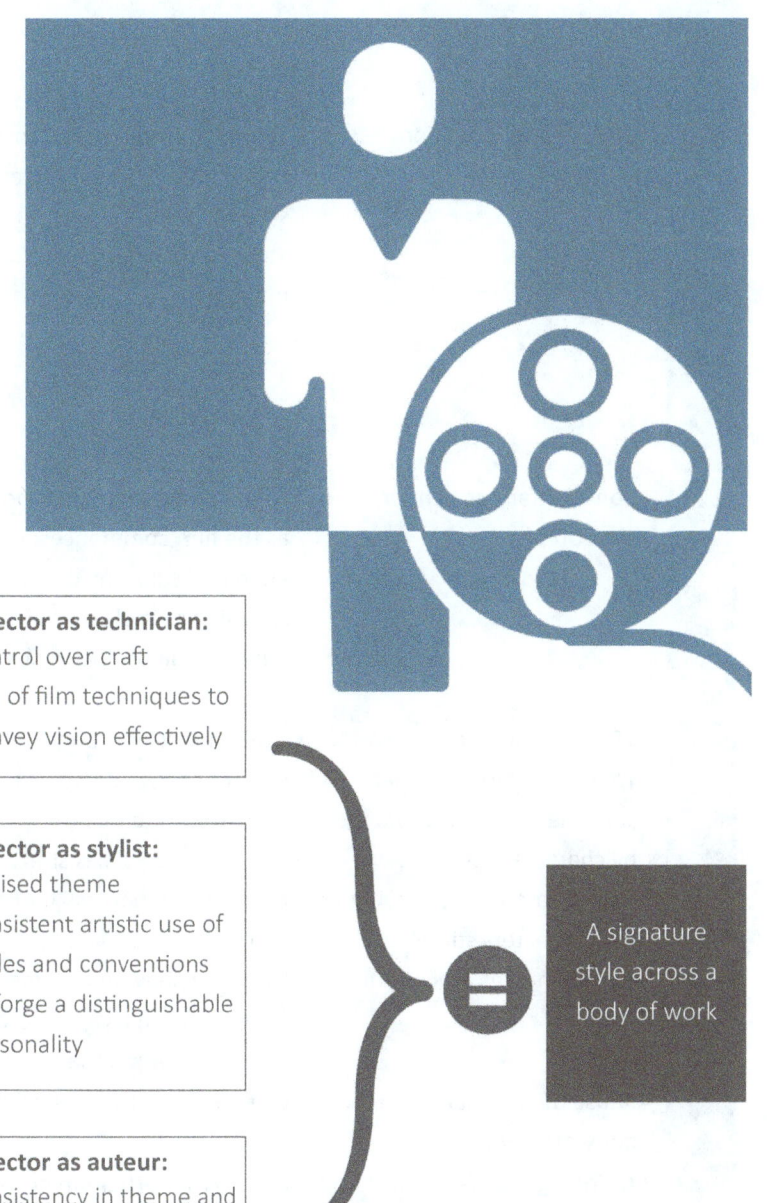

Andrew Sarris, an American film critic, introduced America to the term **auteur.** He furthered the argument begun by French filmmakers in the *Cahier Du Cinema* magazine by proposing that in order for a filmmaker to be considered an auteur, or an author who **shows a clear and distinguishable style**, he or she needed to display three aspects:

1. Technical competence

→ **The director as technician:**
- control over craft
- use of film techniques to convey vision effectively

2. Personal expression

→ **The director as stylist:**
- stylised theme
- consistent artistic use of codes and conventions to forge a distinguishable personality

3. Interior meaning

→ **The director as auteur:**
- consistency in theme and visual style across their work

= A signature style across a body of work

35

Signature style displayed by Tom Tykwer

	Signature element	Film 1: Run Lola Run (1998)	Film 2: Epilog (1992)
Theme	• Relationships and their complexities • Infidelity	• Love, coupled with power: the first two runs see an imbalance in the relationship resulting in the death of either Manni or Lola.	• Power in the relationship is aesthetically represented by having characters move objects telekinetically, initially Rainer moves a chair to ensure his comfort whilst eavesdropping on Nadja while she is on the phone to her lover. A revolver, a phone, and a rubbish bin are used as symbols of power. For instance, Rainer takes a revolver from a beside drawer in the first version and uses it to shoot Nadja, but in the second version Nadja has removed the gun from the drawer and uses it to shoot Rainer. As he collapses, she telekinetically moves the bed out of the way to deny him a comfortable fall.
	• Chance and repetition	• Temporal frequency of three; Lola is given three chances to save Manni's life, with each attempt resulting in a different outcome.	• Temporal frequency of three (or more) as the suggestion is that the narrative sequence plays out in different configurations endlessly. • The same line, "It's so hot...Did I shoot?" is spoken by Rainer when he shoots Nadja, and again at the end when Nadja shoots Rainer.
Issues	• Commentary on gender stereotypes	• Lola is given agency as soon as the film commences; her animated self runs through a spiralling tunnel knocking and punching all obstacles out of her way.	• Nadja tells Rainer to 'Get lost, piss off,' later telling him that he is 'disgusting and pathetic' before shooting him. Through her actions and dialogue, she is shown to be strong, not submissive, she is in control of her life.
Technical codes	• 360° spiralling camera work. Traditional film grammar sees the camera motivated by character action, Tykwer manipulates this by having the characters still while the camera moves around them.	• Camera circles around Lola's mother to reveal important mise-en-scène. • 360° around Lola as she considers who to ask for help. • Circles around Manni and Lola after they find themselves trapped when trying to escape the supermarket they robbed.	• Camera spirals around Nadja and Rainer as they argue about their deteriorated relationship creating a sense of urgency and momentum to reach a resolution.
	• Reuse of crew across the body of his work.	• Cinematographer Frank Griebe	• Cinematographer Frank Griebe
Video Game	• A video game aesthetic	• Lola has superhuman powers; she is able to save lives.	• Both characters can move objects without touching them.

	Signature element	Film 1: Run Lola Run (1998)	Film 2: Epilog (1992)
Symbolic codes	• Mise-en-scène • Artificiality of film world • Visual and aural motifs • Colour palette	• Stylised motifs such as Lola's screams that shatter glass, allowing her to regain control of her environment. • The use of animation to blend the super-hero video game version of Lola to 'real-world' Lola as her physical abilities move between realms allowing 'real' Lola to save a man's life. • Colour palette is red, yellow and green. Red associated with Lola, fiery, passionate, active, has drive. Yellow associated with Manni, suggesting cowardice and being associated with the 'gold' he needs.	• Chair, rubbish bin, phone and bed move on their own. Objects shift position in the room (almost like a reset) to allow for different variations of the same narrative to unfold, who will kill who in this version, what objects will be available to them? • Colour palette is red and yellow. Yellow is a tainted yellow, suggestive of their broken relationship. • Nadja wears a red gown, a red blanket adorns the bed connoting passion and drive as she tells Rainer to 'piss off.'
Sound aesthetic	• Aural motifs • Repetition in dialogue sequences	• Ticking clock, techno beat, Lola's screams used to control her environment all contribute to an artificial world where Lola appears superhuman. • Silence used when Lola is shot by a police officer during the supermarket robbery scene. As an aesthetic the power of silence to focus audience attention onto the intensity of the scene is effective.	• Sparse dialogue, music used to heighten emotion. • Sound is more subtle than RLR. • Silence used to heighten tension as Nadja ends her call with her lover, unaware Rainer is sitting in the room listening to the conversation.
Narrative structure	• Open-ended resolution	• The last run involves active audience participation as we are aware that Manni has given Ronnie the bag of money but some of it is missing as the homeless man took part of the cash to buy a bike and food. Lola too has secured a bag of cash from her casino winnings, hence narrative possibilities abound as Manni turns to Lola and asks, "What's in the bag?"	• An endless loop is implied by the last line of dialogue as it mimics the opening. Nadja says, "It's so hot...Did I shoot?" • Open-ended narrative: the narrative resolution is left open as the audience is asked to project the narrative into the next possible sequence, who will shot next?
	• Non-linear	• Manipulation of temporal order using flashbacks and flash forwards. The premise of the film is revealed through a flashback. The audience learns that Lola's moped was stolen setting up a chain of events that result in Manni leaving a 100 000 DM on a train by accident.	• Opening shows what could be a flashback of a man shooting a woman. This sequence repeats with different variations and outcomes.
	• Temporal manipulation	• Film is episodic and has a temporal frequency of three. Lola has three attempts to save Manni's life, succeeding in the last attempt. She appears to carry knowledge from one run through to the next, building on her knowledge base and allowing her to succeed. For instance, in the first run Lola does not know how to use a gun, in the second run she has learnt how to take off the safety catch and is able to use the gun to effectively assist her with her goal.	• Temporal frequency of two as the film shows variations of Nadja's death and Rainer's death; however, there are limitless permutations to the ending of their relationship, and the question posed by Nadja,"Did I kill Rainer?" hints at an infinite temporal frequency. • The line "It's hot" is used as a reset to start the sequence again.

AUTEUR THEORY
a signature style

MAIN ESSENTIAL CONTENT TO CONSIDER WHEN DISCUSSING THE AUTEUR THEORY:

1. What is the auteur's **signature style**? Supply very specific examples of codes, conventions and techniques the auteur uses **across a body of work**.
2. Discuss **Andrew Sarris' contribution to the auteur theory** by summarising how he privileged the director of the film acknowledging their artistic endeavours despite, or because of, any restraints.
3. Consider scaffolding any answer about auteur theory using **Andrew Sarris' three concentric circles:**
   - The outer circle as technique (**technical quality**). Control over craft highlighting their technical competence to show an innovative approach.
   - The middle circle as **personal style/expression:** supply examples of codes and conventions which exemplify a clear personal style.
   - The inner circle relates to **interior meaning**. Supply examples highlighting the film's theme/s and the auteur's point of view on the issues presented.
4. Consider **Pauline Kael's rebuttal** in her 1963 essay *Circles and Squares* where she argued that any film should be judged on its individual merit, not on any previous landscape of success built by the director.
5. Consider **audience expectations** in relation to the director. What does the audience expect in terms of style, themes, collaboration with actors and so on? How does this connect to **auteur branding** with film marketers trading on the name of the director in order to connect with the intended audience and allow for recognisable marketing of elements?
6. Remember that an auteur is not just a director, **an auteur can be a screenwriter, a cinematographer, an editor, an actor, a costume designer,** basically anyone who has a recognisable signature style across a body of work.

Consider discussing some of the cultural or artistic benefits of auteur driven films:
- **cultural benefit:** films can challenge dominant ideologies and question the status quo.
- **artistic benefit:** experimentation with historical film grammar and narrative structure, thus setting the groundwork for others to experiment with personal expression and engage with manipulation of established structures and techniques.
- allows for **audience recognition** via auteur traits, making marketing more targeted and precise.

Auteur Theory

Review & sample questions

Sample questions containing auteur theory:

1. Analyse how an auteur has used film aesthetics to challenge dominant ideologies.
2. Discuss how a director's personal expression can be a vehicle to construct meaning.
3. Discuss the viability of the auteur theory in relation to audience expectations.
4. Analyse how an auteur uses personal expression to convey theme.
5. Discuss how an auteur combines codes and conventions to construct media art.
6. Discuss audience expectations of an auteur's work.

 **Auteur - main essential content to discuss:**

01
- An **auteur** is someone whose films show **a signature style**, technically and thematically across a body of work. An auteur can be a director, screenwriter, producer, cinematographer, editor, music composer, costume designer, actor, production designer, or even a studio - the defining characteristic is that their filmography shows **a clear and recognisable stylistic or thematic signature.**

02
- **Andrew Sarris'** seminal essay, *Notes on the Auteur Theory* in 1962 highlighted the importance of the director to an American audience who previously had prefaced the actors and story. Sarris stated that **three criteria** needed to be met to classify a director as an auteur (1) **technical competence** (2) **personal signature** (3) **interior meaning**.

03
- **Pauline Kael** responded to Sarris in her essay *Circles and Squares* by rebutting Sarris' criterion with her own (1) technical competence should be based on **audience judgement** (2) why should a director's consistent personal style be celebrated, should it not be seen for what it is—**formulaic** (3) meaning in film should not be judged on stylistic and thematic consistency, instead Kael argues it should be judged on its **individual merit and substance.**

04
- **Commodification of the auteur**: the auteur's celebrity status can be used to market films due to their recognisable aesthetic style.

Chapter Three

Film Movements

- Film movement timeline
- Film movement background
- Film movement conventions
- Suggested 'must-watch' art films
- Sample questions
- Review

Film Movements

Film Movement Timeline

Timeline

Visual representation of some, but not all, film movements:

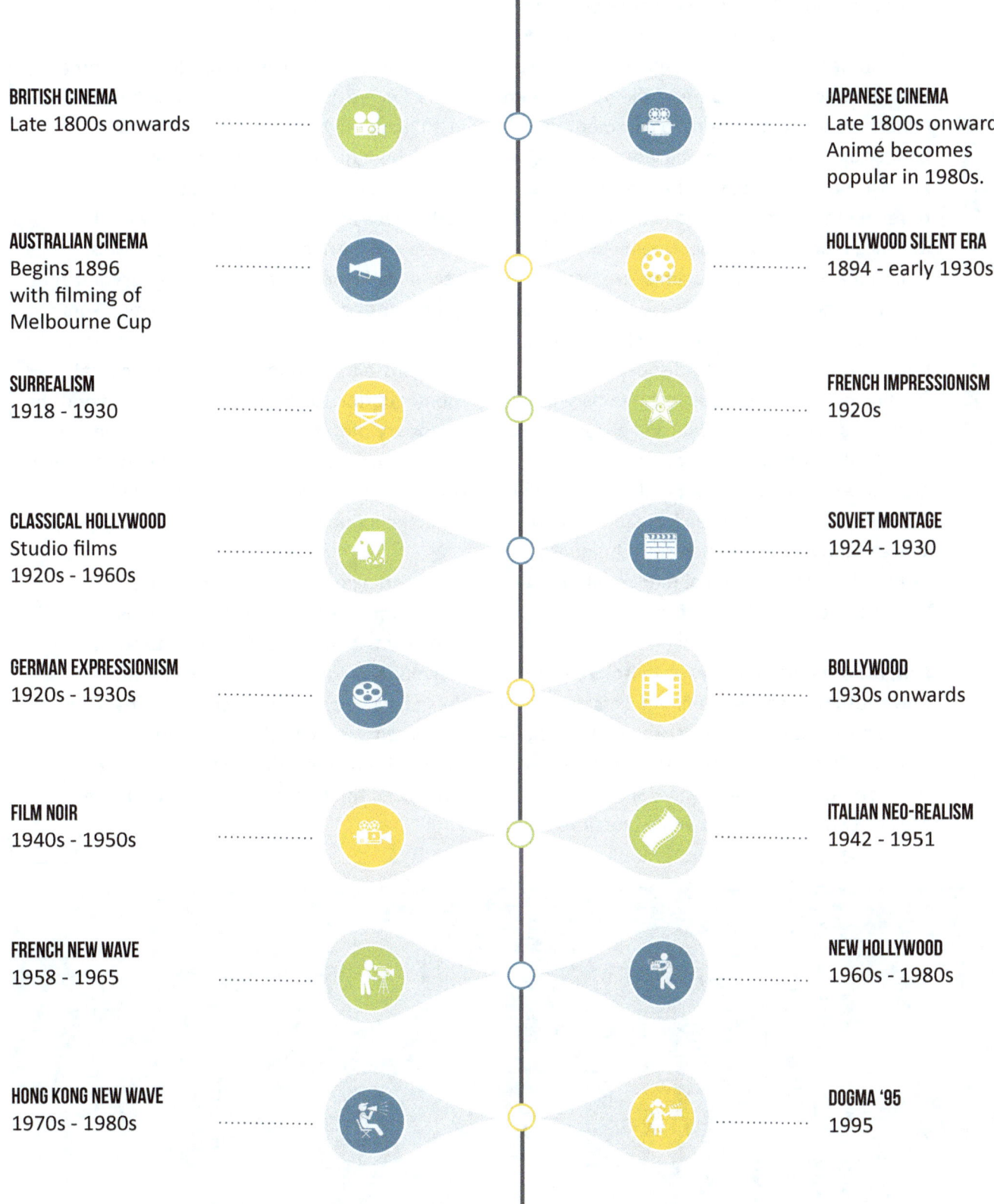

BRITISH CINEMA Late 1800s onwards	**JAPANESE CINEMA** Late 1800s onwards. Animé becomes popular in 1980s.
AUSTRALIAN CINEMA Begins 1896 with filming of Melbourne Cup	**HOLLYWOOD SILENT ERA** 1894 - early 1930s
SURREALISM 1918 - 1930	**FRENCH IMPRESSIONISM** 1920s
CLASSICAL HOLLYWOOD Studio films 1920s - 1960s	**SOVIET MONTAGE** 1924 - 1930
GERMAN EXPRESSIONISM 1920s - 1930s	**BOLLYWOOD** 1930s onwards
FILM NOIR 1940s - 1950s	**ITALIAN NEO-REALISM** 1942 - 1951
FRENCH NEW WAVE 1958 - 1965	**NEW HOLLYWOOD** 1960s - 1980s
HONG KONG NEW WAVE 1970s - 1980s	**DOGMA '95** 1995

Film Movements

Background

Film movements act as a time capsule by reflecting the cultural, economic, political and social elements of the society from which they arose. They highlighted what was relevant and authentic to filmmakers and audiences during that moment in time. Some movements arose as an antithesis or **rejection of the mainstream**. Others grew out of a desire to c**omment on contextual issues**. Others still were **reacting against the old guard**, ushering in change to reflect their altered world landscape. For instance **French New Wave** cinema forms from a combination of change agents; post World War Two France ushers in a new generation of filmmakers with an appetite for change; the technological tools at their disposal allowed for innovation, **lighter mobile cameras** see narratives take to the streets and engage more realistically with their young audience, films are made on a **small budget** and do not follow conventional film grammar, instead the New Wave filmmakers revolutionise techniques by **not following conventional film grammar**, by telling stories in entirely different ways.

Film movements do not exist in isolation from one another, many of the filmmakers directly or indirectly influenced each other. Luis Buñuel, for instance, is one of the foundational **surrealism** filmmakers, his work in France, Spain and Mexico (where he made twenty one films) laid the groundwork for **non-linear, anti-narrative** productions that questioned the foundation of society. Buñuel's surrealistic film conventions made an indelible mark on world cinema.

Moreover, **Sergei Eisenstein**, a Soviet filmmaker spent two years in Western Europe beginning in 1928, in the May of 1930 he arrived in Hollywood, quickly heading to Mexico in 1931 for fourteen months. His **montage techniques** are born out of his early work in Russia and carried with him on his travels, becoming incorporated into the **embryonic film grammar** of early world cinema. Filmmakers such as Hitchcock were greatly influenced by Eisenstein's development of **intellectual montage**. Hitchcock's ability to **push beyond the boundary of the frame** and have the audience actively connect shots to garner a new meaning can be directly attributed to Eisenstein's montage influence.

The interlinking nature and influence **film movements** have had on each other is significant. A **'wave' of films that used similar conventions constituted a movement**; these had a defining impact on cinema. Film movements, specifically their innovative cinematic and narrative techniques, have influenced the film language of world cinema.

"Now why should the cinema follow the forms of theatre and painting rather than the methodology of language, which allows wholly new concepts of ideas to arise from the combination of two concrete denotations of two concrete objects?"

- Sergei Eisenstein, 1942.

FILM MOVEMENTS

film as art

Legitimising **film as an art form** has taken time. Film was originally seen as a novelty, an entertainment medium for the masses. The move towards embracing film as more than a novelty and elevating it to the status of art arose out of a combination of factors:

1. Validation via **film festival** circuits
2. Establishment of **film schools**
3. Recognition via institutions such as **governments supplying finance** in order to highlight their cultural capital
4. **Film critic reviews:** use of a discourse associated with the medium
5. **Authorship:** rise of the auteur theory that attributed status to the director in the same way as an author of a book is acknowledged as the source of creativity, inspiration and skill
6. **Archival films** considered important enough to keep, not just as factual historical records but as a window into the zeitgeist of a culture
7. **Academia:** Film Studies taught in universities.

Film as art—the term 'art' connects the medium to traditionally established sources of art such as painting and drawing, these historical art mediums have a long history with an appreciative audience base who foster a sense of legitimacy and status through their continued championing of the Arts. By associating film with traditional arts, and by surrounding it with the **same discourse**, allows for the creation of **legitimacy.** Moreover, many film movements take their name from their art world compatriots and use numerous **established art conventions**, thus furnishing the film art world with **a similar, and identifiable set of codes and conventions** that audiences, through their knowledge of art, can associate with film. Consider surrealism in painting versus surrealism in film; the mediums differ, however, the conventions of providing incongruities in the form of scale, juxtaposition, texture, distortion, floating objects and dislocation, to name but a few, are used in the same way.

Cinematic culture has, like traditional art, a **divide** between what is considered **high culture** and what is deemed as **popular culture**. High culture film art is intended for a **niche audience**, is considered innovative, the skill and craftsmanship of the director, cast and crew are evident, and the films are frequently independently produced; whereas popular culture films are associated with formulaic blockbusters, lacking in originality and are designed as accessible, consumable entertainment **for the masses**.

Son of Man (1964) Rene Magritte

Surrealism

FILM MOVEMENT 1918-1930

Context

- Surrealist films visually explore the subconscious mind.
- Surrealism made clear that traditional art should be replaced with anything 'anti-art' and it triumphed the ridiculous and the absurd, having a disregard for form.
- Surrealism is a cultural, social and political movement aiming to free minds and liberate individuals and society as a whole.
- While there are numerous films that are true expressions of the movement, many films classified as Surrealist only contain surrealist fragments.
- Film becomes a vehicle for social and political comment, audiences are active in making meaning.

Conventions

- Deliberately anti-narrative, challenging traditional notions of cause and effect.
- Non-linear structure.
- Absence of logic and reason.
- Events and elements are juxtaposed to unsettle, disturb and shock.
- Incorporates sexual desire, ecstasy, violence, blasphemy, and bizarre humour with a disregard for conventional narrative principles and societal norms.
- Discontinuous editing is commonly used to fracture any organised temporal space.
- Diegesis of the film world is not cohesive.
- Objects lose their literal meaning, instead becoming metaphorical or conceptual. E.g., clocks float.
- Attack institutions such as marriage, the church, family, and government.

SOME EXAMPLES OF Early Films

- Un Chien Andalou (1929) Dir. Luis Buñuel & Salivador Dali
- The Seashell and The Clergyman (1928) Dir. Germaine Dulac

SOME EXAMPLES OF Later Films

- Mulhollund Drive (2001) & Eraserhead (1977) Dir. David Lynch
- Eternal Sunshine of the Spotless Mind (2004) Dir. Michael Gondry
- Being John Malkovich (1999) Dir. Spike Jonze

French Impressionism

FILM MOVEMENT 1918–1930s

Context

- The French impressionist filmmakers were reacting against the devastation of WW1 and the influx of Hollywood and German films; they wanted French films to bear the stamp of a French cultural context.
- Taking its name from the art movement, impressionism delves into emotions, it saw film as a vehicle for conveying raw emotions through narratives with characters steeped in inner psychological intensity.
- Operated mostly within the mainstream film industry making avant-garde films.
- As the techniques implemented by the impressionists became more common place, the movement's impact decreased. The arrival of sound, which was too costly for independent filmmakers, saw the movement naturally fade away.

Conventions

- Non-linear editing, cross-cutting.
- Point of view camera work - subjectivity paramount.
- Experimentation with lighting styles.
- Emotional representation through dream sequences and fantasies.
- Aesthetics of the image paramount.
- Manipulation of temporal time and space, flashbacks common.
- Experimentation with editing and cinematography to depict mental state such as iris, superimposition, image distortion, slow motion, and masking. Rhythm of editing reflects emotional calm or angst of character. Camera work highlights emotions through point of view shots and camera subjectivity.

SOME EXAMPLES OF
Early Films

- The Tenth Symphony (1918) Dir. Abel Gance
- Napoléon (1927) Dir. Abel Gance
- Fièvre (1921) Dir. Louis Dellec
- Rose-France (1919) Dir. Marcel L'Herbier
- The Smiling Madame Beudet (1923) Dir. Germaine Dulac

SOME EXAMPLES OF
Later Films

- Elephant (2003) Gus Van Sant
- The Ring (1927) Alfred Hitchcock
- Spellbound (1945) Alfred Hitchcock
- Taxi Driver (1976) Scorsese

Classical Hollywood

FILM MOVEMENT 1908-1960s

Context

- The classical Hollywood narrative designates both a visual, and sound style for making motion pictures. It set the groundwork for film grammar. It became the dominant mode of storytelling and the comparison point for all future filmmakers.
- Classical style is fundamentally built on the principle of continuity editing or 'invisible' style. That is, the camera and sound recording should never call attention to themselves.
- Time and space manipulation are realistic. The viewer is encouraged to believe that space exists outside the confines of the film's frame.
- Suspension of disbelief is paramount.
- Hollywood benefitted from the huge skill base attached to the immigrant filmmakers who found refuge in America.

Conventions

- Linear cause and effect plot construction. Causality is paramount - the principle that everything that happens must have a cause.
- Goal orientated characters.
- Clearly defined conflicts rising to a climax, and a resolution that emphasises closure.
- Narrative economy – characters are developed quickly.
- Multiple plot lines, at least two interweaving plots.
- Invisible continuity editing and camera work. All filmmaking processes are concealed or seamless.
- 30 degree & 180 degree rule, eyeline match and match on action - continuity editing.
- Realism adhered to. Viewer expectation of narrative achieved.
- Three point lighting to imitate a natural look.

SOME EXAMPLES OF
Early Films

- The Squaw Man (1914) Dir. Cecile B. DeMille
- Birth of a Nation (1915) and Intolerance (1916) Dir. D.W. Griffith
- The Jazz Singer (1927) Dir. Alan Crosland

SOME EXAMPLES OF
Later Films

- Gone with the Wind (1939) Dir. Victor Fleming
- Casablanca (1942) Dir. Michael Curtiz
- Citizen Kane (1942) Dir. Orson Wells
- Singing in the Rain (1952) Dir. Stanley Donen & Gene Kelly

German Expressionism

FILM MOVEMENT 1920s–1930s

Context

- German cinema reflects disillusionment after WW1. Shown by stark shadows, corruptible and untrustworthy characters, showing authority figures as villains to highlight that no one could be trusted, e.g., the doctor in *Cabinet of Dr Caligari*. Directors wanted the audience to look beyond the characters and examine their world, hence the importance of mise-en-scène.
- By 1930 Hitler had made his mark on Germany and he discredits German Expressionism as a degenerate art, instead using film for his propaganda purposes.
- Not the end for directors as many left and went to Hollywood, thus shaping American cinema, specifically the horror and thriller genres.

Conventions

- Distorted shapes, actors wear heavy, grotesque makeup, and move in a slow or exaggerated manner.
- Chiaroscuro lighting – extreme contrast in dark/light, thus creating dramatic shadows to convey emotional states.
- Exaggerated sets – seen as an extension of character psychology.
- Set design can be non-realistic, include geometrically angular shapes, with designs painted on floors and walls to suggest light or shadows.
- Symbolism and mise-en-scène used to insert mood and deeper meaning.
- Expressive camera angles, often canted.
- Themes of dark, dystopian worlds, with a gloomy, pessimistic, tormented protagonist.

SOME EXAMPLES OF Early Films

- Cabinet of Dr Caligari (1920) Dir. Robert Weiner
- Nosferatu (1922) Dir. F.W. Murnau
- Metropolis (1927) Dir. Fritz Lang
- Pandora's Box (1929) Dir. G.W. Pabst

SOME EXAMPLES OF Later Films

- The Big Sleep (1946) Dir. Howard Hawks
- Batman Returns (1992) Dir. Tim Burton
- Edward Scissorhands (1990) Dir. Tim Burton
- Barton Fink (1991) Dir. Joel Coen

Soviet Montage

FILM MOVEMENT 1942-1930

Context

- After the Russian Revolution film stock was hard to come by, Lev Kuleshov tried editing together shots from old films, he found audiences responded differently depending on where a shot was placed in a sequence.
- Sergei Eisenstein and Vsevolod Podovkin refined Kuleshov's experiment by looking at how images shown next to each other affect a person's emotions. Eisenstein developed his theory of montage of attractions. He looked at combining and contrasting images and how to maximise emotional impact through the pace and rhythm of editing.
- Soviet filmmakers used cinema as a tool to evoke emotions and drive the audience to support the Revolution. They rejected Hollywood continuity seamless editing, favouring a conflict of ideas or intellectual montage.

Conventions

- Ideation montage or montage of attractions. Shot A + Shot B = Concept C. Juxtaposing of shots to create a world in the viewer's head that is not directly shown to them on the screen. E.g., a close-up of terrified eyes + a close up of a bloodied knife. The viewer comes up with the concept of murder, fear and so on. Active audience participation in linking shots is essential.
- Overlapping editing - the action is repeated from numerous angles thus expanding the time for the action to unfold.
- Elliptical editing - an aspect of an event is left out, thus shortening the time it takes to complete the action. The action jumps between elements that are not connected causing a jump cut.
- Early Russian films emphasised the group over the individual, the narrative lacked an individual protagonist.

SOME EXAMPLES OF Early Films

- Battleship Potemkin (1925) Dir. Sergei Eisenstein
- Mechanics of the Brain (1925) Dir. Vsevolod Podovkin
- Dziga Vertov (1929) Dir. Man with a Movie Camera

SOME EXAMPLES OF Later Films

Some films influenced by Soviet Montage:
- Strangers on a Train (1951) Dir. Hitchcock
- Rocky (1976) Dir. John Avildsen
- The Untouchables (1987) Dir. Brian De Palma

Film Noir

FILM MOVEMENT 1940s–1950s

Context

- France was occupied by Nazis in WW2 and therefore a ban was placed on foreign films. At the end of the war, five year's worth of American films were seen by French viewers. These films had a common thread of a hard-boiled crime detective style narratives, shot using German expressionistic techniques.
- The term 'noir' means black, and was coined to indicate the black, dark and dismal themes found in noir films.
- The noir narrative was influenced by the changing role of women in society after WW2. Women had proven themselves and were not content to return to their traditional pre-war roles. Men feared women would abandon their domestic duties, and thus the femme fatale character negatively highlights women's power by showing her as cunning and seductive.

Conventions

- A complex narrative structure. Resolution is rarely happy.
- Themes of fatalism, disillusionment, and cynicism explore the moral complexity of the characters.
- Illicit desire and sexuality are explored through the femme fatale character.
- Use of chiaroscuro lighting and stark black and white photography.
- Slatted light through blinds falling onto the faces of people engaged in deception.
- Narrative often unfolds as a series of flashbacks.
- First person voiceover narration conveys narrative from the point of view of the protagonist thus connecting the audience to the hero.
- Many conventions taken directly from German Expressionism, such as canted angles and chiaroscuro lighting.

SOME EXAMPLES OF Early Films

- The Postman Always Rings Twice (1946) Dir. Tay Garnett
- Sunset Boulevard (1950) Dir. Billy Wilder
- Double Indemnity (1944) Dir. Billy Wilder
- The Maltese Falcon (1940) Dir. John Huston

SOME EXAMPLES OF Later Films

Neo Noir films include:
- LA Confidential (1997) Dir. Curtis Hanson
- Sin City (2005) Dir. Robert Rodriguez and Frank Miller
- Blade Runner (1982) Dir. Ridley Scott
- Memento (2000) Dir. Christopher Nolan

Italian Neo-Realism

FILM MOVEMENT 1942-1951

Context

- After Mussolini's fall in 1943 filmmakers began to make films that highlighted social and political issues. This was in direct contrast to previous films that had been escapist style melodramas made in the lavish Cinecitta studios.
- Neo-realism was born out of a political climate and a desire to reject Mussolini's contrived plots, instead enjoying the freedom to criticise contemporary society.
- The war saw the biggest film studio, Cinecitta, mostly destroyed, along with the majority of sound equipment. This resulted in Neorealists using actual locations, camera work saw documentary style tracking shots employed, and lighting was limited to the available light source. Hollywood style glamour, including three-point lighting was nowhere to be seen.
- The narrative is looser in cause and effect relationship as a reaction against contrived plots.

Conventions

- Interest in everyday life, particularly that of hardship faced by the needy and poor.
- Dealt with real social and political issues and included a call to reform.
- A bleak, but not entirely pessimistic tone.
- Lack of narrative resolution, intentionally open-ended.
- Location shooting (biggest Italian studio was damaged during the war).
- Unpolished style.
- Use of unknown, or amateur actors.
- Little make-up, not glamorous.
- Long takes, tracking shots.
- Black and white cinematography.
- Style is dictated by lack of film resources and a desire to show the real Italy.

SOME EXAMPLES OF Early Films

- Rome, Open City (1945) Dir. Roberto Rossellini
- The Bicycle Thieves (1948) Dir. Vittorio De Sica
- Ossessione (1942) Dir. Luchino Visconti
- I Vitelloni (1953) Dir. Federico Fellini
- Umberto D (1952) Dir. Federico Fellini

SOME EXAMPLES OF Later Films

Some films influenced by Neorealists:
- Body and Soul (1947) Dir. Robert Rossen
- Salt of the Earth (1954) Dir. H. Biberman
- Padre Padrone (1977) Dir. Paolo and Vittorio Taviani

Bollywood

FILM MOVEMENT
1940s onward

Context

- Bollywood: name of the Hindi film industry. The name comes from a comparison with Hollywood as India is one of the largest film industries in the world, frequently producing over 1000 films annually. Bollywood is an amalgamation of Bombay (now Mumbai) and Hollywood. It is one section of a colossal Indian film industry that makes films in many languages.
- Bollywood films encompass about 20% of the total output of Indian cinema.
- 1947 saw British India divided into India and Pakistan, allowing India to become a free democracy. Ironically this freedom was not extended to its film industry. Censorship tightened; nudity, lustful kissing and sex were not allowed on screen, hence the use of song and dance to display a degree of sexuality and eroticism.

Conventions

- Although Bollywood conjures up the musical genre, it does encompass many genres. These being: topical, mythological, historical, romance and masala (a hybrid of romance, comedy, musical and action genres).
- Use of love triangle narrative structure told through song and dance.
- Moralistic themes of good triumphing over evil.
- Presence of faith and religion.
- Elaborate sets and brightly coloured costumes, usually decorative authentic saris.
- Large cast incorporated into choreographed song and dance extravaganza routines.
- Use of Hindi language.

SOME EXAMPLES OF Early Films

- Sholay (1975) Dir. Ramesh Sippy
- Pyaasa (1957) Dir. Guru Dutt
- Awaara (1951) Dir. Raj Kapoor
- Anand (1971) Dir. Hrishikesh Mukherjee
- Mughal-e-Azam (1960) Dir. K Asif
- Mother India (1957) Dir. Mehboob Khan

SOME EXAMPLES OF Later Films

- Dilwale Dulhania Jayenge (1995) Dir. Aditya Chopra
- Jab We Met (2007) Dir. Imtiaz Ali
- Queen (2014) Dir. Vikas Bahl
- Dangal (2016) Dir. Nitesh Tiwari
- Lagaan (2001) Dir. Ashutosh Gowariker

French New Wave

FILM MOVEMENT 1958-1965

Context

- After the traumatic experience of WW2, a generation gap emerged between the 'old school' of French filmmakers and the younger generation who wanted change.
- In the 50s a collective of French film critics, led by Andre Bazan formed the ground-breaking journal of film criticism *Cahier Du Cinema*. It had two guiding principles:
1. A rejection of classical montage-style filmmaking in favour of mise-en-scène (placing in the scene), preferring reality over manipulation via editing.
2. A conviction that the best films show a personal artistic expression and should bear a stamp of personal authorship, much as great works of literature bear the stamp of the writer. This latter tenet would be dubbed by American film critic Andrew Sarris the auteur (author) theory.

Conventions

- Most discontinuous narratives seen since surrealism.
- Lack of goal orientated protagonist (hero drifts).
- Loose cause and effect narrative.
- Resolution is open and uncertain.
- Jump cuts: a non-naturalistic edit, usually a section of a continuous shot that is removed unexpectedly or illogically.
- Shooting on location.
- Use of natural lighting.
- Improvised dialogue and plotting.
- Direct sound recording.
- Long takes dominate.
- Use of portable equipment, particularly hand-held cameras.
- Breaking of the fourth wall.

SOME EXAMPLES OF
Early Films

- The 400 Blows (Les Quatre Cents Coups) Dir. Francois Truffaut (1959)
- Jules and Jim (Jules Et Jim) Dir. Francois Truffaut (1962)
- Breathless (A bout de souffle) Dir. Jean Luc Godard (1960)

SOME EXAMPLES OF
Later Films

Some films influenced by French New Wave:
- Hannah and her Sisters (1986) Dir. Woody Allen
- Pulp Fiction (1994) Dir. Quentin Tarantino
- Eternal Sunshine of the Spotless Mind (2004) Dir. Michael Gondry

British New Wave

FILM MOVEMENT 1959–1963

Context

- Britain's history is steeped in the cultural construct of class divisions. The New Wave films placed working class characters at the centre of the narrative, not as support or comic relief, showing the protagonist as embodying anti-establishment ideals, being independent and not subservient to those considered of higher class.
- Post war affluence brought a consumer culture linked to higher disposable incomes. However, this did little to remove class boundaries. Thus, these films were born out of a desire to challenge the status quo, to shift the focus from inherited class status to a social landscape based on meritocracy.
- Although the films highlighted the complex class issues, they did not succeed in breaking the stratified social hierarchies.

Conventions

- Films depicted a class divide and gave a voice to the raw reality of urban working life. Known as 'kitchen sink realism' films.
- Social realism portrayed through uncompromising, gritty, raw treatment of the working class, including its alienated and frustrated youth, often referred to as angry young men.
- Sexual content more forthright and frank. Due to changes in censorship, aspects such as premarital sex, abortion, prostitution and homosexuality were dealt with progressively.
- Frequently set in bleak Northern locations rather than the historical studio set up. The landscape was used to elicit emotion.
- Use of natural lighting.
- Use of working class actors rather than studio stars.

SOME EXAMPLES OF Early Films

- Look Back in Anger (1959) Dir. Tony Richardson
- Saturday Night and Sunday Morning (1960) Dir. Karel Reisz
- The Sporting Life (1963) Dir. Lindsay Anderson

SOME EXAMPLES OF Later Films

Some films influenced by British New Wave:
- Kes (1969) Dir. Ken Loach
- Ratcatcher (1999) Dir. Lynne Ramsay
- Brassed Off (1996) Dir. Mark Herman

Japanese New Wave

FILM MOVEMENT 1950s–1970s

Context

- Japan's studio system suffered due to the weakened economy caused by WW2. To save themselves, studios promoted young filmmakers who soon became disenchanted by their lack of freedom and set up independently, making films that contained anti-establishment and social criticism themes.
- The Art Theatre Guild was formed as a means of producing and distributing their films outside of the studio system.
- Post WW2 saw a politically divided country ignited by the signing of the Treaty of Mutual Cooperation and Security between USA and Japan that left many feeling that Japan's autonomy would be compromised. On film, young filmmakers explored what it meant to be Japanese, rejecting aspects of American classical filmmaking.

Conventions

- Narratives centred around delinquent, alienated youth looking to establish an identity in post war Japan.
- Highlighted the fragmented and dysfunctional, nature of society.
- Delved into previously taboo topics of homosexuality, rape and incest. Broadened the exploration of gender roles, social inequality, and xenophobia (particularly in relation to Koreans).
- Honest reflection and investigation of the contextual issues surrounding post war Japan, including generational disconnect.
- No overarching conventions, however common techniques such as use of hand held camera, flashbacks, compositional experimentation, and inclusion of fantasy was incorporated across many films.

SOME EXAMPLES OF
Early Films

- Cruel Story of Youth (1960) Dir. Nagisa Oshima
- Blackmail is my Life (1968) Dir. Kinji Fukasaku
- Tokyo Drifter (1966) Seijun Suzuki
- Branded to Kill (1967) Seijun Suzuki
- Woman of the Dunes (1964) Dir. Hiroshi Teshigahara

SOME EXAMPLES OF
Later Films

- A Clockwork Orange (1971) Stanley Kubrick
- After Life (1998) Hirokazu Kore-eda
- Ghost Dog (1999) Jim Jarmusch

Hong Kong New Wave

FILM MOVEMENT 1970s–1980s

Context

- The 70s saw the First New Wave of filmmakers arise out of a convergence of factors; these directors were young, had been mostly western educated, had experience in television, and made films on the back of the 70s economic boom financed by independent film companies.
- These filmmakers worked outside of the studio system. Their films dealt with local themes and issues, and displayed a synchronicity with western popular culture.
- The 80s saw Hong Kong as the powerhouse of the Asian film industry. This era ushered in the Second New Wave of directors who dealt with West vs. East collusion, particularly the uptake of western popular culture, concern with Chinese take-over, and contextual issues concerning identity and crime via martial arts and crime films.

Conventions

- Explored cultural and social issues specific to Hong Kong, reflecting social unease. E.g., cultural displacement, crime and alienation.
- Inclusion of Cantonese dialect rather than Mandarin, asserting Hong Kong identity.
- Experimentation with narrative and cinematic techniques. E.g., non-linear, multi-layered narrative, use of hand held camera, fragmented narratives.
- Use of synchronous sound.
- Inclusion of urban settings, real and immersive.
- Experimentation with visual and special effects. E.g., motion blur, bokeh lighting.
- Transformation or appropriation of existing genre elements by reframing audience expectation around a particular element, such as how the protagonist is constructed.

SOME EXAMPLES OF
Early Films

First New Wave Films
- The Secret (1979) Dir. Ann Hui
- Father and Son (1981) Dir. Allen Fong
- The Extra (1978) Dir. Yim Ho
- The Butterfly Murders (1979) Dir. Tsui Hark
- Cops and Robbers (1979) Dir. Alex Cheung
- A Better Tomorrow (1986) John Woo

SOME EXAMPLES OF
Later Films

Second New Wave Films:
- Face/Off (1997) John Woo
- Rouge (1987) Stanley Kwan
- Mission Impossible 2 (2000) John Woo
- Chungking Express (1994) Dir. Wong Kar-Wa
- Comrades: Almost a Love Story (1996) Peter Chan

New Hollywood

FILM MOVEMENT 1960s–1980s

Context

- New Hollywood, also known as American New Wave, grew out of the demise of the studio system, a change in the MPAA (Motion Picture Association of America) previously known as the Hays Code, and an audience hungry for more explicit content. The lifting of restrictions on content allowed for narratives to move away from the studio based genre formula, and revel in freedom.
- Narratives were aimed at a younger, more educated audience who were less impressed by escapism and spectacle.
- Hollywood films were hit by the rise of television, an influx of foreign films that shifted audience expectation regarding film narratives, and a rise in independent filmmakers. To ensure survival, mainstream Hollywood turned to significant experimental techniques during this period.

Conventions

- More auteurship. Less studio control, more director control of films.
- Exploration of previously taboo subjects such as sex, violence, and anti-establishmentarianism.
- Exploration of American morality.
- Narrative structure is loose, however, it follows the three act structure of introduction, rising action, and resolution.
- Mise-en-scène focuses on realism rather than stylised glamour.
- Continuity, eye-line match, and adherence to the 180° rule all contribute to suspension of disbelief.
- Use of location shooting as a clear step away from Studio Hollywood.
- Use of popular culture, including music.
- Technological experimentation including 3D cinema and surround sound (Dolby Stereo).

SOME EXAMPLES OF
Early Films

- Bonnie and Clyde (1967) Dir. Arthur Penn
- The Graduate (1967) Dir. Mike Nichols
- 2001: A Space Odyssey (1968) Dir. Stanley Kubrick
- Planet of the Apes (1968) Dir. F.J. Schaffner
- Badlands (1973) Dir. Terrence Malick

SOME EXAMPLES OF
Later Films

- A Clockwork Orange (1971) Dir. Stanley Kubrick
- The Godfather (1972) Dir. Francis Ford Coppola
- American Graffiti (1973) Dir. George Lucas
- Chinatown (1974) Dir. Roman Polanski

Australian New Wave

FILM MOVEMENT 1975-1985

Context

- Reflected and created the overseas image of Australian culture consisting of hard drinking, blokey-blokes, who live in the outback enjoying the land.
- Directors emerged from the newly established Australian Film, Television and Radio School, coupled with government funding saw approximately four hundred films made during this period. It is the volume of films that mark the resurgence of the industry rather than an experimental approach to cinema or a rejection of filmmaking norms.
- Character driven narratives.
- Use of landscape in a variety of ways.
- Introduction of R rating saw a rise in Ozploitation films that were defined as being crass, vulgar, and misogynistic.

Conventions

- Three main categories: period film, genre outback film, and social realist films. Ozploitation films were a sub genre of the above and used Australian slang, were sexually comedic, and embraced the Australian ability to laugh at themselves.
- Defined by use of location shooting in the Australian outback with wide open spaces to express concepts such as isolation or identification (budget constraints necessitated use of natural landscape).
- Male dominance couched in 'ockerism'.
- More violence and sexuality due to relaxation of censorship laws.
- Social realist films tended to veer away from using the landscape as a prop, focusing instead on everyday struggles.
- National identity created, expressing Australian culture.

SOME EXAMPLES OF
Early Films

- Sunday Too Far Away (1975) Dir. Ken Hannam
- Picnic at Hanging Rock (1975) Dir. Peter Weir
- Alvin Purple (1973) Dir. Tim Burstall
- Newsfront (1978) Phillip Noyce
- Mad Max (1979) George Miller

SOME EXAMPLES OF
Later Films

- Muriel's Wedding (1994) Dir. PJ Hogan
- The Castle (1997) Dir. Rob Sitch
- Rabbit Proof Fence (2002) Phillip Noyce
- The Adventures of Priscilla: Queen of the Desert (1994) Dir. Stephan Elliot

New Mexican Cinema

FILM MOVEMENT 1990s–

Context

- 1940s -50s considered the golden age aided by two events (1) The Cinema Bank was set up by government to provide funds to filmmakers and, (2) America provided Mexico with film stock and equipment after they became allies in WW2.
- Film output declined in the 60s due to lack of government support, which unfortunately coincided with the arrival of television, furthering the decline.
- The late 90s-2000s saw the industry crippled by the economic crisis. A lack of government finance, coupled with limited exhibition venues saw many film professionals leave for more fertile grounds, some landing in America.
- The late 2000s saw government incentives return to filmmaking, this, combined with private investments, generated a revival.

Conventions

- Social criticism such as dealing with recurring themes of social division, issues of endemic poverty, family structure and gender roles, political concerns such as liberation and change, issues associated with drug cartels, as well as Mexican immigration to the US, led film content.
- Hand held or shaky camera work, raw and natural evoking brutal realism.
- Use of long takes and tracking shots.
- Sergei Eisenstein spent 14 months in Mexico beginning in 1931, his montage techniques were continually employed to challenge audience perception of realism.
- Luis Buñuel, after fleeing Spain, settled in Mexico in 1946, making 21 films. His surrealist film influence can be seen scattered throughout Mexican films.

SOME EXAMPLES OF Early Films

- *Nosotros Los Pobres* We the Poor (1947) Dir. Ismael Rodriguez
- *Los Olvidados* The Young and the Damned (1950) Dir. Luis Buñuel
- *El Topo* The Mole (1970) Dir. Alejandro Jodorowsky

SOME EXAMPLES OF Later Films

- *Y Tu Mamá También* And Your Mother Too (2001) Dir. Alfonso Cuarón
- *Amores Perros* Love's a Bitch (2000) Dir. Alejandro González Iñárritu
- Pan's Labyrinth (2006) Dir. Guillermo del Toro

Dogme '95

FILM MOVEMENT
1990s - 2005

Context

- Dogme is the Danish word for Dogma. Danish filmmakers, Lars Von Trier and Thomas Vinterberg wrote a ten point 'vow of chastity' or manifesto that constitute the movement.
- Created as a reaction against the vast number of commercial, large budget, gimmicky films, riddled with special effects, the intention was to make pure, smaller budget films, free from copious post-production modifications, showing a desire to showcase the narrative and good storytelling over hiding behind the technical artifice of commercial extravaganzas.
- The 'rules' created a style similar to documentaries due to the location shooting, lack of non-diegetic sound, natural lighting, hand held shots, and no inclusion of additional props to set the scene.
- Disbanded in 2005 after igniting change.

Conventions

- The ten point manifesto written by Trier and Vinterberg asked filmmakers to create realistic films, free from 'illusion.' It stated:
  1. Filming must be done on location. Props and sets must not be brought in
  2. Music must not be used unless it occurs within the scene being filmed
  3. The camera must be hand-held; filming must take place where the action takes place
  4. The film must be in colour. No special lighting
  5. Optical work and filters are forbidden
  6. No superficial action (No murders, weapons, etc.)
  7. No temporal or geographical alienation
  8. No genre movies
  9. The aspect ratio must be 4:3, not wide-screen
  10. The director must not be credited

SOME EXAMPLES OF Early Films

- The Idiots (1998) Dir. Lars von Trier
- Italian for Beginners (2000) Dir. Lone Scherfig
- The Celebration (1998) Dir. Thomas Vinterberg
- Mifune (1999) Dir. Soren Kragh-Jacobsen

SOME EXAMPLES OF Later Films

Films influenced by the movement:
- Donnie Darko (2001) Dir. Richard Kelly
- Hotel (2001) Dir. Mike Figis
- Melancholia (2011) Lars von Trier
- Thomas Vinterberg (2012) The Hunt

Art Films

A few suggestions

 *A film is never really good unless the camera is an eye in the head of a poet."*
Orson Welles

- Citizen Kane (1941) Orson Welles
- Mullholland Drive (2001) David Lynch
- Andrei Rublev (1966) Andrei Tarkovsky
- The Seventh Seal (1957) Ingmar Bergman
- Battleship Potemkin (1925) Sergei Eisenstein
- Tokyo Story (1953) Yasujiro Ozu
- Blow-Up (1966) Michelangelo Antonioni
- Un Chien Andalou (1929) Luis Buñuel & Salvador Dalí
- Eraserhead (1977) David Lynch
- Shadows (1959) John Cassavetes
- Enter the Void (2009) Gaspar Noé
- Eternal Sunshine of the Spotless Mind (2004) Charlie Kaufman
- Melancholia (2011) Lars von Trier
- Donnie Darko (2001) Richard Kelly
- Being John Malkovich (1999) Charlie Kaufman
- 2001: A Space Odyssey (1968) Stanley Kubrick
- Hunger (2008) Steve McQueen
- The Lobster (2015) Yorgos Lanthimos
- Fish Tank (2009) Andrea Arnold
- Bronson (2008) Nicolas Winding Refn
- Biutiful (2010) Alejandro González Iñárritu
- Babel (2006) Alejandro González Iñárritu
- Inherent Vice (2014) Paul Thomas Anderson
- Old Boy (2003) Park Chan Wook
- The 400 Blows (1959) François Truffaut
- I vitelloni (1953) Federico Fellini
- Wild Strawberries (1957) Ingmar Bergman
- Irréversible (2002) Gaspar Noe
- Night and Fog (1955) Alain Resnais
- The Bicycle Thieves (1948) Vittorio De Sica
- Birdman (2014) Alejandro G. Iñárritu
- Elephant (2003) Gus Van Sant
- Farenheit 451 (1966) François Truffaut
- Rashomon (1950) Akira Kurosawa
- La Dolce Vita (1960) Federico Fellini
- Whiplash (2014) Damien Chazel

MUST WATCH FILMS
some suggestions

- The Graduate (1967) Mike Nichols
- Psycho (1960) Alfred Hitchcock
- A Clockwork Orange (1971) Stanley Kubrick
- Breathless (1960) Jean Luc Godard
- American Beauty (1999) Sam Mendes
- Barton Fink (1991) Coen Brothers
- Blackboard Jungle (1955) Richard Brooks
- Blade Runner (1982) Ridley Scott
- The Big Lebowski (1998) Coen Brothers
- The Cabinet of Dr Caligari (1920) Robert Wiene
- Casablanca (1942) Michael Curtiz
- Double Indemnity (1944) Billy Wilder
- Dune (1984) David Lynch
- Edward Scissorhands (1990) Tim Burton
- Fargo (1996) The Coen Brothers
- Fight Club (1999) David Fincher
- Gone with the Wind (1939) Victor Fleming
- Chinatown (1974) Roman Polanski
- Heathers (1989) Michael Lehmann
- In Bruges (2008) Martin McDonagh
- Jerry Maguire (1996) Cameron Crowe
- The Lord of the Rings Trilogy - Peter Jackson
- Mad Max (1979) George Miller
- The Maltese Falcon (1941) John Huston
- Memento (2000) Christopher Nolan
- Muriel's Wedding (1994) P. J. Hogan
- My Own Private Idaho (1991) Gus Van Sant
- The Party (1968) Blake Edwards
- Picnic at Hanging Rock (1975) Peter Weir
- Pulp Fiction (1994) Quentin Tarantino
- Punch Drunk Love (2002) Paul Thomas Anderson
- The Royal Tenenbaums (2001) Wes Anderson
- Rear Window (1954) Alfred Hitchcock
- The Grand Budapest Hotel (2014) Wes Anderson
- Scarface (1983) Brian De Palma
- The Shawshank Redemption (1994) Frank Darabont
- Annie Hall (1977) Woody Allen
- Spirited Away (2001) Hayao Miyazaki
- Star Wars (1977) George Lucas
- This is Spinal Tap (1984) Rob Reiner
- Wake in Fright (1971) Ted Kotcheff
- Rebel Without a Cause (1955) Nicholas Ray
- Jaws (1975) Steven Spielberg
- Rocky Horror Picture Show (1975) Jim Sharman
- The Warriors (1979) Walter Hill
- Princess Bride (1987) Rob Reiner
- Harold and Maude (1971) Hal Ashby

MUST WATCH FILMS
some suggestions

- Metropolis (1927) Fritz Lang
- Monty Python and the Holy Grail (1975) Terry Gilliam and Terry Jones
- One Flew Over the Cuckoo's Nest (1975) Milos Forman
- Sunset Boulevard (1950) Billy Wilder
- The Castle (1997) Rob Sitch
- Rain Man (1988) Barry Levinson
- E.T the Extra-Terrestrial (1982) Steven Spielberg
- Children of Men (2006) Alfonso Cuarón
- Trainspotting (1996) Danny Boyle
- The Godfather (1972) Francis Ford Coppola
- Ferris Bueller's Day Off (1986) John Hughes
- The Breakfast Club (1985) John Hughes
- Forrest Gump (1994) Robert Zemeckis
- Taxi Driver (1976) Martin Scorsese
- Raging Bull (1980) Martin Scorsese
- Dr. Strangelove or: How I Learned to Stop Worrying and Love the Bomb (1964) Stanley Kubrick
- Dr Zhivago (1965) David Lean
- Close Encounters of the Third Kind (1977) Steven Spielberg
- Hero (2002) Zhang Yimou
- Blue Velvet (1986) David Lynch
- Koyaanisqatsi (1982) Godfrey Reggio
- Run Lola Run (1998) Tom Tykwer
- Solaris (1972) Andrei Tarkovsky
- Jules et Jim (1962) François Truffaut
- Kill Bill (2003) Quentin Tarantino
- Kiss Me Deadly (1955) Robert Aldrich
- The Last Wave (1977) Peter Weir
- Pan's Labyrinth (2006) Guillermo del Toro
- Logan's Run (1976) Michael Anderson

Film Movements

Review & sample questions

Sample questions containing film movements:

1. Analyse the aesthetic innovations introduced by a film movement.
2. Discuss how context influences aesthetics.
3. Analyse how globalisation has influenced film aesthetics.
4. Analyse how personal expression appeals to a niche audience.
5. Discuss the artistic benefit of a film movement.
6. Analyse how media trends have shaped film grammar.

 **Film movements - main essential content to discuss:**

01
- Be aware of the **codes and conventions** associated with particular **film movements**. What innovative cinematic and narrative techniques were used to push the boundaries of **film grammar** and show a **distinctive style**?

02
- Have an understanding of **context** and be able to discuss how relevant film movements comment on a point in time, whether that be a cultural, political or social comment, each movement reflects what is **relevant and authentic** to audiences of the time.

03
- Film movements are **interlinked**, either rejecting the elements of established movements (think surrealism rejecting Hollywood film grammar) or endeavouring to **manipulate and innovate** using available technologies (think French New Wave).

04
- Can you discuss how a film you have studied has been shaped by the **conventions** of a film movement?

Chapter Four
Film Aesthetics

- Film as art
- Art film techniques
- Aesthetics in film
- Case study: *Run Lola Run*
- Innovative narrative structure: *Run Lola Run*
- Video game aesthetic: *Run Lola Run*
- Sample questions
- Review

Film Aesthetics

Film Aesthetics

Film as art

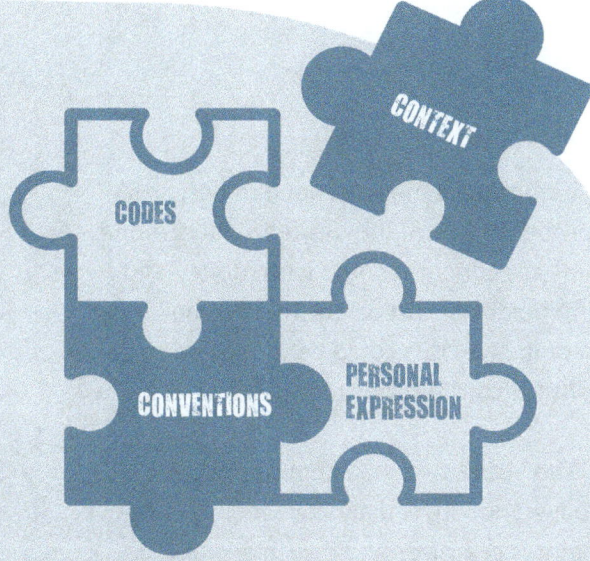

FILM STYLE
A director's personal expression is woven into the film's theme and aesthetic choices. Decisions such as selecting, omitting, and manipulating codes and conventions create a canvas to showcase creative vision. By intentionally manipulating narrative structure, experimenting with innovative camera techniques, using stylised colour palettes, and playing with aural and visual motifs, a film's unique style is created, reflecting the director's aesthetic and contextual influences.

CODES
- creative consideration of aspects such as colour palette, visual motifs, aural motifs
- aesthetic engineering of mise-en-scène
- character subjectivity.

CONVENTIONS
- experiment with narrative structure
- manipulate genre conventions
- innovative use of technology
- manipulates time and space
- experimentation with conventional editing.

CONTEXT
- aesthetics is a consequence of cultural production. Context always affects content; therefore when, where, and who the intended audience is, will shape a film's style and content.

PERSONAL EXPRESSION
- aesthetic intention
- manipulation and innovation with technology and film grammar
- commentary on issues or topics to construct a theme that critiques and questions the status quo.

What is Film Art?

What defines film as art? We can all identify Hollywood blockbuster films, but can we identify an art film? Is it even possible to categorise film as art since art is subjective? There are certain aesthetic considerations to look at in order to differentiate commercial films from art films — is it an art film or is it an ambitious mainstream film?

1. Commercial mainstream film has, as its number one aim, the desire to make money. Art films are concerned less with money and more with **aesthetic intention**. The filmmaker has an objective, this could be to make **a social or political comment or to explore an issue**.

2. The visual style of a commercial Hollywood film is distinctive in that it is seamless and invisible; the filmmaking process is hidden. The narrative structure is linear cause and effect based, the characters are goal orientated, and realism is adhered to. Contrast this with an art film where there is a **loose association given to cause and effect, and narrative closure is not emphasised.** Filmmaking grammar (as defined by the Hollywood paradigm) is quite often deliberately rejected, aspects such as the fourth wall, 180° rule, and continuity editing are experimented with, and **less emphasis is placed on action and more on the emotional driver of the protagonist.** The filmmaker experiments with the expected rules of film grammar in order to **manipulate, experiment and extend the boundaries of accepted film grammar**.

3. Hollywood films are aimed at a large homogeneous, mainstream mass audience. Art films direct their content to a **small, niche audience** of like-minded people. Due to the smaller audience Art Films will often be shown at Art House cinemas rather than a multiplex.

4. Art films have a **distinctive style,** feel and overall aesthetic. The foundations of art film arose out of cultural context, and in some cases in direct opposition to Hollywood.

5. Art films, due to budget constraints and a desire to use actors that the audience do not have a preconception of, will often **use lesser known or amateur actors.**

6. Mainstream films are frequently action orientated and escapist in intent. Art house films require the audience to be more **active in making meaning.** Ready-made, hand fed answers to the narrative dilemma are not provided.

7. Hollywood films are concerned with realism, whereas art house is often the **antithesis of realism.**

> "A good film is when the price of the dinner, the theatre admission and the babysitter were worth it."
>
> Alfred Hitchcock

Film Aesthetics

Aesthetics concerns itself with defining what is artistic, beautiful or stylish. Arising from this definition is the subjective nature of aesthetics. Who defines what is art, or beauty, or style? Aesthetics in film is the study of what makes a film artistic, what makes it visually and aurally appealing, and what gives it an edge.

MEDIA AESTHETICS: DEFINED BY STYLE, FORM, CHOICE OF CODES & CONVENTIONS, & USE OF TECHNOLOGY

Film conventions

Includes:
- How is the narrative structure manipulated? Does it mimic Hollywood linear cause and effect or is it more episodic in construction?
- Does the narrative include a definite resolution or is it open-ended?
- How are time and space manipulated?
- Performance of actors - amateur or professional?
- Continuity editing or experimentation?

Technology

Includes:
- Mobility of camera
- Sound equipment
- Access to lighting
- Film stock
- Cost associated with black and white or colour film
- Editing techniques

Film codes

Includes:
- Deviation from Hollywood standard of aesthetic realism
- Use of lighting - is it three point?
- Use of colour - how is the film colour graded? What connotations are created?
- Motion - consider the rhythm and pace of the film. Are long tracking shots used or short, sharp shots?
- Sound - synchronous or non-synchronous?

Aesthetics is concerned with the **style and form of film,** it is about the filmmaker's **intention,** and the viewer's reception, in terms of appreciating the creative, symbolic and expressive intent. Often these defining factors can be seen as a **deviation from, or a rejection of, the mainstream Hollywood formulaic narrative.**

Art Film Techniques

Aesthetics in film

Techniques found in Art films:

1. **Innovative visual and aural aesthetic**
A distinctive style is shown through aspects such as mise-en-scène, inclusion of visual and aural motifs, choice of colour palette and an experimentation with medium. Moreover, consideration is given to the rhythm and pace of editing; lighting, camera movement, framing, and sound operate on more than a purely technical level.

2. **Manipulation of narrative structure**
Experimentation with the narrative structure occurs within Art films as they frequently deviate from the linear, cause and effect model shaped by Classical Hollywood. Plot events are often traced in a non-linear, circular, multi-layered or episodic manner.

3. **Character subjectivity**
The protagonist often acts as the emotional driver of the film. The audience invests in the main character's emotional journey, can see what they see, and feel what they feel. The narrative is driven by characters rather than action.

4. **Political and social comment**
The intention of the filmmaker is weighted less to financial gain, and more toward making a cultural or political comment designed to engineer social change through aesthetic capability.

5. **Open-ended narrative**
Narratives conclude, but do not necessarily resolve. Open-ended resolutions are a hallmark of Art films. They demand active audience participation.

6. **Manipulation of time**
Manipulation of time can occur through temporal order, duration and frequency. Aesthetic manipulation of **temporal order** considers how the plot events are sequenced; inclusion of devices such as flashbacks and flash forwards can add narrative intrigue. **Temporal duration** refers to the length of time represented by events in the plot. Techniques such as split screen, simultaneous time, jump cuts and slow motion, to name a few, create a stylistic visual aesthetic and add emphasis to plot events. **Temporal frequency** refers to the number of times an event is shown within the plot. Traditionally the main plot event unfolds once, narrative and aesthetic interest can be injected by repeating the plot event to show a differing point of view, to create emphasis or to show how a minor alteration within each repetition alters the outcome of the narrative.

7. **Manipulation of space**
Film space is manipulated primarily through mise-en-scène, montage and sound. Suspension of disbelief occurs when the audience is able to engage with spatial elements such as costumes, setting and performance; aesthetic connection occurs when these elements are elevated by the richness of cinematic language. Consider the symmetrical compositions and centred shots used to manipulate space in Wes Anderson films, the geometric perfection creates a theatrical aesthetic; one that is very pleasing to the eye.

Art Film Techniques

Aesthetics in film

 Manipulation of space continues with the use of montage, particularly intellectual montage whereby the filmmaker aesthetically places two shots together and asks the audience to actively engage to determine a third concept. Moreover, camera work such as depth of field or camera framing and movement focuses the audiences' attention, emphasising specific elements within space and time.

 ### 8. Deviation from realism
Mainstream Hollywood films usually celebrate realism. They seek to replicate the real world through accurate use of mise-en-scène, and by mimicking temporal and spatial reality. Conventions, such as continuity editing are seamlessly employed to convey an effortless version of the real world. Art films, on the other hand, experiment with conventions; stretch the boundaries, tease and play with how we represent our world, extending and manipulating the accepted conventions of film grammar.

Conventions that frequently deviate from realism in Art films are outlined in Bordwell's 1979 essay *The Art of Cinema as a Mode of Film Practice*:
- A loose cause and effect exist within the narrative construction; linear story telling is often absent
- Open-ended resolutions are utilised
- The protagonist is not as goal orientated as his or her Hollywood counterpart
- Emotion is prefaced over action.

 ### 9. Experimentation with rhythm and pace
The pace can be fast or slow to emotionally engage the audience. Pacing should vary to create a suite of emotions from suspense and tension, through to joy and action. The rhythm arises from the film's pace. It creates a flow, a mood and overall style for the film.

 ### 10. Manipulation of the medium
Experimenting with or combining mediums to enhance the visual experience is an aesthetic technique used in some art films. Using mediums such as still photography, animation, video tape and film stock in the one film allows for narrative depth and interest.

 ### 11. Choice of actors
Mostly unknown actors are used, or if known, the actor will play a role far removed from previous audience expectations, using the film as a vehicle for art.

Film Aesthetics

Run Lola Run

Case Study - Run Lola Run

Some ART FILM CONVENTIONS

- innovative visual aesthetic
- manipulation of narrative structure
- character subjectivity
- open-ended narrative
- political and social comment
- manipulation of time and space
- deviation from realism
- experimentation with rhythm, pace, and continuity editing
- manipulation of the medium

Run Lola Run (1998) directed by Tom Tykwer tells the story of Lola, a young German woman who must come up with 100 000 Deutsch Marks in twenty minutes in order to save her boyfriend Manni from a vengeful criminal Ronnie, whose money Manni accidentally left on the subway. The story is segmented into three twenty minute retellings of the same narrative arc, with the ultimate outcome of each altered by the actions of the protagonist Lola.

Innovative Visual Aesthetic

The use of **VISUAL & AURAL MOTIFS:** *Run Lola Run* bears a distinctive **visual aesthetic** constructed from the use of numerous recurring motifs. These include:

Red

Use of a **distinctive colour palette:** the protagonist, Lola, is associated with the colour **red**, she sports fiery **red** hair, uses a fire engine **red** telephone that dramatically flies through the air at the start of each new sequence to signal Manni's request for help and Lola's subsequent leap into action and, a **red** ambulance containing a paramedic in a **red** suit appears in each run. The money stolen from the grocery store is placed in a **red** plastic bag, perhaps foreshadowing Lola's death.

Red interludes create narrative distance from the fast paced action that aesthetically transitions the viewer from the 'death' to 'life' sequences using the monochrome **red** wash to signify a 'reset' or rebirth. The **red** overlay used in these sequences links directly to the topic of conversation being held by Manni and Lola as they lie next to each other in bed. The **red** is suggestive of love and intimacy,

Film Aesthetics

Run Lola Run

Innovative Visual Aesthetic

creating a more subjective feel and developing an emotional rapport between the audience, Lola and Manni. Lola asks Manni, "Do you love me?" **Red** connotes passion, love, action and danger. This scene sees Lola questioning her passion and commitment to Manni. He asks her, "Lola, what's wrong? You want to leave me?" As the scene concludes we transition from the **red** overlaying black and white film and revert to colour. We return to Lola lying on the road, near death, having just been shot in the stomach by a police officer. Lola looks up and states, "But I don't want to. I don't want to leave." The **red** bag of money that was thrown into the air starts to descend, signalling the start of the second run.

Gold & Yellow

Yellow/gold is associated with Manni. We first met him in a **yellow** public phone booth where he is pleading with Lola, "Help me, Lola! I don't know what to do," as he hysterically yells at her to find a way to come up with the 100 000 Deutsch Marks to replace the lost cash he left on the subway. **Yellow**, historically is associated with cowardice. The damsel-in-distress paradigm is reversed with Manni begging Lola for help whilst visually being surrounded by the **yellow** phone booth and the **yellow** Spirale sign on the supermarket wall.

Gold, being a hue of yellow, and having connotations of wealth and extravagance, is attached to Manni as a symbol of his illegally obtained spoils. **Gold**, representing wealth, appears in many trimmings in the casino and bank scenes. The workmen carrying the pane of glass across the road are dressed in **gold/yellow** jump suits, potentially signifying the fragile and precious nature of their load and finally, when Lola legally achieves her aim of obtaining 100 000 Deutsch Marks by winning it at the Casino, her valued money is placed in a **gold bag** suggesting a rich future. Lola wears light **green** cargo pants. Green connotes health and well-being, and the colour can be attached to the concept of money, the 'green back.' The rubbish bag Lola uses to carry the stolen money away from the bank robbery scene is **green.** Lola achieves her goal of obtaining the money in this scene, however, Manni 'dies' rendering the value of the money worthless.

Spirals

Spirals are used to represent the continuity of life; the circle or **spiral** continues on and on. Conversely, **spirals** represent chaos and confusion. The first time we met Lola she is in animated form running at speed through a fast moving, **spiralling** time tunnel. The movement connotes urgency and confusion. Once Lola emerges from the tunnel she enters the real world via a fast pace zooming shot that rapidly journeys from an aerial view of a city, through an open window of an apartment, down a corridor and onto a ringing red phone that Lola (now transformed into her real life form) picks up with a questioning, "Manni?" thus signalling the end of the **prologue** and segueing into the **premise** of the film.

The **mise-en-scène** of spirals continues on the imprint of the pillow cases seen in the **red** overlay scenes.

Film Aesthetics

Run Lola Run

ART FILM CONVENTIONS IN RUN LOLA RUN

Some **VISUAL MOTIFS**

"To the question, 'Is the cinema an art?' my answer is, 'what does it matter? You can make films, or you can cultivate a garden. Both have as much claim to being called art as a poem by Verlaine or a painting by Delacroix...Art is making."

Jean Renoir

Innovative Visual Aesthetic

Additionally, Tykwer used a **spiralling** camera action that moved around Lola in a 360° frantic movement, signifying the haste and confusion in Lola's mind as she tries to decide who is best positioned to help her find 100 000 DM in twenty minutes. We hear her saying, "Okay! Who? Who?" Once Lola selects Papa as her chosen saviour, the camera pans away from her and tracks into a television set revealing an animated Lola running down a hyper-exaggerated **spiral** set of stairs.

Tykwer incorporates many **aesthetic** avant-garde **spiralling** camera movements to reinforce the frenzied and confused nature of the action. In the supermarket robbery scene Lola and Manni are surrounded by police blocking both ends of a road thus effectively trapping the pair. The camera travels with them as they run up and then back, only to realise they are blocked, and escape is impossible, as this dawns on them, rather than have a static camera on the now still pair, Tykwer manoeuvres the camera in a **360° spiral**, continuing the frantic movement. This frenetic motion is jarringly juxtaposed with the slow paced song *What a Difference a Day Made* by Dinah Washington. The **visual pace** of the images is contrasted with the **aural pace** contained in the slow beat and rhythm of the song. This stark difference engages the audience to question the reality unfolding before them. The song's lyrics (sung in English) contain the words, "I'm a part of you, dear" reinforcing the central narrative **theme** of love. This is underscored in the second **red overlay scene** when Manni questions Lola's love for him by asking, "What would you do if I died?" and she emphatically replies, "I wouldn't let you."

72

Film Aesthetics

Run Lola Run

Some **AURAL MOTIFS**

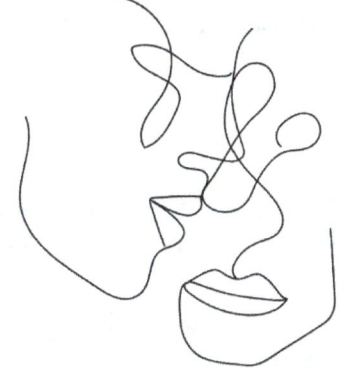

Innovative Visual & Aural Aesthetic

Time

TIME is central to the narrative. The premise of the film is revealed in the opening telephone conversation when Manni says to Lola, "You said, 'Love can do everything' So, find 100 000 marks in **twenty minutes!**" **Time**, or the lack of it, is used as a **narrative device** to propel the characters into action.

The very first sound heard in *Run Lola Run* is the fast paced **ticking of a clock,** which is coupled with a demonic pendulum clock swinging ominously across the screen wiping away the opening credits. The **swishing, creaking, and ticking sounds** are just as ominous as they are foreboding. The use of **sound as an aesthetic device** creates an emotional and intellectual response as the tension builds with each layering of sound, and foreshadows the importance of **time** to the narrative. The camera work positions the audience to engage with the **aural motif of time** by the camera tracking up the face of the pendulum clock, which is set into the wooden body of a monkey, passing over the ticking clock hands and being consumed by the open mouth of the monkey. The all-consuming nature of **time** is shown visually and aurally, thus leaving the audience in no doubt as to its significance.

The **race against time plot premise** is reinforced by the presence of **numerous clocks** throughout the film; the most important of all is the large clock mounted on the wall of the Bolle supermarket clearly seen from Manni's phone booth as he screams at Lola, "In **twenty minutes** I'll be dead unless I steal the money!" This clock is the main reference point for time, it is the **official game time piece** as it counts down the precious **twenty minutes** in each of Lola's runs.

Clocks and watches are seen in Lola's house, in Papa's office, on the wrist of the old lady in the

73

Film Aesthetics

Run Lola Run

ART FILM CONVENTIONS IN RUN LOLA RUN

Innovative Visual & Aural Aesthetic

street who Lola enquires about the time, and in the Casino. The incorporation of a huge **wall mounted clock** into the casino scene reinforces the hyperreal world through which Lola is journeying. **Clocks** do not usually appear in casinos as the absence of clocks allows for **time** to be forgotten and for the players to absorb themselves in their fantasy world.

Time and fate are interlinked. Lola attempts three runs, each with minor variations that have a rippling impact on the **fate** of others. The film is steeped in **causality**, the 'what if' moments that change a person's future. Tykwer's style of highlighting these moments through **still photographs** projected at a fast pace, accompanied by the **clicking of a camera shutter** showing various possible futures for minor characters, examines the impact of **choice, karma and fate**. For instance, in Lola's first run she bumps into a lady (Doris) pushing a pram. Doris yells at Lola, "Watch where you're going! Bitch!" The unfolding series of flash forwards constructed as a montage of still images are startling in their projection into the possible future lives Doris may live, depending on the hand fate deals her. The images shown are of Doris mistreating her child, and drinking too much alcohol, Doris crying as her child has been removed by welfare, and Doris snatching someone else's child from a pram and trying to escape. In her second run Lola only slightly nudges Doris as she runs past. Doris yells, "Watch it, you stupid cow! Fucking bitch!" The still images that follow show Doris buying a lotto ticket, winning the lottery, buying a large house and an expensive car, and appearing to live happily with her husband and child. In the final run Lola avoids bumping into Doris, instead running around her. Doris calls out "Watch out" and the **montage** of images we see predicting her future consist of Doris turning to religion and leaving her husband and child behind.

Causality shows us the link between actions and outcomes, and Tykwer has not walked the mainstream path of showing good actions equating to good outcomes. The concept of one small moment in time having massive repercussions is highlighted through the visual style of **flash forwards. Karma** is questioned as Doris treats Lola badly in the second run by using demeaning expletives, however she appears to be rewarded for her bad behaviour.

Moreover, Tykwer experiments with the **temporal sequencing of time** by relaying the film's back story via the **time manipulation device of a flashback.** Tykwer uses a **black and white montage sequence** to portray the sequence of events leading up to Manni

Film Aesthetics

Run Lola Run

requiring Lola's help. It is here we learn that Manni, a small time criminal, is acting as a courier for Ronnie, a violent and unforgiving crime boss. Manni had expected Lola to pick him up on her moped after he had completed a diamond smuggling transaction. "I went to see that cyclops, and he was finished in no time. And everything was on time, except for you. You were not there." Manni explains that Lola's absence necessitated him walking to the subway carrying a bag containing 100 000 DM. It is on the train that we learn more about Manni's character. Manni bumps into a homeless man and unquestioningly helps him up. Manni recounts, "On the train, there was this bum who somehow fell down. Suddenly, these inspectors showed up. And I got out like always. An old reflex," leaving the bag behind. The **flashback** communicates the essential information regarding the **goal of the protagonist** - replace the contents of the bag or Manni dies, as well as allowing the audience to emotionally connect with the main characters, to care about them successfully achieving their goal even though we know that they are small time criminals. The **flashback** draws the audience into the backstory and allows for emotional connection.

The Number Twenty

The number twenty appears frequently as a **visual motif.** It is, most importantly, the amount of time Lola has to save Manni. All of Lola's runs and actions are centred around the premise that she can achieve her goal in just **twenty minutes.**

The use of real time, rather than compressed time, is a rarity in film. Tykwer uses the **temporal frequency of three** to deliver three versions of the same run using **twenty** minutes of Lola's life shown in **real time.**

Twice, in the casino scene, Lola chooses to place her betting chips on the number **twenty**. The first time Lola anxiously holds her breath, her hands pressed to her face as the roulette wheel spins, finally landing on the number **twenty** and delivering her a win of 3500 DM. She then places all her winnings on the same number, and as the croupier spins the roulette wheel, Lola emits her trademark piercing scream, which allows her to gain control of her environment and will the ball to land on the number **twenty.**

RUN LOLA RUN is no different. We have passionate love, we have a clear action principle, we have a task which runs throughout the film. RUN LOLA RUN works in the same way as the search for the Holy Grail. Only in this case, the grail is worth 100,000 Marks.

Tom Tykwer

Film Aesthetics

Run Lola Run

ART FILM CONVENTIONS IN RUN LOLA RUN

Innovative Aural Aesthetic

Screaming & Shattering Glass

The **aural motif** of Lola **screaming** and **shattering glass** is a recurring **aesthetic device** used to signal Lola's desire to control her environment, to pause the play and gain clarity of direction. The first time we hear Lola **scream** is out of frustration at Manni who is yelling at her down the phone, "You can't get me 100 grand either! He'll rub me out, and all that's left of me will be 100 000 ashes floating down the Spree to the sea. No more Manni! You can't do a thing!" Lola **screams** at him to shut up, and in the process **shatters** a couple of glass bottles sending glass shards clattering to the floor. The distinct **aural juxtaposition** between the explosive shattering glass and the silence that follows is an **innovative aesthetic choice**; not only is the audience intrigued by Lola's ability to break glass with her **screams** but they are now focused on the extreme change in pace from frenetically fast and loud, including jump cuts moving closer into Lola's face, to **virtual silence** with slow push in shots revealing background information about Lola and Manni's relationship. We see a polaroid picture on Lola's pin up board showing her and Manni embracing. The suggestion given is that they know each other well and have been in a relationship for a significant period of time. The camera then slowly pans across a series of discarded Barbie dolls, highlighting the discrepancy between the young adult Lola, who **embodies action and agency**, contrasted with her discarded toys that

represent **stereotypical female passive play**. The **visual aesthetic** is accentuated by a slow moving turtle crossing the floor behind Lola suggesting a **homage** to Aesop's *The Tortoise and the Hare* foreshadowing the outcome of her three runs.

Lola's ability to control her fate through **emitting a high pitched scream** is clearly detailed in the casino scene. It is here that Lola's **lingering scream** defies reason as the continuous sound jolts the ball on the roulette wheel, causing it to land on the number twenty and allowing her to win the required money to save Manni.

> "Her screams are one of her characteristics, a typical sign, as it were. Every time things become tense, and it seems like the chaos is near, Lola tries to gain control of the chaos by means of screaming (by releasing the pressure as it were). Lola's scream is mad, wild a hysterical expression of despair and an effort to take action against the panic and to get things moving."
>
> Tom Tykwer

Film Aesthetics

Run Lola Run

Innovative Aural Aesthetic

The **visual motif of glass** is closely linked to the **themes of fate and chance**. In each run we see yellow clad men carrying a large plate of glass across a road as an ambulance races towards them. **Narrative curiosity** is aroused as the audience is intrigued as to whether the ambulance will smash into the glass, avoid it, or stop in time. The **glass is indicative of the fragility of life** and how just a few moments in time can drastically alter the outcome of a situation.

Sound as an aesthetic creates an emotional and intellectual response to the narrative. Tykwer incorporates the fast pace popular culture techno beat songs, *Wish*, *Running One*, *Running Two* and *Running Three,* all written and composed by him, and sung by Franka Potente (who plays Lola). The constant **frenetic beat is reminiscent of a heartbeat or a ticking clock.** It encourages pace, drive, and pulsating action as we race along with Lola on her three, slightly altered, breakneck journeys to save Manni.

The lyrics of the song *Wish,* written especially for the film, tell the tale of a girl yearning for alternate futures. The **song anchors meaning to the chaotic universe Lola inhabits** and directs the audience to journey with her as she endeavours to find a suitable path. The **non-diegetic song lyrics** give power and agency to Lola, enabling the audience to see her as a figure of control. She wishes she was a hunter, a starship, a princess with armies, a ruler and a writer, to name a few.

The **sound of silence** is used twice as an **effective aesthetic device;** once in the opening when Lola screams at Manni down the phone to shut up, and the scream dies down to complete silence, and again in the bank robbery scene when the teller leaves Lola and her father alone as he goes to the vault to retrieve the required money. The emotionally pained expression and clear discomfort between father and daughter are heightened by the silence. It exacerbates their strained relationship, their lack of communication, and lack of familial bond.

Film Aesthetics: narrative

Run Lola Run

OPENING SEQUENCE OF RUN LOLA RUN

PROLOGUE

Manipulation Of Narrative Structure

Unlike a traditional mainstream film that ensures the audience is aligned with the major protagonist almost instantaneously, the **prologue** of *Run Lola Run* veers away from this well trodden-path. Instead, it introduces the audience to the minor players as the camera spirals through a fog of characters, only occasionally pausing to focus on people whose lives intersect with Lola's. The **aesthetic** images are coupled with a voiceover from Hans Paetsch, a well-known narrator of German fairy tales, potentially chosen to suggest that the narrative is a tale of wonder and possibilities, who says:

*"Man.
Probably the most mysterious species on our planet.
A mystery of unanswered questions.
Who are we? Where do we come from?
Where are we going?
How do we know what we think we know?
Why do we believe anything at all?
Countless questions in search of an answer.
An answer that will give rise to a new question and the next answer will give rise to the next question and so on and so on.
But, in the end, isn't it always
the same question? And always the same answer?"*

The camera comes to rest on a mid-shot of a security guard, who we later learn is Schuster, as he philosophically states:

*"The ball is round.
The game lasts 90 minutes.
That's a fact. Everything else is pure theory.
Here we go!"*

Schuster picks up the ball, kicks it high into the air, and as the camera follows its decent from an aerial view, the fog of people milling about form the letters LOLA RENNT. The ball rapidly falls through the letter 'O' and a graphic match is created with the shape of an animated spiralling tunnel. It is here that we first meet Lola in her cartoon form running through the tunnel. As we have been asked to question what we know, and the **narrative has been framed by a game analogy,** "The ball is round...Here we go!" the appearance of cartoon Lola does not remove us from the diegetic world of the film but rather draws us in more deeply as we are now actively positioned to uncover the **narrative enigma.**

As a **prologue**, the audience is given information about the themes and potential philosophical nature of the narrative. We are asked to question what we believe and embrace the unexpected. Unlike a traditional opening that quickly reveals the protagonist, gives plot clues and establishes a setting, *Run Lola Run* instead uses **epigraphs** from T.S. Eliott, Sepp Herberger and a **prologue** that establishes the themes of fate, chance and destiny.

NARRATIVE MANIPULATION
Run Lola Run

Epigraphs

Run Lola Run opens with the quotes:

We shall not cease from exploration.
And the end of all our exploring
Will be to arrive where we started
And know the place for the first time.

T.S. Eliot

Followed by...

"After the game is before the game."

S. Herberger

FILM AESTHETICS

The film opens with an epigraph from T.S. Eliot's poem *Little Gidding*. The fifth stanza of the poem comments on the cyclical nature of history, what constitutes a beginning and an ending, and about building on past traditions to create a present whereby we learn from previous mistakes. Tykwer's choice to begin *Run Lola Run* with this quote highlights the importance of the narrative journey we are about to embark on, life is a cycle, destined to be repeated many times over. As we arrive back 'where we started' hopefully we have gained experience and a different perspective from the journey, thus gaining an insight and appreciation for what we have.

The second epigraph, "After the game is before the game" is by German soccer coach Sepp Herberger who coached the German soccer team from 1936-1964, winning the FIFA World Cup in 1954. He coined many sayings, including "The ball is round, the game lasts ninety minutes, and everything else is just theory." Herberger's quotes begin the recurring game theme references in *Run Lola Run* and touch on the pace and structure of the narrative. "After the game is before the game" suggests a continuing, never ending cycle in which participants quickly move forward to the next game, not stopping to celebrate success or complain about a loss, simply maintaining focus and moving on.

The epigraphs do not work in isolation but rather in unison as they begin to scaffold the cyclical nature of the narrative and foreshadow the game structure that is to come.

Aesthetics

NARRATIVE MANIPULATION
In Run Lola Run

Narrative

Innovative Narrative Structure

Narrative structure - the framework for how the story events are ordered and may consist of:

- **Multi-layered** includes multiple plot lines
- **Linear cause and effect** create a chronological sequence to the narrative
- **Non-linear** narrative is disjointed or fractured
- **Circular** narrative begins and ends at the same point
- **Episodic** told in flashbacks, flash forwards, chapters.

Run Lola Run constructs a **complex episodic narrative structure** including an opening that provides a framework for the themes that is separate to the main narrative, a triple repetition of a single sequence of events, and a lack of narrative closure.

Each of the film's main segments or **chapters**; namely the supermarket robbery, the bank robbery and the casino scene **follow a linear cause and effect structure,** however the overall narrative design does not follow the traditional mainstream model, instead opting for an **episodic, non-linear structure** in which the narrative is told using **flashbacks, flash forwards** and having distinct chapters or scenes.

Todorov's structuralist approach to narrative advocates that a story is structured around having the beginning in **equilibrium**; events are **disrupted by an enigma**, a **disequilibrium** occurs, and a **return to equilibrium** must take place at the point of narrative closure in order to satisfy audience expectations. *Run Lola Run* **subverts** a number of these classical narrative structural elements. The classical Hollywood model for **establishing equilibrium** is to use the opening few minutes of the film to establish the setting and reveal the major protagonists, preferably engaged in actions suggesting balance or normality. *Run Lola Run* defies this by not revealing a specific location in its opening, although a period is hinted at through the clothing (the protagonist, Lola, appropriates the clothing of Lara Croft from the Tomb Raider video game, placing the time period as the mid to late 90s). Additionally, the opening does not engage with the major protagonists, instead revealing only minor characters and choosing to direct the audience's attention towards the **themes** of the film as seen in the **two epigraphs** (one of which states 'After the game is before the game') and the voiceover by Hans Paetsch, a well-known German narrator of fairy tales. In the **prologue, equilibrium** only exists in the slower reflective pace that asks the audience to consider their lives in terms of **fate, karma, chance and destiny.**

In a classical Hollywood narrative, how the narrative begins establishes character interactions, suggests possible **narrative progression points,** and introduces the audience to the **main themes** or issues. As the prologue only reveals thematic information Tykwer uses the **narrative enigma** to

NARRATIVE MANIPULATION
In Run Lola Run

Film Aesthetics

Manipulation

Innovative Narrative Structure

introduce the audience to the major protagonists. It is through a combination of **time manipulation** techniques of **flashbacks and flash forwards** that the audience learns about Manni's predicament and are given the narrative goal which is for Lola to obtain 100 000 DM in twenty minutes in order to save Manni's life. The audience anticipates the **narrative journey** that Lola must accept to succeed in her **quest. Narrative pleasure** is gained from being **actively** involved in anticipating how the **enigma will be resolved**.

Tykwer breaks the expectations of a traditional narrative as Lola is not successful in restoring **equilibrium** to the narrative, both Manni and Lola 'die' in two out of three runs, the narrative is 'reset', beginning again at the same place, with Lola running past her mother and down the spiral staircase, increasing **audience expectation** for her to successfully **obtain her goal** with each run.

Although the film is **episodic** in its construction, a degree of **cause and effect** exists within scenes. For instance, the black and white **flashback** recounted by Manni and Lola at the beginning of the film creates a **causal relationship between past and present events.** The audience learns that Lola drove her moped to the shop to get cigarettes, leaving the moped outside. The moped was stolen which **causes** Lola to not pick Manni up at the designated time and place.

The **effect** created is that Manni must make his own way, and he decides to walk to the subway with his ill-gotten bag of money. Whilst on the train Manni explains,"... there was this bum who somehow fell down. Suddenly, these inspectors showed up. And I got out like always. An old reflex." The arrival of the guards causes Manni to panic. The **effect** of the panic instigates a reflex and Manni flees, leaving the bag of money on the train. Norbert, a homeless man who is on the train, takes the bag of money creating a **casual chain of events** whereby Manni must now obtain 100 000 DM in twenty minutes to replace the lost money otherwise his crime lord boss, Ronnie, will potentially kill him.

For **narrative closure** to occur the audience must **resolve the enigma** at the start of the film. An audience takes pleasure in anticipating how the enigma will be resolved and participating in the **narrative puzzle**. Tykwer offers three alternate narratives, making each retelling compelling with subtle changes and contrasting endings. The audience anticipates how Lola will respond differently to the sneering teenager with the snarling dog on the stairs, or how Doris' future life will change depending on how Lola interacts with her. **Narrative pleasure** is derived from seeing Lola overcome obstacles to achieve her goal.

Todorov's approach to narrative construction would suggest that **equilibrium** has been restored as Lola achieves her goal, and **audience expectation**, for the most part, has been met. However, by having both Manni and Lola obtain the money, and by showing the audience that some of the money in the original bag was used by Norbert (the homeless man on the train), the audience is left with more questions than answers, therefore creating **new narrative possibilities** with the **open-ended resolution. Viewing pleasure** is derived from leaving the resolution open as Tykwer **actively** engages the audience in the **narrative journey** by positioning them to create their own **flash forward**, their own alternate future for Manni and Lola based on the existing narrative foundation.

Film Aesthetics: Narrative

Run Lola Run

Structuring of Time

Audience knowledge of film conventions associated with the structuring of time is traditionally based on chronological, cause and effect representation of events. Art films frequently experiment with time by manipulating **temporal order, duration, and frequency**, subverting audience expectations and adding interest to the narrative.

Manipulation of Narrative Structure

Temporal Order

Temporal order refers to the sequencing of plot events. *Run Lola Run* is **episodic and non-linear rather than chronological** in its sequencing of events. Tykwer commences the narrative with two **epigraphs**, followed by a **prologue,** and then three reiterations of the same event interspersed with two red overlay scenes. The three occurrences of the same run can be seen as **cyclical** in construction as the audience is returned to the same starting point of Lola frantically yelling at Manni on the phone prior to her frenetic run down the spiral stairs that signals the start of her quest.

 The **flashback** is used as a **temporal sequencing device** as it supplies the audience with the necessary back story information thus using **temporal order** to communicate information of narrative importance. The **flashback** allows the audience to sympathise with Lola and Manni through a constant **montage** of close-ups, displaying emotions of powerlessness and disbelief at the situation Manni finds himself in. Through dialogue and a black and white **flashback** the audience learns of Manni's connection with the crime world and his mistake of leaving the money belonging to his boss on the train. Manni explains that when Lola failed to pick him up that there wasn't even a,"... phone booth. I couldn't even call a taxi, so I walked to the subway station. On the train, there was this bum who somehow fell down. Suddenly, these inspectors showed up. And I got out like always. An old reflex. The bag!" The **flashback** is crucial in conveying the **premise** of the film.

 **Flash forwards** are not common in mainstream texts. The flash-forwards in *Run Lola Run* do little to progress the narrative, however they do reinforce the **themes**. Lola runs into each minor character three times, each time their destiny alters, as shown through the montage of still images displaying their possible life journey. Therefore, the themes of **destiny, karma, and fate** are explored and challenged.

NARRATIVE MANIPULATION
Run Lola Run

Innovative Narrative Structure: Manipulating Time

Temporal duration

Temporal duration refers to the length of time represented by events in the plot. Events can be **compressed or expanded** to highlight their significance within the narrative. The running time of *Run Lola Run* is eighty-four minutes. Within this, Tykwer employs **temporal experimentation** in his use of **compressed, expanded, real and simultaneous time.** Lola's three runs occur in close to twenty minutes of real time, this directly correlates to the film's premise which states that Lola has twenty minutes to achieve her goal or Manni dies. The three variations of Lola's runs comprise sixty minutes of the film.

 The **temporal manipulation** of the duration of the narrative includes the use of **simultaneous time** which Tykwer applies in the form of a **split screen** divided into three segments showing the urgency of Lola's run as she endeavours to stop Manni from robbing the supermarket; the second segment shows the clock about to hit the midday mark, signifying the end of the twenty minutes, and the third segment presents Manni entering the supermarket to rob it. The audience's desire for Lola to triumph is heightened by the **diegetic sound** of the clock ticking, and Lola shouting at Manni from a distance, "Wait! Don't do it! Manni, please! Wait! Wait for me! I'll be right there. Please. Manni, please wait!" The **split screen** focuses the audience's attention onto the crux of the story —will Lola make it in time to help Manni? The conclusion of the **split screen** creates **temporal unity** as Manni and Lola's **disconnected time and space** are drawn together as they are now both in the supermarket and Manni asks Lola, "So, are you with me?" **Narrative engagement** and suspense are increased as the audience is positioned to barrack for Lola and Manni to succeed in their goal. Similarly, in the final run, a **split screen** is used to show Lola trying to reach Papa on time, again **increasing narrative suspense and engagement**.

 **Jump cuts** are used to **compress time** and can be traced back to the French New Wave. **Spatial discontinuity** occurs frequently when Tykwer uses the unsettling effect of the **jump cut** to create tension in several scenes thereby causing a degree of discomfort for the audience. Notably, this occurs in the **prologue** once Lola learns of Manni's predicament. The rapid **jump cuts** into the clock signal the start of the run as we are shown that the time is twenty minutes to midday. Lola flings the red telephone in the air highlighting her frustration. The **jump cuts** continue in a series of ever closer shots as the telephone falls in **slow motion**. The cuts are interspersed with mid shots and close ups of the television set depicting dominoes falling over, reinforcing the **game aesthetic** and foregrounding the **theme of karma** as the domino effect is visually highlighted. The **jump cuts** are repeated as shots of Lola's face are shown in quick succession as she asks, 'Who? Who? Who?' trying to decide who can help her in her quest. The **slow motion** shot of the phone falling into its cradle appears with a cartoon image of the croupier (who appears in the casino scene) saying, "No more bets," another reference to the **game aesthetic** as Lola hurriedly runs out of room to find Papa to assist her in her quest. The **rhythmic pace** of Lola's running is fast

Aesthetics

NARRATIVE MANIPULATION
In Run Lola Run

and energetic. Her urgency is conveyed through **jump cuts** that **fracture the seamless continuity of time and space**. The audience is carried along on Lola's quest by the rhythmic techno beat, rapid **jump cuts,** and fast paced running scenes that allow them to journey alongside her.

Rather than break the suspension of disbelief by drawing attention to the filmmaking process, the **spatial discontinuity** achieved by using **jump cuts** only serves to heighten audience suspense and engagement. The **visual aesthetic** creates pace, rhythm and **temporal connectivity** using disparate, yet unifying **time manipulation techniques** that constantly remind the audience that Lola is in a race against time. For instance:

 **Slow motion**: the use of **slow motion** directly contrasts with the fast pace of the rest of the narrative. As a device it adds emphasis and intensity, it heightens the emotional moment and creates a **stylistic visual aesthetic**.

- **Slow motion** is used when Manni exits the train, slowly turning around when he realises he has left the bag containing the money behind. His despair and fear are captured intently in this black and white, slow motion sequence.

- At the end of the supermarket robbery scene a frustrated Manni throws the red bag of stolen money into the air. The bag rises high in **slow motion**, accompanied by a swishing sound; a policeman has his gun aimed at Lola, but his eyes are diverted by the bag, he accidentally pulls the trigger of his pistol, shooting Lola in the chest. The sound of the gun shot echoes into complete silence as **slow motion** is used to capture Lola staggering backwards and falling to her 'death'. The stark contrast between Lola's high octane run and the intense supermarket scene, coupled with the fact that the heroine of the film has seemingly died less than halfway through the film, delivers a **post-modern aesthetic take on narrative construction.**

- The **slow motion** of the red telephone gradually falling back into its cradle, inter-cut with images on a television set of dominoes falling, create **temporal possibilities** about chance and fate at the start of each run.

- At the end of the second run **slow motion** is used to emphasise Lola dropping the green bag containing the money from the bank robbery after Manni is run over by the ambulance. The underpinning emotional connection is that the money is secondary to their relationship.

Aesthetics

NARRATIVE MANIPULATION
In Run Lola Run

TIME MANIPULATION

Temporal frequency

Temporal frequency refers to the number of times an event is shown within the plot. In a traditional Hollywood film, the event unfolds once, however some New Hollywood films such as *Groundhog Day* and *Sliding Doors* repeat the main story event to create emphasis, to show a different **point of view,** or to show the effect a minor alteration has on the **outcome of a narrative.**

 In *Run Lola Run* a **temporal frequency of three** is used as Lola repeats her run to save Manni three times; each time a **minor plot variation occurs,** altering the outcome of the event. Tykwer explores the idea of one moment in time having a significant impact on a person's life. The 'what if' butterfly effect narrative scaffold questions if our fate is pre-determined or if we control our own fate.

Repetition creates emphasis. Having Lola repeat the same actions, with slight variations, three times, focuses the audience's attention on **similarities and differences** (the causes and their effects), and their importance to the narrative. For instance, in the second run, in her animated form Lola is tripped up by the rebellious teenager, she falls down the stairs and injures her leg, therefore she leaves the apartment grounds a little later than in previous runs, setting in motion a series of **time related events**. Her late start means that now she bumps into Doris' shoulder, Doris calls Lola by an expletive and her **flash forward** shows her future life as luxurious and happy due to a large lottery win. As Lola continues her run, she encounters Mr Meyer's car coming out of an alleyway, her late start means that Lola now has less time to see the car and jump over the bonnet. Unfortunately for Mr Meyer, the distraction of Lola causes him to crash into Ronnie's car. The **repetition** of the same **narrative arc three times** creates variety in the **temporal possibilities** offered to the audience.

Film Aesthetics: Narrative

Run Lola Run

Video Game Aesthetic

Manipulation of Narrative Structure

Run Lola Run's narrative parallels that of a **video game.** The opening **animated sequence** is the first indication of the **video game analogy**. Lola is introduced in cartoon form, she appears as her **avatar**; her hair vividly bright red, wearing cargo pants and Doc Marten boots, paired with a singlet t-shirt. She jumps, runs, and smashes all obstacles in her way, showing power, determination and an ability to succeed. She appropriates the actions and appearance of **Lara Croft** from the *Tomb Raider* role playing computer games. The **video game aesthetic** is established through her character construction and reveals itself in the narrative structure as the film unfolds.

A **video game trope** seen widely in popular culture is the **sidekick** or helper. Lola considers several 'helpers' as the camera rotates 360⁰ around her. The still images projected through this rotation allow the audience a brief look at Lola's extensive support system before she settles on Papa to assist her. Her choice of Papa as her helper is **foreshadowed** negatively in the first run as the camera stops rotating long enough for Lola to exit the scene, beginning her quest by going to Papa's office to request help. Unbeknownst to Lola the camera has focused on Papa who shakes his head in an action suggesting that he will not be open to helping Lola achieve her goal.

Tykwer has repurposed a number of **video game techniques**, one of which is the ability of a character to **learn from past mistakes**. Lola repeats the same run three times, each with slight variations. In the first run animated Lola runs past a rebellious looking teenage boy with an aggressive, spiky collared dog on the stairs; in the second variation the boy trips Lola up and she falls, injuring her foot which briefly slows her in her quest; and in the third variant Lola has learnt to stand up to the boy. In her third attempt, as Lola runs past the boy, his dog snarls and she jumps up and over, thus avoiding the possibility of being tripped. She lands safely, turning briefly to growl back at the dog revealing her intention to **take the play into her own hands**, thus highlighting her agency.

Additionally, we see the **video game technique** of learning from past mistakes being used to progress Lola's ability to use a gun. In the supermarket scene Lola clearly has no idea how to use a gun. After hitting the security guard over the head

86

VIDEO GAME AESTHETIC

Run Lola Run

Lola takes his gun and holds it mistrustfully as Manni says, "The safety catch is on." She fumbles with the gun saying, "How does it work?" before Manni points out that she needs to unlock the lever on the side. Fast forward to the second run when Lola acts decisively, deciding to rob her father's bank, she grabs the gun from the security guard's holster and in one fluid motion releases the safety catch and fires a warning shot, leaving nobody in doubt as to her ability and intention. The audience is positioned to engage with the **complex layering of the narrative** as the security guard says to Lola, "Girl, listen. You don't know how to use that thing," and we are asked to draw on our **intertextual understanding** of how video games allow players to learn from their past mistakes in order to progress to a higher level.

Aspects of the **video game aesthetic** attributed to Lola's character include her **superhero capabilities**. The first hint of her superpowers is seen in cartoon Lola's energy driven run through the spiral time tunnel as she destroys any obstacle in her way. As 'real' Lola and not cartoon Lola we see her talk to Manni through thick glass in the supermarket scene, and most importantly she saves the life of Schuster, the bank security guard, simply by holding his hand and passing her strength to him as he lies in the ambulance. Lola's ability to save his life is contrasted with that of the paramedic who furiously performs CPR to no avail. It is not until Lola holds Schuster's hand that his heartbeat returns to normal. Like a **video game superhero,** Lola is imbued with qualities that portray her as powerful, a person capable of **successfully completing a quest.**

Tykwer favours a **sensory video game experience** and a **subverted narrative structure** over the deep construction of characters. The **sensory assault** of the techno beat music drives the pace in Lola's running scenes. It creates a mood and intensity **reminiscent of a music video.** Tykwer draws together **a pastiche of popular cultural elements** such as fast paced music videos, action films, and video game culture to immerse the audience in a **postmodern narrative.**

The narrative's similarities to a video game include:
- the use of animation
- a temporal frequency of three, thus suggesting the three lives given to a player of a video game, having the characters and plot 'reset' after the characters die
- having a quest, a goal for the character to achieve, complete with obstacles in her way
- imbuing Lola with superpowers
- creating a fast beat techno world like the immersive world of video games
- having the ability to choose characters to assist with the quest
- having a set time to complete the quest
- using split screens, similar to a two player game
- choose your own path
- constructing Lola as an androgynous superhero character allows for narrative similarities to the video game structure.

Aesthetics

Postmodern elements

AESTHETIC MANIPULATION
In Run Lola Run

Aesthetics in Run Lola Run

- Tom Tykwer's *Run Lola Run* showcases the avant-garde film practices that reflect the changing cultural landscape in Germany. Tykwer's strategic use of aesthetic choices in the film are a consequence of cultural production, blending various media forms to create a unique narrative experience.

- Tom Tykwer's 1998 film *Run Lola Run* tells the story of Lola, who must find 100,000 Marks in twenty minutes to save her boyfriend Manni from a local crime lord. The film's aesthetics play a crucial role in engaging its target audience of German youth.

Video Game Aesthetic

- Lola is portrayed using popular culture references to Lara Croft from Tomb Raider.
- The use of animation sequences highlight the hyper-reality of Lola's world, reminiscent of video game aesthetics.
- Lola's ability to 'revive' herself and try again after each failure is a mechanism well-known to a German and international youth audience familiar with the video game structure of having three lives, and resetting the game to start again.
- The manipulation of narrative structure via a temporal frequency of three, where Lola has three chances to succeed, further reinforces the video game aesthetic.
- The inclusion of gaming-related motifs, such as the tumbling dominoes on the television screen, the roulette table in the casino, and the use of a soccer ball to start the 'game' contributes to the game culture aesthetic.

Superhero Aesthetic

- Lola's visual appearance, with her cargo pants, tank top, Doc Martens, and fiery red hair, aligns her with the iconic Lara Croft character, evoking a superhero-like aesthetic.
- Lola's superpowers, such as the ability to control her environment through the visual and aural motif of smashing glass and screaming, further enhance the superhero aesthetic.
- Lola's healing power, demonstrated when she saves the bank security guard Schuster, reinforces her status as a superhero.
- The use of distinctive visual motifs, such as the vibrant red and yellow colours associated with Lola and Manni, respectively, mimics the aesthetic of comic books and superheroes.

Techno-Pop Aesthetic and use of Animation

- The film starts with animated Lola racing against the backdrop of fast-paced techno-pop music. The artistic benefits of animating Lola and using techno-pop music tie into the video game aesthetic that Tykwer is attempting to achieve within his media work.

Aesthetic use of Media Forms

- Tykwer synthesises animation, film, still photography, and videotape into a narrative driven by techno-pop music. All elements contribute to the film's unique visual and aural identity, resonating with the primary German youth audience, and the secondary international audience who related to the cultural shifts

POST MODERN NARRATIVE
Run Lola Run

(technology, modernity, gender roles) happening at the time.
- The use of still photography highlights the theme of karma vs. fate and how choices will impact the direction of a person's life. We see Lola run into the character of Doris, and her life trajectory change depending on what she says (or doesn't say) to Lola.
- Use of 35mm film vs. video tape to physically and emotionally separate Lola and Manni from Pappa and Jutta. The video tape sections are grainy, the camera is hand held, which creates a voyeuristic feel to the emotional scene playing out between Pappa and his mistress Jutta. The 35mm film sequences are clear and allow the audience to connect more sharply with Manni and Lola.
- Black and white segments are used to recount past events.
- Red overlay scenes are used to indicate the reset and rebirth of the narrative and to connect the audience with Lola and Manni's relationship.

Audience Engagement

- The inclusion of popular culture icons such as video game and superhero aesthetics, as well as having younger protagonists in Lola (Franke Potente) and Manni (Moritz Bleibtreu), generates a significant impact on audience engagement, particularly for the German youth market who have engaged with previous work from these two actors.
- By using tropes and aesthetics that the target audience is familiar with, the film creates a conduit between youth culture and the culture within the film, allowing the audience to connect with the film's themes and visually represent their own cultural references.
- This connection encourages a preferred and favourable reading of the film, where Lola is seen as the heroic protagonist, despite her criminal actions, as the audience can sympathise with her quest as it is driven by love.

The strategic use of video game and superhero aesthetics in *Run Lola Run* effectively engages the film's target audience, the German youth, by providing a familiar and relatable visual language that enhances their connection to the narrative and the protagonist's journey.

Tykwer's choice of aesthetic practices in *Run Lola Run* is reflective of the changing German culture, as he explores avant-garde film techniques to engage with the evolving cultural landscape. By blending these diverse aesthetic elements, Tykwer creates a visually and aurally engaging film that reflects the cultural production and transformation occurring in Germany at the time of production.

AESTHETICS
IN FILM

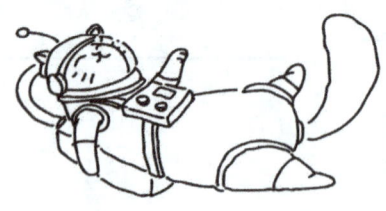

Art films experiment and manipulate with the established codes and conventions of historical film grammar. They subvert, manipulate, and create an innovative visual and aural aesthetic that experiments with established film practices.

CONVENTIONS & CODES

CONVENTIONS

- Narrative structure: deviates from Hollywood traditional cause and effect
  - time and space manipulation
  - experimentation with editing: rhythm, pace, and continuity
  - open-ended resolution
  - character subjectivity
- Manipulation of the medium
- Experimentation with genre
- Establishing film movement conventions
- Intent is to make a political or social comment

CODES

- Symbolic codes include:
  - visual motifs
  - colour
  - settings
  - costume
  - hair and make-up
  - objects
- Written codes include:
  - typography
  - title
- Audio codes include:
  - music
  - sound effects
  - silence
  - dialogue
- Technical codes include:
  - experimentation with camera movements, camera angles, and framing
  - editing: subverting or experimenting with traditional Hollywood seamless, invisible continuity editing style
  - lighting and colour palette have symbolic meaning
  - composition

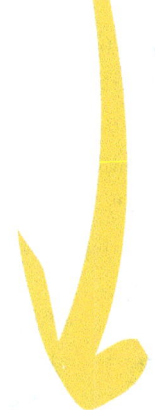

Films are shaped by:
- available technology
- budget
- cast and crew
- institutions
- director's aesthetic vision
- audience expectation of genre
- audience values and beliefs

CONTEXT WILL ALWAYS SHAPE AESTHETICS

Film Aesthetics

Review & sample questions

FILM AESTHETICS - main essential content to discuss:

Sample questions:

1. Discuss the effect the director's aesthetic choices have on audience interpretation.
2. Analyse how a director's personal expression has been influenced by production context.
3. Discuss how film aesthetics have been used to convey theme.
4. Discuss the narrative possibilities signalled in a film's opening scene.
5. Discuss how time and space have been used to structure a narrative.
6. Analyse how a narrative has been manipulated to engage a niche audience.
7. Analyse how an auteur has used mise-en-scène to create film art.
8. Discuss how visual and aural elements contribute to constructing an art film.
9. Analyse how media aesthetics construct representations.
10. Discuss how the aesthetic use of codes and conventions create personal expression.
11. Discuss aesthetic elements used to connect with a niche audience.

01
- **Film style** is constructed from a director's **personal expression** of **theme** that arises out of a **choice of codes, conventions and techniques**; all are encoded by the production context and decoded by the audience's reception context.

02
Techniques found in art films:
- innovative visual aesthetic
- manipulation of narrative structure
- character subjectivity
- open-ended narrative
- political and social comment
- manipulation of time and space
- deviation from realism
- experimentation with rhythm, pace, and continuity editing
- manipulation of the medium
- choice of actors

03
- **Film aesthetics** concerns itself with defining what makes a film art rather than commercial fodder. How and where can the line be drawn? To differentiate a purely commercial venture from an artistic one, firstly look at the **filmmaker's intention**. What social or political comment is being made? Secondly, consider the **manipulation of codes, conventions, and techniques**, including the use of available technology and mediums, do they deviate from mainstream Hollywood? Have they been used innovatively to extend the boundaries of historical film grammar?

Chapter Five

How Narrative Functions in a Text

- Narrative components
- Narrative elements: case study *Everything Everywhere All at Once*
- Story elements
- Genre
- Point of view
- Theme
- Montage
- Narrative structure theory: Vladimir Propp - applied to *Harry Potter and the Philosopher's Stone*
- Narrative structure theory: Joseph Campbell - applied to *The Lego Movie*
- Narrative structure theory: Tzvetan Todorov - applied to *Run Lola Run*
- Narrative structure theory: Claude Levi-Strauss - applied to *Run Lola Run*
- Narrative structure theory: Syd Field - applied to *Everything Everywhere All at Once*
- Sample questions
- Review

Narrative

Narrative

Narrative is the linking of cause and effect to tell a story that arises out of a specific context. Many components combine to form, and shape a narrative, among them are the context of production, the context of reception, audience expectations, story elements, narrative structure, narrative elements and expectations of genre.

Production context: where and when a text is made will influence narrative construction in terms of narrative elements, story elements, narrative structure and genre expectations. A text is not made in a vacuum, it will be shaped by its context.

Audience expectations: narrative construction needs to consider who its primary audience demographic is in order to align expectations, values, and beliefs.

Story Elements:
The components used to convey the narrative's message.

- Plot
- Theme
- Point of view
- Style

Narrative Elements:
The scaffold upon which the plot is built.

- Characters
- Setting
- Conflict
- Resolution

Narrative Structure:
The plot sequence ordering how story events unfold.

- Multi-layered
- Linear cause and effect
- Non-linear
- Circular
- Episodic

Genre Expectations:
Prediction of the plot and story based on genre elements.

- Iconography
- Stephen Neale's theory of repetition and difference

Narrative Theories
Create a framework to scaffold the plot.

- Tzvetan Todorov
- Claude Lévi-Strauss
- Vladimir Propp
- Syd Field
- Joseph Campbell
- Freytag's Pyramid
- Roland Barthes

Reception context: where and when an audience views a text will influence how they decode meaning. An audience viewing a text that was made in 1940 but viewed in 2024 will decode aspects such as representations of gender differently to what was intended. Audience reception is influenced by context.

Narrative

Narrative elements

Discuss the narrative elements used to showcase the film's themes.

Synopsis

Everything Everywhere All at Once (2022) directed by Daniel Kwan and Daniel Scheinert garnered seven Oscars, including Best Picture in 2023. Thematically the film layers the concepts of love, kindness, acceptance of difference, and the importance of family over an even deeper question concerning the meaning of life. Evelyn Wang (Michelle Yeoh) is the matriarch of a family who runs a failing laundromat business. Her marriage to husband Waymond (Ke Huy Quan) is in trouble. At first, he appears to offer limited tangible help as Evelyn tries but fails to organise their finances for a tax audit, set up a birthday party for her visiting father, and attend to customers. Evelyn's daughter, Joy (Stephanie Hsu), adds to the layers of discontent as she would like her mother to openly acknowledge, and approve of her choice of sexual orientation, and introduce her girlfriend at her grandfather's party. Evelyn's initial goals appear to be straight forward, survive the tax audit, pull off a party for her father, connect with her daughter, and find time to work on her marriage. Little does she know that she is one among many Evelyn's who exist in a vast array of multiverses, but she is the only one who can save everyone from catastrophe.

Character

The protagonist, Evelyn Wang, is the central character who embodies the film's themes of love, acceptance, and the search for meaning in life. Through her journey across multiverses Evelyn's character arc explores the regret and longing she feels for the life choices she could have made, whilst also discovering the power of unconditional love, and the importance of cherishing the small moments in life.

The character of Jobu Tupaki, the evil multiverse version of Evelyn's daughter Joy, represents a significant generational and cultural divide. Jobu's quest to find meaning in the "Everything Bagel" (a metaphor for the excess of everything) highlights the film's deeper exploration of the meaning of life, and serves as a foil to Evelyn's own journey of self-discovery. Jobu Tupaki is hell bent on nihilism, she contrasts starkly with Evelyn's husband Waymond whose character traits highlight kindness and integrity: "I don't know. The only thing I do know is that we have to be kind. Please. Be kind, especially when we don't know what's going on." Jobu's lack of hope, use of aggression and lack of compassion are diametrically opposed to Waymond's character, thus allowing the themes of love, hope and finding happiness in life's small moments, to shine through.

The supporting characters of Evelyn's husband Waymond, and the IRS auditor Deirdre, play crucial roles in shaping the film's themes. Waymond's character traits of kindness and integrity contrast with the obstacles placed by Deidre, (both in the form of IRS auditor and the "Bagel" metaverse version of Deirdre) further emphasising the importance of compassion and understanding in the face of adversity. Bagel Deirdre is unkind and uncaring, having one goal, that being the destruction of Evelyn.

NARRATIVE ELEMENTS

Everything Everywhere All at Once

Setting

The primary settings of the film are the laundromat, the family's apartment above the laundromat, and the IRS building. The laundromat represents the mundane and often overwhelming aspects of Evelyn's daily life, whereas the tax office with its cubicles and multilevel office space serves as the backdrop for the conflict between Evelyn and the IRS agent Deidre. These settings, along with the visual cues and symbolic codes used to construct Evelyn's "Laundromat world" (such as her streaks of grey hair, drab clothing, and cluttered home), contribute to the film's thematic exploration of the meaning of life, and the importance of finding joy and purpose in the smallest of moments.

Conflict

The climactic moment of the film occurs when Jobu Tupaki, the evil multiverse version of Joy, tries to convince Evelyn to jump into the "Everything Bagel" in an attempt to see and feel everything as she has scanned the multiverses and found no meaning. Evelyn says to her, "No matter what, I still want to be here with you. I will always, always, want to be here with you." The conflict highlights the film's central theme of the search for meaning in life, and the importance of relationships and unconditional love in staying connected. Evelyn's refusal to let Jobu Tupaki jump into the "Everything Bagel" and her use of her martial arts skills to obliterate the obstacles in her way to save her daughter, showcase the power of unconditional love and the film's theme of being compassionate, not judgemental.

Resolution

In the film's resolution, Evelyn's kindness and compassion are foregrounded as she uses these emotions as the antidote to Jobu Tupaki's nihilistic desire to destroy everything. Rather than resorting to violence, Evelyn uses kindness by tapping into the needs and fantasies of the people blocking her from getting to the "Everything Bagel" where Jobu plans to disappear by being sucked into the Bagel's centre hole which can destroy anything that enters. Evelyn uses kindness to disarm the people who are obstacles between her potentially saving Jobu (Joy in another multiverse) from jumping into oblivion. This binary opposition between Evelyn's empathy and Jobu Tupaki's destructive impulses underscore the film's central message about the transformative power of love and understanding.

Ultimately, Evelyn's journey culminates in her own metaverse, where she successfully navigates the tax audit, hosts a joyous birthday party for her father, and most importantly, reconnects with her daughter by accepting her life choices. Amidst the chaos and multiversal exploration, Evelyn realises that her relationship with her husband Waymond has always been the bright spot in her life, even in the mundane moments of filling out tax forms and doing laundry. The film's resolution celebrates the importance of kindness, family, and finding meaning in the smallest of life's moments, leaving the audience to understand the message of choosing kindness and compassion over violence and chaos, highlighting how order over destruction can be a choice, and allowing the audience to appreciate the small, sometimes supposedly inconsequential, but

Narrative

Narrative components:

STORY ELEMENTS

PLOT

- The plot is the sequence of events that occurs in the world of the story. A story can be plotted according to cause and effect events that progress the narrative.

THEME

- A theme is the main message that recurs throughout the narrative. It is the unifying concept that conveys the story's intention, highlighting why the story is being told and what the audience should take away from it.

POINT OF VIEW

- Point of view is a story telling device used to show the perspective the story is being told from. The audience is positioned to see the narrative unfold from a character's eyes. We see what they see, hear what they hear, therefore aligning the audience with their view of the world.

STYLE

- A film style arises out of the production techniques used by the director. These include a choice of film grammar such as camera movements, shot sizes, camera angles, pace of editing, manipulation of time and space, mise-en-scène, composition, colour palette, sound design, choice of actors, choice of symbolic codes and use of technology; all components combine to form an identifiable style.

Narrative

Genre

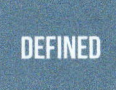
DEFINED
- Genre refers to a classification or category into which films fit. An audience has an expectation of the type of film they will see based on recognisable visual and aural traits. Narrative structure and genre are interwoven as an audience has an expectation of the plot and narrative elements depending on the genre.

ICONOGRAPHY
- The iconic and expected visual and aural elements associated with a genre are referred to as iconography. For instance, the horror genre is linked to tension music, jump scares, isolated settings, lone characters, a dark colour palette, and the expectation of death or something unsavoury occurring.

STEPHEN NEALE
- An influential film scholar, Stephen Neale contributed greatly to the study of genre. In particular, he posited the theory of **repetition** and **difference** whereby he stated that audience members gained pleasure from engaging with recognisable genre elements as they were **familiar and identifiable.** The **familiar and repeated** elements provide comfort as they allow the audience to navigate the narrative using expected and anticipated markers. To stay appealing, a genre must offer **difference**, something **new or novel** to maintain audience interest. Therefore, genres employ **repetition and difference** to stay current and provide audience viewing pleasure (Neale, 1980).
- Genres are not static; they change to accommodate their context.

Film Language - Point of View

Through whose eyes is the audience invited to see the action unfold from?

Techniques used to construct a point of view:

- **Technical codes**: consider the eye line match, which character's gaze is privileged?
- **Camera angle**: which characters have a high camera angle, low camera angle or high eye level?
- **Shot sizes**: who is attributed more close ups?
- **shot duration**: on which characters or objects does the camera linger?
- **Audio codes:** what sounds are associated with characters, what dialogue do we hear, what tone is used to convey the information?
- **Symbolic codes**: consider body language, facial expressions, colours, objects, and settings associated with characters. How are these used to convey meaning?
- **Written codes:** are any positive or negative written codes used to anchor meaning regarding a particular character, issue or idea?
- Consider how the **selection of codes** shapes meaning and constructs a **point of view** regarding the main conflict, the characters in the narrative, and how the audience views the resolution.
- The narrative's **theme** is conveyed to the audience using the **point of view** of the main characters as a vehicle to showcase **values and ideologies** which the audience is invited to align with.

Point of view in The Fresh Prince of Bel-Air

- From **whose eyes** do we see the narrative unfold? **Technical and audio codes** combine to direct audience attention to the character of Will as we see him in aerial view via a close-up that pulls back to a long shot revealing him to be sitting on a throne. A hip-hop song plays and the lyrics of "Now this is a story about how my life got twist turned upside down" immediately invites the audience to connect with Will through the **first person point of view narration** and **camera techniques.**
- As the audience is positioned to see the narrative from **Will's point of view,** we are asked to align our **value system** with his. In the pilot episode the **codes of construction** position Will as the protagonist. The premise of the series is that Will is sent to Beverly Hills to live with his rich uncle, Phil Banks, his aunt, and his cousins to learn 'proper behaviour' and escape the bad neighbourhood of West Philadelphia where he constantly found himself in trouble. The audience would like to see Will integrate successfully into the Banks household even when he is rude (comedically) to Phil Banks. Will's overarching **values** are good, he assists his cousin Ashley with her choir debacle, even though he has only just met her. His actions show he is caring and kind. Therefore, as the

Point of View

Point of view as a narrative device.

audience shares a similar altruistic value system, they are more likely to align with Will's **point of view** whereby he questions the status quo within the Banks household, and in later episodes, in society as a whole.

- **Camera angles and shot size** choice play a crucial role in creating a **point of view.** Technical code choices focus the audience onto Will. When the camera choice is primarily on one person it becomes subjective, focusing the audience onto that character's viewpoint. As an audience, we see only what they see, we experience the world from their **point of view** or narrative stance. Altering the **point of view** can change the way the audience interprets the narrative. For instance, what would happen if The Fresh Prince of Bel-Air was told from the point of view of Phil Banks?

Point of View in Run Lola Run

Through **whose eyes** do we see the narrative unfold? How does this position the audience to engage with the **themes of love, karma, and fate** foregrounded in Tom Tykwer's 1998 *Run Lola Run*? The film tells the story of Lola, a young German women who must come up with 100 000 Deutsch Marks in twenty minutes in order to save her boyfriend Manni from a vengeful criminal Ronnie, whose money Manni accidentally left on the subway train.

The film's opening credits use the non-diegetic **audio code** of the sound of a prison door slamming and a camera shutter clicking, coupled with what appears to be police mug shots introducing the major characters. The **selection of codes** invites the audience to see the characters as criminals right from the start. As the prison connotations conclude the camera dives from the sky into Lola's bedroom showing her engaged in a heated phone conversation with her boyfriend Manni. As the protagonist takes an active role in progressing the plot we see her taking control by yelling at Manni, telling him to wait, she will be there in twenty minutes with a solution to the problem. The fast **montage** of shots, some in black and white depicting past events, unveil a **back story** showing Manni involved in criminal dealings with Lola as his absent getaway accomplice. The universal perception of crime is a negative one, thus it is with interest that the audience finds themselves **positioned to view** these criminal characters, Lola and Manni, from a positive **point of view.** Twyker has used **selection processes** such as **camera angles, shot duration, framing**, as well as **audio and symbolic codes** to cause the audience to reflect on the narrative from the **point of view** of Manni and Lola, showing their desperation and explaining why they are embroiled in a world of crime.

Theme

THEME
- main message
- moral
- lesson
- central idea
- unifying concept
- point of the story

A theme is the main message recurring throughout the narrative. It is communicated via the meaning encoded in the chosen codes and conventions, these visual and aural signifiers are decoded by the audience to arrive at a preferred, negotiated, or oppositional reading of the text, thereby either aligning themselves with the values and ideologies embedded in the theme, or rejecting the film's central message

ELEMENTS USED TO COMMUNICATE THEME

The theme is interwoven throughout the story and is embedded in the codes, conventions, and narrative techniques used to construct the plot and convey the story.

CODES

Visual signifiers such as the symbolic codes of costume, colour, setting, body language, lighting, recurring motifs, and mise-en-scène assist to convey and reinforce the theme. For instance, consider how the symbolic code of colour can be used symbolically to convey the theme of the power of love and what people will do in its name.

Aural signifiers such as music, sound effects, dialogue, and voiceover convey the theme on an emotional and literal level. Consider what a character says and how they say it. The conversations held between characters frequently allow for exploration and expression of the film's central idea.

CONVENTIONS

Genre conventions convey themes through distinguishable features. For instance, the romance genre's narrative structural conventions include obstacles whereby the main characters find themselves separated by an obstacle; only to overcome the obstacle and reunite by the end. The genre convention reinforces the theme of love overcoming any adversity.

Film style consists of recognisable features and conventions. Consider the visual elements employed by Wes Anderson in his films used to underpin the film's main message; the colour palette, composition, mise-en-scène, lighting and stylised visuals combine to convey the theme.

NARRATIVE

The sequencing of a film's events can contribute to theme. A non-linear ordering of events may suggest that time and its importance is central to the narrative.

Narrative elements allow audience engagement with the theme as characters explore the film's message through their actions and dialogue, the setting allows for characters to reveal or reinforce the theme, and the conflict and resolution reveal the lessons the protagonist learned during the course of the narrative thereby revealing values and ideologies connected to the film's central message.

To effectively analyse a film's theme describe it using more than one word such as love, revenge or power. Always discuss the stance the film takes on the stated topic. For instance, in James Cameron's 1997 *Titanic*, the major theme of love is conveyed through the obstacles the protagonists, Rose and Jack, must overcome to be together. Therefore, the film explores how love transcends social class barriers and reinforces the theme of the power of love.

Montage

Meaning is created by editing shots together in a particular sequence to manipulate time and space.

- Narrative montage
- Ideational montage
- Montage sequences
- Juxtaposition
- Communicating theme
- Manipulating time and space

How can montage be used to convey meaning in film?

IDEATIONAL MONTAGE
Images are linked together to suggest a connection, empowering the audience to actively create meaning. For instance, showing a shot of a blood stained floor and then a shot of a bloodied knife, actively positions the audience to link the ideas conceptually (within context) to suggest an idea such as murder.

MOOD
Shot selection, along with rhythmic editing, can establish a mood or atmosphere in a film. Consider Tom Tykwer's 1998 *Run Lola Run* where shots of the protagonist, Lola, running across Germany are edited to the fast pace rhythmic beat of the song *Wish,* conveying her sense of urgency and creating a mood that highlights Lola's desperation as she runs to save her boyfriend, Manni from a vengeful crime boss.

JUMP CUTS
A jump cut creates a disjointed, distancing effect, it fractures the seamless Hollywood invisible editing style. Its jarring effect can be used to disorient the viewer and create stylised manipulation of time and space. In Tykwer's *Run Lola Run* jump cuts are used frequently. Initially the camera circles around Lola, the film's protagonist, to show images of who she thinks would be most useful to help her achieve her goal of saving her boyfriend Manni. Montage and jump cuts are used to compress time and show Lola's unease, disorientation and urgency as she finally settles on her father as a potential person who can help her to get 100,000 Deutsch Marks in twenty minutes, thus saving Manni. The use of montage, including jump cuts reinforces the film's theme regarding the impact of decisions and whether outcomes occur because of fate, karma, or neither.

COMMUNICATING THEME
Montage can be used to build relationships between characters and convey the film's theme by sequencing information. In Coppola's 1972 *The Godfather,* the baptism sequence employs montage to cut between the sacred religious baptism ritual where Michael Corleone is to become godfather to his niece, and the violent assassinations ordered by the Corleone family. Parallel editing takes the audience back and forth between the two scenes highlighting the themes of moral ambiguity, loss of innocence and corruption of power by showing the purity of a baby contrasted with extreme violence in clear juxtaposition.

NARRATIVE MONTAGE
Connections are made between shots, progressing the narrative and showing a relationship between time and place.

Propp's Theory

Narrative Theory

Vladimir Propp, a Russian scholar analysed over one hundred Russian folk tales and saw commonalities in narrative structures. In his 1928 book *Morphology of the Folktale*, he identified eight character roles which he attributed narrative functions to.

 **Hero**

A main character who overcomes obstacles in order to achieve goals.

 **Villain**

A character who attempts to foil the hero.

 **Dispatcher**

A character who sends the hero on his/her way to achieve a set goal or task.

 **Donor**

A character who provides the hero with an essential, sometimes magical object.

 **Princess**

A character who acts as a reward for the hero achieving his/her goal. For instance, it could be a love interest, or it could be someone who delivers peace, truth or justice.

 **Helper**

A character who helps the hero achieve his/her goal.

 **False Hero**

A character who acts like the hero but is deceptive, and will often try to steal the reward or essential object away from the hero.

 **Father**

A character who rewards the hero, and can assist in guarding the magical object.

PROPP'S THEORY

Applied to Harry Potter and the Philosopher's Stone

The roles proposed by Propp are metaphorical not literal. Had he created them in the modern era his Princess role may have been labelled Prize to account for the current gender equity context. When applying his theory consider that a character can fulfil multiple roles.

Harry Potter is a ten year old orphan who is treated poorly by his relatives. On his 11th birthday he learns he has magical powers. His quest is to learn how to be a wizard, find a place to call 'home' and overcome obstacles created by Lord Voldemort's return.

Lord Voldemort is the main villain as his goal is to kill Harry, the story's hero. Additional characters with villainous traits are Draco Malfoy, and Professor Snape who intentionally try to foil the hero by sabotaging him at every turn.

Harry is dispatched into his life of magic by Hagrid, a half-giant, who arrives at Harry's house, and offers for him to attend wizard school.

Hagrid acts as the first donor as he provides Harry with his first wand and Hedwig, the snowy white owl, purchased in the magical Diagon Alley. Dumbledore provides Harry with the key to his magical abilities - stressing that his power comes from his love for his parents.

Ginny Weasley eventually fills this role. However, in the *Philosopher's Stone* Harry, Ron, Neville, and Hermione win Gryffindor the House Cup through their bravery and intellect in assisting to find, and destroy the Philosopher's stone.

Ron Wesley and Hermione Granger are the helpers in the narrative. Ron befriends Harry who assists him to board the train to Hogwarts and helps him on his quest. Hermione assists only after the boys save her from a troll.

Professor Quirrell, a Defence Against the Dark Arts teacher at Hogwarts, in his youth attempted to track down and defeat Voldemort, however, it is revealed that Voldemort inhabits Quirrell's body, feeding off his soul in order to regain his lost power.

Dumbledore, Headmaster of Hogwarts, offers wisdom and advice to Harry. At the story's conclusion, when Harry and Voldemort fight over the possession of the Philosopher's Stone, it is Dumbledore who saves him, ensuring the stone is destroyed.

Narrative

Hero's Journey

Chris Vogler's adaptation of Joseph Campbell's hero's journey can be found in his book *The Writer's Journey: Mythic Structure For Writers* which is considered to be a screen writing 'must-have' text book.

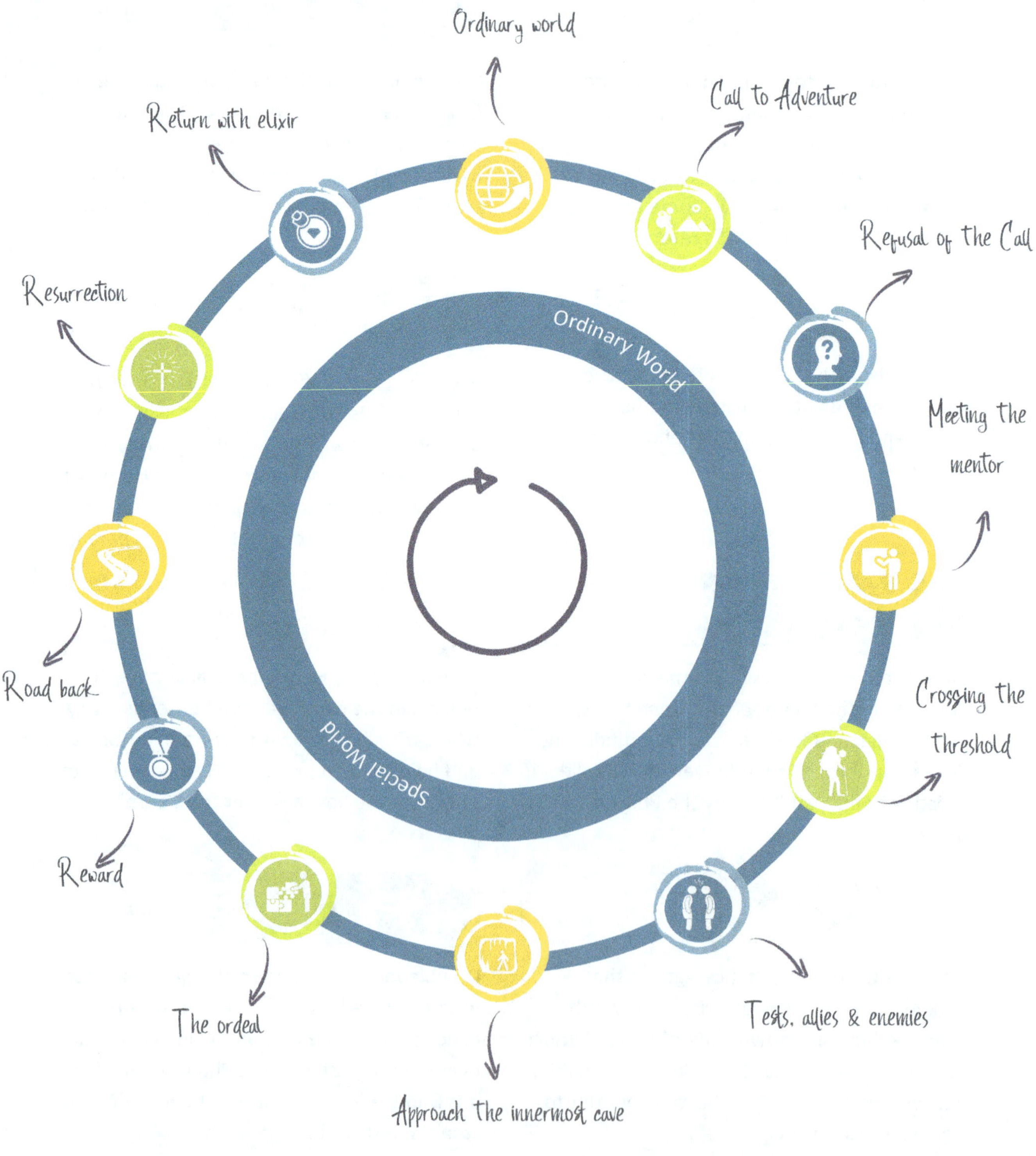

- Ordinary world
- Call to Adventure
- Refusal of the Call
- Meeting the mentor
- Crossing the threshold
- Tests, allies & enemies
- Approach the innermost cave
- The ordeal
- Reward
- Road back
- Resurrection
- Return with elixir

Ordinary World / Special World

THE HERO'S JOURNEY

Applied to The Lego Movie

Joseph Campbell's 1949 plot template refers to the structure of stories that follow the narrative progression of an unwitting hero who finds himself on a journey, learns something about himself, and at a decisive moment in the plot puts this new-found knowledge to use, triumphs over adversity, returning home transformed by his adventure. Below the template is applied to *The Lego Movie* (2014).

1. The Ordinary World:
The audience is introduced to their unwitting hero in his ordinary world. We meet Emmett Brickowski in his hometown of Bricksburg. It is here that we learn that he is a very average, assiduous rule following, overly perky, generic construction worker who wants nothing more than order, simplicity, and conformity.

2. The Call to Adventure:
Emmett moves out of his comfort zone when he steps away from the ordered construction site onto rubble to find his instruction book which had been blown away by the wind. Here he meets Wyldstyle, a member of the Resistance.

3. Refusal of the Call:
Emmett learns he is the chosen 'Special.' His task is to stop Lord Business freezing the world with his 'kragle.' In the opening scenes Wyldstyle tries to rescue Emmett from the police where he is heard to protest the call to adventure saying "I can't do this."

4. Meeting the Mentor:
Once Emmett decides to go on the adventure, he needs help to establish his confidence; enter the wizard Vitruvius who tells Emmett that to succeed all he has to do is believe.

5. Crossing the First Threshold:
Our hero, Emmett, fully commits to the journey and ventures into the unknown leaving the ordinary world behind and crossing into the special world. He leaves the comfort of Bricksburg with Wyldstyle as he is being chased by Bad Cop. He joins with Wyldstyle and Vitruvius to try and assemble all the Master Builders on Cloud Cuckoo Land.

6. Tests, Allies, Enemies:
In the special world there are many tests for Emmett to pass and obstacles for him to overcome. As he, Wyldstyle, and Vitruvius try to outrun the police on their way to Cloud Cuckoo Land Emmett is advised by Vitruvius to trust his instincts. He does just that, turning his head into an axle for a wheel, thus allowing them to escape. During this stage Emmett encounters many more enemies and finds new allies, in particular Batman, who, along with Wyldstyle, are part of the Resistance.

7. Approach to the Innermost Cave:
Emmett leaves Cloud Cuckoo Land, having secured new allies, namely Benny the Astronaut, Metal Beard the Pirate, and Unikitty. Emmett outlines his plan to get inside the Octan Tower and defeat Lord Business.

8. The Ordeal:
Emmett confronts his fear of not being able to use his own initiative, and faces the major hurdle of getting into the Octan Towers to find the 'kragle,' however he fails. Instead, he is captured by Lord Business and tied to a ticking bomb. To save the Master Builders, Emmett sacrifices himself by falling to his 'death' in the real world, thus transforming into a hero.

9. Reward:
After obtaining the 'piece of resistance' Emmett's reward is gaining insight about himself thus transforming him into a true 'special' or Master Builder.

10. The Road Back:
Emmett thinks he has saved his allies but finds that the journey home is not quite what he thinks. He has escaped the bomb but wakes up in a basement with a human child.

11. Resurrection:
Emmett is tested for a final time. He finds himself in an unfamiliar world where Lord Business is now in his human form, he must fight his last battle to ensure the kragle is not used.

12. Return with the Elixir:
Emmett returns to Bricksburg a changed man. His journey allowed him to grow as a person, he no longer slavishly follows instructions, instead he embraces creativity and initiative.

Narrative

Todorov's Theory

Tzvetan Todorov, a Bulgarian-French literary critic and author, proposed a narrative theory which states that all stories follow a similar pattern and use five clear stages. His structuralist approach is outlined in his 1969 book *Structural Analysis of Narrative*.

1. **Equilibrium** — The narrative begins in balance. Harmony exists between characters and events are stable.

2. **Disruption** — An event occurs that disrupts balance and harmony. Also referred to as an enigma, something that tampers with normality.

3. **Recognition** — A recognition that a disruptive event has occurred, and order has been broken. Disequilibrium occurs.

4. **Repair** — Tension exists as an attempt is made to repair the damage.

5. **Reinstatement** — The equilibrium is reinstated. Conflicts are resolved, questions answered, and normality restored.

TODOROV'S THEORY
Applied to Run Lola Run

INNOVATIVE NARRATIVE STRUCTURE

EQUILIBRIUM, DISEQUILIBRIUM AND ENIGMA

Traditional Hollywood films follow a cause and effect linear narrative with a beginning, middle, and contain a definitive narrative closure. Todorov's structuralist approach to narrative theory posits that stories follow a similar pattern consisting of five distinct stages. By examining the narrative manipulation in *Run Lola Run* we can begin to see how Tom Tykwer has experimented and subverted many of the expectations associated with a traditional narrative model.

Equilibrium

Traditionally, the beginning state of equilibrium establishes the major characters, their relationship to each other, and the setting. *Run Lola Run*, instead, introduces us to the themes through a prologue and the use of two epigraphs.

Disruption

The segue from the prologue to the enigma occurs at high speed. The audience is propelled into the **disruptive narrative event** which Manni explains to Lola in a phone conversation outlining the central premise of the film. Manni has lost 100 000 DM, and he needs Lola's assistance to come up with the money in twenty minutes, or he will die. Balance and harmony are thrown into turmoil.

Recognition

Disequilibrium occurs as Lola **recognises that a disruptive event** has caused order and normality to be thrown into chaos. She is forced to find a way to restore order. She begins by choosing the person who will most likely be able to help her, and she decides on Papa.

Repair

Tension exists as Lola attempts, three times, to **repair** the damage done by Manni accidentally leaving the money on the train. Tykwer experiments with the audience's expectations of **repair** as twice Lola fails in her quest.

Reinstatement

In a classical narrative, **equilibrium is reinstated**, and normality restored by the resolution of conflict. However, *Run Lola Run* is open-ended as the film concludes but does not resolve. The enigma is answered, Lola achieves her quest and gains the money, however this act now frames many narrative possibilities and viewing pleasure is derived from interpreting possible endings.

Narrative

Binary Oppositions

Claude Lévi-Strauss, a French structural anthropologist posited the idea that binary oppositions are used in narratives to fuel audience engagement by creating contrasting characters and ideas.

- Luck vs. skill
- Determinism vs. free will
- Fate vs. chance
- Good vs. evil
- Order vs. chaos
- Reality vs. fantasy
- Life vs. death
- Success vs. failure
- Tradition vs. modernity
- Innocence vs. experience
- Rationality vs. emotion
- Individualism vs. collectivism
- Ambition vs. contentment
- Stability vs. change
- Civilisation vs. nature
- Harmony vs. conflict
- Masculine vs. feminine
- Wealth vs. poverty
- Love vs. hate
- Optimism vs. pessimism
- Idealism vs. cynicism
- Happy vs. sad
- Revenge vs. forgiveness
- Public vs. private

- Binary oppositions can function to showcase the film's theme by using juxtaposition.
- For conflict to exist binary opposites must be present to create an opposition between two competing forces, such as good vs. evil, thus progressing the narrative.
- The audience is directed to embrace the values and ideologies underpinning the privileged element. For instance, good succeeding over evil conveys clear societal expectations and ideological beliefs.
- Oppositions are given to the audience in terms of actions, values, appearance, and character development which create a foundation to explore a film's themes. Binary oppositions add narrative interest as they allow for exploration of differences within story elements.
- By inviting the audience to consider the differences between opposites, and to consider the agenda behind one element being privileged over another, allows for meaningful engagement with the film's theme.

BINARY OPPOSITES

Applied to Run Lola Run

In the acclaimed 1998 postmodern German film *Run Lola Run* directed by Tom Tykwer, several binary oppositions exist to propel the narrative forward:

- **Chance vs. determinism:** the film explores whether individual agency has a role in determining the outcome of events, or whether chance has a big impact in shaping one's life. Lola is given three chances to achieve her goal of finding 100 000 Deutsch Marks in twenty minutes to save the life of her boyfriend Manni. Each attempt has slight variations that alter the outcome of the same event, these small changes in Lola's behaviour, such as jumping over a snarling dog, or falling down a staircase alter the course of events, highlighting how chance actions impacted her life. As a counterpoint, determinism is shown in Lola's actions as she learns how to use a gun and is able to bring this knowledge with her during her second attempt to save Manni. Moreover, a sense of determinism is suggested in Lola's actions of going to the casino and successfully betting on the number twenty at the roulette table, specifically Lola's scream ensures the ball successfully lands on the winning number showing that she can influence her own destiny.

- **Individuality vs. conformity:** Lola does not conform to societal expectations of femininity, she is active, powerful and assertive. She wears Doc Marten boots, cargo pants, a singlet top, and has dyed bright red hair to showcase her individuality. In contrast, the casino scene highlights conformity and societal rigidity as Lola is eventually escorted out of the betting room after breaking rules associated with behaviour and dress.

- **Chaos vs. order:** Chaos is visually represented on screen from the film's inception. We see people moving around a field with no purpose or order, this scene segues into an animated Lola running through a chaotic spiralling tunnel as she battles to destroy any obstacles in her path. Lola and Manni's lives are shown to be chaotic with many events converging, such as Lola's moped getting stolen, Manni getting spooked and leaving a bag of money on the train, all highlighting the chaotic nature of their lives. In contrast, order is shown via pattern and repetition, the visual motif of spirals appears throughout to signify the cycle of life, this cycle is represented in the three chances or lives Lola has to achieve her goal. The structured repetition of each of the three lives, with the events playing out with only slight variations, suggests order governs life events and determinism plays a small part.

Syd Field Paradigm

Narrative Theory

Syd Field, an American screenwriter, in his 1979 book *Screenplay: The Foundations of Screenwriting* proposed the three act structure in relation to the narrative construction of films.

The Syd Field Paradigm

The **climax** or the AHA moment. The most important point in the story.

Obstacles: what struggles does the main character have to overcome to achieve their goal?

Plot point 1

Plot point 2

Falling Action (denouement), the obstacles are overcome, issues are explained.

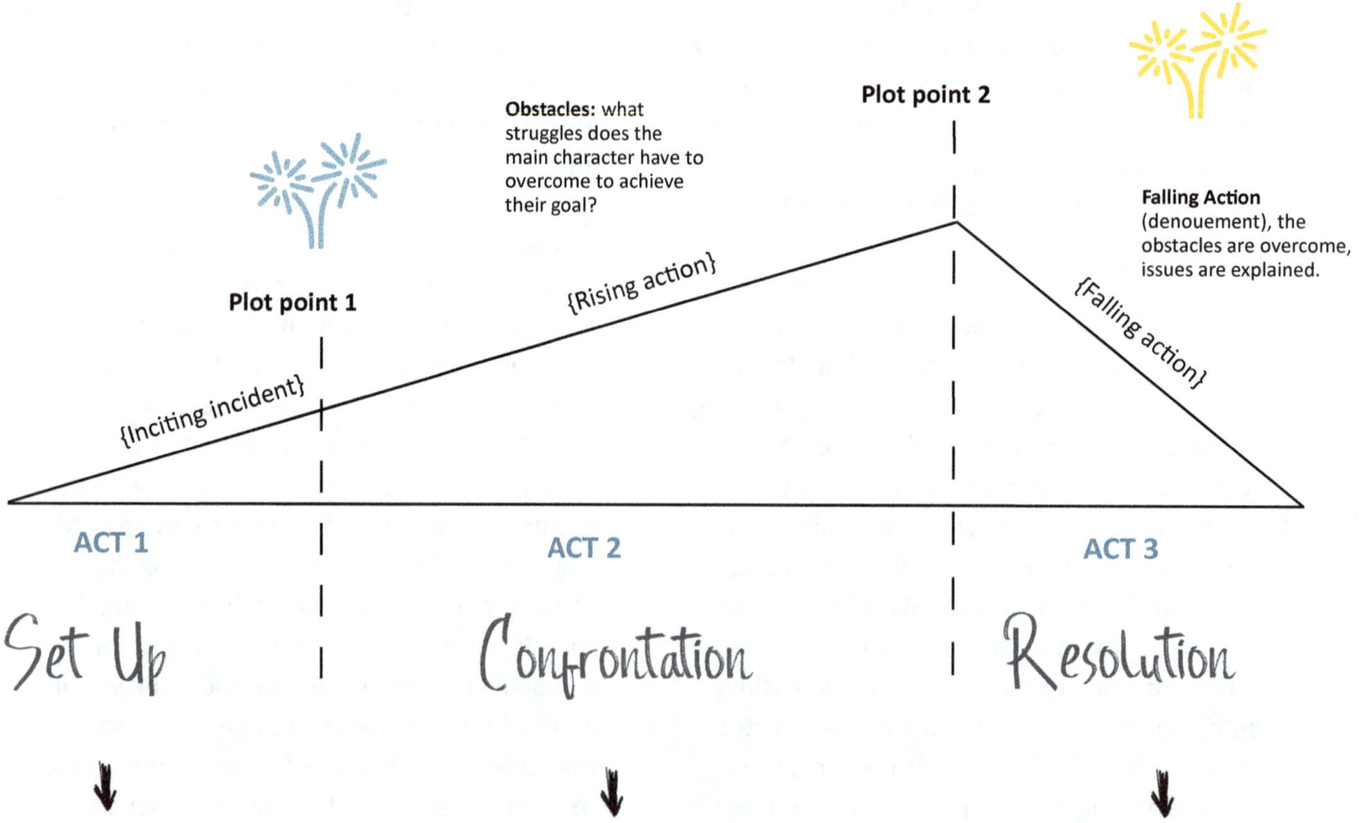

{Inciting incident} {Rising action} {Falling action}

ACT 1 — Set Up

ACT 2 — Confrontation

ACT 3 — Resolution

Exposition: setting the scene and establishing the main characters and the goal he/she needs to achieve.

This is the body of the film.

Resolution: is where we find out if the main character has achieved his or her goal and whether they have changed or grown from the journey.

SYD FIELD PARADIGM
Applied to Everything Everywhere All at Once

Everything Everywhere All at Once (2022) directed by Daniel Kwan and Daniel Scheinert.

Part 1: Everything

Act 1
Set up - establishing Wang family dynamics.
Evelyn Wang (Michelle Yeoh) runs a laundromat with her husband Waymond (Ke Huy Quan). The laundromat business is undergoing a tax audit. Her daughter, Joy (Stephanie Hsu), is trying to connect with her mother and have her accept her girlfriend Becky. To add to the chaos of Evelyn's life her father is coming to visit, and she must plan a birthday party for him. In addition, Waymond is unhappy in the marriage, and is trying to tell Evelyn he would like a divorce.

Inciting Incident 1:
An incident occurs that upsets, or unbalances the harmony of the protagonist.

Evelyn Wang, the protagonist is undergoing an Internal Revenue Service tax audit which propels the narrative as Evelyn arrives at the tax office unprepared. In the elevator on the way up to the office her husband Waymond undergoes a change, turning into Alphaverse Waymond where he tells Evelyn that she may be in grave danger whilst simultaneously placing a set of Blue-tooth earphones into her ears. An intertextual *Matrix* red pill/blue pill reference is made when Waymond issues a challenge saying that when Evelyn leaves the elevator, she can either turn left and go to her IRS tax appointment, or turn right and go into the janitor's closet.

Plot point 1:
The protagonist's journey begins.
Evelyn decides to go on the quest when she understands that her version of Evelyn is the only one who can stand up to the antagonist Jobu Tupaki (the evil version of Joy, Evelyn's daughter). Evelyn accepts going on the Alphaverse mission to take the world back to how it was meant to be. She begins to explore the concept of verse jumping to acquire skills to assist her with her quest. During this time Evelyn learns about Jobu Tupaki and how she is an agent of pure chaos, being nihilistic, without real purpose or desire. However, she has built a black hole called the "Everything Bagel" which consumes and destroys life. It is Evelyn's job to stop her.

Act 2
Confrontation
First half of confrontation.
By travelling to different multiverses Evelyn encounters bizarre versions of herself, including a martial arts film star. She learns that Jobu is looking for a specific version of Evelyn, the ordinary Evelyn who gets tax audited, and runs a laundromat.

Midpoint of confrontation.
Evelyn begins to realise her love for Waymond, additionally she begins to accept the chaotic multiverse and all it offers, instead of fighting it, she embraces it.

Second half of confrontation.
Evelyn's concern grows that she will become evil like Jobu Tupaki. A confrontation occurs when Evelyn tries to persuade Joy/Jobu that life is worth living and everything is not morbid and hopeless. She tells

Syd Field Paradigm

Everything Everywhere All at Once

Joy that she knows that she has feelings that make her want to give up but it is not her fault, instead it is the Jobu who lies within her who is causing Joy to feel nihilistic.

Plot point 2.

Part 2: Everywhere

All appears to be lost. Jobu shows Evelyn every multiverse option to allow her to understand its complex nature. She tells Jobu that she is the version of Evelyn Jobu has been searching for, and she will defeat her. Jobu tells Evelyn that she has been looking for her because she wanted someone who could see what she sees, and feel what she feels, and as her mother in every multiverse Evelyn is the one who Jobu wants to journey into the abyss of the Everything Bagel with.

The audience is shown how Evelyn's life turns out in each version of her many multiverses. The film's title of Everything Everywhere All at Once comes to fruition as we see possibilities of Evelyn's life play out, including her signing the divorce papers as Waymond looks on in shock, and Deirdre, the IRS agent arrives to seize all of their assets.

Act 3
Climax.
Questions are answered as Evelyn accepts Joy's sexual orientation by introducing Becky, Joy's girlfriend to her father. A montage of Joy and Evelyn physically fighting in each multiverse is shown with an overarching sound bridge of Jobu saying that the Bagel is the only place to find peace as she is slowly sucked into the centre of it. Evelyn's love is overpowering and we hear her shout at Jobu/Joy, "I am your mother" as she grabs her around the waist to stop the Bagel from pulling her in. The camera pulls back to reveal that while Evelyn is holding on to Joy, Evelyn's father is holding onto her, behind him Waymond is holding fast in a united show of love, strength and unity.

The act of love pulls the audience back into Evelyn's Laundromat universe where she must confront the pain she has caused her daughter by not acknowledging her sexuality, or giving her the love and attention she craved. The climactic scene sees Evelyn telling Joy that no matter what, she always wants to be with her daughter, she will cherish the moments she gets to spend with her.

Waymond and Evelyn reconcile. We see Waymond watching Evelyn and Joy find common ground, he ignores the divorce papers as he lovingly smiles at his family.

Part 3: All At Once

Resolution: equilibrium is restored to the Wang family.

The film comes a full circle as we return to the dining room table covered in receipts, but this time Evelyn is not alone in trying to prepare for the tax audit, her father, husband and daughter are all helping.

The entire family travel to the tax office in Becky's car, showing inclusion, inside the tax office we see Evelyn and Waymond kissing as they wait for the lift to take them up to their appointment with Deirdre. The juxtaposition between their old and new relationship is clear; by showing love, kindness and positivity the character of Evelyn found the version of herself she is happiest with. While Deidre discusses their successful tax filing, Evelyn briefly returns to alternate versions of herself, only to return to her Laundromat universe where she is now surrounded by everyone who she loves, and is loved by in return.

Narrative

Review & sample questions

Sample questions containing narrative:

1. Discuss the narrative elements used to showcase the film's theme.
2. Analyse how values and ideologies influence narrative elements.
3. Discuss how the narrative element of conflict conveys meaning.
4. Discuss the narrative possibilities created by a film's opening.
5. Discuss how a narrative is structured to engage with audience expectations.
6. Discuss how time has been structured to create meaning in a studied text.
7. Discuss how setting functions in a narrative.
8. Analyse the strategies used in a media text to construct a point of view.
9. Explain how a narrative theory applies to a media text.
10. Discuss how editing techniques contribute to audience engagement.
11. Analyse the relationship between narrative techniques and audience expectations.

NARRATIVE - main essential content to discuss:

01
- **Narrative elements:** the elements used to build a story and plot, and showcase the film's themes are characters, setting, conflict, and resolution.

02
- **Genre:** Stephen Neale's genre theory of repetition and difference posits that audiences have expectations of genres which are fulfilled by familiarity and repetition being supplied in genre iconography and narrative structure. However, difference is injected to maintain continued interest in the genre.

03
- **Point of view:** Through whose eyes is the audience invited to view the action from? Point of view can shape audience understanding of characters, conflict, resolution, and the underpinning story themes.

04
- **Theme:** A theme is the main message recurring throughout the narrative. The theme is interwoven throughout the story and is embedded in the codes, conventions, and narrative techniques used to construct the plot and convey the story.

05
- **Narrative structure:** the sequence of plot events showing how the story unfolds. How does the sequence of events impact audience understanding? Is the story linear cause and effect, circular, multi-layered, episodic or non-linear?

06
- **Narrative theories:** such as Vladimir Propp's theory, Joseph Campbell's Hero's Journey, Tzvetan Todorov's theory of equilibrium, disequilibrium and enigma, Claude Levi-Strauss' binary oppositions and Syd Field's paradigm create a framework for sequencing events in a narrative.

Chapter Six

Codes, Conventions & Techniques

- Film codes: symbolic - applied to *Memento*
- Film codes: written - applied to *Monsters Inc.*
- Film codes: audio - applied to *Boy*
- Film codes: technical - applied to *Three Billboards Outside Ebbing, Missouri*
- Film conventions
- Manipulation of space
- Manipulation of time
- Point of view
- Selection and omission
- Sample questions
- Review

Codes & Conventions

Codes & conventions

Codes and conventions are used by producers to construct the **preferred meaning** of a production. The audience uses the **selected codes and conventions** to deconstruct meaning based on their previous viewing history, context, demographics, and experience to arrive at either the preferred meaning, a negotiated meaning, or an oppositional reading of the text.

The preferred meaning is shaped by a selection process involving a choice of:

CODES

- **SYMBOLIC**: costume, colour, setting, objects, body language including hair, makeup and facial expressions.

- **WRITTEN**: titles, credits, captions, headlines, speech bubbles, typography choice.

- **AUDIO**: music, sound effects, dialogue including accent and vocabulary choice, voiceover narration, use of silence, consideration of rhythm, volume, pace and pitch.

- **TECHNICAL**: camera angles and movement, shot sizes, lighting, depth of field, compositional devices, special effects, editing techniques.

CONVENTIONS

- **GENRE** conventions such as iconography, narrative elements and narrative structure.

- **NARRATIVE** conventions include the accepted use of characters, setting, conflict, and resolution to form identifiable genres.

- **STRUCTURAL** conventions include narrative structures such as linear cause and effect, non-linear, circular, and multi-layered stories.

- **EDITING** conventions include the manipulation of time and space, use of montage, eye-line match, screen direction, continuity editing, and so on.

The combination of **selected codes and conventions** combine to form a narrative which either **supports** (through expected use), **or challenges** (through innovative use), the traditional audience expectations of **genre and style**.

Selection processes shape the meaning of media texts. The chosen combination of **codes and conventions** unite to convey the narrative's **theme**, and influence meaning.

CODES are the building blocks used to construct meaning. CONVENTIONS are the established ways of using codes and techniques to form meaning in media texts.

Symbolic codes

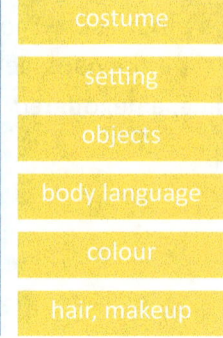

Codes function to symbolically indicate meaning based on the audience's understanding born out of context and experience. Connotative meanings quickly convey information without the need for lengthy explanations.

COSTUME
A character's clothing can relay information about historical time and place, socioeconomics, lifestyle, occupation, and personality.

OBJECTS
Objects can function to create realism, propel the narrative, and support the theme. An object can be a MacGuffin, something that motivates a character to achieve a goal.

SETTING
Setting is defined by time and place, and is conveyed via location, clothing, dialogue, weather, objects and context. It is used to construct atmosphere and support or challenge audience expectations.

BODY LANGUAGE
Used to succinctly convey information about emotions, actions, and relationships with other characters. Body language is a technique used to communicate feelings and intentions.

COLOUR
A film's colour palette indicates its mood and tone. Colours can be used symbolically to convey meaning about characters, to evoke emotion, and to foreshadow events.

HAIR, MAKEUP
Cohesive characterisation is formed through the selection of hairstyle and makeup chosen to define and construct characters suitable for their role.

Analyse the symbolic codes used to construct characters, convey the world of the narrative, and progress the plot in the opening sequence of Chris Nolan's *Memento*.

Chris Nolan's *Memento* (2000) is a complex, interwoven narrative that manipulates time and space to actively engage the audience in piecing together its maze like dual plot lines. The film centres around the character of Leonard Shelby (Guy Pearce) who has anterograde amnesia, meaning his long term memory is intact but he is unable to form any new memories. He clearly remembers the rape and murder of his wife, and this plot point is what propels the narrative forward as Leonard's central goal is to find the person responsible. The clear obstacle in the way of Leonard achieving his goal is his inability to remember any new information, hence his need to use tools such as Polaroid images, tattoos, and pen and paper to try and capture and retain information that he can no longer remember. However, as the film begins the audience is unaware of any of this.

The film opens with tense, dark, slow music playing as we see the title *Memento* appear in blue serif text. A **point of view** shot looking down at a close up of a Polaroid photo held by a male hand fades onto the screen behind the title. The photo shows a blood splattered tiled wall with what appears to be a male's body

Symbolic codes in Memento

lying face down in a pool of blood in the corner of the frame. The names of cast and crew continue to play over the confronting Polaroid image as it is occasionally given a shake in the mistaken belief that the image will develop faster, however, rather than seeing the image become clearer, we begin to see it fade away, foreshadowing the time manipulation to come. The **visual motif** of a Polaroid photograph is used to set the scene and jump start the narrative.

The music fades to reveal the first of Nolan's **time manipulation techniques** as we witness the Polaroid being feed into the camera. Audience expectation and knowledge suggests that the Polariod should come out of the camera, however, the flash goes off, shattering audience understanding of the sequence of events, and firmly bringing the audience around to the fact that what they are seeing is playing in reverse. It is here that we met Leonard Shelby, his face splattered in blood as he places the Polaroid camera to his side. His **clothing** consists of a light brown suit jacket and pants with a blue business shirt underneath. The juxtaposition of his blood splattered face, with his calm impassive, **body language** and professional attire raises a few questions. The **symbolic codes of clothing and body language** have been manipulated by Nolan, as they feed into the narrative enigma.

A **montage** of disorientating shots consisting of blood running backwards across a tile, the shell of a bullet on the floor, blood stained reading glasses lying on the tiles, and finally the image of a gun appearing from the floor and landing in Leonard's hand, all move in reverse with the bullet arriving in the gun chamber, the glasses lifting back onto the face of the man as his head lifts from the ground as we see Leonard pull the trigger, firing into the back of the man's head. Any notion that we may have had of Leonard being at the crime scene for the purposes of taking a polariod image to uncover the killer are quickly broken as we are shown that he is the killer. The minimalist mise-en-scéne connotes a murder scene but has the audience querying their previous understanding as Nolan artfully toys with **temporal sequencing,** showing us the ending at the beginning.

Up until this moment the film's **colour palette** consists of muted hues, everything slightly darker to replicate the darker enclosed space of what is potentially an abandoned building where the murder takes place. At the precise point that Leonard is revealed to be the murderer the **colour palette** switches to black and white and we find ourselves transported to an extreme close-up panning up the side of Leonard's face, all in shadow except for his eye, the accompanying voiceover states, "So where are you? You're in some motel room. You just wake up and you're in a motel room. There's a key. It feels just like the first time you've been there but, perhaps you've been there for a week, three months, it's kinda hard to say. It's just an anonymous room." Nolan uses the **objects** of the motel key, a pan across an empty dresser showing generic hotel products, and a cut to an empty closet revealing wire hangers with no clothes to build the groundwork around understanding Leonard's emptiness. The impersonal motel **setting**, coupled with Leonard's inner voiceover suggests that this is not unfamiliar territory for Leonard; his confusion is palpable.

The **exposition** suggests that Leonard's confusion is a constant state of mind, echoed by the **non-linear** story line which allows the audience to feel what Leonard feels. The **symbolic codes of setting, objects, colour, and body language** used in the film's opening combine to convey meaning about where Leonard is, and what he has done. Nolan's use of **temporal manipulation** means that audience expectation of the noir/crime genre is subverted as we begin to piece together the goal of the protagonist based on the given **symbolic codes** which hint at possible plot progression points.

Written Codes

WRITTEN
- title sequence
- word choice
- typography
- captions
- credits
- headlines

Written codes anchor meaning by directing the audience to decode the text according to signifiers such as word choice, typography, colour, and positioning.

The opening title sequence in a film or TV show orients the viewer by signalling important narrative considerations such as genre, mood and tone. The use of typography, combined with all visual and aural elements function as a launching pad for the story, and indicate what the story has in store.

Title sequences do more than relay the name of the production. Here are several title sequences worth investigating as they function to showcase the essence of each production and draw the audience into the story:
- Dr Dolittle
- Catch Me If You Can
- Se7en
- Grease
- The Fresh Prince of Bel-Air
- The Pink Panther
- Dr No

Several **title sequence** designers have had **auteur status** attributed to them due to their signature film title designs. **Saul Bass** is noteworthy as his authorial attributions span decades of work. His signature content and design frequently consist of animated 2D silhouettes that function to encapsulate the story.

Some of his title sequences include:

- The Man with the Golden Arm (1955)
- Around the World in 80 Days (1956)
- Anatomy of a Murder (1958)
- North By Northwest (1959)
- Vertigo (1956)
- Psycho (1960)
- Spartacus (1960)
- West Side Story (1961)
- Goodfellas (1990)
- Cape Fear (1991)
- Casino (1995)

Deconstructing the Monsters, Inc. (2001) title sequence.

Monsters, Inc. (2001) a Pixar film directed by Pete Docter centres around two monster type characters, Sully and Mike who work for the power company Monsters, Inc. Their job requires them to scare human children as the resulting screams are needed to power the city of Monstropolis.

The opening **title sequence** was designed by Geefwee Boedoe and is reminiscent of **Saul Bass** as **2D collage cut-out shapes** animate around the screen underscored by music composed by Randy Newman. The 2D shapes appear on the screen to the beat of jazzy upbeat music, the shapes bounce and actively move around to form the shape of a door, a clear **visual motif** for the film as doors are the gateway to the human world. The door opens

Title sequence in Monsters, Inc.

to reveal a child's closet containing clothes, toys and sporting equipment. All innocuous and innocent items. As the door quickly slams shut and reopens to reveal an extreme close-up of a stylised monster's mouth with sharp pointy teeth and green scaly skin we begin to see the **binary oppositions** at play in the film. A dull monster's roar is heard as the door slams shut yet again and is lifted out of the frame leaving only purple rectangles in the corner of the screen. These shapes quickly animate to form numerous doors that move across the screen in a choreographed, synchronised dance. The dance ends with the doors all in a horizontal line, now open and showing the **title** Walt Disney Pictures as one letter behind each door. In place of the letter P for pictures stands an eyeball that fills the door frame, a potential nod to the character of Mike whose one eye dominates the centre of his face.

The **colour palette** for the doors consists of purple and pink, the **font** for the Walt Disney title has a thick white **stroke** with a light purple **fill**. The font is reminiscent of chalkboard writing, neat yet child-like. The **design elements** evoke a fun, school days feel, anchored by the audience expectation of Walt Disney films, designed to fulfil a brief of an engaging narrative for children.

Prior to the Walt Disney **title** disappearing a scream is heard. The **aural motif** of screams and the visual **motif** of doors is repeated to indicate their important foundation for the up-coming story. To remove the Walt Disney title from the screen a larger door opens, and the long arm and talons of a monster reaches out and scoops up all of the letters, dragging them inside the door and slamming it shut.

An orange door appears next, it falls open vertically and the **text** A Pixar Animation Studios Film animates onto the screen. As before, more doors appear, one opens to let out a snake like monster who gobbles up all of the letters in its path. Far from appearing scary, the monsters have a hand drawn child's imaginative quality to them, and apart from the occasional stylised screaming, the jazzy upbeat **musical score** ensures the **hybrid genre** of comedy/children's drama is made clear.

Geefwee Boedoe uses a selection of colourful doors bordering the frame, with doors opening at random to reveal varying monsters picking up **letters** to form the title *Monsters, Inc.* The final letter M is placed into its spot by the mouth of the snake-like monster dropping it into the sequence with a firm swishing sound. That being done, the snake slithers across the screen, hits the title with its tail causing it to form the thick bold blue child-like *Monsters, Inc.* **title** with the iconic eyeball placed in the centre of the letter M, the doors that were static now **animate** across the screen to form a virtual curtain covering the title. The jazzy music changes into a calmer melody, the door colour changes from orange to the iconic blue and purple associated with the large monster Sully, and the **title sequence** ends with the audience being pulled into a singular open blue door, the inside totally black, drawing us into the unknown.

The **title sequence** functions to set the light comedic tone, hint at possible **plot progression points,** and draw on **audience expectations** via the signalled **visual and aural design elements.**

Audio codes

MUSIC
- score
- instrumental
- lyrics
- pace
- rhythm
- pitch

Music creates a mood and signals the film's genre. Instrumental music underpins moments of emotional intensity. Music with lyrics, often created for the film, anchors meaning by reinforcing or foreshadowing plot points.

DIALOGUE
- intonation
- content
- accent
- word choice
- volume
- pace

Dialogue directs audience understanding about characters and their motives. What a character says is equally as important as what a character does. Dialogue functions as a vehicle to deliver important plot information.

SOUND EFFECTS
- hard effects
- ambience
- foley
- silence
- atmosphere
- synchronous

Sound effects immerse the audience in the world of the film. Layering ambient sounds, sound effects, and foley enhances the realism, sets a mood and assists with suspension of disbelief.

VOICEOVER NARRATION
Voiceover is usually non-diegetic, emanating from outside of the film world. The audience is invited to see events unfold from the narrator's point of view and to connect with their beliefs.

PARALLEL SOUND
Parallel sound, also known as synchronous sound, mirrors the mood of the events in the scene. E.g., happy music accompanies a celebration or tense music plays during a suspense scene.

CONTRAPUNTAL SOUND
Sound that contrasts with the vision. In other words what you see and what you hear are in opposition. E.g., hearing bright, cheerful music whilst viewing a brutal crime.

SILENCE
Silence can be impactful. Juxtaposing a loud sound with silence signals an intensity, it directs the audience to look for visual cues such as facial expressions or actions.

DIEGETIC SOUND
Originates from a source within the film. E.g., a radio playing on a table, a character speaking, or the sound of a car passing are all diegetic sounds as they belong in the world of the film.

NON - DIEGETIC SOUND
Originates from outside of the world of the film. Sounds that cannot be heard by the characters such as a musical score, voiceover, or anything without a visible source within the film world is a non-diegetic sound.

Audio codes in Taika Waititi's Boy

Audio codes influence meaning by delivering clarity in plot progression points via:
- character dialogue
- creating realism through ambient sounds and sound effects
- creating emotional poignancy via music.

A film's **sound design** is a constructed process that layers **dialogue, music**, and **sound effects** to allow the audience to be transported seamlessly into the world of the film. **Audio codes** shape meaning by positioning the audience to side with a particular character, understand a point of view or feel a signalled emotion. For instance, in Taika Waititi's 2010 film *Boy* the audience is welcomed into the film through a traditional New Zealand **folk song** sung by an all-girl **choir** which delivers us to the Bay of Plenty highlighting the remote location. Placed to the right of the screen is a road sign stating *You are entering the tribal lands of Te Whanau-A-Apanui* which is accompanied by the **fast beat** of the **choir music**, thus inviting the audience to positively connect with the New Zealand location and its Māori inhabitants. The **choir music** continues, **volume fading** a little as we transition to a shot of the protagonist Boy, standing in front of blackboard that reveals the date as being 1984 written in chalk. The shot cuts to a question "Who am I?" written on the board which Boy begins to answer as he steps into frame, breaking the fourth wall and speaking directly to camera saying "Kia ora," a **Māori-language greeting** that roughly translates to hello or be well in English. The choice of opening the film with a Māori greeting positions the film geographically and assists to connect with an initial **primary Māori audience**, and later a **secondary global audience** due to the **universal themes** of coming of age, love, masculinity, and identity. The **selection of music** influences the audience to identify the setting as New Zealand and begin to understand the pointers which suggest the narrative will be a **comedy/drama genre**. Moreover, the **dialogue** delivered by Boy allows the audience to see the world through his perspective thus aligning us to his **point of view**.

Narrative progression begins as Boy looks at the audience and says, "My name is Boy. And welcome to my interesting world." The **montage** of accompanying images anchored by Boy's continuing **voiceover** deliver on Boy's statement; his world is interesting. He introduces us to his young brother Rocky, his cousins, his grandmother, his aunt, his pet goat, his school friends, his love of Michael Jackson, and his dad. The fantasy father that Boy constructs for the audience consists of him **describing** his father as, "a master carver, a deep sea diver, and the captain of the rugby team." Waititi uses a montage of images including Boy holding a cardboard sign bearing childlike bubble writing saying, "Welcome Home Dad" accompanied by an image of Boy dropping the sign as he is heard to say, "My dad's not here right now. He's a busy man." The **body language** of Boy suggests this scenario has been played out many times before and Boy's disappointment at his dad's absence is nothing new, hence the audience begins to understand Boy's fantasy creation of his father engaging in a variety of occupations which keep him away from home.

Boy completes his **speech to camera** by referencing his father saying, "When he comes home, he's taking me to see Michael Jackson. Live. The end." The **hopeful certainty in his voice** sets the audience up to understand that the narrative will deliver many obstacles in the way of Boy accepting his father for who he is rather than who Boy imagines him to be.

The opening scene emphasises the **audio codes of music, and voiceover** to intensify the viewing experience by clearly signalling who the protagonist is and shaping his potential goal in this coming of age story.

Technical codes

TECHNICAL
- camera angles
- camera movement
- shot sizes
- lighting
- composition
- editing

Technical codes are constructed from deliberate choices made when using filming equipment to effectively convey the narrative's meaning.

TECHNICAL

SHOT SIZES
Shot sizes convey information. For instance, by revealing specific emotions seen in a **close-up**, such as anger or sadness, we can understand character intentions and interactions.

CAMERA MOVEMENT
Camera movements signify meaning such as a **push-in** to highlight intensity, a tracking shot to move with the character, or a **tilt** to reveal an object or person of importance.

CAMERA ANGLES
Angles function to signal relative importance such as an **eye level** showing equality, a **high camera angle** suggesting vulnerability, and a **low camera angle** creating a feeling of dominance.

LIGHTING
Lighting functions to create an atmosphere and set a mood. Recognisable genre conventions see **bright lighting** used for comedies and **darker lighting** for horror films.

COMPOSITION
Devices used to lead the viewer's eye within the frame include the **rule of thirds**, using **leading lines**, juxtaposition, contrast, positioning, look room, eye-line match, lead room and head room.

EDITING
The film's pace, mood, and rhythm can be established using editing techniques such as **cross cutting**, **split screen**, **graphic match**, **jump cut**, and so on to effectively manipulate time and space.

APERTURE & SHUTTER
Aperture choice effects the **depth of field** and **exposure** of the subject. Shutter choice impacts the degree to which movement is **sharp** or **blurry**.

SPECIAL EFFECTS
Effects can come in a **physical form** such as makeup or prosthetics, or by chromakeying in a new background, or by using **computer generated imagery** to create the world of the film.

LENS CHOICE
The lens used will impact the **field of view, depth of field, bokeh,** and sharpness of the image.

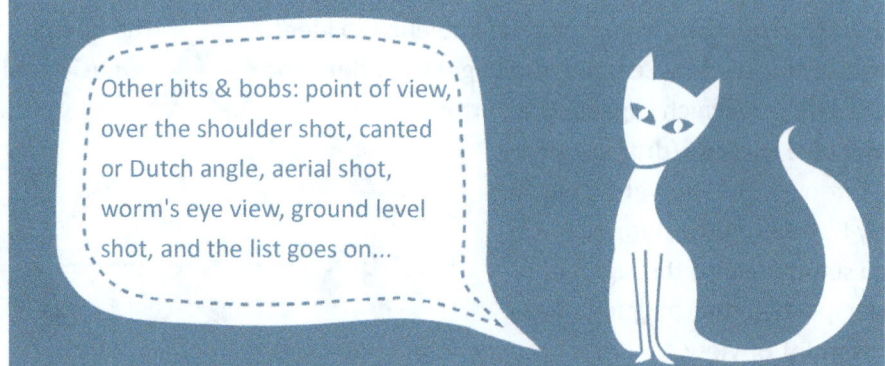

Other bits & bobs: point of view, over the shoulder shot, canted or Dutch angle, aerial shot, worm's eye view, ground level shot, and the list goes on...

Technical codes in Three Billboards Outside Ebbing, Missouri

Three Billboards Outside Ebbing, Missouri (2018) directed by Martin McDonagh received a Best Picture nomination and won the Best Actor and Best Supporting Actor roles at the Oscars. The film's content is gritty, connecting with audiences through the poignant portrayal of a grieving mother whose daughter has been raped and murdered. Francis McDormand received the best Actress award for her convincing characterisation of Mildred Hayes, a mother who is grieving yet has the strength and determination to stand up to the police who have bungled the investigation, leaving her daughter's murder unsolved. She rents three billboards to call attention to the farcical investigation, thus propelling the film's plot as we journey with Mildred on her quest for justice.

The film begins with fog encasing the countryside of the fictional town of Ebbing, Missouri as McDonagh introduces the film's **Macguffin**, the three billboards which are shown in **long shot, cutting into close up**s to reveal their dilapidated state, clearly not having been used in years. An **extreme long shot** reveals the three billboards proximity to one another, suggesting that a motorist passing would see each billboard in quick succession, being no more than one hundred metres apart.

The fog encircled billboards disappear as a **transition** into a black background reveals the title *Three Billboards outside Ebbing, Missouri* written in white using a typewriter like font. The **typography** choice functions to create an efficient, precise report feel, ironically the exact opposite of how the police have handled Mildred's daughter's murder case. The title anchors meaning for the audience in terms of place, Ebbing, Missouri, and signals the importance the billboards will play to **progress the narrative**.

The title fades away to reveal the billboards in **long shot**, now no longer surrounded by fog but instead lush green trees and a bright sunny day greets the audience as a car comes into view, travelling over the crest of a hill and moving slowly past the still dilapidated billboards. The shot **cuts** to inside the car and the audience is presented with a **close-up** of the rear view mirror revealing that Mildred Hayes is driving the car.

An **extreme long shot** shows the rear of the car passing the billboards, the car stops as we cut to a **mid shot** of Mildred looking pensively at the billboards. She places the car in reverse driving backward to the first billboard. A **close up** shows the text 'Ebbing Advertising Company' in faded writing at the bottom of the billboard. Mildred chews her nails, places the car into drive and zooms off down the road. Meaning is **encoded** in the opening minutes of the film by the **choice of codes**, as yet Mildred has not said a word, however, the combination of technical, symbolic, written and audio codes have delivered a

Technical codes in Three Billboards Outside Ebbing, Missouri

wealth of **encoded** meaning to the audience who now ponder what Mildred is planning on doing with the billboards.

Manipulation of time and space occurs via the **close up** of a mirrored window containing the written code, Ebbing Advertising Company, seen in a reverse reflection. The title has been used as a pseudo **graphic match** to deliver the audience to the new location, linking Mildred's billboards to the advertising office. The **camera pans** down the window showing a blurry Mildred walking towards the office in its reflection. In the background, equally blurry we can make out a police car in front of what appears to be a police station. The camera **pulls focus to a close up** of Mildred's determined face as she enters the office, the **bokeh** separates the background from the foreground thrusting Mildred forward.

A pan, stopping at an **over-the-shoulder shot** of a man sitting at a desk, reveals that he should be reading the aptly titled *A Good Man is Hard to Find* by Flannery O'Connor, however, he is in fact voyeuristically watching his female co-worker stack shelves. His pretence is interrupted by Mildred entering the room asking, "You Red Welby?" A series

of **over-the-shoulder shots** unfold with Red being viewed from **a high camera angle,** and Mildred from **a low camera angle** perspective establishing her dominance in this scenario. Mildred makes it clear that she would like to rent the billboards for a year, asking Red about any laws which constrain the content posted on a billboard. The **camera pans** with Mildred as she hands the money, and a few pieces of paper containing the text for what is to be written on each billboard to Red.

Interestingly, Martin MacDonagh chooses to include a **close up** of a bug upside down on a windowsill that Mildred is now standing in front of. The bug moves its legs helplessly, and it is at this point that Red says, "I guess you're Angela Hayes' mom," as Mildred reaches out to turn the bug back onto its feet. The seamless inclusion of this act of kindness speaks volumes about Mildred's character.

Speaking to Red, Mildred asks how long it will take before the billboards are put up. The audience hears the conversation unfold however their attention is turned outside of the office as McDonagh has **framed** Mildred to the left of the window and a **pull focus** sees the scene out of the window become clear. Ebbing Police Department, with its blue front door, blue window frames, and large America Flag

Technical codes in Three Billboards Outside Ebbing, Missouri

become clear. Red states that the billboards will be up by Easter Sunday. MacDonagh uses a **close up** showing Mildred looking out of the window across at the police department whilst saying, "That'd be perfect."

Without yet having learned that Mildred has lost her daughter to a violent crime, and that the police have done little to solve the murder, the audience is given clear **visual and aural clues** to **signal potential conflict** via the **combination of codes** used to create meaning. MacDonagh's **selection process** of placing the Ebbing Police Department directly across the road from the Ebbing Advertising Company allowed for the use of a variety of **technical codes** to assist the audience to begin to **deconstruct the preferred meaning** regarding a bereaved mother wanting justice for her murdered daughter.

Conventions

Conventions are the expected practices or established ways of using codes and techniques to construct meaning.

The medium chosen to tell the story (film, TV, radio, social media, magazine, book and so on) becomes the starting point for a narrative as audience expectations begin with the medium. What do you expect from a YouTube short as opposed to something on Netflix, or something on free-to-air television? Once the medium (let's say film) and the genre (say horror) are chosen to convey the story, then these elements influence aesthetic and structural choices. For instance, consider conventional expectations for the use of audio codes, or narrative structural choices, or narrative elements, or editing choices in a horror film. How do you expect the codes, and narrative techniques will be conventionally employed to construct the film? The chosen elements can either reinforce conventional understanding, subvert, or challenge audience expectations of established practices.

GENRE consider the accepted ways of using conventions such as iconography, narrative elements, narrative structure, lighting, sound, technical codes, and typography in genres. The next few pages cover the expected conventions associated with the **horror genre.**

Conventional use of **NARRATIVE ELEMENTS** includes the accepted use of:
- **Characters** are often stereotypes or archetypes. Consider how a villain is often encoded using conventional visual signifiers of body language that suggest they are tough, violent, or trying to hide something. In addition, they demonstrate behaviour that shows they are selfish and uncaring.
- **Settings** are associated with specific genres. Bright, light, open settings tend to be used for comedies whereas more confined, darker, isolated settings tend to be used for horrors.
- **Conflict and resolution** usually follow expected practices to form identifiable genres.

Consider the conventional use of **DOCUMENTARY** conventions:
- interviews, testimonials
- archival and black and white footage
- re-enactments, dramatisation
- use of emotional appeal
- voiceover, narration
- authority figures
- selection and omission
- oversimplification, card-stacking, straw man, common man, bandwagon.

Conventions

Audience expectations have shaped narratives in relation to genre iconography, narrative structure, narrative elements, and use of conventions associated with each medium.

Conventional narrative storytelling STRUCTURES and techniques include:
- Narrative structures such as linear cause and effect, and multi-layered stories.
- Use of Syd Field's three act structure.
- Todorov's equilibrium, disruption and return to new equilibrium.
- Creation of a point of view.

EDITING conventions include:
- the manipulation of time and space
- use of montage
- eye-line match and the use of screen direction
- continuity, seamless, invisible editing
- creation of rhythm and pace.

FILM MOVEMENT conventions include the expected techniques and codes seen in:
- French New Wave: such as the use of jump cuts, long takes, and open-ended resolutions.
- Film Noir conventionally uses chiaroscuro lighting, femme fatale, and first person voiceover narration.
- Classical Hollywood films have goal orientated characters, a linear cause and effect plot line, and seamless editing that does not draw any attention to the filmmaking process.
- German Expressionism centers around dark themes, uses chiaroscuro lighting, has exaggerated sets that are extensions of the characters, and employs canted angles to unsettle the audience.

Consider how codes and techniques are conventionally used to construct a:
- film trailer
- film poster
- podcast
- YouTube short
- TikTok
- Instagram post
- advertisements for print, television, radio
- news
- current affairs
- tweet
- genre.

Conventions

What are a mainstream audience's expectations for the conventional use of horror film structural and aesthetic elements?

Established ways of using codes and techniques to construct meaning in a horror film:

Narrative Elements

Protagonist - hero
- must embark on a mission to achieve a goal
- has strength, skill, persistence, intelligence, and moral fortitude to overcome all obstacles
- quite often good-looking and athletic
- will not give up despite the odds

Antagonist - villain
- has some abnormal characteristic, could be a monster, ghost, demon, serial killer etc.
- often wears a disguise such as a mask
- has strong fighting abilities, impervious to hero's attempts to shoot/stab/hit/kick
- appears to have superhuman strength

Victim/s
- is often weak, stupid, or just plain ditsy
- a good person in the wrong place at the wrong time

Iconic settings
- isolated and dark setting
- haunted or abandoned houses
- basement
- cemetery
- hospital, asylum
- woodlands

Iconic conflicts can involve:
- a sacrifice, whereby one character will sacrifice themselves for the sake of others
- a confrontation in which the protagonist stops the antagonist, usually by lethal force

Iconic resolutions can involve:
- an escape whereby the protagonist survives, achieves all goals, and returns to a new equilibrium.
- a twist
- a revelation occurs, the protagonist learns new information about the antagonist, changing their original goal.

Narrative Structure

The conventional narrative structure of a horror film frequently follows **Syd Field's three act structure** whereby the **setup** gives backstory and establishes the goal of the protagonist; the **confrontation** is where the audience sees the horror and might of the antagonist, it is here that the protagonist must overcome obstacles; the **resolution** is where the hero and villain confront for the final time, it is here that a twist may be injected as the audience waits to have all of their narrative questions answered.

Editing

- Use of jump scares
- Fast pace to create tension
- Slow pace for anticipation and suspense
- Parallel editing: cutting between events to create tension
- Slow motion to exaggerate or draw attention to an element of the narrative
- Cut-away to point of tension or to foreshadow events
- Point of view shots: used to show main character's perspective and create empathy
- Split screen: showing events occurring simultaneously
- Montage: a series of shots edited together to convey information succinctly and convey a mood
- Flashback: a scene that provides backstory and contextual information for the audience.

Conventional use of codes

Conventional ways of using codes to encode meaning in a horror film:

Symbolic

- **Colour palette** tends to be earthy, brown, reds, and blacks
- **Iconography:** can be religious icons, weapons, masks, candles, creepy paintings, blood and gore
- **Settings** tend to be isolated, old, dilapidated or confined spaces
- **Clothing** is contextual but can include tattered clothes, masks, uniforms or costumes to hide someone's identity
- **Body language** expectations include fearful emotional expressions, shaking or trembling to indicate fear, cowering to try and escape danger, aggression from both the antagonist and protagonist, tense or frozen stance due to fear or shock, and desperation shown via screaming, yelling or pleading.

Written

- Often a one word title such as *Scream* or *Psycho*
- Typography conventionally uses fonts related to blood, uses Gothic fonts, or uses all caps as this is a solid font type
- Colour palette is darker to convey the ominous horror genre.

Audio

- Diegetic sounds such as footsteps, thunder, lightning, rain, screaming, squeaky doors, floorboards and so on
- Non-diegetic sounds such as a heartbeat, haunting sounds, suspense music, intense music, horror music
- While diegetic sounds can be used to create suspense, silence is also very important to create unease and tension
- Sound effects are iconic as heightened noises such as wind, twigs snapping, and doors creaking all function to build tension
- Suspense and tension music are used to shape audience emotions in relation to events.

Technical

- Lighting tends to be low key with lots of shadows, flickering lights, unusual shapes and use of darkness
- Chiaroscuro lighting employed – half light half dark, throwing suspicion onto characters
- Low and high camera angles to suggest fear and uncertainty
- Point of view shots to create tension and highlight an impending threat
- Hand held shots to suggest urgency
- Close ups and extreme close ups, especially on the victim and hero to highlight emotions
- Canted angle: slight tilt to create an unstable feeling
- Camera framing: camera placed behind (tree, window etc.) to make it appear as if the character is being watched.

Manipulation of time

Real time: events occur in the same time frame as would occur in real life. Often used for sports events or music concerts.

Screen time: the length of time it takes for the events to unfold within a film (a day, a week, a year and so).

Compressed time: time is shorter than real time. This is the most frequently used time manipulation technique and involves editing out actions unnecessary to the plot. For example, the audience does not need to see a character move from one setting to the next if the journey is not integral to the plot.
Techniques to compress time include:
- editing techniques such as cuts, graphic match, jump cuts
- editing transitions such as dissolves or fade to black
- time lapse or fast motion
- time remapping - video is sped up
- simultaneous time - split screen, parallel cutting.

Expanded time: time is slower than real time thus giving dramatic emphasis to the event. Techniques to expand time include:
- freeze frame
- slow motion or time-remapping (the speed of the clip is reduced thus increasing its duration)
- replay
- repetition (using many different angles and cutaways to enhance the suspense of an event).

Time manipulation techniques
- flash back: character remembering past events, thereby supplying crucial missing background information for the audience.
- flash forward: gives an indication of what occurs in the future.
- dream sequence
- long take
- real time interlude.

- **Temporal order:** the sequence in which the story's events are ordered within the plot. Events can be out of chronological order by using devices such as flashbacks or flash forwards.
- **Temporal duration:** the length of time represented by the events in the plot.
- **Temporal frequency:** the number of times an event is shown within the plot. Repetition creates emphasis.

Manipulation of space

Open frame: characters enter or exit as they desire, indicating a space beyond the frame.

Closed frame: characters are contained within the frame. Visual space does not extend beyond the frame.

Sound from a source outside of the frame suggests the surrounding space and atmosphere. The film frame is an artificial boundary, space can be extended beyond the frame through devices such as:
- Sound effects, for example, the audience hears a siren, they don't need to see an emergency vehicle as they will extend the space outside the frame simply by hearing the siren.
- Off screen dialogue extends the artificial boundary of the frame. For example, in Hitchcock's *Psycho* Marion Crane hears, but never sees, Norman Bates' mother berating him. This off-screen sound adds a further dimension to the story and encourages the audience to construct a space beyond the frame.

Diegetic sound: exists within the world of the narrative.
Non-diegetic sound: emanates from outside the story space.

Mise-en-scène assists the audience to suspend their disbelief and engage with the fictional film space. The director, working with the set designer, will use spatial elements such as props, setting, costume, colour, and acting performance to create the fictional film space.

Film space is primarily manipulated through sound, montage, and mise-en-scène.

Does any action take place off screen? How does this occur? Does this allow the audience to know more than the characters?

Montage contributes to creating a world outside the frame, particularly through intellectual montage whereby the audience is asked to connect two shots together in order to come up with a third concept. For example:
- Exterior location shots are edited and placed next to interior shots to create the sense that the interior is part of the established exterior.

131

Selection and omission

SELECTION & OMISSION
- What's selected?
- What's excluded?
- What's emphasised?
- Whose agenda is served?
- Whose point of view is privileged?
- What codes of construction are chosen?

All narratives are created using selection processes, specifically what to include and what to exclude. In so doing a point of view is constructed. When considering how a point of view is created analyse selection and omission in terms of who or what is being privileged and why?

Selection of codes & conventions

AUDIO CODES
Consider audio codes in terms of voiceover, dialogue, and accompanying music. Whose dialogue is foregrounded? What connotations can be attached to the choice of words? What is the discourse surrounding a topic? Are competing discourses allowed? Who speaks as an authority figure? How does this frame the narrative? Is all power and knowledge spread along equal gender and racial lines or is it concentrated among an elite few? How are music and sound effects used to signal emotional relatability or used to signal distance? How do the audio codes combine to form a pathway for the audience to adopt the preferred meaning and viewpoint of the text?

CAMERA
Camera positioning and framing: consider who is given more/less screen time? How do camera techniques such as angle, framing and composition position the audience to engage with a character?

WRITTEN CODES
Consider written codes and how they anchor meaning. What is the title? Are there subtitles for authority figures, quotes or statistics? How does the selection of written information convey meaning?

Aesthetic choices
Selection includes stylistic choices such as mise-en-scène, colour palette, and all aesthetic choices.

SYMBOLIC CODES
What a character wears, where the narrative is set, and the accompanying mise-en-scène position the audience to engage with the text's preferred point of view.

EDITING
Ordering of shots: how the narrative begins establishes the foundations for the text's point of view. Which character is shown first? Whose eyes do we see the story unfold from? The way a text is structured is crucial in relaying and supporting its themes, ideas and point of view. Consider how binary oppositions are used to clearly highlight a text's preferred meaning.

NARRATIVE
Whose point of view is privileged? What character representations are used? How is the narrative sequenced? Does the way the events unfold favour a character, issue or idea, revealing a theme or agenda?

VALUES
Texts are made in a historical context. How does the selection of codes and conventions convey values on any given topic?

Selection and omission

Bias by omission

SOCIAL MEDIA
Consider the algorithms that select and feed content to your device; what you see shapes your version of reality. What perspectives have been omitted? How does this form a bias?

MEDIA
Omission occurs in the casting of films where certain genders, ethnicities, and ages are excluded thereby highlighting what is privileged within society (frequently heterosexual, white males of any age). Think about older females, people of colour, or people whose sexual identity is not heteronormative, are they given positive coverage or inclusive roles that are not tokenistic? Consider what ideas, beliefs, values or perspectives are excluded? Whose agenda does it serve to omit these representations or ideas?

FICTION AND NON-FICTION MEDIA
Bias occurs when constructing media texts through selection and omission of aspects such as:
- Placement
- Time
- Coverage
- Word choice
- Codes of construction
- Representations
- Selection of source (authority figure, testimonial)
- Selection of content
- Who to cast
- How, and what to edit to form meaning.

OMISSION
What information is left out? Why? Whose agenda is served?

SELECTION
What elements are included to construct the narrative? Why? How do they shape audience understanding of representations, values, and ideologies?

Selection and omission

Preferred meaning — Embedded with **values and ideologies** foregrounded by the **selection process**

Constructed via the **selection and omission** of information

Selection
- Codes and conventions
- Genre conventions
- Narrative conventions
- Conventions associated with form, such as documentary conventions or podcast conventions
- Aesthetic and stylistic choices.

Omission
- Omitting representations
- Excluding ideas, beliefs, perspectives, or values that do not align with or support the production's preferred meaning.

Bias

Media productions contain some form of **bias** as they are carefully crafted constructions with an agenda. The **agenda** may be to:
- entertain
- inform
- persuade or sell
- artistic expression
- social commentary
- advocacy

Therefore, the production contains the **point of view**, bias, aesthetics, and agenda of its maker.

The choice of **selected and omitted** codes, conventions, and techniques form a **representation** of the topic, event or person.

Audience

As **selection and omission** are an inevitable part of the production process audiences need to be critically aware of how the choices made throughout the production process shape meaning. Examine the choices to determine any bias and agenda embedded in the content.

Codes and conventions

Review & sample questions

Sample questions containing codes, conventions, techniques:

1. Discuss how codes and conventions are used to construct gender.
2. Discuss how sound conveys meaning in a studied media text.
3. Discuss how setting contributes to meaning.
4. Discuss how codes and conventions are manipulated to create tension.
5. Analyse how time and space are manipulated in a studied media text.
6. Discuss how codes have been used to shape a character.
7. Discuss how technical codes influence meaning.
8. Analyse how audio codes create audience engagement.
9. Discuss how selection and omission of content shapes a media text.

 **CODES, CONVENTIONS, TECHNIQUES - main essential content to discuss:**

01
- **Codes** are the building blocks used to construct meaning. A preferred meaning is constructed from a choice of symbolic, written, audio, and technical codes.

02
- **Conventions** are the expected practices or established ways of using codes and techniques to construct meaning. Audience expectations have shaped narratives in relation to the conventional use of genre, form, narrative structure, and film grammar.

03
- **Manipulation of time:** deals with how events are ordered within the narrative. Time can be compressed, expanded, or manipulated using a multitude of techniques.
- **Manipulation of space:** occurs through manipulating sound, mise-en-scène, and using editing techniques to create the fictional film space.

04
- **Selection and omission:** what content is included and what is left out? What codes and conventions have been deliberately chosen to represent people, places or ideas? What has been omitted? Whose agenda is served? Who or what is privileged by this choice? What values or ideologies are embedded in the foregrounding of the chosen content?

Chapter Seven

How Context Affects Content

- Context defined
- How context shapes content
- Context analysis applied to *Run Lola Run*
- Context analysis applied to *The Bicycle Thieves*
- Context analysis applied to *The True Cost*
- Sample questions
- Review

Context Affects Content

Context

Context relates to the parts of the environment that surround a text (such as a book, film or television show) that can throw light on its meaning. Contextual elements may include:
- time
- place
- culture
- technology
- specific events, people, issues
- ideas, beliefs, values, ideologies.

In a media text the contextual information provided informs meaning by giving the audience greater understanding of characters and their intentions by providing the circumstances that shaped the character's persona, beliefs and purpose. Different audience members will decode the text's content differently depending on their contextual circumstances.

SOCIAL CONTEXT
- Language
- Fashion
- Entertainment: music, films, TV, games...
- Social norms
- Representations of groups

POLITICAL CONTEXT
- Political leaders
- Wars
- Political ideology
- Military
- Agenda setting

GEOGRAPHIC CONTEXT
- Location
- Language
- Cultural references
- Natural resources

HISTORICAL CONTEXT
- Inventions/technology
- Values and attitudes: gender, equality, race
- Education
- Religion
- Cultural movements
- Revolutions

ECONOMIC CONTEXT
- Economic systems
- Labour markets
- Recessions
- Depressions

CULTURAL CONTEXT
- Cultural icons or symbols
- Language
- Customs and traditions
- Values and ideologies
- Art and literature
- Social structures and organisations

CONTEXT always affects CONTENT

The **CONTEXT** subheadings are all interlinked. Elements have been placed under a subheading in a 'best fit' scenario. For instance, 'Wars' could fit into other contextual headings but have been placed under Political Context as this is often where they arise.

CONTEXT
shapes content

- Context shapes the meaning of media content by providing contextual clarity regarding the background or circumstances surrounding an event, issue, or story.
- Cultural context encompasses factors which inform the audience about societal attitudes, values, and ideologies that shape the text's content. Some factors include historical events, economic considerations, religion, gender, time period, language, relationships, historical figures, location, and age of the audience member engaging with the content. Different audiences will decode the content differently depending on their context.
- How are codes used to encode contextual meaning? For instance, symbolic codes of clothing, objects, setting, and colour are contextual signifiers as they signal important contextual information about class, location, culture, age, and gender to the audience.
- Cultural context shapes representations in media as those with power can shape and direct the representations of others. For instance, consider how minorities and women have historically been represented in the media.

- Representations of historical events/figures – how have these been constructed? Whose agenda is being served? Discuss the iconography used to portray the historical context?
- Does the film use codes and conventions from a particular film movement? Does this situate it in a historical period?

- Historical context informs cultural context as it includes events that shape media content such as wars, inventions, word choice, clothing, food, religion, entertainment, gender roles, beliefs, values, ideologies, social structures, literature and language use.

- Where is the film set? What visual and aural markers signify the geographic context? How does the film portray the setting, negatively or positively? How is meaning encoded? How are places and their people conveyed? What codes and conventions are used to construct either positive or negative portrayals?

- A political context such as capitalism, communism, social-democrat, conservative-Christian can indicate an agenda behind a media text. A political context can be reflected in the text's content via its themes, character representations, conflict, resolution and their associated values and ideologies.

Context

Contextual factors influence how the audience will interpret media content

- Economic context, particularly the labour market, shapes media content. What job roles are portrayed as powerful? Who has access to these roles? Why? How are economic systems such as capitalism portrayed? Whose agenda is served by privileging this system?

- Where is the text consumed? How are family structures, genders, sexuality, and subcultures represented? How is language used? Social context is built on shared values and ideologies in relation to behaviour, appearance, norms and traditions. How does the social context influence the perception of media content?

- What tools does the filmmaker have at his/her disposal? How does technology impact production, distribution, marketing, and circulation? Consider traditional marketing methods such as print and television vs. the use of social media, and virtual reality, specifically Netflix using billboards in the Metaverse to advertise up and coming films.

- Which institution made the film? Commercial or independent? Is there an agenda attached? Analyse the political or social commentary encoded in the film. Whose agenda is furthered by the political or social commentary? Whose viewpoint is critiqued? Consider controls and constraints, budgets and regulations.

- Who owns what? Why does this matter? Is there an agenda associated with ownership or institutions? Is the production commercial or independent? How was the production made, distributed and exhibited? What regulations and controls and constraints impact the text's content?

- Where is the content being delivered? In a classroom? In a shop? At the beach? What country is the text being viewed in? When was the film made versus when it is set? How does this influence interpretation of the preferred meaning?

Run Lola Run Context Analysis

A text cannot be separated from its context. **Context will always affect content**. When analysing a media text, it is important to research the production context (when, where, and why the text was made), as well as the reception context (who is consuming the text and why).

Context in Run Lola Run

Run Lola Run, a 1998 film directed by Tom Tykwer tells the tale of a young woman, Lola, who is issued with the task of obtaining 100,000 Deutsche Marks in twenty minutes in order to save the life of her boyfriend Manni from the vengeful crime lord Ronnie, whose money Manni accidentally left on the train.

The film reflects changes in the **cultural and political context** of Germany in the 90s through its representation of women and its use of the video game culture to frame the narrative.

Cultural Context

The construction of Lola is influenced by **contextual factors** such as **Lara Croft's character in the Tomb Raider video games** which were first released in 1996. Lara Croft was a **pop culture icon** of gaming, acting as a strong female protagonist who frequently assaulted male villains and saved the world. Lola's dress style of khaki pants, combat boots, a singlet and fiery red hair mimic Lara Croft's clothing. When we first met Lola, she is in animated form and her decisive actions emulate those of her video game doppelgänger. She is seen running past various obstacles such as a growling dog, an ominous clock mouth, and she is seen smashing glass. Her animated form and ability to overcome the obstacles in her way imbues her with superhero like qualities. The film's opening animated sequence establishes Lola as a virtual hero, being indestructible, powerful and driven. As Lola transitions from the animated world into the real world the audience continues to attach these qualities to her. **Contextual understanding** of Lola's ability is **gained from her appearance and actions** being aligned with those of the popular cultural icon of Lara Croft.

The superhero aesthetic connects to the **video game popular cultural appeal** of the 90s that saw German youth embrace American popular culture, particularly Atari video games. Tykwer **appropriates many video game structural conventions** in the construction of his post-modern narrative. Like a video game, his **protagonist is goal orientated** and has an objective to achieve in a given time limit. In this case Lola must obtain 100 000 marks in twenty minutes or risk having her boyfriend, Manni, killed. A video game player is given three chances to achieve their objective before the game ends. *Run Lola Run* has a **temporal frequency of three**, as Lola's quest to obtain the money and save Manni's life occurs three times, each time an obstacle stands in Lola's way, and she secures her place as the protagonist by being determined to achieve her goal. The **video game context** has influenced the aesthetic construction of the narrative, engaging a primary niche German youth audience and a secondary international audience by aesthetically experimenting with a video game structure.

The **pop culture references to video game aesthetics** are littered throughout

Context

the film. Most notably Lola has the ability to save lives by her touch. In the final run she wins 100 000 DM at a casino and hitches a lift in an ambulance in an attempt to get to Manni within the allocated twenty minutes. Inside the ambulance Lola finds Schuster, the bank security guard who has had a heart attack. Schuster's heart stops, evidenced by the slowing of the non-diegetic sound effect of his heartbeat. Lola takes Schuster's hand in hers and the audience begins to hear his heartbeat return to normal, thus appearing to save his life simply by her touch. A **contextual understanding surrounding superheroes** having the ability to achieve superhuman feats is transferred to Lola from the video game context.

The audience's previous **contextual knowledge of video games** allows them to transfer their understanding from one medium to another. For instance:

- Like a video game, the **laws of space and time are manipulated.** In the supermarket run Lola has the ability to talk to Manni through the thick supermarket window as if it were not there.
- Lola's **'superpowers'** manifest in the form of her screaming which results in glass smashing as a means of Lola taking control of her physical environment. These **visually and aurally aesthetic motifs** are first introduced to the audience in the opening title sequence where the audience sees an animated Lola smashing through glass, and breaking the names of the cast and crew that are superimposed on the tunnel she is running through. Her superhero powers are established, and narrative possibilities are suggested by Lola's actions, thus the **contemporary video game context** has shaped the film's aesthetic and created interesting narrative possibilities.

Contextual knowledge of historical events feed into the **reception context** of the film. For the audience to effectively decode meaning they need to be aware of a few contextual factors:

- Lola represents a shift in the cultural identity of post-unification Germany, embodying values of courage, determination, and risk-taking that were encouraged post the fall of the Berlin Wall. The **merging of East and West Germany** is seen through the symbolism of Lola running between the formally divided East and West Berlin as she runs over the red brick bridge known as the Oberbaumbrücke, which was a border crossing before the fall of the wall.
- Lola's self-reliance, optimism, and agency act as an agent of change which contrasts with the disapproval of the older generation who are represented in the casino scene, signalling a **generational divide**. Their disapproval of Lola's dress style of khaki pants, singlet and Doc Marten boots, and her screaming is clear. In the **wake of reunification**, the film highlights a rejection of traditional values, moving away from conservatism and embracing chance and change.
- A construction of a **new German identity** included a representation of women as having determination, strength, and agency as seen by Lola's powerful physical actions of doing whatever is required to save Manni. In contrast Lola's mother, who represents the old femininity seen in Germany, is passive, more ornamental, and has no agency of her own.
- The **context of the third wave of feminism** shapes the film's content as Lola's character aligns with the goals of empowering women to make their own decisions and not be constrained by societal expectations. The feminist ideological lens through which

Run Lola Run Context Analysis

the audience sees Lola can be seen as being shaped by, and in turn shaping, the third wave of feminism's goals of expanding female agency.

- By reversing the damsel-in-distress paradigm, the film calls upon **contextual understanding of the historically subservient,** passive nature of female roles in order to understand Manni's frantic screaming down the phone at Lola, begging her for help. Manni calls Lola from a phone box, and his utter vulnerability is represented in high angles and close ups that communicate his volatile and helpless state as he begs, "...help me Lola, help me." The **traditional patriarchal power structure** is called into question by rejecting traditional gender roles. Lola appropriates 'male' traits such as strength, bravery, risk-taking and determination that reflect a change in societal discourse, highlighting a desire to shift the boundaries away from a patriarchal view and to **privilege the female experience** as highlighted by Lola's expanded agency, her clothing aesthetic, and her mobility across East and West Berlin.

- The film's rejection of traditional Christian values in favour of embracing the random nature of life reflects the **cultural shift** away from religion towards secularism.

- The film's fast-paced editing and **video game-inspired narrative structure** tap into the zeitgeist of 1990s Berlin as an emerging hub of youth culture, technology, and electronic dance music.

Tom Tykwer's *Run Lola Run* engages with the **cultural and political zeitgeist of Germany** in the late 80s early 90s by appropriating traits traditionally attached to a male protagonist and using the character of Lola to embody change, thus showing that **gender equality is not a deficit model**. Lola's strength, agency, and determination do not weaken Manni's masculinity, rather by both characters showing agency, their goal is achieved.

Context always affects content; the **production context** of the late 90s saw copious contextual elements shape *Run Lola Run*; these included having **powerful female characters** such as Lola aligning with the goals of the **third wave of feminism**, a **questioning of religion** by rejecting Christian doctrines of fate and instead embracing chance and the random nature of events, and **a shift towards risk-taking** as highlighted by Lola's actions to obtain the required money to save Manni's life.

Context has shaped many of Tykwer's stylistic and thematic choices in *Run Lola Run,* from his use of techno music to the aesthetic of a video game, to his character construction, he has created an experimental and **contextually relevant** film for his primary niche German youth audience, as well as for an older progressive international audience who found the universal themes resonated with them despite the film's specific **cultural and political context.**

Context: Run Lola Run

The Three Runs

Run Lola Run (1998) an independent film directed by Tom Tykwer foregrounds the **contextual liberalised gender values** of 1990s Germany. Tykwer experiments with narrative structure and mediums to **subvert traditional gender norms**. Lola, the protagonist, first appears as her animated self signally strength and determination as she battles all obstacles in her way positioning the audience to engage with her power and agency. The film is non-linear and is constructed using three 'runs' or chapters, in each run Lola starts the same sequence of events with slight variations causing major changes to the outcome of the run.

Run 1: Lola races across Berlin to find 100 000 Deutsche Marks in order to save her boyfriend Manni from the hands of criminal diamond smuggler Ronnie. Manni, a small time criminal himself owes Ronnie the money from a job gone wrong. Manni's desperation leads him to robbing a supermarket with Lola arriving too late to stop him. The unfolding outcome sees them leave the supermarket with the stolen money, only to be surrounded by police, one of whom shoots and kills Lola. Although Lola 'dies' in this run she is shown to be determined, powerful and resourceful, learning to use a gun in an attempt to help Manni flee the supermarket.

Run 2: Events restart with Lola heading to her father's bank in an attempt to convince him to give her the money to save Manni. Her father refuses, lashing out at Lola and telling her that she is not his biological child. Anger, disbelief, and sadness lead Lola to stealing the bank security guard's gun and robbing her father's bank, taking off with the money just in time to stop Manni entering the supermarket to rob it. The butterfly effect showing the change of events means that an ambulance that Lola caused to slow down in her first run, has now arrived on the road in front of the supermarket at the exact time that Manni steps out on to the road as he responds to Lola's shouts for him to wait. This results in him being run over, and 'dying' at the scene of the accident.

Run 3: In her final attempt Lola places a few bets at the casino, winning the money she needs to save Manni. Meanwhile, Manni has found the homeless man who took the money from the diamond smuggling deal that Manni accidentally left on a train and bargains with him to get it back. Both Manni and Lola independently succeed in obtaining the money. Manni is seen giving his bag of money to Ronnie, and Lola walks up to Manni with her bag of money dangling by her side. The **context of gender equity** can be explored as the audience views the last scene and actively participates in determining what will result from Lola having won the money as Manni asks her, "What's in the bag?"

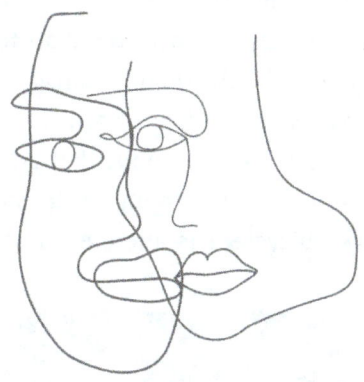

WHAT'S IN THE BAG?

The Bicycle Thieves: Context

'The Bicycle Thieves' (1948) directed by Vittorio De Sica remains relevant to a universal audience as it embodies timeless themes of love, family responsibility, and family connectedness in times of hardship, contrasted with familiar issues such as unemployment and the disconnection this causes.

Vittorio De Sica, a pioneer of Italian neo-realism, reaffirms many of the conventions of the movement in his 1948 film *The Bicycle Thieves*. De Sica's film highlights the abolishment of contrived plots and the move towards narratives focused on contemporary social issues. The **cultural context** surrounding the film contributes to its content significantly as *The Bicycle Thieves* represents the lives of the Ricci family in **post WW2 Italy** and documents their struggle against adversity, homing in on social issues arising from the end of the war such as **unemployment and poverty.**

The bleak, yet realistic depiction of Italian society in 1948 was embraced by Italian cinema goers as under Mussolini their cinema diet had been entertainment value over substance. Film was not used as a vehicle for social comment but rather for pure escapism. Hence, after the **fall of Mussolini**, post WW2 the neo-realist film makers used their films to satisfy the Italian audiences' desire for reality and truth, the need to see their real lives and **issues acknowledged on screen**. The film opens with Antonio Ricci (Lamberto Maggiorami) being selected from many men for the opportunity to work for a company that puts up bill posters; the only requirement being that he must have his own bicycle. The audience quickly learns that Ricci

has

been waiting a while to **secure a job** and is willing to go to great lengths to get one. The employment controller tells him "Remember if you haven't got a bike, there's nothing doing, right?" To which Ricci replies, "Think I'm going to wait another two years? I'll be there with a bike." Ricci shares his good news with his wife Maria (Lianalla Carell) who is at a water pump arguing with the local women about the **shortage of water.** The opening minutes establish the **bleakness of their environment**, the hardships they suffer, and suggest a glimmer of hope that should Ricci manage to obtain his bicycle from the pawn shop, his family might have a brighter future.

Ricci does manage to get his bike back but only after pawning the family's bed linen. Things appear to be looking up as he heads out on his first day on the job to learn how to put up posters without causing too many wrinkles to the paper as he pastes it onto a wall, hoping not to make too many mistakes as it will come out of his pay packet. The task involves him standing on a ladder and pasting glue to a wall with one hand, whilst securing the poster with the other. As the title of the film suggests, whilst occupied with this task his bike is stolen, and as he must have a bike to do his job **the quest of the film** becomes inevitable; he must find the bicycle. Ricci's responsibility to provide for his family is tied to the bicycle, and it

Context

is here that the film starts to explore the bonds of **familial love** and what families will do for one another. Ricci enlists his young son Bruno and some friends to assist him with the search as they take up any leads in pursuit of the bicycle thief.

Films like *The Bicycle Thieves* embody universal themes of love, family, and relationships in times of hardship. Moreover, alienation and loneliness are explored as cornerstones of the social issue of unemployment. Although **contextually set in 1948 Italy** the film remains relevant to a universal audience as it comments sharply on issues familiar to all – **unemployment, family responsibilities, religion** – it may be dated in conventions but not in its ability to convey timeless values.

The **class divide** is highlighted throughout the film. The restaurant scene is particularly poignant as Antonio and his son Bruno sit at a table where Di Sica has positioned a much richer family in the foreground. The **binary opposition between rich and poor** is highlighted through the mise-en-scène, particularly the contrast in treatment Antoni and Bruno receive from the waiter. The cutlery and plates are simply placed on the table for them to organise themselves, whereas the rich family at the next table have a waiter who fawns over them, bringing them wine and food to excess. This social divide is further emphasised by Bruno struggling with the use of a knife and fork, finally giving up and eating his pizza with his hands. De Sica hammers home his point by showing the rich young girl at the next table, who, with exceptional table manners, cleanly and politely eats her food, including an extravagant cake that is clearly out of the financial reach of the Ricci family. As Antonio states, "To eat like that, you'd have to earn at least a million a month."

De Sica **questions the institution of the church**. In post WW2 Italy, religion is strongly connected to the working class. The church scene in *The Bicycle Thieves* exemplifies this by showing a large crowd attending the sermon. The morality attached to choices such as "thou shalt not steal' is supplanted by Antonio's drive to get his bicycle back. **Social issues such as unemployment** and Antonio's desperate need to work supersede his religious beliefs.

As an auteur, De Sica used context to engage his audience with relevant content that shaped the narrative of the text and its preferred audience reading.

CONTEXT
Notes for The True Cost

Historical Context

- Released in 2015
- Environmental awareness, pollution, global warming
- Rana Plaza collapsed April 24th, 2013
- 1134 workers killed and 2500 injured when the 8 story building collapsed
- Working conditions, safety, health impacts
- Genetically modified crops
- The need for a sustainable fashion industry as it is currently second only to the oil industry in its pollution. Exploitation of workers in third world countries for profit (with no consequences)

Social Context

- Vlogging, fashion influencers, YouTube clothing haul videos
- Fashion trends
- Materialism
- Mindless consumerism, over consumption
- Surrounded by advertising
- Clothing consumption/disposable clothing
- Shop ethically, ethical consumerism

Political Context

- Capitalism (huge profits for those at the top)
- Globalisation
- Wages - fair pay for work required
- Minimum wage, worker's rights
- Human rights violations
- Human capital
- Structural poverty

Cultural Context

- Humanitarianism
- Fast fashion
- Gender equity, gender roles
- Materialism - consumer culture
- Employment opportunities
- Consumerism
- American context (shops, adverts, people, references to American authority figure)
- Environmental sustainability
- Issues with the fashion industry
- Ethical and sustainable fashion (clothing should not be a 'single use item')
- Fair trade

The True Cost Context Analysis

The **production context** (time and place a production is made), as well as its **reception context** (when and where an audience member watches the production), will shape interpretation of the text's content. When analysing the context surrounding a production consider the following drop-down list of elements to scaffold deconstruction of a text:

1. State the **production context** (when and where was the text produced). How does this influence the point of view taken on issues?
2. Specify any **contextual elements** that shaped the production. Consider discussing overarching **cultural context** and any supporting **political, social or historical contextual elements** that are relevant to the production.
3. State the **reception context** (only if this differs from the production context). How do audience values, ideologies, beliefs, and expectations of narratives position them to decode meaning?

Content does not arise in a vacuum but rather exists within a framework of existing cultural and historical social norms.

Andrew Morgan's participatory documentary on the fast fashion industry **anchors meaning** via its title *The True Cost* by telling the audience that a hidden cost is embedded in their clothing purchases and that his investigation will show them the true cost involved in purchasing cheap, disposable clothing items. The documentary takes the audience on a journey to discover the **environmental and humanitarian costs** associated with unethical, capitalism-driven, fast fashion industry practices.

The True Cost documentary's **production date** of 2015 means it draws on the **cultural and historical context** of the era to inform its content. Equally, the **year of reception** will influence how an audience **decodes the preferred meaning** that environmental abuse and ignoring humanitarian concerns will have severe consequences. The early 2000s (**reception context**) was an era of environmental degradation with humanitarian issues ranging from poverty to inequality. Therefore, the film's intended audience of 13+ predominantly western viewers will have their **viewing experience shaped by their contextual knowledge** of:

- the harmful effects caused by disregarding the environment,
- their understanding of humanitarian issues such as equal pay for equal work, the Black Lives Matter movement, the #MeToo movement,
- and a desire to align their values of environmental and humanitarian concern with those found in the text.

Historical context is injected into the documentary via **archival footage** showing the collapse of a few garment factories, none more prominent than

147

The True Cost: Context Analysis

the Rana Plaza, an eight storey garment factory workshop which collapsed in Dhaka, Bangladesh on April 24th, 2013, killing over one thousand workers, and injuring two and a half thousand others. Morgan leans into the collapse of this building by showing confronting images of emergency workers trying to save trapped people, bodies being pulled out from under rubble, and wailing onlookers dreading the loss of loved ones. By using historical news footage Morgan can show authentic and **contextually relevant content** whilst emotionally connecting with his primary audience. Morgan elicits sadness, and then anger at the poor conditions the workers are forced to work under, and in some cases, die under.

The True Cost's **cultural and historical production and reception context** of environmental concern is showcased throughout, most notably Morgan's voiceover imparts the startling information that the fashion industry is a two and a half trillion dollar sector and is the second most polluting industry in the world, second only to the oil industry. His voice is anchored by images of dirty waterways showing their banks teeming with discarded human textile and plastic waste. The use of **persuasive facts and figures** directs the audience to consider how their clothing purchases impact the natural ecological system, and more importantly, how their purchasing power can positively influence corporate practices, knowing that **environmentally aware audience members** are invested in sustainability, not disposability.

Morgan uses a **montage** of advertising billboards showing fast fashion giants Zara, H&M, Forever 21, Topshop, Gap, and Joe Fresh coupled with a **voiceover** describing the newest H&M store opening in Manhattan. He explains that many more stores just like it will be opened around the country to entice people into the fast fashion model whereby they buy clothes with frequency

throughout the year with little regard for the longevity of the item. Rather the consumer is asked to enjoy the "new" thus buying into the **capitalist, consumeristic model** with **no consideration for the environment or sustainability**. The scene serves to highlight consumerism, materialism, and the relentless drive of capitalism at all costs. The link to **humanitarianism** is clear; capitalism does not care about humanitarian or environmental impacts, it only cares about profit. Orsola De Castro, a fashion designer highlights the **capitalistic ethos** by stating that the fast fashion model, "... is moving ruthlessly towards a way of producing which only really looks after big business interests," she explains that fast fashion is solely about generating profit with no regard for the environment or the workers at the bottom of the supply chain. The combination of western **fast fashion consumerism**, high pressure advertising and a head-in-the-sand approach towards why fast fashion is so cheap, has created consumers who either don't know, or don't care about the people who make their clothes and the environment that is desperately trying to avoid the **effects of over-consumption**.

The **reception context** for a current day audience has more urgency surrounding **environmental sustainability** as they view environmental damage through a plethora of environmental disasters such as global warming from fossil fuels, loss of biodiversity, pollution of waterways, air pollution,

Context

bush fires, earthquakes, and floods to name but a few, and therefore view textile and fast fashion waste as significant issues. The **core audience values** of environmental awareness and environmental sustainability are used to **showcase corporate capital greed** as Morgan presents the fast fashion industry as having no regard for how it pollutes waterways, produces excessive greenhouse gas emissions, and has created a fashion cycle built on the base of discarding clothes at a ridiculous rate, thus creating vast amounts of non-biodegradable textile waste.

Morgan states that the average American discards around **eight two pounds of textile waste in a year which ends up in landfill**. He shows discarded clothing towering high in rubbish dumps in Bangladesh, coupled with images of natural resources such as forests being abused. Morgan states that the natural resources used to produce clothes are ignored and not measured as part of the cost of creating fast fashion. The **authority figure** of Mike Schragger, Founder of the Sustainable Fashion Academy, adds weight to the film's stance regarding the negative effects of fast fashion by explaining that because natural resources have been so abundant people wrongly assume that they can draw on them forever. The audience is asked to ponder their own textile waste and to consider how they are contributing to the huge problem of textile pollution. Christina Dean, Founder and CEO of Redress discusses the extent to which clothes and textiles are **contributing to landfill**. She states that we now can't deny that the fast fashion industry is having a massive impact on developing countries. Her interview is **juxtaposed with images** of an enormous rubbish tip showing textile rubbish in the foreground and bulldozers moving the rubbish in the background. We segue into Morgan's **voiceover** telling us that the average American discards a significant amount of textile waste every year,

most of which is non-biodegradable caused by the fast fashion industry. The audience's **historical and cultural context of environmental awareness** makes them susceptible to the film's **preferred environmental message;** mother nature's resources are not infinite, and we need to make changes now.

The film was two years in the making, Morgan began filming in 2013, with the film being released in cinemas in 2015. A western audience viewing the film in this time period would do so looking through **a lens of significant feminist movement upheaval**. Debate surrounds the blurred start of the fourth wave of feminism that was carried forward on a wave of social media interaction starting in 2010 and mobilised women to speak out, demonstrate, and stand up for the right to be safe at home and in their workplace. **Digital connectedness** allowed for a surge of female backlash against sexual abuse and workplace discrimination culminating in the #Metoo movement and the Women's March4Justice. **Context influences content** as the primary western audience are aware of the feminist movement's continued fight for equal economic, social and political rights for women. Morgan uses the **audience's contextual knowledge** by incorporating Shima Akhter, a twenty three year old female garment factory worker who highlights the inequity in her working environment by addressing the camera and explaining how she and her co-workers wrote a list requesting a safe working environment and a liveable wage. She

The True Cost: Context Analysis

describes that when she submitted it to her boss an altercation ensued whereby she and some of her fellow workers were beaten with sticks, stabbed with scissors, punched, and kicked. The emotional and physical result of Shima attempting to achieve fair and equal pay is viewed through a western lens, one that positions the audience to not just understand, but to expect a safe working environment, and fair wages for their skills and effort. The **fashion industry is villainised** as it is shown to only want profits, and to **disregard any humanitarian or environmental issues** associated with the production of garments. Shima's working conditions are examined through a western window of humanitarianism highlighting how an **audience's reception context can shape the deconstruction of a text**.

The **cultural and political context of capitalism and globalisation** bring the materialistic and interconnected nature of the fashion industry production supply chain into clear focus. It is made abundantly clear to the audience, "Cinderella's singing mice aren't working behind the scenes to sew garments in your bedroom. Real people are doing it, who have real lives. Far from the eyes of the world, companies are getting away with murder — literally. Factory fires, building collapses, and diseases have all killed factory workers recently. And these aren't isolated incidents. Workers are getting skin cancer as well as digestive and liver problems — all health issues directly related to the chemicals found in those factories. It doesn't seem to be slowing down either. The U.S. was producing 95% of the clothes domestically in the 1960s. Today, it's more like three percent." The **context of capitalism** which is enshrined with a materialistic drive is questioned by Morgan who asks if this system is environmentally sustainable. He uses Tim Kasser PhD, Psychology, Knox College, to position the audience to **decode the preferred meaning** of rejecting fast fashion and instead embracing a model of ethical consumerism by discussing how people have been groomed to focus on materialistic values and to embrace status and possessions to achieve happiness. He discusses how studies have shown that people who privilege materialism and status tend to be more depressed and anxious. He points out how this is at odds with the messages being sold to consumers via advertising. Kasser's voice is used as a **sound bridge over a montage** of billboards showing Victoria's Secret models, Nike, Coca-Cola, and Forever 21, to name but a few, as he explains how the pursuit of happiness being promised by these companies is founded on empty promises; they want their customers to believe that their needs will be met by purchasing the advertised products. And when the person feels dissatisfied, not to worry, a new product is available to ensure the whole cycle can continue over and over again. The materialistic concern with one's own happiness in this model leaves no room to consider the true cost of fast fashion and how it impacts others.

The ubiquitous use of social media in a **twenty-first century context** allows the audience to easily identify with the shopping haul scenes. Morgan uses the superficiality of the YouTube clothes haul scene to draw the audience in to considering the humanitarian and environmental consequences of the western capitalistic fast fashion industry. Specifically, he highlights the important facets that are often ignored by consumers as they coo over their cheap clothing purchases. Mark Miller, professor of Media Culture at NYU provides insight into the shopping haul scenes by discussing advertising as a clear **form of propaganda** as companies tie their products to people's emotional needs, making it clear that there will always be

The True Cost: Context Analysis

products to fill the void. Morgan uses a **montage** of product advertisements to highlight how adverts suggest that people can be competent, successful, beautiful, loving and so on if they purchase the advertised product. The end of the **montage** delivers the audience back to Tim Kasser who pointedly states that advertising teaches us that the way to solve life's problems is through consumption. YouTube social media vloggers are used to highlight the extreme of clothing purchases done with little thought for sustainability. One vlogger says she went insane and bought so many things, and in the next breath states that she might not even wear it now that she owns it. The notion of **instant gratification** is underscored by Morgan who notes that only 10% of clothing items donated to charity will be recycled, the majority will end up in land fill. Even if the clothing haul shoppers use their disposable income to buy clothing they never wear and then think they will altruistically donate it to charity, the harm is already done. **Over-consumption** has consequences. Morgan uses the clothing haul scene to highlight how the **context of a materialistic consumer culture** privileges western capitalistic cultures whilst ignoring the problematic and unethical nature of the fast-fashion industry.

An **American production context** is used to ground the film creating a decidedly western point of view. References are made to American products; American authority figures are used throughout, and references are continually made to clothes being made for American consumers. *The True Cost's* primary American 13+ western audience is positioned to engage with the **preferred meaning** of the text which is that the fashion industry is only concerned with profit, not with the environmental impact of producing its clothes, nor with the humanitarian impact of the people who produce the clothes. **Context shapes understanding of content,** and therefore as well as connecting to its primary audience, the film appeals to a secondary international audience who cannot deny the devastating effect the fast fashion supply chain is

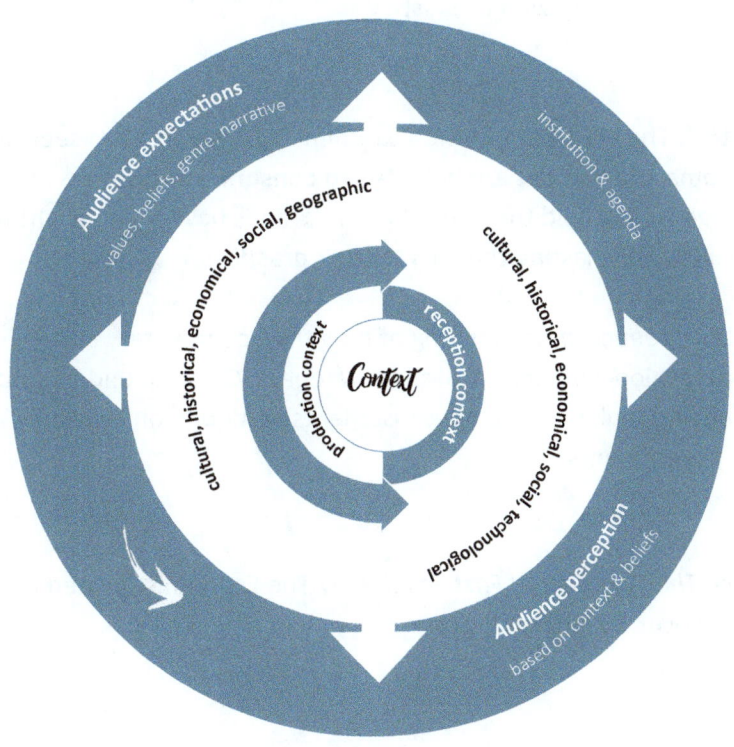

CONTEXT
shapes content

The True Cost's agenda was to raise awareness about fast fashion's environmental impact on the planet. The director and writer, Andrew Morgan had no connection to the fashion industry prior to filming the documentary. His production was supported by people who are prominent in the fashion industry, particularly professionals in the fashion world focused on sustainability and fair trade. Consideration needs to be given to how Morgan incorporated their expertise as these people are also executive producers for the film. Is there a conflict of interest in having Livia Firth, the creative director for Eco-Age, and Lucy Siegle, a journalist who writes on environmental and ethical issues as major **authority figures** in the film? **Is objectivity called into question** as their dual roles potentially shaped the direction of the narrative due to their strong advocacy positions creating bias on fast fashion? Or is **selective use of content** made clear from the outset when Morgan states that his **agenda** was to expose the environmental and humanitarian costs created by the fast fashion industry. He wanted the audience to critically analyse their clothing consumption habits; he wanted them to be aware of the environmental footprint they created when engaging with the fast fashion machine.

Funding can influence content and place commercial pressure on a director as economic success is paramount for big film studios. *The True Cost* is made by the production company Untold Creative on a small half a million dollar budget. Money was raised via Kickstarter which allowed Morgan freedom from corporate commercial pressure.

Feedback mechanisms created by the film and driven by audiences include a response to the film's **social media presence** and a **call to action** by encouraging viewers to change their consumption habits and purchase sustainable clothes. The question is, did it work? Nearly a decade since the film's release what has changed? Are consumers more mindful of their choices and whether they involve fair trade and environmental consideration?

Context influences content. The aftermath of the 2015 film *The True Cost* has seen small changes in the fast fashion landscape. Some key changes are **heightened consumer awareness** and a **rise in sustainable practices.** However, change is slow, and the major fashion brands have a significant way to go to transform the industry and make substantive lasting changes to their practices.

Scan the QR codes to gain a deeper understanding of how the documentary added pressure to the already growing cracks in the fast fashion industry by raising awareness. Growing understanding of the impact of fast fashion is now being seen in popular culture advertisements, critiqued on Ted Talks, analysed in the news media, and taken up by governments.

Watch *The True Cost of Fast Fashion* by The Economist posted in 2018 that has been viewed over 1.2 million times

Context

Watch the advertisement Vinted: *Too Many* by Ads of Brands. The advert highlights the ridiculous nature of over-consumption.

Read the Reuters article *French lawmakers approve bill to apply penalties on fast fashion*, March 15, 2024.

France has approved a bill banning fast fashion. How will it impact companies like Temu, Shein, Zara and H&M? The bill prohibits them from advertising, and will also allocate a surcharge of five Euros to each item of clothing, the surcharge is set to rise by ten Euros by 2030, making the clothing items financially unattractive to consumers. Proceeds from the surcharge will go towards Fair Trade sustainable retailers, thereby allowing them a more equal footing to compete in the market.

Due to current financial hardships faced by many, low income earners are stating that these added costs are too much to bear, and they buy fast fashion as it is affordable.

In addition, manufacturers will need to make visible their environmental impact.

Do you think these changes should be introduced worldwide?

Read the ABC News article *Plibersek warns clothing industry must turn back on 'fast fashion' as she considers intervention.* Posted 21 February 2024.

Watch the Ted Talk by Josephine Philips *The Simple Solution to Fast Fashion,* September 22, 2023

Context shapes content

When discussing context consider some of the following:

PRODUCTION CONTEXT — When and where a media text is CREATED shapes its content.

1. CULTURAL & HISTORICAL CONTEXT

- How the time and place of production affects content, aesthetics, and themes.
- Values and ideologies: are they supported or challenged?
- What key events or movements influenced the text's content?
- Are representations supported or challenged?
- What social trends and issues shape the text? Consider language, clothing, beliefs, technology use and so on.

2. ECONOMIC & INSTITUTIONAL CONTEXT

- How does the text's budget impact scale and quality?
- Commercial interests: do advertisers or sponsors shape content?
- Agenda: is an institution or person's agenda served or promoted?
- Policies and regulations: how have regulatory bodies, policies, and censorship impacted the production?

3. TECHNOLOGICAL CONTEXT

What role has technology played in shaping the text's content?
What impact has advancements in technology had in shaping the narrative and engaging the audience?

4. POLITICAL CONTEXT

- How has the political climate surrounding the government of the day shaped the content?
- Consider if propaganda or bias is prevalent, does this suggest agenda setting?
- Consider if misinformation or disinformation has been used. If so, whose agenda is being served?

5. RECEPTION CONTEXT — When and where a media text is CONSUMED shapes its content.

RECEPTION CONTEXT

- Consider all the elements (1-4) from above when analysing the reception context and how the audience decodes meaning.
- Consider the audience's demographic metrics and how their expectations shape media content.
- Audience feedback: consider any feedback mechanisms used to shape future productions.

Context

Review & sample questions

Sample questions containing context:

1. Discuss how production context shapes content.
2. Analyse how values and ideologies reflect their production and reception context.
3. Discuss how representations are shaped by context.
4. Analyse how context influences the theme conveyed in a media text.
5. Discuss how cultural context shapes the intended audience's reception of the text's preferred meaning.
6. Discuss how context influences character construction.

 **CONTEXT - main essential content to discuss:**

01
- **Context** refers to the background behind a fact, event or period, or the circumstances surrounding an event. Context deals with the society of the text including the time and place, values and attitudes, and how the culture impacts behaviour and opportunities.

02
- Audience, context, and content are interlinked to create the text's **preferred meaning.**

03
- **Cultural context** is an umbrella term that includes historical, social, political, and economic contexts that surround the interpretation of an event, issue, or group. Contextual elements frequently can be categorised under many headings, an event could be historical context but could also speak to the cultural context of the era.

04
- A text cannot be separated from its context. Context will always affect content. Discuss the **production context** (when, where, and why the text was made), as well as the **reception context** (who is consuming the text, where they are consuming it, and why).

05
- Consider the political, social, cultural, and historical context surrounding the text and how this shapes meaning for characters, themes and representations.

Chapter Eight
Stereotypes & Representations

- Representations: how are they constructed?
- Stuart Hall: representation theory
- Representation analysis: *Run Lola Run*
- David Gauntlett: representations, digital media and audiences
- Media as a tool to challenge stereotypes
- Representation: timeline for women's rights
- Problems with stereotyping
- Sample questions
- Review

Stereotypes & Representations

Representations

A representation is a likeness or re-presentation of reality; it is not the real world but rather a constructed, mediated, portrayal of real world issues, people, groups, concepts, objects and places.

When used repeatedly representations form stereotypes. Stereotypes can be problematic as they use simplified traits as a short cut in meaning. When used repeatedly stereotypes can become naturalised or appear to be the natural way of viewing a group, issue, concept, or place.

How are representations constructed?

CODES & CONVENTIONS

The choice of codes and conventions shapes the construction of the representation. Consider how symbolic, written, audio, and technical codes create meaning.

SELECTION & OMISSION

What is deliberately included and what is excluded when representing a group, issue, or place? The codes that are foregrounded, as well as those that are excluded, privilege certain views.

VALUES & IDEOLOGIES

Values and ideologies are circulated via representations. The choice of codes used to represent the group, issue, or event have been deliberately chosen and therefore a value judgement has been made. Have positive or negative codes been chosen?

CONTEXT

Representations are not made in a vacuum; they are influenced by cultural and social norms. They are not static, rather they change to reflect their cultural and historical context.

SIMPLIFICATION

Simplification occurs when a narrow choice of codes is chosen to represent an entire group. Simplification leads to inaccuracy associated with labelling an entire group with a few selected codes.

 REPRESENTATIONS HAVE THE POWER TO CONTROL THE CONSTRUCTION AND CIRCULATION OF MEANING.

Stuart Hall: Representation theory

Representation Theory

Stuart Hall

Professor Stuart Hall's study of **representation** investigated how media texts can shape perceptions of people, individuals, places, issues, and events by analysing how they are **constructed via a choice of codes and conventions** to convey meaning. The encoded representations are not neutral, the choice of codes is **value laden**, and reflects the agenda of those with power.

Choice of codes

➤ Representations are constructed from a **choice of codes and conventions.** Stuart Hall describes the idea of people in society needing a **'shared cultural map'** or a common conceptual roadmap to assist them in deconstructing meaning. He states for a society to function effectively it needs to have a shared frame of reference or roadmap to **encode and decode meaning**. Hall discusses this process of constructing meaning as occurring through 'language' choice. He specifies that **'language' is any sign or symbol system** used to communicate meaning. 'Language' choice includes the words we use, how we speak (tone, volume, pitch), the writing we use to anchor meaning to images, visual codes chosen such as clothing, colour, and body language, as well as aural codes used to communicate meaning. Hall states that **'language' is a privileged vehicle** through which meaning is **constructed and disseminated.**

Sign systems

➤ 'Language' choice or sign systems are frequently **culturally specific** and **embedded with values and ideologies**. For instance, in Middle Eastern cultures clothing such as the hijab represent religious devotion and indicate modesty, whereas in a western culture the same clothing choice can be seen as a symbol of oppression.

Agenda

➤ Representations and power are linked: those in powerful positions in media institutions can influence how events, issues, places and people are represented. It is important to look at the media you consume and critically consider who has the power to progress certain representations and why they would want to? What is their **agenda**?

Think of a famous person, someone like Donald Trump. What is your immediate mental representation of him? Where did you get this information to form these ideas and images about him? Most likely it was from a media source. The power of the media to fix meaning to representations is significant.

Dominant, emerging, oppositional

Representation & Reception Theory

Encoding and decoding
→ The media attempt to 'fix' meaning to representations by using the same ones **repeatedly** until they form **stereotypical representations** of people, places and ideas. However, meaning is contestable as theorised by **Stuart Hall's Reception theory** whereby he posits that media producers encode media texts using 'language' choices or codes and conventions in order to create a **preferred meaning** and propagate their **values and ideologies**, however, audience members can decode meaning differently depending on their **cultural context** and **demographic metrics** resulting in a move away from the preferred or dominant reading to a **negotiated or oppositional reading** of the text.

Oversimplification
→ **Representations,** when used repeatedly **form stereotypes**. Stereotypes are used by media producers as **short cuts in meaning** as they are **simplified**, often **inaccurate** depictions of people, places, objects and ideas. By choosing a few characteristics to represent the whole a **generalisation** is made that reduces something complex to something simple. By taking a few main characteristics to represent a whole group **oversimplification** has occurred. This oversimplification leads to inaccurate understanding regarding groups as it uses a **narrow range** of ideas and characteristics to represent the whole group. **Oversimplification** and **naturalisation** are significant issues associated with stereotyping, both can lead to prejudice and bias forming due to the one dimensional representation presented by the media. When used repeatedly, the stereotype can become **naturalised**.

Consider the agenda of media texts, whose agenda is benefitted by having representations a particular way? Which groups are privileged? Why? Where does the power lie?

Representation: Stuart Hall

> "Representation is the process by which members of a culture use language (broadly defined as any system which deploys signs, any signifying system) to produce meaning."
>
> (Stuart Hall, 1979)

	EXAMPLE 1:	EXAMPLE 2:
CULTURE 	People exist within a **mainstream national culture**.	How does mainstream **western culture** represent the colour **red**?	How does mainstream **eastern culture** represent the colour **red**?
LANGUAGE 	**Meaning** is produced when a **code** (word, image, gesture or sound) is assigned to **represent** a concept or object.	**Red** can represent passion, anger or danger depending on context.	**Red** is worn as a clothing choice on major occasions such as a wedding or New Year to connote good luck.
REPRESENTATION 	**Circulation** of meaning can occur as **representation** starts to take shape through 'language' choice.	The visual choice of **red** on an emergency vehicle represents danger or a **red** rose represents love.	**Red** is associated with happiness, good luck and prosperity.

Are representations linked to the politics of language? How a culture describes, and visually represents a concept, event, issue, group or idea shapes how meaning is framed, constructed, and conveyed. **Language matters.** A culture's *language* includes its gestures, dress, written word, spoken word, visual signs, and aural signs. Culture, language choice, and representations are linked. They exist within a historical context and are therefore not static. Representations will change, reflecting a change in 'language' choice and culture.

Representation

LANGUAGE CHOICE

- The words, images, gestures, and sounds chosen to describe a group, event or issue will influence whether a positive or negative representation is constructed.
- 'Language' controls the construction of meaning.
- Discourse shapes how people perceive a representation, and by doing so embeds values.

MEDIA CONSUMED

- Television, films, magazines, social media, newspaper, advertising, and any media we consume, and how often we consume it, can impact how we perceive representations of groups, issues or events. Whether you engage with media that is considered right wing, left wing, or centre, your consumption of constructed representations will alter your version of reality.

REPRESENTATION SHAPED VIA:

LIFE EXPERIENCES

- What you experience personally, as opposed to the constructed, filtered version of reality consumed on any media platform, will impact your understanding of representations. Did you personally experience an event represented in the media? How did your experience differ from the mediated version? Do you personally know groups who are represented and stereotyped by the media? How does your real life experience compare to the represented version of reality?

SOCIETAL INSTITUTIONS

- Societal constraints arise from institutions such as the government, educational institutions, media institutions and so on. The purpose and agenda behind each institution needs to be carefully considered as each has a role in shaping representations.

REPRESENTATION
Run Lola Run

> **Main essential content to discuss when analysing representations and stereotypes:**
>
> 1. **Codes and conventions** – discuss how the choice of codes shapes the construction of the representation.
> 2. **Values and ideologies** – representations are value laden. Have positive or negative codes been chosen to represent the group?
> 3. **Simplification** – when a representation is continually used it produces a stereotype due to the simplified visual and aural traits being used as a short cut in meaning.
> 4. **Selection and omission** – what is excluded what is foregrounded? Representations privilege certain views, ages, ethnicities, genders and so on.
> 5. **Context** – representations are not made in a vacuum; they are created within a set of cultural and social norms.

Codes & Conventions

> 1. **Codes and conventions:** how the choice of codes shapes the construction of the representation.

Professor Stuart Hall, a British cultural studies theorist, examined how sign systems, such as language and image choice shape representations. *Run Lola Run*, a 1998 film by Tom Tykwer, utilises a system of representation to construct meaning regarding gender roles. Tykwer's use of **aural and visual codes** positions the audience to deconstruct the **preferred meaning** of valuing women who show agency, willing them to obtain equal access to power and success.

Run Lola Run recounts the story of Lola, a young German woman who must come up with 100,000 Marks in twenty minutes in order to save her boyfriend Manni from the vengeful criminal Ronnie, whose money Manni accidentally left on the subway train. The story is segmented into three twenty minute re-tellings of the same narrative arc, with the ultimate outcome of each altered by the actions of the protagonist Lola.

A representation of contemporary femininity, Lola is constructed to defy traditional gender stereotypes. With her bright dyed red hair and androgynous clothing and tattoos, Lola is represented as an 'anti-heroine' who defies the historically traditional visual representation of femininity. Lola's dress indicates a strong and determined personality; she has fiery red hair, green cargo pants and Doc Marten boots. In contrast, her mother's attire consists of long flowing hair and a soft pink dressing gown; a colour associated with femininity, passivity and sweetness. Lola's clothes are functional, suggesting purpose and direction, not flowing and aesthetic like her mothers, thus the **choice of symbolic codes** shapes the construction of traditional femininity, contrasted with modern progressive femininity.

Additionally, symbols of 'flightiness' such as astrology are incorporated by Tykwer to create a binary opposition between mother and daughter, "I should

Run Lola Run Representation Analysis

have known that Sagittarius was your ascendant," Lola's mother says as she talks on the phone to a presumably male friend whilst reclining on a lounge chair, consequently reinforcing a traditional female passive, mercurial role. **Binary oppositions** further the extreme in representations between Lola and her mother as her mother is constructed using the **visual codes** representative of a stay-at-home wife and mother who enjoys leisure over work and who is more worried about her social life than her daughter's predicament. To ensure the audience **decodes the preferred reading** Tykwer confines Lola's mother to the domestic realm, she is never seen outside the house and is a flawed character due to her suggested alcoholism and infidelity. **Visual and aural signifiers** that direct the audience to decode this meaning include Lola's mother drinking what appears to be scotch or something similar, whilst lounging on the couch in her flowing dressing gown and leisurely talking on the phone. We only hear her side of the conversation, "Sure, the more I think about it. I don't know. Yes, but you're married too," however her reference to marriage, coupled with the **visual signifiers,** indicate infidelity.

Representations are constructed via a **choice of codes.** When visual traits are continually used a **stereotype** is produced that relies on an understanding of the simplified traits as a **short cut in meaning.** Lola's mother is not needed to further the narrative, her stereotype of a self-centred, superficial, passive female is needed as a contrast to Lola's active, fierce determination. The **choice of codes** to construct Lola's mother is a short cut in meaning using historical connotations attached to housewives with rich husbands, and the superficial desire for beauty as shown through the choice of soft pink for Lola's mother versus red for Lola.

Lola subverts the traditional **representation** of a weak, damsel-in-distress, historically subservient female. Instead, she embodies the characteristics of strength, determination, initiative, and vitality. The incorporation of the **aural motif** of Lola's scream creates a sense of strength and control, lifting her out of the **damsel-in-distress paradigm**. Her trademark piercing scream is a recurring **aesthetic device** which allows Lola to gain control of her environment. Rather than being self-pitying, it projects her forward and gives her determination to complete her goal. For instance, in the casino scene Lola's scream acts as a force which sees the ball on the roulette wheel jump and land on the number twenty, consequently allowing her to win the money needed to save Manni.

The audience is introduced to Lola in the middle of action. We see her in her animated form running through a tunnel breaking any obstacle in her way. Her **actions** give Lola power in the narrative, they shape her as a forceful character. Immediately the audience is positioned to reconsider historically soft **feminine stereotypes** and embrace the historically male traits associated with Lola. Her aggression, drive, and **active representation** are all attributes often associated with a male. Tykwer has **appropriated the characteristics** of a male hero and applied them to Lola as the heroine. He subtly

Representation: Run Lola Run

reinforces this by using the **technical code of camera movement** to constantly track Lola. Even when she is stationary, the camera will often spiral around her. Contrast this with Manni, who although not feminised, is still represented as weaker than Lola at the beginning of the narrative by his inaction. The **camera tracks Lola,** whereas with Manni it is often still.

Lola is **represented** as a person who takes matters into own hands, she shows agency rather than passively accepting her fate and waiting for someone else to rescue her. For instance, during the bank robbery scene when Lola's father refuses to loan her money to help Manni, Lola initially leaves her father's office, however, when she passes Schuster, the bank security guard she decides to take matters into her own hands. She takes Schuster's gun and threatens to shoot her father. When Schuster says, "kid you don't know how to use that," referring to the gun, she coldly looks at him, flicks off the safety and takes control. Her **actions represent** her as being assertive, in control and determined to succeed.

As the film has a temporal frequency of three, Lola has three opportunities to achieve her goal of saving Manni. In the first two attempts, although Lola is **represented as active and goal orientated**, she still turns to her father for help. However, in the third run, Lola bypasses her father, instead going to the Casino in an attempt to win the money. It is here that Lola succeeds in her goal independently of male assistance. The **representation of women** shows that when Lola is self-reliant, she achieves her goal, when she is subservient, she fails. *Run Lola Run* challenges the status quo of the **patriarchal ideology** by appropriating and subverting traditional narratives of knights saving the princess (damsel-in-distress) to reflect the changes in the social landscape of **female representation** today.

Representations, through their **choice of codes,** shape how we think about concepts such as gender construction. Tykwer has used *Run Lola Run* to highlight the societal shift in viewing females as passive, as shown by Lola's mother, to **privileging females who show agency,** as viewed by the techniques used to facilitate the **representation of Lola as a strong,** driven female who is able to overcome obstacles, learn from previous mistakes, and be self-reliant.

REPRESENTATION
Run Lola Run

Simplification

Selection & Omission

2. **Simplification**: when a representation is continually used it produces a stereotype due to the simplified visual and aural traits being used as a short cut in meaning.

3. **Selection and omission**: what is excluded what is foregrounded? Representations privilege certain views, ages, ethnicities, genders and so on.

The **oversimplification** of the stereotype of women as weak and passive is used as a tongue-in-cheek weapon against itself in *Run Lola Run*. For instance, in the bank robbery scene criminal activity goes unpunished as a result of **perpetuated gender stereotypes**. After Lola robs her father's bank, she exits, only to discover the building is surrounded by police pointing guns at her. The police are all male, their body language is firm and commanding, carrying connotations of the 'macho' male culture that relies on the relative weakness of others, particularly young women. As such, it makes sense for them to tell Lola to 'get out of the way kid' as they think her incapable of robbing a bank, therefore casting her as a victim of crime, not the perpetrator. As the audience is introduced to Lola's power and drive at the outset of the narrative, this apparent **oversimplification** of women is shown to cause social problems, specifically justice has been disrupted as Lola is a criminal but has evaded the natural outcome of her actions due to the **oversimplification** of the female stereotype. This **oversimplified** approach highlights the resulting consequences of **stereotyping**.

Run Lola Run purposefully appropriates the typical **damsel in distress paradigm**, subverting gender roles and challenging ingrained societal expectations by making a clear statement against the **naturalisation** of women as perpetual victims. The film explores the social problems associated with the limited **representation of women** in the media, and advocates for females to have their own agency and power.

Classical Hollywood narratives have conventionally **selected** the female-as-victim plot point. Invariably she is a victim, or damsel, who needs to be rescued by a male protagonist. The female character only serves as a **means of progressing the male protagonist's actions and has no agency herself**. This **naturalisation** of the female-as-victim **stereotype** has been perpetuated since early fairy tale narratives. The archetype Prince Charming consistently saves the Princess, who has no personal control over her fate, instead relying on her male hero to rescue her. These historically **traditional representations privilege** the power and dominance of the male character, attributing him with the required attributes to be a saviour. By **omission**, the female is inferior, not being allocated the same abilities, power and agency to succeed.

Tykwer challenges the **naturalisation of gender stereotypes** by reversing the roles traditionally associated with males and females.

REPRESENTATION

Run Lola Run

Context

4. **Context:** representations are not made in a vacuum; they are created within a set of cultural and social norms.

The construction of Lola is influenced by **contextual factors** such as Lara Croft's character in the Tomb Raider video games which were first released in 1996. Lara Croft was a pop culture icon of gaming, acting as a strong female protagonist who frequently battled male villains and saved the world. Lola's dress style of khaki pants, combat boots, a singlet and fiery red hair mimic Lara Croft's clothing. When we first met Lola, she is in animated form and her decisive actions emulate those of her video game doppelgänger. Like a video game character, Lola is constructed to be goal orientated, having an objective to achieve in twenty minutes. She is tasked with getting 100,0000 marks in twenty minutes or risk having her boyfriend, Manni, die. Similar to a video game whereby the player has three chances to achieve their objective, Lola too has three attempts to gain the money. The video game context has influenced the construction of the narrative and its characters. The choice of using video game **conventions** and their attached **codes of construction** allows Tykwer to critique traditional pervasive passive representations of females by imbuing Lola with power and agency. Her strength acts as a powerful statement to question the **naturalisation** of female **stereotypical** helplessness.

Stuart Hall's concept of representation deals with people having **'shared maps of meaning'** which arise from their cultural and social experiences. Therefore, for the audience to understand the **contextual representation** of the narrative as a video game construct Tykwer encoded meaning by utilising the temporal frequency of three, imbuing Lola with superpowers and employing the medium of animation to clearly give the audience access to **decode the preferred meaning** of seeing Lola as a representation of a superhero style character within a video game world who has three chances to achieve her goal.

Feminism is society's response to assumptions about gender roles and how they have marginalised women. Until the emergence of feminism women were largely overlooked, mostly treated as **passive agents in a male world.** The history of feminism needs to be understood for the audience to think critically about the representation of Lola versus her mother, the use of binary oppositions shows how patriarchal structures played a complex role in creating subservient women and the subversion required by females to challenge this constructed version of femininity.

Both the construction of a representation by a media producer, and the interpretations made by audiences are shaped by historical, cultural, technological, and social context. **Nothing is made in a vacuum. Context will always affect content.** The interconnected relationship between audiences, media producers and texts is complex and dynamic, resulting in a constantly changing environment where representations evolve in an ever-changing landscape.

Representation

Values & Ideologies

5. **Values and ideologies:** representations are value laden. Have positive or negative codes been chosen to represent the group?

As Stuart Hall states, how something is described and constructed attributes positive or negative connotations, therefore evoking a **value judgement**. All media texts are constructions. It is because **representations are constructed** that they reflect the **cultural values** of the period of production. For instance, Tykwer subverts traditional representations of masculinity and embeds Manni with vulnerability, desperation, and a clear dependence on Lola in the first two runs as he is shown to rely on Lola to save him, thus reversing the traditional Hollywood storyline of the maiden in distress. Manni calls Lola from a phone box, and his utter vulnerability is represented in **high angles and close ups** that communicate his volatile and helpless state as he begs Lola for help. The value of men being self-sufficient, unemotional, and not needing female help is challenged by Manni's actions.

Tykwer represents the **trend of liberalisation of gender values** in Lola's sexual relationship with Manni. Not only does the film portray it as socially acceptable for the two to be in a relationship outside of wedlock, but Lola is presented as the dominant partner which challenges the traditional **patriarchal** power dynamic.

Stereotypes are value laden. Lola's mother is portrayed as passive as she is seen watching daytime television, drinking alcohol, and wearing a soft pink dressing gown whilst sitting in an armchair. The **choice of codes** suggests women have limited **value** beyond the home. In addition, as Lola asks a **patriarchal** figure, her father, for the money to help Manni it implies that women have limited financial resources and cannot be relied on for help. In contrast Lola's father is **valued** for his earning power. He complains to Lola that she and her mother 'sponge off' him showing how the **naturalisation** of women as subservient to men gives men control, especially over money. This is Lola's downfall, as her father uses his power over her and refuses her the money in her first run, causing her to 'fail' in her quest. In the third run, Lola wins the money herself, showing self-reliance and a departure from the naturalisation of women as weak and incapable, therefore showing the benefits of **subverting the stereotype**.

Values and ideologies are circulated via representations. By showing Manni needing and accepting Lola's help in the first two runs allows for the self-reliant **patriarchal male representation** to be critiqued as the **value** of showing emotion and being vulnerable progresses societal expectations of gender roles by normalising a greater range of emotions for men. By promoting powerful female traits such as Lola's tenacity, drive, and emotional strength encourages a healthier balance of gender roles and expectations.

The **values and ideologies privileged** in a text will showcase who has power in a society and how power dynamics shift and change.

David Gauntlett: Representation

David Gauntlett, a British media and sociology academic explores the relationship between digital media, audiences, and content creators. He examines how individuals shape their own representations and broader social discourse through the creation and dissemination of online content.

Gauntlett argues that identities are shaped through social interaction, construction, and negotiation. An audience draws a sense of their own identity from the media they consume, be it gender identity, sexual identity, or cultural identity. What does an audience learn about themselves from their media consumption and production? Media consumption is hard to avoid, we drive past billboards, scroll past advertisements in our digital feed, and engage with social media posts; however social media production on platforms such as Twitter (now X), Instagram, YouTube, and Facebook is a choice involving specific codes used to represent our constructed selves. How do people negotiate and construct their identities in a media saturated world?

Consider what representational aspects have been foregrounded:
- sexual identity
- race
- gender
- age
- ethnicity
- appearance
- socio-economics

What codes of construction have been employed to encode the representation? Consider:
- what costuming has been chosen?
- what body language has been used?
- how does dialogue shape the representation?
- what setting has the representation used?
- what technical codes have been chosen?
- whose point of view do we see the representation from?
- who has more close ups, or more screen time?
- is a written code incorporated to anchor meaning?

 Media techniques encode meaning into the representation by privileging specific aspects. For instance, Cristiano Ronaldo, regarded as the top performing football player in the world, is represented on social media via his Instagram account. At the time of writing his follower count is at 640 million. Due to his massive audience reach advertisers pay over a million US dollars to post on his Instagram feed. Therefore, his constructed representation will be closely linked to their brand. His posts consist of privileging his football wins, his success, his sporting prowess, and occasionally a humanising post shows him as a loving family man. The codes of construction preface action shots when on the football field, using a mixture of long shots to show action, and mid shots to extract the emotion of joy linked to his success. In contrast, the images posted of Ronaldo's family contain an amateurish aesthetic; a posed image taken at a holiday location,

Digital media and audiences

REPRESENTATIONS REINFORCE DOMINANT IDEOLOGIES
Do media representations circulate and reinforce existing stereotypes or do they challenge and subvert them? Representations constructed by media influencers are encoded using codes of construction to create an ideal version of the self, one that represents the media influencer in a chosen way, reinforcing the values of their brand.

or an equally posed family shot to mark an event such as a birthday. The juxtaposition between the professional football images and the family snaps create a representation of a skilled sportsman and an authentic family man. Ronaldo's Instagram account creates a representation, a curated identity that he projects to the world and uses to influence others. As David Gauntlett explains in his book *Making is Connecting,* the digital age has allowed for people to instantaneously construct their own representations.

 Gauntlett explores the impact of media consumption on how we think about gender identity. Specifically, he looks at how the media we consume influences our identity in relation to gender construction. A person is born a particular sex but learns their gender. Clearly a person's family, friends, and daily interactions with society will impact their understanding of how gender is constructed and represented. Within each culture a person learns how to be a girl or a boy. Moreover, the impact of the media each person consumes cannot be discounted in this learning process.

Why is this important? When we consider the enveloping nature of media it is crucial to analyse how the media landscape represents gender, culture, sexuality, marital status, ethnicity, appropriate behaviour and so on, and try and understand how an active audience is shaped by their media consumption. Even if you think the media has no influence, think again. According to Pew Research individuals average four hours a day on their devices, of this about 50% is allocated to the top five social media platforms: YouTube, Instagram, TikTok, Snapchat, and Facebook. Nielson research increases this time to eleven hours a day for the average person when listening to music, watching TV, being on a computer, or being engaged with a game console is factored into the equation. The over-saturation of media content in the form of digital devices, as well as people engaging with traditional media such as billboards, magazines, and newspapers has a role in shaping society's representations of gender, culture, sexuality, age and ethnicity.

Take, as an example, how representations of gender appear in films. Dr Martha M. Lauzen's article, *It's a Man's (Celluloid) World: Portrayals of Female Characters in the Top Grossing Films of 2018* presents quantitative analysis of the top 100 domestic grossing films and compares this to historical data dating back to 2002. Her study found that:

- Women made up 36%, down from 37% in 2017, while men accounted for the remaining 64%.
- Female characters tended to be younger than their male counterparts with 29% being in their

David Gauntlett: Representation

20s and 28% being in their 30s. In contrast, 35% of male characters were aged in their 30s and 25% in their 40s.
- In 2018 white actors dominated speaking roles holding two-thirds of available roles, followed by black actors, with other ethnicities being underrepresented (Lauzen, 2019).

As Dr Martha M. Lauzen's study found, certain aspects are privileged within representations. Younger, white women are given more screen time than their non-white older counterparts. In contrast males represented 64% of major film characters. By linking Dr Lauzen's findings to David Gauntlett's idea that our identities are a process of construction and negotiation, influenced in part by the amount of media we consume, we can see that older non-white females were very under-represented in mainstream movies in 2018. As a male it is easier to find media that models a successful pathway. However, representations of success for females and minorities are harder to come by.

David Gauntlett, in his book, *Media, Gender and Identity*, states that traditional media representations tended to stereotype gender roles within a narrow viewpoint constricted by historical boundaries of gender expectations. This can by evidenced by clear binary gender representations. Specifically, representations of men were constructed from visual signifiers showing them to be strong, powerful, and dominant. Contrast this to female representations which constructed women to be weak, submissive, and emotional.

Within a culture people acquire a gender identity. Through social interaction and media consumption we learn what it is to be a man or a woman. As Gauntlett states, historical representations about ideal male and female identities tended to use stereotypical iconography of masculinity and femininity. Current representations are much broader, and significantly more complex, incorporating more diverse, fluid representations of sexuality and gender. This larger range of representations allows for a diverse audience connection with a wide range of gender, sexual orientation, and culture choices, rather than a narrow, white-centric, heterosexual world view. For instance, in *Orange is the New Black,* the Netflix

series created by Jenji Kohan, representations of lesbians abound. These include the stereotypical butch lesbian but branch out to encompass a wider range of lesbian representation such as women of colour, a transwoman, and bisexuality. The show allows for a discussion regarding not just what is represented in terms of sexuality and race, but how it is represented. By including high profile actors such as Ruby Rose, a model, TV presenter, actress and advocate for LGBTQ rights who identifies as being gender fluid, increases the visibility of lesbian representation on mainstream media.

Representations influence media messages. What is

> How does a lack of representation in the media in respect to power and privilege shape a person's identity?

REPRESENTATION

David Gauntlett

encoded as being feminine, masculine, heterosexual, homosexual, lesbian and so on can influence the creation of identity. Therefore, by being inclusive of sexuality choices, and showing a diversity in racial representations allows for people to create diverse identities rather than being cornered into a white, gender binary world view.

The economic agenda of mainstream media means that the desire to move beyond normative boundaries is driven by slow cultural change. Contemporary portrayals of gender, race, age, and culture are intertwined with mainstream and social media representations in productions. If an audience member feels marginalised by mainstream media, they can consume and produce content on social media platforms that allow them to actively construct their identity by consuming and producing their own media products.

> David Gauntlett in *Making is Connecting* discusses how digital creation and interaction empowers individuals through self-expression, identity creation, and global connection.

Creating identity in an on-line world that is borderless, transformative, and international can allow for diversity. However, the curated spaces made by the internet means that behaviour can be steered, making culture not as diverse or interesting due to filter bubbles and algorithms that constrict the user's worldview.

Gauntlett discusses how digital media platforms offer creative venues through new technologies. He looks at how people can construct their representations using different platforms to showcase facets of their identity through channels such as blogging, Facebook, Instagram, YouTube and so on. Consider what a person posts and how it constructs their ideal representation of self to the world. Does having the access and ability to create your own identity, to represent your ideal self to the world broaden the landscape of available representations, or does the very nature of the narrow curated internet world mean that representations are just as limited in the digital world as they were in the analogue world?

In *Media, Gender and Identity* Gauntlett explains that self-identity in the online space has evolved from curating media to creating media. The effect of social media culture on the construction and representation of gender cannot be under-estimated. Deconstructing how individuals make considered decisions when negotiating their on-line representation will reveal dominant ideologies about race, sexuality and culture.

Gauntlett claims that individuals actively select and construct their personal narratives to shape their concept of self. The complex relationship between media and audiences means that active decoding, selection, and omission are tools used to craft representations of self-concept. How does the consumption and construction of social media shape the representation and identity of individuals?

Greta Thunberg, the Swedish climate activist is a good example of how a person can embrace the digital tools available to disseminate a message that embraces her environmental ideology and constructs her political activist identity. Her representation encodes environmental activism with values of

REPRESENTATION
David Gauntlett

youth, determination, and passion. Her social media voice has allowed for others to connect and view the representation of environmental activists more positively thus eschewing the negative stereotyped traits of militant or eccentric hippie tree huggers which often distance people from the cause. Her positive representation of the environmental movement has inspired hundreds of thousands of students across the world to relate to her cause and begin to build their own climate change identity.

Does the audience mediate and shift their identity according to what is consumed? Does the plethora of coverage of Greta Thunberg allow for a shift in how people view environmentalists? Do younger people see that Greta is capable of spurring change, and her activist representation, which encompasses youth, passion, and sensibility broaden their landscape of possibilities? Gauntlett describes this succinctly by stating that people use the media 'as navigation points for developing our own identities.' The process of consuming and producing media will be different for each person. However, to have access to a world of representations, to a diversity of viewpoints, even in an algorithmic driven digital world, allows for a variety of navigation points to create a diversity of constructed and negotiated identities.

Gauntlett contributes to the analysis of representations by providing the idea that media texts and social media platforms allow a modern audience to shape their own identities. Whereas historically media engagement was limited, and singular in the availability of representations of sexual orientation, race, body image, culture, age and so on. Nowadays a diversity of representations can be found due to the ease of access of independent media content found on the internet, which in turn influences mainstream practices. Therefore, people who previously struggled to find characters or stars to identify with now have a wider range of representations available to them.

However, it is important to be critical and consider what the social media giants gain from people engaging in creative spaces. Do Google and Meta subvert these spaces, instead of letting them be individual digital places for personal representation have they instead become homogeneous money-making advertising machines? **Representations matter.** Be critical of who constructed it and for what purpose, as representations circulate meaning.

Representation

MEDIA AS A TOOL TO CHALLENGE STEREOTYPES

By challenging existing representations and promoting diverse depictions in both traditional and social media we can counter the narrow, one-dimensional portrayals that have dominated narratives. The world is diverse; accurate and authentic representations are needed to shift public perceptions and promote inclusivity.

Media is used to challenge perceptions of gender identity and gender roles. For instance, some advertising campaigns are leaning into the social issue of gender politics and challenging gender stereotypes:

Ford Explorer Men's Only Edition: is a tongue-in-cheek advertisement poking fun at what cars would be like without the contributions made by female inventors.

Fearless Girl: is a statue commissioned by Wall Street to encourage gender diversity on business boards.

#MeToo is a viral movement challenging stereotypes about sexual harassment.

#thisgirlcan is a viral advertising campaign promoted by England's National Lottery designed to get more females involved in sport or simply to be more active.

How does media consumption of gender roles and sexual identification impact our own construction and representation of gender.

Strong, powerful representations of women (and in fact any marginalised group) are needed to promote inclusivity and equity. By showing marginalised people who occupy powerful places, such as Kamala Harris, the Vice President of the United States (currently campaigning to be the 47th President), who is a female of mixed Indian and Jamaican heritage, normalises minority groups in leadership roles. In addition, by celebrating female athletes such as Serena Williams who has won four Olympic gold medals and numerous Grand Slam tennis tournaments, inspires women to participate in male dominated sports.

Media can be used as a tool to challenge stereotypes by providing positive, diverse, and powerful representations of marginalised groups. By making the invisible visible we can begin to shift societal norms by promoting equality and diversity, thus benefitting all of society as open-mindedness allows for innovation and critical thinking to foster.

REPRESENTATION
Timeline for Women's Rights

Historical context: When discussing how context affects representations it is important to be armed with some facts. By studying the four waves of feminism students can examine how media representations of femininity have been shaped by context, these media representations in turn shape societal understanding of gender identities. By analysing depictions of females in different media contexts students can decode the choice of codes used to construct them, the values embedded in the choice of codes, and the agenda behind their representation. The fight for gender equity is global. By having diverse and inclusive representations of femininity we can begin to dismantle negative representations of gender and build a media landscape that is equitable for all.

FIRST WAVE 1848 - 1920S
Focus is on women's suffrage, their legal rights and access to education.

1848	Origin of women's rights launched by the Seneca Falls Convention whose purpose was to demand equality for women via the Declaration of Sentiments.
1869	Wyoming is the first state in America to grant the right to vote to women as the National Women Suffrage Association is formed in order to secure female voting rights.
1877	New Zealand enacts compulsory education for all children, enforced through the Education Act.
1880s	The Married Women's Property Act (and subsequent Acts) gradually allowed married women to be independent of their husbands as they could own property in their own right, enter into contracts, and earn an independent salary.
1893	New Zealand is the first country to grant women's suffrage. Women could vote, but they could not be a political candidate.
1902	In Australia, women were given the vote, and the right to be elected.
1920	In America, the 19th Amendment granted women's suffrage (voting rights).
1922	The Country Women's Association was founded, allowing a space for women to support each other and advocate for their rights.

SECOND WAVE EARLY 1960s - 1980s

The second wave dealt with inequality in the work force, specifically pregnant or married women having to leave their job as the assumption was that they would be the main family caregiver. In addition, it dealt with property rights, reproductive rights, and legal reforms such as attempts to deal with domestic violence and criminalising rape in marriage.

1960 — Sirimavo Bandaranaike of Sri Lanka is the world's first female Prime Minister.

1963 — Equal Pay Act passed in US which attempted to connect the wage disparity divide by providing equal pay for equal work.

1963 — Betty Friedan published *The Feminine Mystique* which voiced what many were thinking, women were tired of being confined to the domestic sphere, and being seen as 'less than' men.

1964 — Equal Civil Rights Act - prohibited discrimination based on race, sex, religion or nationality.

1966 — Ban on married women working in the public service is lifted in Australia.

1969 — The Australian Conciliation and Arbitration Commission established the principle of equal pay for equal work. Although a step towards pay equity, it was not as comprehensive as the US Equal Pay Act.

1973 — Roe v. Wade legalises abortion.

1974 — Until 1974 in America and 1984 in Australia women were not allowed to open a bank account, take out a mortgage, or get a line of credit without a man as guarantor. The introduction of the Equal Credit Opportunity Act prohibited discrimination based on gender or marital status thus allowing women financial independence.

1979 — Margaret Thatcher becomes Prime Minister of the United Kingdom. She stays in power for 11 years.

1981 — Sandra O'Connor is elected to the US Supreme Court as the first female justice.

THIRD WAVE 1989 - EARLY 2000s

Third wave feminism is more general in application in that it is a continuation of trying to achieve equal pay for equal work, trying to break the 'glass ceiling,' expanding to include an acceptance of all women no matter what creed or colour, championing diversity, and drawing attention to intersectionality.

1989 — Kimberle Crenshaw's article *Demarginalizing the Intersection of Race and Sex: A Black Feminist Critique of Antidiscrimination Doctrine, Feminist Theory, and Antiracist Politics* foregrounds the idea of intersectionality which propelled the idea that people with multiple identities such as being female, black, and in poverty have layers of discrimination that overlap and intersect; they are not distinct from one another, therefore treating gender, race, and economic status as intersecting entities allows for multiple complex inequalities to be seen and addressed.

1990s — Girrl Power is a slogan coined by US punk band Bikini Kill. They advanced discussion on female issues such as domestic violence and rape whilst championing female empowerment.

1991 — Anita Hill is an African American law professor and attorney who testified at the 1991 American Supreme Court Confirmation hearings for Clarence Thomas about the sexual harassment she faced at his hands. Thomas was confirmed as a supreme court judge by an all-white, all-male committee who dismissed Hill's candid and composed testimony thus shining a spotlight on sexual harassment in the workplace and highlighting how little regard is given to women's testimony. The public's outraged reaction led to meaningful change to workplace sexual harassment procedures and legislation.

1992 — Ms. magazine published an article by Rebecca Walker titled *Becoming the Third Wave*. The seminal text coined the term 'third wave' as Walker critiqued Thomas Clarence's appointment to the Supreme Court despite him being accused of sexual harassment. She urged women to be vocal and to become the 'third wave' recognising that the fight for equality was far from over.

1995 — Beijing Declaration and Platform for Action was a gathering of representatives from 189 governments. The platform addressed key critical women's concerns such as poverty, violence, health, and education acknowledging obstacles and setting goals for gender equality and women's rights.

FOURTH WAVE 2010 - present

The fourth wave of feminism concerns itself with digital activism in that it harnesses social media to raise awareness regarding women's issues regarding their on-going fight for bodily autonomy and reproductive rights, their continued push for workplace equality, their on-going commitment to fighting violence against women, and a focus on body positivity and inclusivity.

2010	Julia Gillard becomes the first female Prime Minister of Australia. She remained in power for three years.
2017	#MeToo movement is driven by the trend of social media use. Largest protest for a Women's march with an estimated three and half million people protesting worldwide in support of women's rights with the bulk being in Washington, D.C.
2017	The Australian Marriage Amendment Act stated that marriage was between two people (rather than defining gender), thereby legalising same-sex marriage.
2018	Ireland repeals abortion ban.
2002	The International Criminal Court formally recognises rape as a war crime.
2020	Kamala Harris becomes the first female, and person of colour, to be the US Vice President.
2021	Taliban seized control of Afghanistan; girls are banned from secondary education.
2023	Andrew Tate, a controversial figure used social media to push the idea that men are oppressed leading to a significant backlash against advancements in women's rights. Historically, women have met resistance when they have attempted to gain equality (not superiority), men like Tate spread a misogynistic ideology, one that wants to suppress women and regress their rights rather than accept equality.
2024	Supreme court of America overturns Roe v. Wade making abortion illegal.
2024	Kamala Harris runs as presidential nominee for the Democrats against Donald Trump's Republican party.

Representation

Representations depict people, places, concepts or events by using certain codes and conventions to convey meaning. By selecting specific signs and symbols to construct the representation a subjective value judgement has been made that conveys the agenda and bias of its creator. Representations are not neutral, they are shaped by context, institutions, and those with power. The use of one-dimensional, stereotypical representations in media productions can lead to inaccurate portrayals and narrow perspectives which do not show the complexity behind people, places, groups, or concepts.

Scan any of the QR codes on the following pages. Look at the timeline for Women's Rights on the previous pages and analyse what historical and cultural events have influenced the representation of gender. Deconstruct the media texts by looking at:
- Codes and conventions chosen to convey meaning
- Values embedded in the choice of codes
- How has context influenced the construction of the representation
- What problems arise out of simplifying representations?

E.L.F. beauty: *So Many Dicks* advertising campaign.

#LikeAGirl advertising campaign.

The Matilda Effect – why *brilliant women were erased from history.*

Caitlin Clark, is an American basketball player who is selling more tickets for games than her male counterparts, but is paid less. The video shows that actions speak louder than words as she responds to the chants by male spectators of 'overrated.'

Chief NFL cheerleaders – shows what they do for full time job as well as the time commitment needed for cheerleading.

What if male athletes were asked the same questions or spoken about in the same way as female athletes? *#overheardinthepatriarchy*

Representation

 Mothers for democracy is an advert on gun violence. The number one killer of children in the US is gun violence. The advert is an interesting representation of gun reform.

 *Ted Talk on Fan girls* – young girls screaming for pop stars is considered crazy, a bit hysterical, whereas young boys screaming at a sports match is considered passionate.

 *Taylor Swift Effect* – swaying younger voters to vote. Tweeted for people to register to vote. Vote.org stated that their site saw 25 000 per hour register to vote after Swift endorsed the Democrats.

 *Orange France* - Women's Soccer Deepfake video manipulation advertisement that uses the faces of male soccer players superimposed on the action footage of female soccer players.

 Dove - *The Code* campaign carries on with the Real Women representation by critiquing the use of artificial intelligence in shaping beauty standards.

 P&G *Thank You, Mom* campaign is a good one to look at for representations of families, gender roles, and mothers.

 Nike *Dream Crazier* advertisement uses powerful representations of female athletes as role models for all women wanting to defy the odds.

Problems with stereotyping

PROBLEMS ASSOCIATED WITH STEREOTYPING

1. OVERSIMPLIFICATION

Stereotyping reduces something complex to something simple by choosing a few codes to represent the entire group, concept, or issue. Simplification means that nuances are missed, and generalisations are highlighted, often exaggerating negative traits that can then be used to represent the entire group.

2. NARROW VIEWPOINT

As stereotypes use limited codes to represent the entire group or issue their portrayal is very one-dimensional. The limited representation creates a narrow, biased viewpoint about the group or issue which frequently focuses on negative traits rather than considering the complexities associated with the issue or group.

3. REPETITION

The choice of codes used to form the stereotypes are repeated with frequency as they are a short cut in meaning and ease the cognitive load for audiences. However, the repetitive use reinforces, and eventually naturalises how we categorise people or groups based on factors such as appearance, race or gender making them more resistant to change.

4. NATURALISATION

When stereotypes are perceived as natural, they become resistant to change as they are seen as a societal norm. Naturalisation perpetuates bias, prejudice, and social inequality, normalising discrimination. As naturalisation occurs due to repeated exposure it is important to be critical about the construction and agenda behind the choice of codes used to represent a group. Who benefits from this representation?

5. INTERSECTIONALITY

Due to simplification, stereotyping does not consider intersections of identity. People and issues are nuanced and layered, often having multiple overlapping identities to do with race, gender, economic status, and culture. Stereotyping simplifies and ignores the intersecting layers.

6. MISREPRESENTATION

Stereotyping can result in misrepresentation as only a few biased codes are chosen to represent the entire group or issue. The simplified, often inaccurate portrayal can shape how people decode meaning and influence their perception of the group or issue. The inaccurate portrayal can perpetuate discrimination.

Review

Sample questions containing representation and stereotypes

1. Analyse how media representations are constructed to influence audience values and perceptions.
2. Discuss how the naturalisation of stereotypes impact individual and collective perceptions and attitudes.
3. Discuss the processes that lead to the naturalisation of stereotypes, allowing them to become naturalised in cultural narratives?
4. Discuss how the media can be used as a vehicle to challenge and transform established representations?
5. Analyse the relationship between encoding, decoding, and contextual factors to explain how a representation is shaped by the media producer and received by the audience.

 **REPRESENTATION - main essential content to discuss:**

01
- **A representation** is a likeness or re-presentation of reality; it is not the real world but rather a constructed, mediated, portrayal of real world issues, people, groups, concepts, objects and places.

02
- Representations are constructed using a **choice of codes and conventions**. By selecting and omitting certain codes to represent a group, a **value laden choice** has been made.

03
- Representations are not made in a vacuum; they are influenced by cultural and social norms. They are not static, rather they change to reflect their **cultural and historical context.**

04
- Professor **Stuart Hall's study of representations** highlighted that representations are not neutral, the **choice of codes** used to construct them is **value laden** and reflects the agenda of those with power. He stated that people need a **'shared cultural map'** to encode and decode meaning in an understandable manner. Hall outlines how representations are formed using **'language'** which is any sign or symbol used to communicate meaning including visual and aural signifiers.

05
- **David Gauntlett** explores the relationship between digital media, audiences, and content creators, examining **how identities are shaped through social media interaction**, construction and consumption.

06
- **Problems associated with stereotyping** include: oversimplification that ignores the intersectional layers shaping each person's identity, using a narrow viewpoint to represent the group, repeating the choice of codes to represent the group until the construction becomes naturalised, and misrepresenting a group through a simplified, inaccurate portrayal.

07
- Representations have the power to control the **construction and circulation of meaning.**

Chapter Nine

Values, Attitudes, & Ideologies

- Values, attitudes, and ideologies defined
- Key terms
- Dominant, emerging, and oppositional values and ideologies
- How a text disseminates values and ideologies
- Values and ideologies embedded in the short film *Hair Love*
- Values and ideologies embedded in *The Bicycle Thieves*
- Sample questions
- Review

Values & Ideologies

Values, attitudes, & ideologies

Values

Values are the beliefs we deem worthy, desirable, and aspirational. They are something we aspire to or believe in. Positive values guide our behaviour. They represent what is important to individuals, shaping attitudes and actions. Examples of values:

- Optimism
- Honesty
- Compassion
- Independence
- Equality
- Loyalty
- Friendship
- Kindness
- Peace
- Love
- Respect
- Trust
- Tolerance
- Teamwork
- Curiosity
- Health
- Security
- Diversity
- Resilience
- Humour
- Sustainability
- Accountability
- Responsibility
- Ambition
- Courage
- Spirituality
- Humility
- Adaptability

Attitudes

Attitudes reflect how a person feels about an issue and are conveyed through language and actions. Attitudes are how values are displayed. They are a learned mental disposition and are susceptible to change. Examples of attitudes are:

- Pessimistic
- Optimistic
- Friendly
- Hostile
- Enthusiastic
- Indifferent
- Open-minded
- Lazy
- Responsible
- Generous
- Selfish
- Honest
- Cautious
- Dishonest
- Judgemental
- Appreciative
- Diplomatic
- Motivated
- Punctual
- Cynical
- Idealistic
- Hopeful
- Easy-going
- Emotional
- Careless
- Principled
- Nurturing
- Naive

Ideologies

Ideologies are a culturally determined shared set of beliefs, values, customs, and practices that shape our view of the world. They often represent beliefs and attitudes about political, economic, and social structures. Examples of ideologies:

- Capitalism
- Socialism
- Feminism
- Environmentalism
- Conservatism
- Materialism
- Patriotism
- Patriarchy
- Familial
- Consumerism
- Minimalism
- Rationalism
- Post-modernism
- Individualism
- Determinism
- Globalism
- Liberalism
- Fascism
- Nationalism
- Heteronormative
- Matriarchy
- Equality
- Racism
- Sexism
- Ageism
- Classism
- Multiculturalism
- Pacifism

Key terms

1. HEGEMONY
Is a top-down structure whereby dominant ideologies appear to be natural and therefore unquestionable.

2. IDEOLOGY
The structure or system of beliefs, values, attitudes, and ideas that, when combined, form a lens through which members of a society see the world.

3. ATTITUDE
Attitudes are how values and beliefs are displayed. Attitudes are constructed from values and beliefs and change according to life experience.

4. VALUE
A value is something we aspire to or believe in. It is our sense of right and wrong, often socially constructed and conveyed via hegemonic institutions such as the media, family, education, government and the law. Values govern actions.

5. BELIEF
A belief forms the basis of values and attitudes. It is often not evidence-based, rather it is a feeling derived from life experiences which scaffolds our beliefs.

6. CONTEXT
Beliefs, values, attitudes, ideologies, and ultimately hegemonic constructs arise from a social, historical, political, and cultural context. Our ideas do not form in a vacuum, they are created and shaped by our contextual experiences.

Dominant, emerging, oppositional

- Media texts can reinforce or challenge dominant values and ideologies.
- Media texts play a role in shaping social values and ideologies.
- Audiences negotiate media texts in relation to their own ideological positions.

Ideologies

Dominant ideologies are held by the vast majority of a society and represent the beliefs, values, and attitudes of those in power positions. These ideologies influence social and political structures, as well as social norms. E.g., feminism, multiculturalism, democracy, environmentalism and racial equality.

Emerging ideologies are shared practices and beliefs held by an increasing group of people within that culture. They challenge the status quo. Often the tide of emerging ideologies shifts to become the dominant view. E.g., Post-genderism is challenging the concept of binary genders and making it more fluid. Or eco-socialism as an alternative to capitalism due to the disillusionment and negative impacts created by capitalism.

Oppositional ideologies are views and practices that directly contrast with those held by most people in a culture. E.g., neo-Nazism is an ideology in opposition to racial equality, egalitarianism, and multiculturalism.

Values

Dominant values are those held by the majority of people in a society. E.g., freedom, personal autonomy, justice, education.

Emerging values are beliefs or attitudes held by a growing number of people in a society. When studying historical texts, these values may eventually become dominant. E.g., mental health, digital privacy, ethical consumerism.

Oppositional values are beliefs that are in direct opposition to those held by the majority of people in a society. E.g., gender roles based on traditionalism, no bodily autonomy for females (no abortion rights).

Ideologies

Imagine for a minute that you have on glasses that allow the invisible structures scaffolding the world around you to be seen. Picture springing up in front of you, institutions like the government (if this was bricks and mortar you would see police stations, court houses, political offices and so on) but instead of the actual buildings you see the concepts that surround those institutions. Now imagine how you navigate your way through these concepts. For example, potentially your family will influence your political leanings, your friends and family might influence your ideological understanding of gender construction, possibly your on-line and social media interactions move you into an echo chamber whereby you hear and see significant amounts of information about a selected topic.

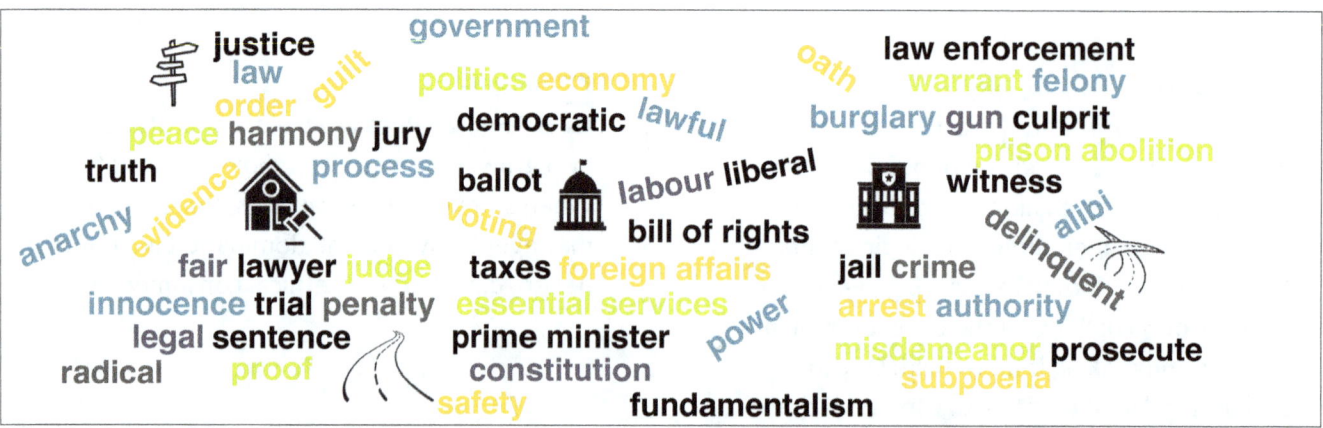

The pathway you take when navigating these concepts is littered with ideological constructs which are mostly invisible—these ideologies scaffold what you believe and how you function. Think about the way your family and friends talk about gender and sexuality. Consider the words used to describe the attributes and emotions associated with boys versus girls. These words are steeped in beliefs, attitudes, and values.

There are numerous pathways to choose from, but your direction is heavily influenced by family, friends, colleagues, media consumption, and institutions like the church, the government, the law, and education institutions.

> Look at the image above. Consider how your ideological understanding of the law or politics would be shaped by your beliefs, attitudes, and values. What words do you see as being associated with a dominant ideology and which do you associate with an oppositional ideology?

Ideologies & values

Dominant, emerging & oppositional ideologies

Media texts carry ideological messages to the audience. For instance, a narrative can uphold the dominant ideology and reinforce historical gender roles by having a classic damsel-in-distress who is rescued by a male hero. Picture this scene in your mind, the main characters are most likely good-looking, fit and healthy, and following the dominant ideological narrative arc, will probably be Caucasian. As a carrier of ideological meaning this narrative has reinforced long-standing social structures regarding gender roles and race. It clearly privileges Caucasian, good looking males. It tells the audience that what is valued in society is good looks, being strong and healthy, and if you happen to be a male who is white, this is preferenced above all else. The volume of films and television shows that fit this paradigm is staggering.

Dominant ideologies are challenged by competing or emerging ideologies. Media texts do reflect cultural shifts in values, attitudes, beliefs, and ideologies. Considering the damsel-in-distress narrative described above, the ideological world view represented is one of patriarchy which highlights the agenda that men actively engage in problem solving, show intellect and strength, whilst women are passive, needing the aid of a man. This serves the patriarchal agenda. Consider what is absent in stories like these —women of strength; minority groups, and people of different sexual orientations are either absent or subservient. By excluding these representations the narrative services the dominant ideology of patriarchy, highlighting the power structures at play. Why do women, or people of colour, or people of a differing sexual orientation still engage with these narratives? The assumption that the audience passively views a text and does not understand its ideological underpinnings is condescending. According to Stuart Hall's reception theory audience members will either make a dominant reading of the text, embracing its ideological position, or a negotiated reading whereby they accept aspects of the text's message but question other underlying meanings, or finally, they may make an oppositional reading by rejecting the text's message entirely.

For instance, a female audience member watching a heterosexual romance set in an exotic holiday location could be doing so for pure escapism. She understands that the preferred message of the text is about accepting that love conquers all and that everyone will find their perfect match. However, a negotiated reading may query unrealistic expectations of love existing within an unequal patriarchal structure. She considers how power dynamics could see the practical realities of life crashing in once the holiday is over. Practical considerations such as the equal division of household labour that will need doing once the exotic holiday is over can place extreme pressure on any relationship. An oppositional reading rejects the dominant ideologies posited by the text by critiquing traditional gender norms and querying why personal fulfilment for a female can only occur by finding love in a heteronormative romantic relationship. A dissatisfaction with a patriarchal power structure does not equate to a rejection of romance or a rejection of men; it means that an active audience is questioning the romance trope genre and its underlying values and ideologies that distribute power unevenly across the cultural landscape.

Disseminate values & ideologies

MEDIA TEXTS AND HOW THEY DISSEMINATE VALUES AND IDEOLOGIES:

- **Character selection and construction**: who is selected to play the protagonist and antagonist? Is it a male, a female, person of colour, older person, younger person? What values are embedded in their **appearance and actions?** The codes of construction used to represent the major characters push the audience towards deconstructing the **preferred meaning** of the text by visually and aurally signally what is valued in terms of actions, appearance, behaviour, and outcomes.
- What **actions** are displayed by the protagonist? Do they embed characteristics society sees as good such as kindness, courage, or determination?
- The **conflict and resolution** of the narrative are crucial as the expose the values and ideologies that are privileged in the text. For instance, is justice served? Does good win over evil? For mainstream texts, dominant ideologies are usually foregrounded in the text's resolution.
- Values and ideologies are shaped by **contextual factors.** For instance, what is the political climate? What social movements are gaining momentum? What historical events have occurred? The **cultural context** of an era will influence values and ideologies; in turn these same values and ideologies will shape the representation of characters, ideas, and issues in media texts.

IDEOLOGY & VALUES
Short film Hair Love Analysed

VALUES AND IDEOLOGIES EMBEDDED IN THE SHORT ANIMATED FILM HAIR LOVE:

Synopsis:
Hair Love (2019) a short Oscar winning animated film written and co-directed by Matthew Cherry, Everett Downing and Bruce Smith aims to break stereotypes in relation to African American fathers and how they involve themselves with their daughter's lives; in particular the minutiae of everyday life such as styling their child's hair. The premise of the film is simple, Zuri, a young child, has one goal, she wishes to style her wayward hair into a tamed fashionable style. In the absence of her mother, Zuri's father Stephen is required to step up and assist his daughter to control her unruly hair. Zuri's mother Angela, is in hospital receiving chemotherapy for cancer, and today is the day she comes home, prompting Zuri to want to look nice for her mother's return. Angela has left her daughter a video tutorial showing her how to style her hair, eventually, using the tutorial as a guide Stephen succeeds in giving Zuri the hairstyle she desires.

Character selection and construction:
Protagonist
Zuri, a young African America aged around seven years old is constructed as the film's protagonist. Her **goal** is to have her hair styled for the special event of picking her mother up from hospital to bring her home after an extended chemotherapy stay. This single desire drives the plot forward. **Codes of construction** used to create Zuri's character include her pink pyjamas complete with a pink bed hat used to contain her unruly hair. The connotations embedded

Ideologies & values

suggest femininity and insecurity regarding setting her hair free. Zuri's **actions** demonstrate that she is a **determined and loving** person. She initially views her mother's hair tutorial and attempts to follow the instructions with disastrous results. Seeing her struggle, Zuri's father steps in to have his first attempt at styling his daughter's hair. The **action displays love, support, and compassion** for his daughter's plight. The audience is made aware that time is of the essence as Stephen looks at his watch several times, indicating that they need to get moving to pick Angela up from the hospital on time. Despite time ticking away Stephen can see how important looking good for her mother's return is to Zuri and **perseveres** in taming her hair into a selected style.

Antagonist

The villain of the piece is Zuri's hair. **Visual and aural codes** set up the fight Stephen is about to face in taming Zuri's unruly hair. An **extreme close up** of Stephen's eyes, sweat dripping down his brow, is framed by Zuri's hair, the accompany beating heart sound overlaid with **tension music** positions the audience to understand that Stephen is about to have a very difficult time. The **ideology of familial love** is highlighted as despite facing many obstacles, including Zuri's hair growing into a monster which Stephen must battle in a boxing ring, he is **determined** to help his daughter. Unfortunately, he too is unsuccessful, resulting in him giving up and placing a hat onto Zuri's head in defeat. Zuri's tears and disappointment spur her on as she runs out of her father's room into the bathroom. Sitting outside the bathroom door Stephen hears Angela's voice emitting from the hair tutorial saying: All it takes is some confidence and a willingness to get started. And even though I'm not there, I'll guide you through this. The **value**

Ideologies & values

of family bonds, connectedness, and using each other for support, is foregrounded as Stephen enters the bathroom to assist his daughter once again. A **high camera angle** is used to position the audience to view the small and vulnerable Zuri hold the iPad up for her father to see the image of his wife with a younger Zuri calmly expressing her **love** for her family and letting the vlog audience know that the 'road ahead might look rough but you can make the journey with a little bit of work and a whole lot of love.' Angela hugs the younger Zuri as the camera pulls back to reveal current Zuri holding the iPad as her eyes beseech her father to help her. The underlying **values of love, compassion, and perseverance** are encoded in Stephen's **actions** as he uses his wife's video tutorial to overcome the challenge of never having styled his daughter's hair before. The audience understands that he is challenging traditional care giving roles as his wife has clearly always done Zuri's hair, but he is **determine**d to be more involved.

Stephen's **actions** of **persevering** with styling Zuri's hair, not getting annoyed at his daughter for being late, and understanding the importance of looking good for her mother's return from the hospital, reveal the **ideology of familial love** and its importance in ensuring strong family bonds.

Conflict and resolution

The **conflict and resolution** of the narrative are crucial as they expose the **values and ideologies that are privileged in the text.** The film's conflict of Stephen's literal and metaphorical battle to style Zuri's hair reveals many societal challenges. Firstly, the stereotypical care giving notion that family 'chores' such as assisting children to get ready, including brushing and styling their hair,

Ideologies & values

traditionally fall to the mother, is **challenged** by *Hair Love*. It is unfortunate that cancer propels Stephen to this realisation, however, he does step up without angst or anger, showing that his own personal insecurities need to be left behind as he **models problem solving** and **love** for his daughter. In turn, Zuri shows her father how to be **resourceful** by using her mother's hair tutorial to assist with their dilemma.

The **resolution** showcases the strength of the family unit when it is built on **love, support, and perseverance.** The **familial ideology** is foregrounded in the final scene when the audience is shown Zuri giving her mother Angela a drawing in the hospital as she sits in a wheelchair with a scarf covering her head. Zuri's drawing is clearly a portrait of her mother depicting a bald head with a gold crown slightly above it, revealing how Zuri sees the **strength and power** in her mother despite, or because of, her cancer ordeal. The **value of unconditional love** is prefaced as Angela takes off the headscarf to reveal her bald head which Zuri strokes whilst hugging her mother. Stephen joins in the hug and a medium close up reveals their happiness and family unity.

Context

Matthew Cherry, a Black ex-NFL American football player who has made two previous independent films (and has several mainstream directing credits to his name) was inspired to challenge the negative absent-father stereotypical portrayal of Black fathers and to instead show positive representations. He chose to do this using the experience of African American's everyday experience, particularly their battles with hair. The inspiration arose from seeing online videos highlighting fathers struggling and succeeding in doing their daughter's hair. Moreover, the film arose in an environment where Black people's struggle with their hair was trivialised, marginalised, and often criticised. Perry invited DeAndre Arnold to the 92nd Oscar awards when he heard about the Texan teen and his cousin getting in trouble at school for having dreadlocks which the school deemed in violation of their policy of having a clean and well-groomed presentation.

The **value of self-confidence and embracing cultural differences** highlights the need stated by Perry to have positive representations of marginalised cultures to allow for connections to grow through understanding, empathy, and compassion.

Hair Love: short film

Ideologies & values

AN EXAMPLE OF VALUES & ATTITUDES IN VITTORIO DE SICA'S "THE BICYCLE THIEVES"

The 1948 Italian Neo-realist film *The Bicycle Thieves* directed by Vittorio De Sica centres on Antonio Ricci's quest to retrieve his stolen bicycle, whose value lies in its ability to deliver him much needed employment to feed his family.

Antonio and his young son Bruno search all over Rome attempting to find the bicycle. He is told the man who stole the bike might be in a church. The church officials are less concerned with helping Antonio find his bike then ensuring he is quiet and reverential, insisting that he and his son leave rather than disrupt the service. Antonio's **attitude** towards Christianity shows minimal respect, as highlighted by the church scene where he continues to try to elicit information about his stolen bike from an acquaintance despite the surrounding avid church goers "shushing him" to obtain silence and respect for the reverence in which they hold their religion. Thus, the **value** of the Christian religion is questioned through Antonio's disrespectful actions. In addition, Vittorio De Sica set these actions on a Sunday; a day known to all Christians as a day of rest and worship. In doing so the underlying Christian **ideology** is subtly questioned as De Sicca juxtaposes abstract worship with Antonio's physical need to obtain information to secure his bike, regain his employment, and therefore support his family.

Ideologies are culturally determined and refer to the shared beliefs, values, customs, and practices that shape a society. Texts can support or challenge ideologies.

Some dominant ideologies are:

- Familial: the belief that the nuclear family model is the foundation of a good society.
- Feminism: advocates for equality between men and women.
- Patriarchal: privileges male dominance in work and home spheres.
- Heterosexual: the belief in heteronormativity as the preferred sexual orientation.
- Capitalist: advocates that private ownership, free market enterprise, and profit making are the best economic system.
- Individualism: Primacy is given to an individual's goals, rights, worth, and autonomy.
- Materialism: an emphasis is placed on consumer culture and its ability to fill any emotional void, achieve higher social status, find success, and ultimately find happiness.
- Bourgeois: the belief in self-advancement and moving up the social strata.
- Patriotism: devotion, loyalty and commitment to one's country shown through active citizenship.

Sample questions

Sample questions containing values and ideologies:

1. Discuss how an auteur expresses values and ideologies through their production.
2. Analyse how representations in media texts can challenge or support dominant ideologies and values.
3. Discuss how media aesthetics can function to critique societal values depicted in a media text.
4. Discuss how cultural context shapes audience interpretation of a film's themes, values, and ideologies.
5. Discuss how independent media subverts dominant ideologies and values.
6. Discuss how a media text adapts content to connect with the values of a niche audience.
7. How have narrative elements been used in a media text to convey values and ideologies.
8. Analyse how persuasive techniques are used in a media text to promote specific values and ideologies.
9. Analyse how propaganda is used to influence the audience into accepting dominant values and ideologies.
10. Discuss how values are encoded into a media text and decoded by the primary audience.
11. Discuss how a media text uses codes, conventions, and techniques to influence audience attitudes.

Values and ideologies are not created in a vacuum, they are shaped by contextual factors that inform beliefs, which then shape values and influence attitudes; combined these elements form ideologies, thus creating a cycle of influence within society.

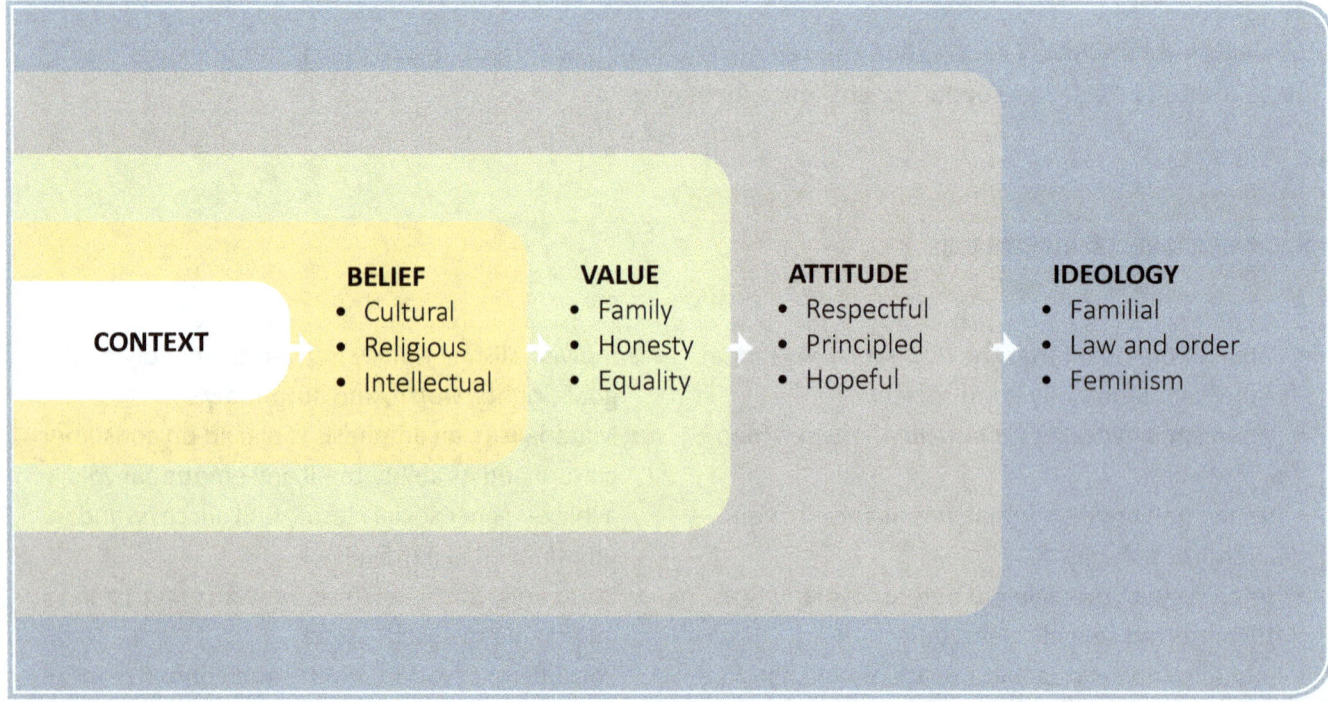

Values and ideologies creation cycle

Review

 **VALUES, ATTITUDES, & IDEOLOGIES - main essential content to discuss:**

01 Values
- Values embedded in the protagonist/antagonist: the protagonist embeds values society sees as good, the antagonist is embedded with values society sees as bad.
- Values revealed in the conflict and resolution: e.g., does good win over evil, does love reign supreme?
- Values revealed through character actions and appearance: e.g., is the hero good looking?

02 Attitudes
- How are attitudes displayed via actions and speech? As an attitude is how a character displays what they are feeling about an issue, person or event, discuss their actions and dialogue to determine their values and beliefs. Attitudes are how values and beliefs are displayed.

03 Ideologies
- Dominant ideologies: the shared practices and beliefs held by the majority within a society.
- Emerging ideologies: the shared practices and beliefs held by an increasing number of people within a society.
- Oppositional ideologies: the views and practices that directly contrast those held by the majority.
- Does the text promote, challenge, reinforce, confirm, endorse or subvert the dominant ideologies?
- What values are embedded in the text via actions, appearance, dialogue, discourse, and chosen representations?
- Film and TV have a language of their own within which values are suggested, attitudes reinforced, and statements conveyed about society, family, and relationships.

04 How do media texts disseminate values & ideologies:
- Characters are constructed through chosen codes and conventions.
- Values are embedded in the chosen codes, usually through appearance and actions.
- A text's conflict and resolution reveal values and ideologies. Discuss what values and ideologies are privileged.
- Context will influence which values and ideologies are privileged through the representation of characters, issues, and ideas.

Chapter Ten

Audience and Communication Theories

- Intended, mainstream, and niche audience
- Audience demographics
- Audience reach
- Audience engagement and reception
- Audience values, attitudes, context, and interpretation
- Communication theory: Hypodermic Needle theory
- Communication theory: Two Step Flow theory - Paul Lazarsfeld
- Communication theory: Reinforcement theory - Joseph Klapper
- Communication theory: Diffusion of Innovation - E.M. Rogers
- Communication theory: Agenda Setting theory - McCombs and Shaw
- Communication theory: Uses and Gratifications - Blumler and Katz
- Communication theory: Spiral of Silence - Elizabeth Noelle-Neuman
- Communication theory: Semiotic theory - Saussure
- Communication theory: Cultivation theory - Gerbner and Gross
- Communication theory: Reception theory - Stuart Hall
- Communication theory: Fandom theory - Henry Jenkins
- Communication theory: End of Audience - Clay Shirky
- Uses and Gratifications theory applied to *The True Cost*
- Agenda Setting theory applied to *The True Cost*
- Reception theory applied to *The True Cost*
- Sample questions
- Review

Communication Theories

Audience & Communication Theories

Intended Audience

Audiences are categorised into identifiable segments to be easily accessed by marketers. Their socio-demographic, psychographic, and geographic variables are used to engage and target groups with shared demographic metrics who collectively engage with media content. A clearly defined **target audience** informs all aspects of media content from planning through to production, marketing, and distribution.

Mainstream Audience

A **mainstream audience** is large and diverse. Media content needs to appeal to popular values in order to connect with its audience by considering:
- Mass appeal in terms of themes (good triumphs over evil), or love reigns supreme.
- Narrative and genre follow audience expectations with some inclusion of difference for interest.
- Budget is large, allowing for effects to be included and realism to be constructed.
- Well-known, popular choice of cast and director.
- Wide release into cinemas and on streaming platforms.

Niche Audience

A **niche audience** is when media content caters to differing cultural values and experiences, focusing on smaller more specialised groups with defined interests, beliefs, and attitudes, and catering to a clearly defined demographic. The media content can:
- Push boundaries with themes and content.
- Narrative structure can experiment with manipulation of time and space.
- Unconventional use of actors, often unknown, however, well-known actors can play unexpected roles.
- Director has creative freedom to experiment with technology, narrative structure, content, casting, and themes.
- Budget is smaller.
- Alternative mode of release such as film festivals, YouTube, social media, smaller independent specialised cinemas.
- Marketing and distribution is targeted to a fan base.

Audience demographics

Demographic Metrics

Socio-demographics:
- gender
- age
- occupation
- ethnicity
- education
- religion

Psychographics
- lifestyle
- values, beliefs, attitudes
- likes and dislikes, interests
- opinions, needs, wants

Geographics
- country
- city
- urban
- suburban

How demographic metrics can shape the filmmaking process

1. Story creation: how will the content connect and resonate with the primary audience? Is the theme accessible? Is the narrative progression clear? Is the genre suitable?
2. Casting: do the actors represent or appeal to the primary audience? Has representation in terms of age, gender, sexual orientation, culture, and religion been considered?
3. Marketing and distribution: What medium and platform is best for the intended audience? Do they mostly engage with social media, streaming services, or traditional mediums such as free-to-air television and cinema?

Audience Demographic

- By understanding the audience composition in terms of socio-demographics, psychographics, and geographic variables, filmmakers can create, market, and distribute films to connect with their primary audience. Although demographic metrics are useful, a film's secondary and tertiary audience allow for demographic boundaries to be blurred.
- Knowing their intended audience allows media producers to effectively construct narratives with appropriate themes, cast characters who resonate with the primary audience, and effectively market and distribute their content:
  1. The primary audience is the main target audience or the film's intended audience for its content.
  2. The secondary audience are one step removed from the primary audience. They engage with the content because of the primary audience. They often influence the primary audience due to familial, friendship, or work bonds.
  3. The tertiary audience are outside the direct intended circle of recipients. They may come in contact with the media content by accident such as when flicking channels or swiping through social media.

Audience

Audience reach

- For a film to connect with its audience it needs to know who they are targeting. By pinpointing their primary audience filmmakers can create narratives that connect via characters, settings, conflicts, and relatable themes.
- Audience preferences can influence casting and aesthetics.
- By knowing their audience filmmakers can have a tailored marketing and distribution strategy to effectively reach their audience demographic.
- Audience reach is measured using metrics such as box office numbers, ratings, and platform track views including how long a person engages with the content and whether they like, comment, or share it.

Audience engagement & reception

- How does the intended audience interact with media content? Do they privilege social media and streaming platforms above traditional mediums such as the cinema or television?
- Are they interactive users, engaging in cross-platform consumption of media content? Do they use social media to share or comment on characters, issues, or moments?
- Active audience participation has seen engagement in terms of transmedia storytelling and user-generated content in terms of remixes, commentary podcasts, and fan films increase.
- Binge watching culture has shaped the flow and structure of narratives to secure audience engagement.
- How does the intended audience consume media?
- Personalised feeds on the home screen of streaming platforms like Netflix offer algorithmic suggestions for viewing.

Audience

Audience values & attitudes

- Media content shifts to suit societal values and the prevailing attitudes of its intended audience. For instance, audience attitudes and expectations towards diversity in terms of gender, sexual orientation, and ethnicity have shifted significantly in the last decade. Consider how mainstream films such as *Black Panther* (2018) feature a majority black cast with strong female leads, or *Everything Everywhere All at Once* (2022) which features a predominantly Asian cast, also with strong female lead characters and LGBTQ+ representation.
- The cyclic nature of films reflecting changing audience values feeds into the continuous shifting landscape of how audience values and attitudes shape media content.

Audience context

- Context always affects content. The audience's **reception context** will shape how they decode meaning. Their demographic metrics including their values and attitudes will position them to decode meaning using their life experience and perspective to interpret the media content. For instance, the 2012 film *The Perks of Being a Wallflower* is a coming of age story which could resonate with teenage viewers whose life experience with high school is about friendships, fitting in, and discovering their identity.
- The **production context** or where and when a media text is made will heavily influence its content. The forces shaping a film include:
  → societal norms and expectations,
  → the political climate which may include beliefs around civil rights, gender equity, and environmental concern,
  → and technological advancements, for example the use of artificial intelligence or advancements such as drones to capture aerial shots.
- *Gone With the Wind* (1939) exemplifies how the production context shaped themes, narrative, and character construction. Made in America and set in the Deep South, the film reflects the agenda and racial attitudes seen in white 1930s America. The character of Mammy, a black slave, is romanticised and the harsh reality of slavery is omitted from the narrative to drive the ideology of white supremacy. The film's **production context** reflects the racial attitudes of the time and would not be accepted by a tolerant modern audience whose landscape on diversity, inclusion, and acceptance has shifted significantly.

Audience interpretation

- Stuart Hall's reception theory (encoding/decoding model) positions the audience to be active participants in the meaning making process. Media producers encode meaning by considering how their intended audience might decode meaning in relation to language choice, costume, mise-en-scène, narrative elements, themes and intertextual cultural references.
- The producer would like the intended audience to have a preferred meaning of the text, thus aligning with the values and beliefs embedded in it. Audience interpretation may include a negotiated meaning, whereby they understand the preferred meaning but don't necessarily subscribe to it, or the audience interpretation could extend to an oppositional reading, whereby the reject the film's intended message.
- Audience interpretation shapes media content as the cyclical nature of encoding is driven by how the audience decodes meaning, thereby shaping media content.

Communication theories

By studying communication theories and applying them to media texts we can begin to examine the connection between media, society, and people. In addition, we can:

- Analyse how the audience shapes, and is shaped by media content by providing a framework to examine how and why media content is selected, and why audiences embrace or reject it.
- Build foundational knowledge in critiquing media's role in society.
- Gain insight into how the media functions, how it shapes values and attitudes, and how it contributes to crafting society's ideological landscape.
- Gain knowledge into how media theories allow us to examine audience values, attitudes, and perceptions.
- Examine how media content can instigate behavioural changes.

Communication theories are many and varied. Twelve curated and summarised theories can be found in this chapter. Extensive detail on most theories is provided in the Year 11 textbook *Media Analysis: Understanding and Applying Media Theory Year 11*.

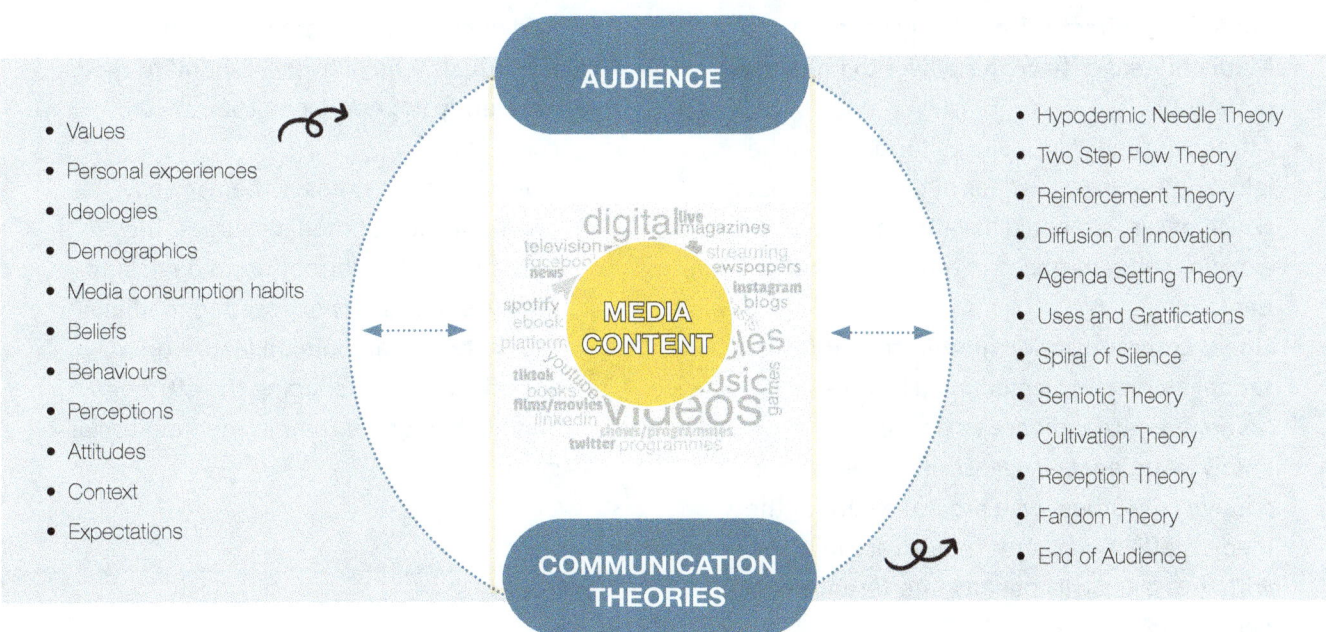

It is important to understand that you need to select the communication theories that best apply to your media text. Be specific and detailed by choosing only a few theories that assist to explain how the audience, media content, and society influence each other. Ensure you can apply your media theory, using it as a scaffold to discuss how or why media content was created, distributed, and interpreted by audiences in varying contexts and with differing demographic metrics.

Communication theories

Hypodermic Needle

Frankfurt School & Payne Fund

Define: A linear communication theory whereby media content is injected directly into the brain of a passive, homogeneous audience without the individual filtering or mediating the message.

Main points:

- Immediate, **direct effect** on audience.
- Media messages have the power to influence behaviour.
- Attractive theory as it allows for blame to be laid, and excuses given for negative behaviour which otherwise could have been hard to explain. Still referenced in times of **moral panic.**
- **Linear communication model** straight from sender to receiver, assuming a passive, homogeneous audience as its base.
- **Passive Audience** - suggested audiences are passive consumers who are not aware of the media's effect on them. They all are injected with messages without any interference or negotiated meaning.

1920-30s

Two Step Flow

Paul Lazarsfeld

Define: Media information moves in two distinct stages. First, opinion leaders who pay close attention to the mass media and its messages receive the information, then opinion leaders pass on their own interpretations in addition to the actual media content.

Main points:

- Audience members are seen as unique individuals who actively respond to media differently depending on their social context.
- Opinion leader exposes themselves to a multitude of media sources; they then filter this information to peers and family who are less exposed to media, thus acting as an opinion leader on a specific topic and shaping the attitudes and behaviours of their immediate social group.

1948

Communication theories

Reinforcement Theory

Joseph Klapper

Define: Promotes the idea that audiences would be more likely to accept and support an idea if it already aligns with their pre-existing values and ideas.

Main points:
According to this theory the power of the media is limited as socialising factors such as family, peers, education, religious affiliation, and community ties play a much larger role than the media in moulding one's beliefs, attitudes and behaviour.

Klapper frames his theory around three main cornerstones:

1. **Selective Exposure:** the audience selectively chooses what media to consume to align the content with their pre-existing views, attitudes, and values.
2. **Selective Retention:** the audience chooses to remember information that aligns with their ideas and interests and forgets, or pushes to the background, information which does not support their beliefs.
3. **Selective Perception:** the audience will seek out information and actively notice content that validates their pre-existing beliefs while avoiding information that contradicts with their views.

- Media can only influence if a new concept or idea is introduced.
- Audience is active, media has a limited effect in shaping a person's perception of their world.

1960

Diffusion of Innovation

E.M Rogers

Define: Examines how and why an innovation (new idea, product, behaviour, technique, belief, process, service or new technology), spreads over time and space in a predictable manner.

Main points:
Diffusion of ideas starts slowly with an uptake by innovators, then accelerates with early adopters and an early majority, before levelling off in a predictable, patterned, time sequence.

Rogers categorised people into five groups to determine their characteristics and how these assist the 'innovation' to spread throughout a society.

- **Innovators:** receptive to new concepts, risk takers.
- **Early adopters:** their advice is sought out and valued, many of this group are opinion leaders.
- **Early majority:** need proof that the innovation is worthwhile and better than what already exists, risk averse.
- **Late majority:** cautious, sceptical, wait for others to test and try, cave to peer pressure.
- **Laggards:** tied to old traditions, reluctant to try new innovations.

- The media influences the diffusion process by continuous and repetitive broadcasting of a message, signalling its importance and triggering an increase in its dissemination.

1962

Communication theories

Agenda Setting

McCombs & Shaw

Define: The media can't tell the audience what to think but they can tell them what to think about. The news media has the power to influence by deciding which stories are presented to the public, how often, how long, where they appear, and how the discourse will set the terms of reference regarding the perceived importance of the issue.

Main points:
Characteristics that filter and shape how an audience might engage and think about important issues:

1. **Framing:** what news information is selected and what is omitted in order to 'frame' or compose news items using a coherent narrative and contextual framework.
2. **Selection occurs** by prioritising certain issues over others. News is selected based on its conflict and potential to trigger or engage the audience.
   - **Emphasis:** highlighting an issue.
   - **Exclusion:** omitting items from the news agenda.
   - **Elaboration:** expansion of ideas and details which explain an issue in more detail.
3. **Priming:** refers to the time, space, and coverage provided to an issue, making some issues prominent and ignoring, or giving minimal coverage to others.
4. **Gatekeeping:** refers to people, such as a news editor, who decides (through selection and omission) the content of media publications. These decisions are based on the values of the news outlet, deadlines, and policies.
- The media has the power to set the agenda by making media content visible for the audience to engage with.

1972

Uses & Gratifications

Blumler, Katz, McQuail, Lull

Define: Looks at what people do with the media, rather than what the media does to people. Use media to gratify social and psychological desires. Audiences actively and deliberately engage with media content to suit their individual needs.

Main points:
The theory has had many proponents who have categorised how an audience uses the media:

- **Diversion:** the media is used as a diversion from reality, a means of relaxation and escape.
- **Personal relationships:** the media can contribute to personal relationships by adding connections in the form of topics of conversation. At times, the media can also function as a substitute companion.
- **Personal identity:** the media can be used as a 'guide' for understanding normal behaviours and values.
- **Surveillance:** keeping abreast of world news, current affairs, and engaging with informational media.
- In the 1980s Denis McQuail refined the theory by using the four headings of entertainment, information, personal identity and integration, and social interaction.
- James Lull furthered the theory in the 90s by looking at what people got out of the viewing experience: aspects such as **Communication Facilitation, Affiliation** or **Avoidance, Social Learning,** and **Competence/Dominance** were the main categories for highlighting what audiences extracted from their viewing experience.

1970 - 90s

Communication theories

Spiral of Silence

Elisabeth Noelle-Neumann

Define: Examines why people stay silent on issues of importance when they judge that their view differs from the majority.

Main points:
- In society conformity is often rewarded and deviance from the norm punished, mostly in the form of social isolation that works to constrain members of a society and direct them to conform to the dominant view, silencing their own, supposedly minority opinion to fit in.
- The theory claims that the media contributes significantly to the climate of fear and isolation by formulating public opinion through priming and framing of an issue. What the media reports about an issue, how long they report about it, and where they position the news item, creates a landscape of perceived importance about the topic.
- This in turn signals the dominant ideology, and the audience interprets this as being the dominant public opinion, regardless of whether it is or not, it appears to be the case.
- Minority groups do voice their opinion publicly to counter the dominant narrative on moral issues. E.g., regarding gender and race equality.
- Opinions of the vocal elite are not necessarily the same as the working class, yet they get more airtime and therefore appear to have strength in forming the dominant opinion.

1974

Semiotic Theory

Saussure

Define: A model showing how signs and symbols are used in a text to attribute meaning. The theory posits that media texts are **encoded** by producers and **decoded** by the audience who share a conceptual understanding of the codes. This allows them to interpret the constructed message using a familiar framework.

Main points:

Ferdinand de Saussure posited that a sign is made up of the **signifier** (physical form of sign) and the **signified** (the conceptual links).

- A sign is any word, image, action, object or sound that refers to something else. It can be **iconic**, physically resembling the thing or idea it is trying to represent (e.g., a photo of a dog looks like the dog it is representing). It can be **indexical**, having a direct link between the sign and signified displaying evidence of what is shown (e.g., smoke and fire). Or, it can be **symbolic**, showing no direct relation between the signifier and the signified, the only link being the socially constructed meaning attributed to the signs (e.g., the letters R.E.D do not look like the colour, but we agree conceptually that the letters refer to the colour).
- A sign's meaning is constructed by its denotation (literal meaning), its connotation (the deeper meaning constructed via social and cultural practices) and the cultural context in which the sign is used.

1960s -70s   Resurgence of idea

Communication theories

Cultivation Theory

Gerbner & Gross

Define: Looked at the effect of habitual, **cumulative exposure** of television and how this impacted people's beliefs and perception of their social reality.

Main points:
- Television's ability to **cultivate** or shape viewers perceptions of their world, including ideologies and values, lies at the heart of this theory. As TV presents an artificial world, how does this influence the formation of ideas about gender, minority groups, politics, occupation roles, and all ideas and beliefs that scaffold a society?
- Heavy viewers of television **cultivated** what Gerbner and his colleagues coined the **'mean world syndrome'** (Gerbner et al, 1986, p28). They found that people who continuously viewed violent TV shows saw their real world as dangerous and were more fearful, suspicious, and less trusting of other people.
- The original study concentrated on television as a medium. How has the addition of a 24/7 connected world, particularly through social media and binge watching contributed to the potential for **cultivating or shaping** a viewer's world, depending on their degree of exposure?
- The power of the media to construct our **social reality** is not limitless, but in areas where we have little or no personal experience, the media diet we consume can shape our perception of reality and can distort our world view.

1970-80s

Reception Theory

Stuart Hall

Define: How an audience is positioned to view a text: **dominant, negotiated,** or **oppositional reading**.

Main points:
Stuart Hall promoted the idea that texts are **polysemic** or have more than one meaning. Audiences differ in their ideological beliefs and values and will make a different reading of a text depending on whether it aligns with the dominant value system operating in their cultural and social landscape. Hall placed a clear bounded framework around how an **active audience** can **decode** or read a text.

1. **Dominant or preferred reading** - the audience shares and accepts the intended meaning. The sender and receiver share similar ideological perspectives.
2. **Negotiated reading** - where the audience understands the dominant position but doesn't necessarily subscribe to that ideology. For instance, females frequently view action films in which the male repeatedly plays the role of hero and saviour; here the female viewer understands the existence of the patriarchal ideology at play within the narrative but doesn't necessarily subscribe to the 'damsel-in-distress' paradigm.
3. **Oppositional reading** - whilst understanding the dominant meaning, the audience chooses to reject it.

1973

Communication theories

Fandom Theory

Henry Jenkins

Define: Examines how the participatory culture of fans shapes the media they consume. Fans are active contributors not passive consumers; for instance, they create art, attend conventions, critique content, participate in online forums, and are a powerful force in shaping popular culture.

Main points:
Active textual participation and fan engagement with media texts is foregrounded. Reinterpreting media content is viewed as a legitimate fan practice.
- The role of fans in constructing and circulating media content is crucial for driving content. They can share, comment on, reinterpret, and even supply original ideas to producers to shape content.
- Textual poaching, a term popularised by Jenkins, is where a fan appropriates aspects of the original media, such as a character or storyline, and uses this as a starting point to create alternative content and meaning not intended by the original producer.
- Fan products such as art, websites, podcasts, blogs, reviews, fan fiction, fan insta-stories, YouTube channels, memes and so on often use a transmedia model to extend the original story into a different version from the original media universe.
- The fandom community base has a significant place in participatory culture as they are innovators of content and can be used by producers to collect ideas and to tap into a ready-made niche audience for marketing and promotional purposes.
- Digital technology has allowed producers and fans to connect closely, thus changing the traditional power dynamics of the audience/producer relationship.

1992

End of Audience

Clay Shirky

Define: Digital technology has democratised media production. Audiences are more interactive in their media consumption and production as they like, share, tweet and make original content. The active participatory behaviour of audiences is now an expectation; passive audience viewing is at an end.

Main points:
A shift away from a passive audience to an active audience as there is a desire to interact with media content.
- Digital technology has allowed for a change in audience behaviour and expectations of media. Active audience participation is now an audience expectation, the desire to connect via live tweeting, or share opinions adds an added layer of engagement and enjoyment.
- Speed and user-generated content has seen a reduction in checks and balances due to the participatory and interactive experience. Traditional media has gatekeepers to filter content, user-generated content is unmediated.
- Shirky's theory shines a light on how traditional media companies have needed to adapt to accommodate the digital technology landscape in order to satisfy an active audience who want personalisation, engagement, and interactivity.
- The audience now has more power to shape media content as they can connect to the media producer in a more effective and timely manner via mechanisms such as social media comments, feedback loops, or fandom communities.

2010s

COMMUNICATION THEORIES
Application of Theories

> There are no right or wrong communication theories. Rather, when applying a theory to a text, look at the framework provided by the theory. Communication theories investigate the influence the media has on the audience or, they try to determine what the audience does with the media. On the following pages three communication theories have been applied to the 2015 documentary text *The True Cost* in order to gain an understanding of a variety of audience responses within different interpretative frameworks.

01 Uses & Gratifications

Uses and Gratifications Theory Applied To *The True Cost.*

Andrew Morgan's 2015 documentary *The True Cost* aims to convince its viewers that purchasing cheap, virtually disposable clothing comes at a hidden cost, paid for by the environment and sweat shop factory workers. Morgan leads his audience on a journey across many continents to enlighten them about large profit driven western garment companies who are outsourcing to third world factories to harness a cheap labour force, avoid safe work practices, and ignore environmental concerns. As a documentary, the film takes advantage of the audience's expectation of the genre's **codes and conventions**. By applying the **uses and gratifications theory**, which looks at what people do with the media, rather than what the media does to people, we can investigate if part of the audience's sense of **gratification** is derived from **decoding** the delivery of content in accordance with techniques aligned to the **perception of truth**.

Morgan **encodes** the film with chosen **codes and conventions** to position the audience to align with the **preferred meaning** of the text, that of questioning the validity of fast fashion by examining the impact it has on the environment and its human rights violations.

By applying the uses and gratifications theory we can further understand the text's meaning.

According to uses and gratifications theorists an audience engages with a text to **satisfy specific uses and to gratify needs.** Notable contributors to the field are Blumler and Katz (1972), Denis McQuail (1980s) and James Lull (1990), who promoted the idea that the audience engages with texts in order to gratify needs and desires, such as the **need for information or a desire to further explore their personal identity.** When applying this theory to *The True Cost* several factors can be extracted to align the audience's needs and desires with the text's preferred meaning.

Theorists who fall under the uses and gratifications umbrella have all, in some form, cited **information gathering** as one of the uses an audience gains from a text. Blumler and Katz termed it **surveillance**, McQuail simply named it **information**, and Lull proposed a concept of **competence and dominance** whereby the information gathered is used to conquer an argument. No matter what the name of the category, the audience can use the information

Communication theories

gathered from the documentary text to **gratifying the need for knowledge**. The significant amount of **statistical information** supplied by Andrew Morgan in *The True Cost* illustrates this point. He employs several documentary conventions to gratify the audience's thirst for knowledge or information. He uses **authority figures and statistics** which create an authorial voice and lend a sense of legitimacy to his content. For instance, Morgan explains the fashion industry spreads far and wide by claiming that 'one in every six people work in some part of the global fashion industry, making it the most labour dependent industry on earth,' he **relays knowledge based information** that the audience may have previously been unaware of. Morgan **narrates** over images of a large factory warehouse, showing line after line of women sitting at sewing machines, repeating the same procedural process. He states, 'Only ten percent of donated clothes get recycled or up cycled, and thrift stores can't sell a lot of the garments that come in, so they end up in landfill. This textile waste comes in at eleven million tons produced by America alone.' The viewer can **gratify their personal need for information** by learning about the detrimental effects of fast fashion on the environment and its human capital. The accumulation of specific information fulfils a need for knowledge and allows for **gratification to occur through learning**.

The documentary **common man** technique is employed by Morgan to position the audience to sympathise with his **point of view** on fast fashion and create a link between himself and his audience. In his **expository voiceover** he remarks 'I went into this story without having any experience in fashion, starting with only a few simple questions. What I've discovered, has forever changed how I think about the clothes I wear, and my hope is that you do the same thing.' Additionally, he mentions that the Rana Plaza collapse connected with him on a fundamentally moral level when he learned about the hidden side of fast fashion. The Rana Plaza was a building in Bangladesh that collapsed killing one thousand one hundred and thirty four garment factory workers and injuring numerous others. Morgan explains that the structural validity of the building had been called into question for some time; pointed out by the workers themselves who were forced to continue working in unsafe conditions. This **common man** technique connects with the uses and gratification theory by supplying the audience with a **pathway to connect and develop their personal identity.** Morgan asks the viewer to do this on a moral and ethical level, to put themselves in the place of the factory worker and question whether their moral compass sits comfortably with purchasing cheap fashion items made by workers being paid less than three dollars a day to work in an unsafe environment.

Morgan creates the **narrative as a journey** which the audience can participate in, add to, and assist with resolving. He does not claim to have all the answers in reducing the safety, environmental, and health impacts associated with fast fashion, but he hooks the audience into being **active**, he asks them to engage and prove their **personal identity** by making statements such as 'It's over to you' or 'Will we continue to turn a blind eye to the lives of those who are behind our clothes?'

McQuail's furthering of the **personal identity** category within the **uses and gratifications theory** highlights the understanding that viewing a text can act as a guide to understanding normal behaviours

Communication theories

and values. Morgan employs this by appealing to the audience's moral principles and asking them to question whether it is morally acceptable to allow garment factory employees to continue to work in unsafe conditions, on low pay, and with no regard for the environment, all for the sake of western fast fashion trends. The audience is asked to question western, materialistic, consumer capitalist habits and question their own role, moral compass, and **personal identity** in relation to their engagement with the fast fashion process.

Furthermore, McQuail suggests that the media can be employed to satisfy the 'use' of **integration and social interaction** which he aligns with social empathy, or

the ability to gain insight and see another perspective on an issue. In *The True Cost* Morgan positions his audience to align with the character of Shima Akhter, a twenty three year old Bangladeshi garment factory worker. Morgan **gratifies** the audience's desire to empathise with others by aligning Shima with the universally identifiable **familial ideology.** He portrays her in mid-shot, standing with her young daughter, tears in her eyes, voice cracking, as she discusses how she has to bring her daughter to the factory even though it is very hot and there are 'chemicals inside the factory which are harmful' she continues to explain that there is no-one else to look after her daughter in the city, and so she must leave her

with family in the country, and therefore does not get to see her for months at a time. The universal identification with the right of the child to be safe, loved, and nurtured is brought into question as Morgan plays on the audience's ability to empathise. He evokes the **integration and social interaction category** within the uses and gratifications theory by playing on the value of humanitarianism, asking the audience to sympathise or empathise with Shima as a victim of the fast fashion industry.

Additionally, he positions the audience to align with Shima by intercutting the story of her life as a **mini-narrative** and presenting images of the hardships she suffers as a result of the fast fashion industry. Specifically, Morgan constructs Shima as proactive, positive, and kind, only wanting to improve her world and her workplace. He **narrates** Shima's story of trying to set up a union to create better working conditions only to be beaten, stabbed with scissors, punched, and kicked after requesting a salary rise to the minimum liveable wage, and asking for safe and humanitarian working conditions. The image shown is of Shima, in a mid-shot, relaying her personal story to Morgan, who is just off camera. The **personal appeal** is used to enforce the audience's **value of security, fairness,** and **humanitarianism,** and gratifies their need for **information and personal identity.**

The uses and gratification theory maintains that the audience (according to Blumler and Katz) is

Communication theories

'sufficiently self-aware' to explain their reasons for using a media text. They are **active participants** in the creation of meaning. In the process of the active audience gratifying a use or desire the question is raised as to whether the 'use' or 'gratification' in relation to the reception of statistical information such as 'the fashion industry, a $2.3 trillion dollar sector is the second most polluting industry on earth, to oil' or emotional manipulation though characters such as Shima Akhter who struggle to maintain a basic living as a garment factory worker, and later, we see her at home in her rural village where she emotionally introduces us to her parents who she rarely gets to see as the camera follows her embracing her mother, **does the content gratify an emotional or educational need**?

Morgan uses this emotional platform to segue into an **interview** with Shima outside her family home, where she implores the audience to consider who made their clothes. She declares, 'People have no idea how difficult it is for us to make the clothing. They only buy it and wear it. I believe the clothes are produced by our blood.' Does the **selection** of emotionally charged information and the heavy reliance on **documentary conventions** such as statistical information translate into action? Does the audience make a behavioural shift in their fashion purchasing habits? Do they consider the environment and the concept of fair trade before purchasing clothing items? Do they abandon fast fashion and instead consider the longevity of a clothing item, willingly paying more to ensure the money trickles back to the factory garment worker? Is the audience **sufficiently self-aware** in the viewing process to actively engage with the content and make a difference? Or did they simply watch the program to **gratify a need** for entertainment and have no intention of taking it any further?

Critics of the theory suggest that audiences do not necessarily have a **predetermined purpose** for their viewing choice. There may not be an active, **goal orientated use or gratification** being sought or obtained by the audience. By happenstance, an audience member landing upon *The True Cost,* decides to view it, and by default, will **extract a use or gratification** of some sort; be it surveillance, diversion, personal relationships, or personal identity. Supporters of the theory, however, argue that as the audience member has actively chosen to view the text, and has not changed channels or left the cinema theatre, therefore a degree of selectivity has occurred.

Notwithstanding, an audience, choosing to engage with the documentary *The True Cost*, does so, according to the uses and gratification theory, in order to **fulfil a need or gratify a desire**; be it the need for entertainment, information or self-reflection on their identity. Andrew Morgan does not disappoint, supplying a plethora of statistical information, engaging emotive appeal to allow for reflection on personal identity, and rounding it off by gratifying a modern audience's desire for entertainment.

Communication theories

02 Agenda Setting Theory

Agenda Setting Theory Applied To *The True Cost.*

The agenda setting theory developed by Maxwell McCombs and Donald Shaw in the 1970s puts forward the idea that the **media cannot tell us what to think but can tell us what to think about.** The theory suggests that the power of the media lies in how it filters and shapes how an audience might engage with issues through **framing (selection and omission), priming (allocating time and space to an issue),** and **gatekeeping (people such as producers and directors who filter content).** The main characteristics of framing, priming, and gatekeeping can be applied to better understand how the audience varies in their interpretation of the text.

The theory states that a text's content is **framed** via certain techniques such as deliberate and considered **selection and omission** of content that moulds the text's preferred meaning. *The True Cost,* a 2015 documentary by Andrew Morgan introduces the filmmaker's position on the fast fashion industry via a **non-diegetic voiceover** stating, 'This is a story about clothes, ... poverty, and greed.' He unequivocally reveals his stance on the destructive impact fast fashion and mindless consumerism is having on the environment. Additionally, Morgan explores the oppression and disregard for the lives of third world factory garment workers and the heartless nature of capitalism. He **selects** a specific **discourse**, when discussing the environment and working conditions that includes words such as 'dying planet', 'vulnerable', 'catastrophic' and 'horror story,' coupled with **montages** interspersed throughout the narrative of fashion models on catwalks and designers based in first world countries, contrasted with workers in third world countries working in harsh, cramped, unsafe conditions, painstakingly making each garment on old sewing machines. These **images are anchored** by comments from television celebrities such as Stephen Colbert who point out, 'The global marketplace, where we export work to have happen in whatever condition we want, and then the product comes back to me cheap enough to throw away without thinking about it,' highlights how **framing** is implemented within the text, forcing the viewer to confront the so called 'invisible cost' of the outsourcing of labour.

A sub-category of framing is **emphasis,** Morgan **emphasises** the inhumane and unsafe working conditions endured by workers in Bangladesh who work for fast fashion manufacturers. He uses **archival footage** and a **montage** of emotionally captivating images such as Bangladeshi women at home with their young children engaged in familial activities which engender emotions of caring, nurturing, and sympathy. The **selection** of this emotional footage

Communication theories

is accompanied by the **voiceover** of Lucy Siegle, a journalist and writer on environmental issues, who questions the capitalist model of the enormous garment industry companies such as Zara and H&M who generate an incredible profit for only a handful of people, '...why is it that it is unable to support millions of its workers properly? Why is it that is not able to guarantee their safety? We're talking about essential human rights. Why is it unable to guarantee that whilst generating these tremendous profits?' The **emphasis** of what Ms Siegle is saying is displayed as a **binary opposition** that creates a clear emotional divide by showing the haves and the have nots. The viewer sees a polluted river filled with small rickety crafts carrying workers to and fro, we are invited inside the corrugated tiny homes of the Bangladeshi workers, and these images are juxtaposed with the light, airy, large room, we assume, based on the western luxury mise-en-scène, is Lucy Siegel's home. By making the contrast so great, Morgan is vilifying the large garment companies by **emphasising the stark difference** between third world sweat shop garment workers, and the first world consumers who often show little regard for their efforts.

Additionally, Morgan **selects and emphasises** the 2013 Rana Plaza building collapse in Dhaka, Bangladesh. The commercial eight storey building housed shops, apartments, a bank, with the top four floors being devoted to a garment factory. Structural damage was evidenced in the building days before its collapse. Despite being aware of the safety hazards, workers were ordered to return to the building. The building collapsed on the 24th of April, leaving 2500 people injured and 1,134 people dead. To expose and **emphasise the scale of the tragedy** Morgan includes a **montage of archival news clips** showing powerful footage of the result of cost cutting and disregarding of safety measures within the fast fashion industry. Viewers are shown the collapsed Rana Plaza building,

hectic scenes of emergency workers, coupled with diegetic wailing and crying of women **emphasise the primal heartache** caused by the unnecessary loss of loved ones. The shift from loud crying to a quieter rural setting immediately gives prominence to the **interview** being conducted with a survivor of the Rana Plaza collapse. The audience is positioned to see a young woman in mid-shot describing her harrowing experience to Morgan. She recounts how she tried to get to the stairs, but as she reached them the building collapsed, trapping both of her legs. The shot size switches to a long shot, revealing that the woman is sitting in a wheelchair and has had both legs amputated. The **selection and emphasis** of the Rana Plaza collapse and its victims encourages the audience to **vilify the fast fashion industry** and reflect on how their fast fashion shopping habit impacts others.

Priming is an integral aspect of **agenda setting;** it seeks to allocate importance to the **time, space, and position** given to media items and content. Within *The True Cost* Morgan accords more screen time to Shima Akhter, a young Bangladeshi garment factory worker. By interspersing her personal story throughout the narrative Morgan creates an **emotional pathway** between her and the audience. He initially depicts her via long shot, crouching next to her child outside her city home using a bucket of water to wash her daughter's face and hands. The shot changes to Shima walking along a crowded, dirty street, holding the hand of her daughter. Morgan narrates, 'Shima is one of about forty million garment

Communication theories

factory workers in the world. Almost four million of them are here in Bangladesh working in almost five thousand factories making clothing for major western brands. Over 85% of these workers are women, and with a minimum wage of less than $3 a day they are among the lowest paid garment workers in the world.' **Somber music plays** as we see Shima sewing garments on an old machine, a practice repeated by the numerous other women surrounding her in the crowded factory.

The screen **time and space** given to the **selection** of Shima Akhter, a twenty three year old factory worker constitutes a **mini narrative** within the documentary. Morgan uses her **point of view** and emotional appeal to tell the tale of her journey as a Bangladeshi garment factory worker. The audience is directed to connect with her emotional journey by **emphasising the pain and suffering** caused by Akhter having to leave her daughter in her local village to be cared for by relatives as Akhter cannot afford the cost of childcare on her salary of $3 a day. The audience is positioned to see the hardship she suffers by not being able to be with her child for months at a time. This connection aligns the audience with Akhter's **point of view** when we see footage of the Rana Plaza disaster showing its collapse and learning about the eventual deaths of over one thousand people. This incident led to Akhter forming a union that submitted a list of demands to the employer. The demands were not well received and resulted in Akhter being beaten. Morgan portrays this scene by keeping the camera on Shima and allowing her personalised story to seep into the minds of the viewer. There is no need for **visual re-enactments** as the emotion in Shima's voice as she relays how she was locked in a room and attacked by thirty to forty staffers who beat her with sticks, chairs, scales, and scissors for daring to question structural poverty and human rights violations experienced by her and her co-workers is distressing.

Morgan uses **priming** to scaffold his point of view by according Shima numerous interviews and a large amount of screen time. In contrast, the time given to business owners of large corporate fashion companies is negligible. Morgan, does however, offer a counterargument which is delivered by Benjamin Powell, Director of the Free Market Institute and author of *Out of Poverty,* and Kate Ball-Young, the former sourcing manager for Joe Fresh. Ms Ball-Young states that, 'there is nothing intrinsically dangerous with sewing clothes' in comparison to other jobs

such as mining. She is supported by Benjamin Powell who reminds the viewer that the alternatives for people working in third world countries are not the same alternatives for people who live in first world countries. A safety net of welfare does not exist and therefore a job, although unsafe and low paying, is better than no job at all. He argues, 'This low wage manufacturing or so called 'sweatshops,' they're not just the least bad option workers have

Communication theories

today, they are part of the very process that raises living standards and leads to higher wages and better working conditions over time.' Morgan includes a shot of Fox News presenter Kennedy who speculates, 'Is it possible that sweatshops are actually good?' The shot changes to Kennedy interviewing Benjamin Powell who has been asked to define sweatshops, 'We're talking about places with very poor working conditions as us normal Americans would experience it, very low wages by our standard, maybe children working places that might not obey local labour laws but there's a key characteristic ... and that's that they're places where people choose to work, admittedly from a bad set of options.' The time allocated to the **counterargument** given by Powell and Ball-Young is approximately two and half minutes and its position in the narrative is sandwiched between Morgan's exposition and his supporting arguments. The use of **priming**, specifically **allocating minimal time** and the **placement** of the counterargument, between two deductive arguments, attempts to nullify the counterargument.

Gatekeeping, within the agenda setting theory, refers to people, such as producers and directors who decide (through **selection and omission**) the content of texts. These decisions are based on the agenda of the production company, its ethos and values, deadlines and policies. *The True Cost* was produced by Andrew Morgan's Untold Creative company in association with Life is My Movie Entertainment. The film was written and directed by Morgan and included in its list of executive producers are Livia Firth and Lucy Siegle. In terms of **gatekeeping** why is this important? Executive producers are often a source of funding for films, either contributing to it themselves or finding backers. As both Siegle and Firth are executive producers for the film, and appear in the documentary, their desire to act as completely **impartial gatekeepers** is something to keep in mind. Lucy Siegle is an author and journalist who writes on environmental issues and ethical consumerism for the BBC, The Guardian, and The Observer. Livia Firth is the founder of Eco Age, a consultancy company that works to bring about sustainable change to industries such as fashion and jewellery by giving them clear connections to fair trade dealers within the supply chain. Her company highlights the need for championing the environment and ensuring workers are not exploited. Considering their values, their desire to advocate for the environment and low paid third world garment workers comes as no surprise.

The **budget** for the film was half a million dollars. It was partly financed by Kickstarter crowdfunding where nine hundred and three backers pledged $76,546. The pitch on the Kickstarter website, which was used to raise money prior to production, included the film's **agenda** of highlighting the unsustainable environmental impacts of fast fashion, as well as its human cost. Accountability exists within the Kickstarter fund raising structure to ensure that filmmakers deliver what has been promised. **Gatekeeping**, therefore, in terms of **selection and omission** of content, needed to further the film's agenda to ensure it delivered on what was promised.

Andrew Morgan's company Untold Creative has a history of using films to communicate social and

Communication theories

human rights issues such as discussing grief and loss in *After the End*, and religion's connection with science in *The Heretic*. The films and television series made by Untold Creative engage with issues that shape our lives, Morgan's narratives encourage the viewer to delve deeper into events and issues and reconsider how they contribute to making the world a better place. In terms of **gatekeeping** his values align strongly with his film production company's ethos and moral direction to create a better world.

The **gatekeepers** of *The True Cost* have a role in shepherding the content of the film, funnelling it through the lens of their **ideological agenda**. Their interest in the environment and social justice issues forms the framework for the film, and through careful **selection and omission** allows for a narrative to be built that reflects their humanitarian and environmental ideals.

The **agenda setting theory**, through **priming, framing,** and **gatekeeping** has incorporated a selection of codes and conventions that position the audience to engage with Andrew Morgan's stance on ethical consumerism, to reveal worker exploitation in third world countries, and to understand the dire effect the fast fashion industry is having on the environment. Morgan constructs a film that removes the smoke and mirror aesthetic manipulation and instead shows the devastating true cost of the fast fashion industry. His **agenda** is clear as he pleads with all involved, including the consumer, to make sure this fast fashion cycle does not continue unhindered.

Communication theories

03 Reception Theory

Reception Theory Applied To *The True Cost*.

The 2015 documentary *The True Cost,* directed by Andrew Morgan journeys through the production and manufacturing stages of the fast fashion industry revealing its underbelly in the form of negative environmental impacts due to the overuse of toxic chemicals, the significant amount of landfill caused by the disposal of unwanted fashion items, and the effect the low-pay-high-profit paradigm has on the workers who produce cheap, virtually disposable fashion items.

Stuart Hall's **encoding/decoding** theory (1980) contributed significantly to **Reception Theory** by stating that texts are **polysemic** or have more than one meaning. Audiences differ in their **ideological beliefs and values** and will make a different reading of a text depending on whether it aligns with their value system. Texts such as *The True Cost* are polysemic and meaning emerges from a **context** dependent process of interpretation. Therefore, an audience's reception context becomes important when **decoding** the **preferred, negotiated, or oppositional readings** of the text. Audience decoding of the text can, and does, diverge depending on the viewers' demographic metrics.

The **preferred meaning** of *The True Cost* is **encoded** using **codes and conventions.** Hall's model of encoding and decoding relies on the sender and

receiver sharing an understanding of the codes and conventions used to construct the message. A successful or **dominant reading** of the text would occur if the audience members' values and beliefs align with Andrew Morgan's and they engage critically with the human rights violations, structural poverty, and the environmental unsustainability revealed in the fast fashion industry. Morgan **encodes** meaning by incorporating a documentary **testimonial device**. He uses twenty three year old Bangladeshi garment factory worker, Shima Akhter, to emotionally engage the audience with the harsh realism of her working life. We first met Shima interacting with her young daughter in a familial manner. The intimate task of washing her daughter's face and brushing her hair is one recognisable to all and creates a nurturing caring atmosphere. Thus, when Morgan presents Shima in a mid-shot as she relays how she was locked in a room and attacked by thirty to forty staffers who

Communication theories

beat her with sticks, chairs, scales, and scissors for daring to form a union and submit a list of requests that included a pay rise to cover minimum living costs, we identify with her right not to be violated, and to try and rise above structural poverty. The **preferred meaning** of the text aligns with the viewers **values and ideologies** of humanitarianism, equality, fairness, and workplace safety. The viewer can sympathise with Shima's lack of workplace rights, therefore a **dominant reading** of the text is achieved.

The **encoding** of the **preferred message** continues with the use of the documentary techniques such as **archival footage** and **authorial voice.** Morgan shows a **montage** of news clips from CNN portraying the devastating Rana Plaza collapse. The reporter's **voiceover** states, 'Many survivors are asking how they could have been forced to return to work when management already was aware of the cracks in the building and workers' concerns on the very day of the collapse.' The **montage** continues with a newsreader from CBS who states, 'A lot of clothes in American stores are made in Bangladesh by workers who earn about $2 a day. Last month there, a garment factory collapsed, killing more than one thousand, and a few months before that, a factory fire killed more than one hundred.' The **voiceover** is accompanied by **sombre music** and a slide show of still images depicting the collapsed building, relatives weeping over bodies in a makeshift morgue, a pool of blood, and scenes of the evacuation as bodies are pulled out of the rubble of the collapsed Rana Plaza building. As a **documentary technique** the news footage shown, and the authority attributed to the news anchor creates a sense of authenticity and power, legitimising Morgan's **preferred meaning**. His underlying **values and ideologies** of humanitarianism, ethical consumerism, and anti-corporate greed are embedded in the footage and clearly **anchored in the voiceover** positioning the intended audience with a similar value set to have a dominant or **preferred reading** of the documentary.

The **preferred meaning** that the environment is not an infinite resource to be used and abused is aligned with the intended audience's **ideology** of environmental sustainability. As the narrator's voiceover is a key **documentary convention** that directs the audience towards the **preferred meaning** it is justifiable that Morgan points out that, 'Fashion

today is the number two most polluting industry on earth, second only to the oil industry.' Morgan continues to hit home his point by cutting to Mike Schragger, founder of Sustainable Fashion Academy, who is framed in mid-shot saying, 'Because they've been so abundant, these resources, it's been assumed that they're going to be there forever.' Morgan then cuts to environmentalist Vandana Shiva who notes, 'The first economy on which our lives rest is nature's economy. Nature has an economy. That economy is huge. It's not counted.' The use of **repetition as a device** to emphasise the importance of the environment and the cost we are all paying at its expense is effective in highlighting how fast fashion is draining our natural resources. The capitalist ideology and associated consumer materialistic desire lies at the root of the problem. *The True Cost* carries the **ideological message** of the imperative for environmental sustainability and suggests a change is needed in the capitalist mode of

Communication theories

production. A **preferred reading** of the text is achieved if this message aligns with the intended audience's pre-existing **value system** of environmental concern and an awareness of the harm caused by over consumption.

Stuart Hall's reception theory proposes that meaning is not absolute or fixed, an audience can have three main responses to a text - **dominant, negotiated, or oppositional**. A **negotiated reading** of a text occurs when the audience understands the dominant or

preferred position but doesn't necessarily subscribe fully to that ideology. In *The True Cost* the **ideologies** of environmental sustainability, humanitarianism, and ethical consumerism occupy positions of primacy in the text. As multiple factors such as age, culture, and gender influence the audience to **decode** a text differently a **negotiated reading** can occur with audience members who understand Morgan's humanitarian and environmental intent but question his attacks on capitalism as he fails to offer any viable alternative solution.

When we consider audience members bring different life experiences to the viewing of a text we might find divergence away from the **preferred reading**. A **negotiated reading** could occur on behalf of audience members who do believe in capitalism as an ideology but do not engage in over-consumption. The concept of consumer-capitalism is depicted by Morgan when he shows **archival footage** of YouTube clothing haul videos. The audience is shown several young women pulling clothing items out of numerous shopping bags from Zara, H&M, and Forever 21. We hear one young woman explain, 'I went shopping and literally went insane and bought so many things.' Another YouTube presenter exclaims, 'I don't even know if I'm going to wear this, now that I got it, because I don't know if I like it that much.' Morgan constructs these young YouTube presenters as shallow, being focused solely on materialism and consumerism to feed their self-esteem. Audience members with different life experiences may make a **negotiated reading** as part, but not all of the content, aligns with their **value system**. They may view capitalism as necessary to produce free markets that allow for industries such as fashion to flourish, however, they do not agree with over-consumption and the unethical and environmentally dangerous waste that this entails.

An **oppositional reading** is deemed to occur when audience members reject the message altogether as it does not align with their **values and ideologies.** Viewers whose values align more with Benjamin Powell and Kate Ball-Young would **reject the preferred meaning** of the text, instead opting for the **oppositional reading** that sweat shops are not inherently bad as they do offer a form of employment, be it unsafe and low paying, but better than the alternative, which we are led to believe is unemployment and eventual starvation. Benjamin Powell, Director of the Free Market Institute and author of *Out of Poverty* and Kate Ball-Young, the former sourcing manager for Joe Fresh, offer a counterargument within the documentary. Mr Powell asserts that in relation to sweatshops that, 'They are not just the least bad option workers have today, they are part of the very process that raises living standards and leads to higher wages and better working

Communication theories

conditions over time.' His argument is that sweatshops stimulate the economy they are based in, and rather than viewing them as villainous we should see them for the positive employment benefits they provide. Powell states that although people in the West may view the working conditions in sweatshops as unsafe and the wages as paltry, he asks that we consider what other employment alternatives there are for the millions of people who are unskilled labourers. His **counterargument** is supported by Ms Ball-Young who states that, 'There is nothing intrinsically dangerous with sewing clothes. We're starting out with a relatively safe industry. It's not like coal mining or natural gas mining.' Right wing conservative viewers could identify with Powell and Ball-Young as their desire to justify the growth and momentum needed to sustain **capitalism** outweighs any misgivings they may have about the **environmental** or **humanitarian** costs associated with fast fashion. The **oppositional reading** isn't just about embracing capitalism at all costs, it is about being realistic and answering the questions Morgan is not prepared to answer in his documentary. If impoverished third world people do not work in sweat shops or something similar, what happens to them? Audience members whose life experiences, values and ideologies do not align with the text may reject its message as they have decoded the signifiers and arrived at an **oppositional reading.** Their reading is not pleasant, it is not a fairy tale ending, but it is realistic, arriving at the conclusion that sweat shops do offer a small lifeline to impoverished workers.

Stuart Hall, in his **reception theory** examines how an audience uses and consumes media through his encoding/decoding model to arrive at a preferred, negotiated, or oppositional reading of the text. Hall proposed that all stages of the model are equally relevant in creating meaning, from production through to consumption. Part of the reception model Hall termed as '**reproduction**.' Here he looked at whether the viewer had been influenced after decoding the message, had they been entertained or affected enough to take action? In *The True Cost,* after raising awareness of the effects of fast fashion, Morgan ultimately concludes that the power lies with the consumer, they hold the ability to withhold their fashion dollars and make the fashion companies more accountable. He urges the audience to engage with the Fashion Revolution campaign by going to fashionrevolution.org. Here consumers are urged to act by using the hash tag #whomademyclothes? The **active audience** drives the Fashion Revolution campaign by reminding large garment companies that consumers want ethical, sustainable, and environmentally aware fashion, not fast disposable fashion.

Unlike other media theories, Hall focused heavily on the **decoding process.** A successful decoding process results in a **dominant preferred reading** of the message and is based on the sender and receiver sharing similar context created **values and ideologies** as the creator and receiver of the message. Andrew Morgan's film *The True Cost* embeds a **preferred meaning** that targets the consumer **capitalistic ideology** and tries to dissuade viewers from buying into the fast fashion conveyor belt of excess consumption. Additionally, Morgan covers the universally identifiable topics of environmental sustainability, social inequality, structural poverty and human rights violations. His model allows for audience members to mentally subscribe to, **negotiate, or reject** the preferred meaning due to factors such as race, class, age or gender.

Review and sample questions

Sample questions containing communication theories:

1. Analyse how a communication theory can be applied to understanding media content.
2. Using a communication theory, discuss the role of the audience in deconstructing meaning.
3. Discuss how a media theory can explain media influence on its intended audience.
4. Discuss how audience values and attitudes shape their interpretation of a media text.
5. Analyse the role of media in reinforcing or challenging audience perception of social norms.
6. Discuss how context affects audience interpretation of media content.

COMMUNICATION THEORIES & AUDIENCE - main essential content to discuss:

01
- The **intended audience** is a collective group with some shared demographic metrics who engage with the media content.
- A **mainstream audience** is a diverse, large group and therefore media content appeals to popular values to ensure mass appeal.
- A **niche audience** has media content tailored to their specific beliefs, interests, values, and specialisation. The content targets the smaller audience segment in a focused manner.

02
- **Demographic metrics** shape the filmmaking process. Ensure you know the composition of the audience by analysing socio-demographics, psychographics, and geographic variables to determine how they position the intended audience to deconstruct the text.

03
- The **audience's reception context** will shape how they decode meaning. The **production context** of a text will influence its content. Consider the reception context in relation to the production context. Context will always affect content.

04
- **Communication theories** provide a framework to analyse the connection between media, society, and people. Consider:
  - Hypodermic needle theory
  - Two step flow theory
  - Reinforcement theory
  - Diffusion of innovation
  - Agenda setting theory
  - Uses and gratifications
  - Spiral of silence
  - Semiotic theory
  - Cultivation theory
  - Reception theory
  - Fandom theory
  - End of audience

Chapter Eleven
Documentary Techniques

- Documentary defined
- Documentary conventions
- Documentary techniques
- Bill Nichols: documentary modes
- The documentary dilemma
- Documentaries to watch
- Documentary deconstruction: *The True Cost*
- Sample questions
- Review

Documentary Techniques

Documentary

> "In feature films the director is God; in documentary films God is the director."
>
> Alfred Hitchcock

Can a documentary provide the viewer with an unbiased truth?

Audience expectations of the documentary genre are:
- the content deals with real world occurrences and issues,
- uses real people and not fictional characters,
- the events are not staged, rather what occurs in front of the camera is unscripted, and is observed and presented to the audience with minimal mediation and intervention on behalf of the filmmaker,
- the narrative structure allows for engagement in terms of entertainment, information, and education.

Documentaries are a slice of real life, constructed by filmmakers who make copious decisions about what story to tell, who to tell it to, and for what purpose.

A documentary aims to construct a convincing sense of truth and has the potential to influence the beliefs and attitudes of its audience.

> " A documentary, like any text, be it fiction or non-fiction, is a construction. It is a representation of an event, issue or person, not the reality itself.

Documentary Techniques

Documentary

Subjective vs. Objective

The documentary form, as a non-fiction text is associated with realism, with its aim being to convey factual information about a social or political message. A documentary, like any text, be it fiction or non-fiction, is a construction. It is a representation of an event, issue or person, not the reality itself. The representation shows the viewer a small 'window on the world.' The perspective given through this metaphorical window contains the point of view of the filmmaker and has a preferred meaning created through selection and omission of information, choice of codes, and structuring of the narrative. As a carefully crafted construction, documentaries contain the bias, perspective, agenda, and aesthetics of the filmmaker. The challenge for the audience is to interpret the information critically, to question the nature of objective reality versus subjective perception.

Documentaries use the fundamental relationship humans have with storytelling as a basis for engaging the audience with their content.

- Like fiction film, documentaries still need to consider the importance of narrative structure and narrative elements.
- The narrative structure may be linear cause and effect, starting with a specific cause and logically revealing the effects. Or the narrative structure may be non-linear.
- A narrative arc that includes rising tension, obstacles in the way of achieving the goal, a climactic moment, and a conclusion are important for audience engagement.
- Narrative elements, including characters such as a host, setting (often involves binary oppositions), conflict to elicit emotion, and often a conclusion rather than a resolution shape meaning.

Documentary films manipulate their content through construction processes consisting of numerous decisions in relation to:

- choice of topic
- voiceover and discourse used to position the audience
- presence of the camera and crew — how do they influence the unfolding events?
- technical codes: lighting, camera angles, camera movement, framing
- audio codes: mode of address, diegetic/non-diegetic music and sound effects, dialogue and narration
- written codes: how do they anchor meaning?
- choice of visual information such as graphics, archival footage, visual effects
- editing: pace, placement, duration
- use of binary oppositions — is space made for a competing discourse?

DOCUMENTARY
Conventions, Modes, Language & Techniques

Documentary Conventions

- voiceover
- testimonial, interview
- archival footage
- black & white footage
- authority figures
- exposition
- juxtaposition
- re-enactment

Documentary Modes

- poetic
- observational
- expository
- participatory
- performative
- reflexive

Persuasion Techniques

- bandwagon
- assertion
- card stacking
- glittering generalities
- name calling
- oversimplification
- stereotyping
- common man

Terminology

- discourse
- representation
- globalisation
- cultural imperialism
- agenda setting
- rhetoric
- propaganda

Documentary Conventions

Documentary techniques used to create a sense of realism.

- **1. Voiceover Narration**
  Positions the audience using specific discourse and rhetoric to direct them to accept the filmmaker's point of view. The choice of language is often emotive and value laden, thus assisting the audience to align with the filmmaker's perspective.

- **2. Testimonial, Interview**
  The recording of information or opinion by witnesses, experts, or other participants. May involve direct address to the camera, or a voiceover which lends authority.

- **3. Black and White Footage**
  Historical attachment with news and history makes it appear more authentic.

- **4. Re-enactments**
  Attempt to represent events and people in such a way that they construct a sense of realism. It can position the audience to believe it is a truthful depiction of events.

- **5. Archival or Stock Film Footage**
  Carries a degree of credibility because of the fact it was considered important to be stored in the first place, includes stills, news footage...

- **6. Juxtaposition**
  Use of binary oppositions to make a point.

- **7. Exposition**
  Use of a voiceover or direct address at the beginning of the film to provide the central themes and argument.

- **8. Authority Figures/Expert**
  Associated with specialist knowledge, an expert in their field. An authority figure adds weight and credibility, serving as the support system for the central documentary argument.

- **9. Emphasis**
  Repetition of visuals or repeating the central thesis. By harnessing the similar but slightly differing points of view of authority figures, witnesses, and participants, emphasises the topic's importance.

- **10. Statistics**
  The use of facts and figures to persuade the audience about the validity of the documentary's claims.

- **11. Montage**
  A sequence of visuals placed together in a specific order to elicit an emotional response. Used as a device to manipulate time and space.

- **12. Actuality Footage**
  The unscripted, raw footage of real events as they unfold in real time, about real people, in real places.

- **13. Selection & Omission**
  Material is selected or omitted to support the argument and create a cohesive narrative.

- **14. Emotive Appeal**
  Appealing directly to the audience's emotions motivates and potentially provokes the audience into action.

Persuasive Techniques

Documentary propaganda techniques used to persuade the audience of a point of view.

1. Bandwagon
Jump on the bandwagon, do the same as everyone else, links to fear of missing out. Encourages people to adopt a belief or behaviour to fit in.

2. Card stacking
Telling a small portion of the truth. Influencing the audience by stacking the deck in the user's favour. Selects certain information and deliberately omits any opposing views.

3. Glittering Generalities
Use of appealing, simplistic, yet vague words to elicit a positive response. E.g., a brighter future, make America great again, or change we can believe in. Words are vague enough to allow people to insert their own interpretation.

4. Name calling
Used to label a group, person or idea and cause division and fear. Used as a derogatory technique to attack rather than having to address the argument or issue at hand.

5. Oversimplification
Very simplistic solutions presented for complex problems. Ignores specific details.

6. Stereotyping/labelling
Using a few codes of construction to represent the entire group causing generalisations and prejudice to arise.

7. Common man
Appears to show an everyday, no-nonsense common-sense approach, used to appear relatable and to gain trust from the audience.

8. Emotional appeal
Use of language or visuals to appeal to human emotions such as fear, isolation, belonging. Designed to influence attitudes and behaviours.

9. Scapegoating
Blaming others to distract from own flaws and avoid responsibility for failures.

10. Assertion
To assert that your point of view is factual not opinion based.

11. Repetition
Repeating a message until it appears natural and common-sense. Designed to reinforce the message through reiteration.

12. Transfer
Making an idea more palatable by transferring the power or authority from a well-known and liked person to make it appear more acceptable. Works equally well with negative qualities as the transfer assists to discredit the person, idea, or issue.

13. Testimonial
First-hand accounts are given to add weight and authenticity to the issue, idea or product, usually from an authority figure or celebrity.

14. Loaded Words
Influence the audience using emotionally charged words such as freedom, fight, security, prosperity or power as they evoke an emotional response and work to influence an audience's attitude through emotion.

Documentary Techniques | Documentary

Documentary films, like fiction films, involve choices about what codes and conventions are used to represent their version of reality. The querying of the notion of objectivity that surrounds documentaries arises from the tension existing between a documentary's claim to truth and accuracy, versus the actuality of choices made by documentary filmmakers when constructing their representation of an occurrence.

REALITY → **CHOICE OF CODES & CONVENTIONS** → **REPRESENTATION**

Such as:
- events
- issues
- people
- places
- nature
- occurrences

Choice of codes and conventions to shape reality:
- **Authorial voiceover** or personal voice.
- **Point of view** - from whose eyes do we see most of the event or issue unfold from?
- **Ordering of events** - how has the narrative been structured? How does the opening position the audience in relation to the issue or event? What content is **selected,** and what **omitted**?
- What **audio code** choices have been made? What does the music direct the audience to feel? What discourse underpins the narration? What dialogue has been included? Who does most of the speaking?

Representation of reality:
What we see in the documentary is not the actual reality, it is a selective view of reality **constructed from a choice of codes and conventions** that shape the validity and credibility of the filmmaker's message.

- Consider **technical codes** in terms of the choice of lighting, the duration of shots, who is afforded more close-ups, who or what is **emphasised** and repeated?
- How do **written codes** anchor meaning? What is the title of the documentary? How have titles been used to label people within the film?
- What **symbolic choices** have been made? What locations are used? If the documentary maker appears on film, what does he or she look like, formal or casual - why? What colours and objects are used?
- Consider if **conventions and techniques** such as statistics, re-enactments, archival footage, experts, testimonials, card stacking or common man are used — how do they shape the message?

DOCUMENTARY

The documentary dilemma

Documentary films claim the privileged position of telling the 'truth.' Unlike fictional texts that celebrate their constructed realism, documentary films often **disguise their construction**. Their role in society in delivering information is invaluable; however, it is important for audiences to recognise that a **documentary is a representation, a constructed version of reality** encoded by the filmmaker from a choice of codes and conventions that allows them to give voice to their issue and construct their narrative **point of view.**

Documentary filmmakers have an **agenda**, usually it is to relay information, uncover new facts, or present a side of the story that may not have been told. The filmmaker's agenda drives his or her **point of view.** The **selection, omission, and privileging** of certain information will be determined by their agenda.

When viewing a documentary ask yourself:
- How can a filmmaker tell the entire objective truth when the exercise of production suggests a **subjective process**?
- How can a film, which invariably has a **time constraint**, present information without **selection and omission**?
- What information is foregrounded or **emphasised**?
- From whose **point of view** does the narrative unfold?
- How does the presence of camera and crew impact or **manipulate** the actual event being filmed? Is reality altered because of their presence?
- Consider the connotations created by film language choices such as:
  - **Technical codes**: what shot sizes, camera angles, editing (sequencing of events), pacing (time spent on the main issue and counter issue) have been employed?
  - **Audio**: what voiceover, discourse, narrator, and music choices have been made to accompany the footage?
  - **Written titles**: how do they anchor meaning and position the audience?
  - **Symbolic codes**: how do the clothes worn by the presenter position the viewer? Are the clothes formal, such as a suit connoting professionalism, education and a sense of authorial distance from the viewer; or are they every-day common man clothes that suggest a sense of bonding and down-to-earth reliability on the part of the presenter? What settings have been chosen? Do they create binary oppositions? What colours are used?
- What is the filmmaker's **agenda**? How is the film being funded? Does the institution or money source come with an agenda attached?

A documentary is a filmmaker's observation, and subsequent **interpretation** of an event, issue, or occurrence. The fact that the filmmaking process mediates the issue, or event is not something to be villainised, it is simply that this carefully **crafted process** needs to be considered when digesting the information to determine the **bias, perspective,** and **agenda** embedded in the information.

DOCUMENTARY

The documentary's claim to truth

When viewing a documentary text, the audience uses their prior knowledge of the genre to decode documentary conventions in good faith. An **active audience** understands that conventions such as statistics, authorial voice, or even the use of an expert opinion is going to form a **degree of bias**, however, this does not necessarily make the text inaccurate, it simply means that a position is being put forward and the audience is asked to reflect on the accuracy of the information using their real life assertions or knowledge. The audience **actively** shapes meaning by comparing their life experiences and knowledge with that shown to them in the text.

Tension exists between the documentary's claim to truth and accuracy, and how the audience decodes the film's representation of reality. Documentary filmmakers choose certain **codes and conventions** to manipulate meaning to construct their chosen message. By choosing specific conventions such as testimonials, authority figures, voiceover, use of statistics and so on, the filmmaker enters an informal contract with the viewer that what is being presented has **credibility**. The historical legacy of the documentary form suggests that the validity of the genre remains. The informal contract between audience and filmmaker indicates that should the filmmaker deliberately set out to deceive, then the validity and legitimacy of the documentary form erodes; however, should the filmmaker's intention be decoded as honest and reliable then the audience is more likely to accept the credibility of the film's message. Therefore, the public's right to know information that is true and correct underpins the discourse shaping the documentary genre. The relationship between filmmaker and audience is built on a **foundation of trust and reassurance.** Documentaries can shape an audience's understanding of the world. Therefore, being active in decoding the codes and conventions used to shape the filmmaker's message allows for critical questioning of a necessary genre. Documentaries **give voice to issues**. They are an essential tool to critique a society, to allow citizen's the right to know, and to act as a watch dog to ensure ideal values are upheld in society.

Historically, documentaries, by their very nature involved a significant degree of **selection, omission and manipulation.** Early cameras were heavy and lacked mobility, when sound equipment entered the field it added a further degree of technical angst. It was not uncommon in a documentary to do many 'takes' to ensure technical quality. The realism of capturing what was unfolding before the camera was limited by the camera's lack of movement and the cords needed to connect sound recording equipment. Wireless technology had yet to be

> You don't get truth by turning on a camera you have to work with it. You don't get it by simply peep hole camera work. There is no such thing as truth until you have made it into a form. Truth is an interpretation, a perception."
>
> John Grierson

Documentary — Claims to truth

birthed and therefore early documentary topics were constrained by available resources. Early documentaries, known as 'actualities,' captured real life without including a narrative structure. For instance, the Lumière brothers 1896 actuality entitled *A Train Arrives at Ciotat Station* documents the train arriving at a station in one continuous long shot.

In contrast, *Nanook of the North,* a 1922 documentary filmed by Robert Flaherty has a cemented place in history as it is one of the first feature length documentary films, and more controversially, it **blended fact with faction**. Unlike actualities, Nanook of the North has a **clear narrative framework** as it follows the major characters of Nanook and his family who show how they survive in a barren, Arctic environment. The film uses written subtitles to convey information, frequently representing the Inuits through a colonial lens. The film pioneered technical and narrative innovations which laid the groundwork for the documentary genre. Flaherty included a clear **narrative structure in a non-fiction film** as he showed the daily struggles of Nanook's family as they hunted, traded, and built an igloo. The technical innovations included the mobility of his hand-cranked Akeley camera, the field processing of negatives, and the collaborative filmmaking process whereby Flaherty would often have Nanook and his family reinact events or stage them to ensure the required aspect was captured to allow for plot progression. The **authenticity and subjectivity** of documentary filmmaking has been questioned since the genre's inception. The audience needs to be aware of the **agenda, bias, and craft** of filmmaking when taking in its **preferred message**.

The advent of television saw a new outlet for a content hungry medium. Documentaries evolved to **entertain as well as inform** the audience. Structured narratives and engaging techniques such as **persuasive voiceovers, interviews, testimonials** and cinema vérité became popular. As an example, David Attenborough's expository documentary series *Zoo Quest* (1954-1967) used a scripted voiceover to anchor meaning to the visuals showing wild animals in their natural habitats and in so doing created a sub-genre of natural history documentaries with Attenborough's style, technique, and substance creating a high level of documentary filmmaking still followed today.

The rise of online platforms such as YouTube and TikTok have provided a new avenue for filmmakers to convey their message using the medium of film to address global and cultural issues. Traditional film outlets are influenced by **government censorship, editorial control, and regulatory bodies**. The decentralisation of social media platforms allows for a wider global audience reach; however, they do impose community guidelines and exert algorithmic control. For instance, TikTok's @60secdocs or YouTube's The New York Times' Op-Docs offer high quality, impactful short form documentaries that allow for immediate feedback and engagement to occur.

The evolving documentary form has seen a significant shift from capturing 'actualities' in a passive manner, to actively engaging the audience in real life issues using a combination of traditional media and social media to increase audience engagement, make content more accessible, allow for interactivity and connectivity, which then drives attitudinal and behavioural change.

A few Influential documentaries:
- Black Fish (2013)
- The Cove (2009)
- Gasland (2010)
- The True Cost (2015)
- The Social Dilemma (2020)

Documentary Modes — Bill Nichols

Bill Nichols, an American film scholar, in his 2001 book *Introduction to Documentary* theorised that documentaries could be **categorised** according to **common recurring features**. He created **six modes** that formed loose categories into which documentaries from particular eras and with particular traits could be categorised. The modes are not rigid, the lines can be blurred in that many documentaries are hybrids, falling into a number of Nichols' modes. He established a schema consisting of six main categories: poetic, expository, observational, participatory, reflexive, and performative. Although at times criticised for being too reductive and having inconsistencies, Nichols' documentary modes have stood the test of time in that they allow for categorisation according to the film grammar associated with documentaries to be clearly deconstructed using the given features of the modes.

Poetic Mode Documentary

Poetic Mode: Reassembling 'fragments of the world', the real world is shown through a non-linear, lyrical, abstract lens. Time and space are disrupted by using a montage of images arranged to evoke emotion. People exist on the same plain as any other living being. Meaning is created via visual and aural associations.

Examples of Poetic Mode Documentaries:
- Rain (1928) Joris Ivens
- Fata Morgana (1971) Werner Herzog
- Koyaanisqatsi (1982) Godfrey Reggio
- Baraka (1992) Ron Fricke
- Samsara (2011) Ron Fricke
- Sans Soleil (1982) Chris Marker

Poetic documentaries embraced the **non-narrative form** and were a reaction against linear-cause and effect structured editing. In order to engage the audience a **contrast** in pace, tone, colour, music, and fragmented visuals are used to create a representation of a place, issue, or mood. Often **binary oppositions** in terms of rhythm and arrangement of visuals emphasise the intended meaning by directing an active audience through association. The poetic mode is the filmmaker's **subjective aesthetic expression** of an aspect of the real world that is constructed to evoke emotion through creating associations between visuals, pace, patterns, and textures. The goal is to **evoke emotion** by creating a viewing experience that represents 'fragments of the real world' (Nichols: 2001).

Main features:
- Non-linear, fragmented, abstract, ambiguous.
- Evoke emotion rather than logic.
- Rhythm, pace, and visual tone emphasised.
- Meaning often created by juxtaposing images and/or sounds.

DOCUMENTARY

Bill Nichols Documentary Modes

Expository Mode: Often known as 'voice of God' or 'voice of authority' as its purpose is to directly address the viewer and propel the filmmaker's argument. The visual images illustrate and guide the viewer as a form of evidence to support the spoken argument and posit the preferred meaning.

Expository Mode Documentary

Examples of Expository Mode Documentaries:
- Nanook of the North (1922) Robert Flaherty
- The Plow That Broke the Plains (1936) Pare Lorentz
- Trance and Dance in Bali (1952)
- An Inconvenient Truth (2006) Davis Guggenheim
- Nature documentaries such as Sir David Attenborough's Frozen Planet or Planet Earth
- March of the Penguins (2005) Luc Jacquet
- Night Mail (1936) John Grierson
- Television news programmes

The **expository mode** uses the oldest form of documentary convention, the '**voice of God**'. The on-screen events are usually directly **narrated** from a script for the audience by an off-screen **omniscient voiceover**. The vision is explained and interpreted by the **authoritative sounding narrator**, and in so doing meaning is anchored by the choice of words whose connotations link meaning to the vision.

The **voice of authority** comes in the form of an **expert** such as a scientist, doctor or any specialist in the field under discussion. Moreover, additional documentary techniques such as **testimonials, archival footage, and interviews** are deployed as **tools of persuasion** which are designed to position the documentary maker's argument as common sense, logical, truthful, trustworthy, and objective.

The main aim of expository documentaries is to **educate** the audience about a specific topic, the content is researched, based on facts rather than opinions. Like all documentaries, selection and omission creates a directed **point of view** about the filmmaker's topic.

Main features:
- Authoritative 'voice of God' narration.
- What is heard relates directly to what is on the screen.
- A linear cause and effect narrative structure is used.
- Argumentative logic is present, filmmaker presents a clear preferred reading of the text.
- Objectivity is emphasised.

DOCUMENTARY

Bill Nichols Documentary Modes

Observational Mode Documentary

Observational Mode: The occurrence being filmed is **unstaged**, the filmmaker records the subject with minimal influence. The objective is to be a fly on the wall, to capture the essence of the subject as naturally and spontaneously as possible **without intervention**.

Examples of Observational Mode Documentaries:
- Titicut Follies (1967) Frederick Wiseman
- Hospital (1970) Frederick Wiseman
- Etre et Avoir (2002) Nicolas Philibert
- Hoop Dreams (1994) Steve James
- Public Housing (1997) Frederick Wiseman
- Salesman (1969) Albert Maysles, David Maysles, Charlotte Zwerin
- Armadillo (2011) Janus Metz Pedersen
- Seven Up (1964) Michael Apted (hybrid: also performative)
- Metallica: Some Kind of Monster (2004) Joe Berlinger and Bruce Sinofsky

The observational mode's style is described in its title — its purpose is to **observe in an unobtrusive manner**, allowing the action to unfold before the camera. The mode is derived from the cinéma vérité French film movement of the '60s which was characterised by natural actions, settings, and dialogue to capture occurrences as **realistically** as possible. The period saw the invention of smaller, more portable hand-held, inexpensive cameras, lenses that could shoot in low light, and less cumbersome synchronous sound recording devices which created the fertile ground for these types of documentaries to flourish. Documentaries that fall into this mode are categorised by conventions such as the use of location shooting, handheld camera work with excessive long takes, narration is frequently absent, common conventions such as formal interviews, or historical re-enactments do not occur, and the subject's being filmed do not break the fourth wall by speaking directly into the camera. The appeal of the style is in its **construction of authenticity**, the audience feels **voyeuristic**, as if they watching a private moment unfold.

Main features:
- No intervention, action is natural.
- Long takes and unobtrusive camera style dominates, voyeuristic style creates feeling of objectivity.
- Hand-held camera follows the action evoking a sense of immediacy and authenticity.
- Sound is synchronous (matches what is seen and creates realism).
- Shot on location.
- No voiceovers.

Documentary Modes

Bill Nichols

Participatory or Interactive Mode: as the title suggests, the filmmaker actively participates in the narrative, framing their point of view. They become a subject within the film who interacts with other subjects to direct the narrative.

Examples of Participatory Mode Documentaries:
- Behind Bars in San Quentin Prison - Louis Theroux: aired January 13 2008 on BBC
- Bowling for Columbine (2002) Michael Moore
- Sicko (2007) Michael Moore
- Icarus (2017) Bryan Fogel (Hybrid - performative)
- The Fog of War (2003) Errol Morris
- Kurt and Courtney (1998) Nick Broomfield
- Enron: The Smartest Guys in the Room (2005) Alex Gibney
- Supersize Me (2004) Morgan Spurlock (Hybrid - performative)

The **participatory mode** invites a **direct relationship** between the social **subject and filmmaker** who is seen directly involved with the lives of the film's subjects. The filmmaker asks questions, gently probes their subjects for more information, and shares their own experiences with the audience. This method of conveying information via **interviews and testimonials** is heavily reliant on the film subjects being truthful in their accounts as their retelling of events is considered a **credible source** of information. Equally, the narrative goal is made clear to the audience, **subjectivity is recognised** as the filmmaker's presence and influence on events is acknowledged. Indeed, the filmmaker's presence is critical to driving the narrative, the encounters he or she has is what allows for the **testimonials** to occur and the narrative to unfold via interviews which characterise this mode. The film's credibility is built on the variety and number of subject's interviewed whose voices are used to persuade the audience that what is being presented is **credible and accurate.**

Main features:
- The filmmaker is a central 'character' visible to the audience, interacting and speaking directly with the film's subjects.
- Shot on location, often with hand-held camera work.
- Informal interviews dominate, the source is considered credible and honest in their relaying of information.
- Voiceover narration by the documentary maker anchors meaning to the visuals.
- Archival footage is used to underpin importance of issues.
- Subjective point of view acknowledged.

Documentary Modes

Bill Nichols

Reflexive Mode Documentary

Reflexive Mode: The filmmaker deliberately experiments with and foregrounds the filmmaking process. The traditional seamless, invisible style is replaced with an acknowledged construction.

Examples of Reflexive Mode Documentaries:
- The Thin Blue Line (1988) Errol Morris
- The Man with a Movie Camera (1929) Dziga Vertov
- This is Spinal Tap (1984) Rob Reiner
- Exit Through the Gift Shop (2010) Banksy
- The Spaghetti Story (1957) BBC (Hybrid - expository)
- The War Game (1966) Peter Watkins

The **reflexive mode** acknowledges the artifice of the filmmaking process and deliberately **exposes or exaggerates** aspects of lighting, sound, cinematography or editing. The audience is encouraged to be very aware that what they are viewing is a **highly constructed version of reality**. In this mode the crew may be seen using a camera, or operating a boom microphone. Or, in the case of Errol Morris' *The Thin Blue Line*, the codes used to convey the events concerning the murder of a Dallas police officer are steeped in construction, coloured lighting connects to innocence and guilt, the exaggerated choice of codes reminds viewers that what they are seeing is a construction, not reality itself as Errol Morris deliberately draws attention to the **constructed nature of the narrative**. The theatrical and aesthetically manipulated re-enactment of the murder used in the film combine to form a cinematic style reminiscent of fiction film. The **audience is active** in deconstructing meaning, they are not told information from a 'voice of God' rather they are presented with raw material and asked to arrive at a conclusion using the filmmaker's signposts conveyed via editing, emotive music, and lighting.

Main features:
- Acknowledges the constructed nature of the filmmaking process.
- Appropriates fiction film techniques such as emotional engagement of the audience via dramatic music and lighting.
- Re-enactments act as suggestions rather than fact.
- Editing is deliberately manipulated to provoke questioning on the subjective nature of the filmmaking process.

DOCUMENTARY

Bill Nichols Documentary Modes

Performative Mode: these documentaries are often autobiographical in nature with the content being subjective and emotional as the filmmaker has a personal, passionate connection to it. The aim is to show a personal perspective regarding the event or issue.

Examples of Performative Mode Documentaries:
- Waltz with Bashir (2008) Ari Folman
- Tongues United (1989) Marion Riggs
- Night And Fog (1955) Alain Resnais
- Forest of Bliss (1986) Robert Gardner
- Paris Is Burning (1991) Jenny Livingston
- Supersize Me (2004) Morgan Spurlock
- That Sugar Film (2014) Damon Gameau
- Gasland (2010) Josh Fox
- Icarus (2017) Brian Fogel

The **performative mode** has many similarities to the participatory mode. The main difference is that in the performative mode the **subject matter is very personal to the filmmaker** and the content reflects the **subjective representation** of what the filmmaker holds to be true. In the participatory mode the filmmaker has a keen interest in the subject, but the subject they are investigating did not happen to them personally. Examples of performativity occur in Damon Gameau's *That Sugar Film.* His narrative begins with his personal and emotive back-story highlighting his girlfriend's pregnancy, his bad eating habits, and his desire to discover the effects of sugar on his diet before his child is born. Thus, as the impetus for his quest is set in place he embarks on a personal journey to discover the effects of consuming forty teaspoons of sugar a day. **Performativity** is foregrounded in the emotional images and message attached to the **personal quest** taken by Gameau. Predictably his health suffers, and the filmic techniques draw the audience in to question their own consumption of sugar. The emotional happy ending arrives with the birth of Gameau's daughter, a return to a diet without sugar, and his health restored. The audience is positioned, through this personal journey, to learn about the serious health risks posed by excess sugar consumption.

Main features:
- Emotional, subjective, first person point of view.
- Director's personal opinion and vision foregrounded.
- Subjectivity acknowledged as audience is positioned to see the narrative unfold from the filmmaker's perspective, we learn directly from their encounters with subjects.

Documentary
Andrew Morgan

The True Cost

Andrew Morgan's 2015 hybrid expository/participatory documentary *The True Cost* aims to convince its viewers that purchasing cheap, virtually disposable clothing comes at a hidden cost, paid for by the environment and sweat shop factory workers. The film uses documentary techniques, codes, and conventions to carefully construct its content to convey an environmental and humanitarian agenda, critiquing the fast fashion industry and challenging its audience to do the same.

The True Cost (2015), an **expository/participatory** mode documentary created by Andrew Morgan positions its intended PG 13+ audience to decode the **preferred meaning** that the fast fashion industry is extracting a high cost from the environment and the workers who toil away for only a few dollars a day to make highly disposable fashion

garments. Documentary codes, conventions, and techniques such as **selection and omission**, **authority figures** and **statistics** persuade the audience to side with the text's **dominant ideology** of environmental awareness and concern for factory garment workers who suffer human rights violations.

1 Selection and omission to create a point of view.

Pointedly, the selection of the opening footage showing a calm body of water, a beautiful sun rising, and fishermen in traditional boats going about their business is immediately **juxtaposed** with a **montage** of fashion designers readying their models for a catwalk, interspersed with images of Bangladeshi workers making off-the-rack garments. Through **selection** and arrangement of footage Morgan directs his audience to decode the three cornerstones of his film — the environment, fashion, and the people who make the clothes—without yet having said a word. He immediately **anchors meaning** to these visuals in the exposition by employing a **personal voiceover** narration that clearly states his narrative goal, "This is a story about clothing, it's about the clothes we wear, the people who make these clothes and the impact it is having on our world. It is a story about greed and fear, power and poverty." Like fiction texts, documentaries are **constructed representations**. They use **selection and omission** to selectively foreground details of importance. In the opening imagery Andrew Morgan has **foregrounded** his environmental and human rights themes, allowing the audience to understand his **agenda** as he intentionally sets out to persuade the viewer to align with his **point of view** regarding his perceived importance of these issues. He uses **emotive appeal** to engage the audience in the worth of his journey.

2 Authority figures to add credibility.

Andrew Morgan constructs his version of reality by encoding the film with a **choice of codes**, conventions, and documentary techniques that allow him to give voice to the issues and construct his **narrative point of view**. He uses the documentary convention of having an **expert or authority figure** weigh in on the effects of fast fashion. The audience hears from Lucy Siegle, a UK journalist and author who states that she

DOCUMENTARY

Codes, conventions & Techniques in The True Cost

has, "... been obsessed, consumed with the environmental and social impacts of the fashion industry for about a decade." She argues that the fashion industry has been reinvented, rather than having two fashion seasons there are now fifty-two. A fast fashion culture has been born, driven by off-the-rack stores such as Zara, H&M, and Topshop who have a need to sell products quickly and frequently to make more and more money. This is supported by Orsola De Castro, a fashion designer who states, "The shift is moving ruthlessly towards a way of producing which only really looks after big business interests." These **talking head interviews** add **weight and credibility**, serving as the support system for the central documentary argument regarding the harm caused by the fast fashion industry.

3. Statistics, use of facts and figures to persuade the audience about the validity of the argument.

Statistical evidence is used liberally to reinforce Morgan's stance. He begins by reminding the audience that in America, "...as recently as the '60s, we were still making 95% of our clothes. Today we only make about 3% and the other 97% is outsourced to developing countries around the world." By highlighting the shift in manufacturing practices Morgan draws on the audience's **contextual knowledge** of the cheap labour force found in developing countries thereby trying to **emotionally connect** them to the process required to bring cheap, fast fashion to western countries.

Statistical information adds **credibility and power** to the topic as the audience hears that one in six people worldwide are involved in the fashion industry which sells eighty billion pieces of clothing annually. Morgan then stresses that this "$2.5 trillion sector—is the second most polluting industry on Earth, right behind oil." The effect of these staggering statistics serves to highlight the detrimental effects caused by over consumption of fast fashion.

To ensure the audience is not complacent by thinking that if they donate their clothes, they can continue to replace their wardrobes at warp speed without feeling guilty about waste and environmental effects, Morgan quickly dispels this with, "As a consumer, don't think you are doing your part to offset increased consumption by donating excess clothing to charity." He claims that the average American discards eighty two pounds of textile waste a year, however only about 10% of what's donated gets sold in charity stores. The rest is dumped into landfill or is shipped to third world countries, often being worn by the very people who originally made them. The **statistics** are used as **a tool to focus attention** on a western materialistic, consumer lifestyle and direct the audience to question why they continue to purchase excess clothing knowing the damage it causes the environment.

4. Juxtaposition used as binary opposites to make a point.

The key editing technique of **juxtaposition** is used to highlight the fast fashion industry's revolution occurring in major western shops as the audience sees images of happy, excited consumers purchasing their fashion items cut to a **non-diegetic** fast tempo beat. This is contrasted with images of Dhaka, Bangladesh where the composition of the shot is initially framed behind bars, giving a prison-like feel and then cuts to inside the garment factory showing cramped working

DOCUMENTARY
Codes, conventions & techniques in The True Cost

conditions. These shots are coupled with emotionally sad **music** and a **voiceover** of the factory boss explaining how the West's dominance in the fashion sphere allows them to bargain down prices, and if he is unable to comply the large fashion company simply takes its business elsewhere. He explains that in order to survive in this ruthless business model something must give, costs are cut and safety measures ignored.

The documentary technique of **repetition** reinforces this point as Morgan's voiceover reiterates, "Cutting corners and disregarding safety measures has become an accepted part of doing business in this new model." **Repetition and juxtaposition** are effectively employed to highlight the exploitative nature of the supply chain.

5 **Archival footage, used to show historical events.** The documentary persuasive device of incorporating **archival news footage** to authenticate the importance of historical events further develops the film's **preferred meaning** of the human and environmental price paid for the western desire for fast fashion. The audience hears from the news anchor of CNN News who informs them that the eight story Rana Plaza building in Dhaka Bangladesh has collapsed, initially killing more than seventy people and injuring hundreds of others. This number rises steadily over the course of the news broadcast reaching a staggering one thousand one hundred and thirty four people dead and two and half thousand injured. The news footage shown is a **montage** of bodies being removed from the site, coupled with grieving, wailing relatives. John Hilary from *War on Want* points out that large cracks in the building were evidenced days before it collapsed. Despite being aware of the safety hazards, workers were forced to return to the building. The human face of the price being paid for fast fashion is laid bare. The **emotive appeal** of this distressing footage is hard to miss. Morgan's desire is that the scale of the tragedy and the visible human impact will motivate the audience into taking action to ensure that human rights violations for factory garment workers are addressed.

The weight of the **archival footage** is furthered by having a **montage** of news items, all repeating variations of the same theme — a CBN news anchor reports on one hundred garment factory workers being killed in a fire, CNN reports another factory fire which killed eight people, two hundred and eighty nine dead at Ali Enterprises, and at Tazreen fashion one hundred and twelve people died in factory fires. Morgan uses these extensive **historical facts** to expose social inequities. His **voiceover** states that, "...as the death toll rose, so did the profits generated...the global fashion industry is now an almost three trillion dollar annual industry." The chasm between those at the top of the supply chain and those at the bottom is starkly obvious.

6 **Testimonials, interviews-the use of witnesses or experts who directly address the audience attributing weight to the preferred meaning.** The **validity** of the film's argument regarding the human price paid by fast fashion is initially supported by a **testimonial** given by a survivor of the Rana

240

Documentary
Andrew Morgan

The True Cost

Plaza collapse who recounts her harrowing experience to Morgan in a mid-shot. She describes how she tried to get to the stairs, but as she reached them the building collapsed, trapping both of her legs. The **shot size** switches to a long shot, revealing that the woman is sitting in a wheelchair and has had both legs amputated. The direct **testimonial** address humanises the Rana Plaza collapse and gives a face to its victims. The **emotional interview** encourages the audience to vilify the fast fashion industry and reflect on how their fast fashion practices impact others.

The film's **narrative structure** assists to achieve the purpose of highlighting the toll the fashion industry has on the environment and factory garment workers. It **appropriates from fiction film** by having the audience align with the main 'character' of Shima Akhter. Using the documentary **testimonial device**, she relays the harsh realism of life as a factory garment worker. She recounts how she was locked in a room and beaten by thirty to forty staffers who attacked her with scissors, chairs, and scales for daring to form a union that wanted access to basic worker rights such as a pay rise to cover minimum living costs and the right to have a safe workplace. As a dominant 'character' in the text Shima's **values** of humanitarianism, kindness, equality, and fairness align with those of the film's intended audience therefore creating a **conduit to decode the preferred meaning** of rejecting fast fashion and righting the wrongs regarding safety issues and cheap labour involved in its manufacturing practices.

7 Discourse and counter discourse

Ideas are imparted through numerous **dominant and competing discourses** which help to shape the viewer's understanding of the effect of the fast fashion industry.

Andrew Morgan relays the dominant **environmental and humanitarian discourse** of the text using several documentary devices. Primarily the use of **authority figures** support and convey the film's **dominant ideologies** of environmental and garment worker safety concern via interviews. Lucy Siegle poses a critical rhetorical question

whilst being interviewed at her dining room table. She asks, "This enormous rapacious industry that is generating so much profit for a handful of people, why is it that it is unable to support millions of its workers properly? Why is it that it is unable to guarantee their safety? We're talking about essential human rights, why is it unable to guarantee that whilst generating these tremendous profits? Is it because it doesn't work properly? That is my question." Morgan uses **binary oppositions** in terms of setting as we see Ms Siegle in a clean white, well-cared for first-world dining room while she asks these questions which he then contrasts with a dirty river and third world wooden boats which appear to transport the workers to work. The unjust nature is signalled via this stark difference in setting, thus repeating his theme of those with, and those without, financial resources.

A **competing discourse** regarding human rights and safe work practices is delivered by Benjamin Powell, Director of the Free Market Institute and author of *Out*

Documentary
Andrew Morgan

The True Cost

of Poverty and Kate Ball-Young, the former sourcing manager for Joe Fresh. Mr Powell asserts that in relation to sweatshops that, "...they are not just the least bad option workers have today, they are part of the very process that raises living standards and leads to higher wages and better working conditions over time." His argument is that sweatshops stimulate the economy that they are based in and rather than viewing them as villainous we should see them for the positive employment benefits they provide. Powell states that although people in the West may view the working conditions in sweatshops as unsafe and the wages as paltry, he asks that we consider what other employment alternatives there are for the millions of people who are unskilled labourers. His **counterargument** is supported by Ms Ball-Young who states that, "...there is nothing intrinsically dangerous with sewing clothes. We're starting out with a relatively safe industry. It's not like coal mining or natural gas mining." Ideas about garment factory workers and their lives are imparted via the **competing discourse** which gives the **counterargument** that sweat shops or garment factories allow people in third world countries, whose choices are very limited, to at least have some form of employment. This, we are told, is better than the alternative, which is unemployment and eventual starvation.

Morgan argues that large fashion companies who use human capital without recompense in terms of safety and liveable wages, do so because they know that people in third world countries have limited alternatives and therefore these companies excuse away their exploitation. He bookends Benjamin Powell and Kate Ball-Young's argument by presenting a solution to factory garment worker exploitation and the environmental disregard shown by large fashion companies. He introduces Safia Minney, the founder and CEO of People Tree, a fair trade fashion brand, and a second fashion company, Patagonia, who encourage their customers to buy less whilst marketing themselves as environmentally and ethically aware companies. Morgan's **dominant discourse** is one that calls for fairness, equality, and safety for workers. People Tree offers this, but on a micro level. The workers share in the profits and the raw materials are environmentally sustainable, correcting the injustice laid at the feet of large fashion brands. However, Morgan uses the documentary technique of **oversimplification** as he fails to explain why this model has not been scaled up to include larger fashion corporations. Therefore, the **dominant discourse** surrounding fast fashion is one of greedy corporations who take from the environment, ignore workers in terms of safety and fair wages, and pay homage to consumerism at all costs. The **dominant discourse** surrounding the topic scaffolds how an audience **decodes the preferred meaning** in *The True Cost,* they are asked to preface environmental and human welfare and villainise large fashion companies who so easily ignore these factors in favour of excessive profit margins.

8 **Narrative structure and elements.** **Characters, setting, conflict, and resolution** constitute the **narrative elements**. A documentary, although non-fiction, does **appropriate narrative elements** from the fiction form. For instance, the creation of the basic **hero/villain character dichotomy** is shown through the vilification of global fast fashion corporations, and by using victims and authority figures as 'heroes.'

DOCUMENTARY
Codes, conventions & Techniques in The True Cost

These saviours are represented by Fair Trade Fashion owner Safia Minney, Shima Akhter, a garment factory employee fighting for the rights of workers, and Larhea Pepper a cotton farmer who champions the organic cotton market drive. Their contributions act as vehicles to carry the narrative's **humanitarian and environmental themes.**

The film is **set** in a number of locations:
- glittering fashion catwalks in America,
- sweatshops in Bangladesh,
- the production process on cotton farms in Texas,
- a summit for the future of fashion in Copenhagen,
- a Fair Trade meeting in Tokyo Japan,
- a cotton seed farm in Punjab India,
- Port-au-Prince Haiti showing the sheer volume of clothes dumped into developing countries,
- and violent protests regarding minimum wages in Cambodia.

The settings defines the scale of the issue. The vast trek across continents gives breadth and depth to the scope and effects of fast fashion, allowing the viewer to **journey in a clear narrative cause and effect path,** to understand the cumulative problems associated with all stages of the fast fashion industry.

The True Cost **segments its narrative**, moving from country to country following the process involved in the garment supply chain. At each stage Morgan includes **interviews** with journalists, scientists, fashion designers, factory workers, cotton farmers and experts in the environmental sustainability field to better understand the "perfectly engineered nightmare for the workers trapped inside" of fast fashion's web.

The **climatic** moment of the film is revealed in the single line uttered by Shima Akhter, a Bangladeshi factory worker who states, "I believe those clothes are produced by our blood." This defining **audio code** brings the human cost of fast fashion into sharp focus. If the audience had never previously given a thought to the origins of their consumable fashion garments, the heartfelt reality displayed by Shima should put them on a path to considering ethical consumerism. The systematic poverty of factory garment workers in third world countries is nothing short of exploitation. Western consumers enjoy a steady supply of abundant and cheap clothing, fashion companies reap large profits, while the fashion garment worker does not earn a fair living wage.

The film does not **resolve** any issues, rather it **concludes** by asking the audience to re-consider their fashion consumer driven desires. Morgan returns to each major **authority figure** and has them suggest what needs to happen next for positive change to occur. Lucy Siegle sums it up by saying, "You change all consumers into activists, all consumers asking ethical questions, all consumers asking quite simple questions about where their clothes come from, all consumers saying I'm sorry it's not acceptable for someone to die in the course of a working day." Only then, she suggests, will change happen, because it is occurring at the grass-root level, driven by the consumer.

After raising awareness regarding the effects of fast fashion, Morgan

DOCUMENTARY

Codes, conventions & techniques in The True Cost

ultimately **concludes** that the power lies with the consumer, they hold the ability to withhold their fashion dollars and make the fashion companies more accountable. He beseeches the audience to stop turning a blind eye and to engage with the Fashion Revolution campaign. He reminds us that everything we wear is touched by human hands. The documentary **concludes** by urging consumers to act by going to truecostmovie.com. Here they will find a plethora of information, the most useful being the hashtag #whomademyclothes? By engaging with this hashtag the audience can ensure transparency is added to all levels within the supply chain. Additionally, this website offers a Fashion Transparency Index which ranks two hundred and fifty fashion companies according to their environmental and social practices. The index is the first step in holding large companies publicly accountable for their actions. The **conclusion relies on an active audience** driving the Fashion Revolution campaign by reminding large garment companies that consumers want ethical, sustainable, and environmentally aware fashion, not fast disposable fashion.

Narrative elements such as **character, setting, conflict, and resolution** scaffold the delivery of the documentary in an engaging and humanising manner.

9 **Symbolic, technical audio, written codes.**
Codes are used to construct meaning within a narrative. A director will manipulate and choose specific codes — **symbolic, written, audio, or technical** to create a **preferred meaning** for an intended audience. As *The True Cost is* a documentary, the director, Andrew Morgan uses **selection and omission** to shape the raw footage to suit his **agenda**. Within this **technical codes** create meaning by **selecting** and lingering on certain characters such as Shima Akhter, a Bangladeshi factory fashion garment worker. We first met her framed in a **long shot** in the doorway of what is presumably her house as she washes the hands and arms of her daughter, scooping water from a bucket. By using her **body language** to connote nurturing Morgan creates a pathway for audience identification. Her character creates **emotional appeal** for the audience and supports the **preferred meaning** of raising awareness about the systematic poverty brought about by fast fashion. As Shima is the human face of garment factory workers, we have significantly more mid-shots and screen time devoted to her **point of view**. For example, we view Shima sewing in the garment factory. She is placed in the foreground of the shot, **framed in a mid-shot**, while the background allows for numerous other workers, all engaged in the same sewing activity to be seen. This shot is coupled with Morgan's **voiceover** as he states, "...that with a minimum wage of less than $3 a day, they are among the lowest paid garment workers in the world." The **voiceover anchors meaning** and gives emotional resonance to the footage.

Audio codes constitute emotional markers within the narrative. This is evidenced by the sad **music** score used when we see Shima shopping in a market stall with her young daughter Nadia in tow. The **music underpins** the harsh reality stated by Shima as she explains

Documentation
Andrew Morgan

The True Cost

that she doesn't have anyone to care for her daughter in the city. We later learn that Shima's parents, who live rurally, care for Nadia for much of the year. The sad **music signposts** the expected audience reaction to seeing Shima only having small moments of time with her child. As Shima cannot afford the cost of childcare, her child must live far away from her. Morgan explains in a **voiceover** that, "The same low wages that have made Bangladesh so attractive to do business have left millions of workers working incredibly long hours, unable to afford to keep their children with them, even in the city's worst slums. In order to give their children an education, and the chance of a better future than life in factories, many garment workers here, like Shima, are leaving their children to be raised by family or friends in villages outside the city, only getting to see them once or twice a year." Shima becomes the **emotional connection** between the subject matter and the audience, we see her hardships and feel her suffering.

Morgan positions the audience to see the effect of the fast fashion industry through the eyes of Shima. He aligns us with her emotionally and then lets the audience hear her harrowing story. Filmed in **mid-shot** against the backdrop of a city window, using only the **ambient sound** of factory workers, we see Shima **recount** her experience. She tells the audience that she formed a union that submitted a list of demands to management. She explains that after meeting with management, the doors were locked and she along with her co-workers were beaten by thirty to forty staffers who hit them with chairs, stick, scales, and scissors. They were punched and kicked and their heads hit against the wall. Shima's **testimonial** to camera, which initially only uses **ambient sound** is powerful as it chooses to let her words create the **emotional drive**, rather than signal the required emotional reaction through music.

This connection is further strengthened when we see Shima introduce her parents to the audience. Her **body language** exudes happiness, she hugs her parents, smiles widely and explains that she hasn't seen them for a year. It is here, outside the familial home that Shima **recounts** how hard her life is.

She explains that people only see a limited side to fashion, they buy the clothes, wear them and don't give a thought to who made them. She says, "I believe those clothes are produced by our blood." Morgan uses **emotive appeal and body language** as Shima begins to cry, explaining how many garment factory workers die in the course of their job, and how little is done to rectify the situation. Her words and their **emotional intensity** appeal to the **intended audience,** acting as motivation to provoke them into carefully considering how ethical their consumer habits actually are.

Written codes anchor meaning to the content of a text. Andrew Morgan's choice to **title** his documentary *The True Cost* connotes meaning regarding the human cost of exploiting factory garment workers and the environmental impact created by the global fast fashion industry. The **title** suggests that the true cost is paid for by the people and mother nature who can

Documentary
Andrew Morgan

The True Cost

least afford it. The documentary technique of **repetition** is used to reinforce the connotation of the **title** as we see the organic cotton farmer, Larhea Pepper, reinforce the need to question the true cost of fast fashion by stating, "One of the problems we have in the current model is that it is all about the profit. It doesn't take into consideration...the cost of polluting the water; the cost of labour; the cost of bars on a window when people die when a fire breaks out in the factory, the cost of farmers that don't have access to education and healthcare. And so, we haven't really factored in what the true cost is." *The True Cost* is **encoded using symbolic, audio, written, and technical codes** chosen by Andrew Morgan to form the **preferred meaning** which targets western consumer capitalistic

ideologies and questions the validity of fast fashion by examining the impact it has on the environment and the human rights violations inflicted on garment factory workers.

Morgan manipulates **documentary codes and conventions** to dissuade viewers from buying into the fast fashion conveyor belt of excess consumption.

10 Agenda

In this **participatory/ expository documentary** Andrew Morgan uses several features of Bill Nichols' **modes** of documentaries. The film is partly **expository** in that what is heard relates directly to what is seen on the screen with argumentative logic being present. However, unlike the objective nature of the expository mode *The True Cost* falls partly into the **participatory** mode with its content being subjective. Andrew Morgan clearly acknowledges his **subjective agenda** in a voice over that states, "This is a story about clothing, it's about the clothes we wear, the people who make these clothes and the impact it is having on our world. It is a story about greed and fear, power and poverty."

In the **exposition** Morgan engages the subjective **common man documentary trope** delivering the film's central narrative **agenda** in a colloquial and inviting manner. He claims that, "I came into this story with no background in fashion at all, beginning with nothing more than a few simple questions, what I've discovered has forever changed the way I think about the things I wear, and my hope is that it might just do the same for you." The audience is positioned to engage with Morgan's stance on the unethical nature of fast fashion as he clearly presents his **argument**, supporting it with numerous **emotional appeals, authority figures and statistics**, thus inviting the audience to join him in **decoding the preferred meaning** which shows the lack of care fast fashion companies have for ethical and environmental consumerism.

The **subjective** nature of the film is highlighted via its source of **funding**. Andrew Morgan raised funds via a Kickstarter campaign and from high profile backers such as Olivia Firth and Lucy Siegle. The question needs to be asked as to whether a **conflict of interest** exists as the major executive producers of the film, Lucy Siegal who is a journalist and author of *To Die For: Is Fashion Wearing Out the World?* and Livia Firth the Creative Director of Eco-Age, a sustainability consultancy

DOCUMENTARY

Codes, conventions & techniques in The True Cost

firm, both appear throughout the film as **authority figures** to convince the viewer to side with Morgan's **point of view** regarding the negative impact fast fashion is having on the environment and garment factory workers. As major financial backers and authority figures in the film, Siegle and Firth's, **objectivity** is in question.

Does Andrew Morgan's **agenda** culminate in raising awareness about the effects of fast fashion to the point of provoking his audience into action? The film has been criticised for being broad on content but lacking in depth and specificity, especially in relation to concrete solutions. It has been lambasted for its lack of clear citations. However, taking all of this into consideration the efficacy of the film is in its ability to **motivate its audience**. Since the film's release in 2015 a continued spotlight has been shone on the effects of fast fashion.

Nature Reviews Earth & Environment, an on-line journal, is just one of many organisations who have continued the fight. In their article *The environmental price of fast fashion* published in 2020 the authors reiterate Morgan's stance that the fashion industry needs to change. **Slow fashion** needs to take effect to mitigate the negative environmental impacts caused by fast fashion. The article stresses the need to increase sustainable practices by decreasing garment output and increasing the life span of all garments purchased by consumers.

The ultimate aim is a **cultural shift** in getting people to treat clothes as **non-consumable items**, something that is worth investing in and wearing for long periods of time, and not seeing clothing as wear-once obsolete items to be discarded. Additionally, the consumer needs to champion the wearing of **fair trade clothing**, prefacing garments that have been ethically sourced and made throughout all stages of the supply chain. Therefore, changing the **consumer culture mindset** is paramount. Within this paradigm shift *Nature Review* encourages a clothes rental scheme for 'special occasion' clothes and convincing buyers that second hand clothing should not attract a stigma. *Nature Review* offers clear recommendations and solutions for all stages of the garment making process from those involved in policy, to the manufacturing industry, the retailers who sell the clothes, and the consumers who buy them. Andrew Morgan's **agenda** was to raise awareness about the negative effects of the fast fashion industry. His film *The True Cost* may not have caused an immediate halt to fast fashion, but it has furthered the conversation, spread the word, and allowed for many other organisations and individuals to move in a more sustainable direction.

> Fast fashion isn't **FREE.** Someone, somewhere is paying.
>
> ———
>
> Lucy Siegle

Documentary Films

> In feature films the director is God; in documentary films, God is the director.
>
> Alfred Hitchcock

- That Sugar Film (2014) Damon Gameau
- 2040 (2019) Damon Gameau
- Blackfish (2013) Gabriela Cowperthwaite
- Rise Of the Eco Warriors (2013) Cathy Henkel
- They Shall Not Grow Old (2018) Peter Jackson
- Man on Wire (2008) James Marsh
- Touching the Void (2003) Kevin Macdonald
- Sicko (2007) Michael Moore
- Icarus (2017) Bryan Fogel
- Racing Extinction (2015) Louie Psihoyos
- The Pixar Story (2007) Leslie Iwerks
- The Greatest Movie Ever Sold (2011) Morgan Spurlock
- Side by Side (2012) Christopher Kenneally
- The Thin Blue Line (1988) Errol Morris
- Hoop Dreams (1994) Steve James
- Bowling for Columbine (2002) Michael Moore
- Inside Job (2010) Chris Ferguson
- The Hunting Ground (2015) Kirby Dick
- Waiting for Superman (2010) Davis Guggenheim
- An Inconvenient Truth (2006) Al Gore
- Page One: Inside the New York Times (2011) Andrew Rossi
- Samsara (2011) Ron Fricke
- The Act of Killing (2012) Joshua Oppenheimer
- The Central Park Five (2012) Burns, Mcmahon
- Capturing the Friedman's (2003) Andrew Jarecki

- The Up series (1964) Michael Apted
- The True Cost (2015) Andrew Morgan
- Baracka (1992) Ron Fricke
- Koyaanisqatsi (1982) Godfrey Reggio
- O.J Made in America (2016) Ezra Edelman
- The Times of Harvey Milk (1984) Rob Epstein
- Nanook of the North (1922) Robert Flaherty
- Roger and Me (1989) Michael Moore
- Man with a Movie Camera (1929) Dziga Vertov
- Grizzly Man (2005) Werner Herzog
- Triumph of the Will (1935) Leni Riefenstahl
- Fahrenheit 9/11 (2004) Michael Moore
- Citizenfour (2014) Laura Poitras
- Exit Through the Gift Shop (2010) Banksy
- Night and Fog (1956) Alain Resnais
- The Queen of Versailles (2012) Lauren Greenfield
- The September Issue (2009) R.J. Cutler
- Spellbound (2002) Jeffrey Blitz
- Super Size Me (2004) Morgan Spurlock
- 9/11: The Falling Man (2006) Henry Singer
- Enron: The Smartest Guys in the Room (2005) Alex Gibney
- Crumb (1994) Terry Zwigoff
- The Corporation (2003) Archbar and Abbot
- Manufacturing Dissent: Noam Chomsky and the Media (1992) Wintonick & Achbar
- Capitalism: A Love Story (2009) Michael Moore

SUGGESTED FILMS

some suggestions

- Gasland (2010) Josh Fox
- Miss Representation (2011) Jennifer Siebel Newsom
- Bra Boys (2007) Abberton & De Souza
- The Big Short (2015) Adam McKay
- The Cove (2009) Louie Psihoyos
- Three Identical Strangers (2018) Tim Wardle
- Louis Theroux documentaries
- On the Way to School (2013) Pascal Plisson
- YouTube 60 second documentaries
- Murbah Swamp Beer (2002) Tropfest Australia. Gary Doust
- Education for Death (1943) Clyde Geronimi
- Alive Inside (2014) Michael Rossata-Bennett
- Being George Clooney (2016) Paul Mariano
- Teenage Paparazzi (2010) Adrian Grenier
- Twinsters (2015) Futerman & Miyamoto
- Metallica: Some Kind of Monster (2004) Sinofsky & Berlinger
- Frackman (2015) Stack & Todd
- Stories We Tell (2012) Sarah Polley
- Searching for Sugarman (2012) Malik Bendjelloul
- Wormwood (2017) Errol Morris
- American Teen (2008) Nanette Burstein
- High School (1968) Frederick Wiseman
- This is Spinal Tap (1984) [Mockumentary]. Rob Reiner

- Zeitgeist (2007) Peter Joseph
- Exposed: The Case of Kelli Lane (2018) Ben Lawrence
- Font Men (2013) Andreev & Covert
- Score: A Film Music Documentary (2017) Matt Schrader
- I Am Not Your Negro (2017) Raoul Peck
- Get Me Roger Stone (2017) Pehme et al
- Generation Like (2014) Frontline PBS
- Instafame documentary: Teenager's relationship with fame through the lens of Instagram (2014)
- Hypernormalisation (2023) Adam Curtis
- Capturing Reality: The Art of Documentary (2008) Pepita Ferrari
- This Changes Everything (2015) Avi Lewis
- The Toys That Made Us (2018) 3 Seasons
- Consuming Kids: The Commercialization of Childhood (2008) Barbaro & Earp
- How the Kids Took Over (2006) ABC
- Story of Stuff (2007) Louis Fox
- Betsy Tells Her Story (1972) Liane Brandon
- Unprecedented (2022) Alex Holder
- New Kings: The Power of Online Influencers (2017) Maria Rodriguez
- After Truth: Disinformation and the Cost of Fake News (2020) Andrew Rossi

Documentary Essential Content

DOCUMENTARY FILMS ARE A REPRESENTATION OF REALITY, CONSTRUCTED FROM A CHOICE OF CODES AND CONVENTIONS TO SHAPE THE VALIDITY AND CREDIBILITY OF THE FILMMAKER'S MESSAGE.

Main essential content to consider when analysing documentary films:

1. **Codes:** Discuss how the choice of codes shapes the representation of the issue, event, or person. Consider the connotations of the:
   - technical
   - symbolic
   - audio and
   - written codes

2. **Documentary conventions:** How do the chosen conventions privilege the filmmaker's point of view. Consider the use of:
   - voiceover
   - testimonials and interviews
   - archival footage
   - re-enactments
   - juxtaposition
   - exposition
   - authority figures
   - statistics
   - selection, omission, emphasis
   - emotive appeal
   - montage

3. **Documentary techniques:** How do they shape the film's message?
   - bandwagon
   - card stacking
   - glittering generalities
   - name calling
   - over-simplification
   - stereotyping
   - common man
   - emotional appeal
   - scapegoating
   - assertion

4. **Point of view:** From whose eyes do we see the story unfold?
   - What codes and conventions construct their point of view?
   - What values and ideologies are attached to this person's actions?
   - What dominant and competing discourses appear?

5. **Ordering of events:**
   - How has the narrative been structured?
   - How does the opening position the audience in relation to the issue or event?
   - What content is selected and what omitted?
   - Have binary oppositions been used?
   - Consider how narrative elements such as character, setting, conflict, and resolution have been employed.

6. **Agenda:** How does the agenda drive the filmmaker's point of view.
   - What is the filmmaker's agenda?
   - How is the film being funded? Does the institution or source of the money come with an agenda attached?

7. **Documentary modes** such as those posited by Bill Nichols: expository, poetic, reflexive, observational, participatory, and performative.

8. **Context:** Discuss how any contextual elements may have shaped the content.

Documentary Review

Sample questions containing documentary concepts:

1. Analyse how media producers construct perceptions of issues using the documentary genre.
2. Discuss how a filmmaker can manipulate selection, emphasis, and omission to construct a preferred point of view on a topic or issue.
3. Discuss the effect of selection of codes, conventions, and persuasive techniques on constructing an effective documentary.
4. Analyse how the genre of documentary is used to deliver a message to a niche audience.
5. Discuss how the influence of documentary films can be understood by applying a communication theory.

Documentary - main essential content to discuss:

01 A documentary text is a **construction**. It is a representation of an event, issue or person, not the reality itself. The filmmaker has a **preferred meaning** created through **selection and omission** of information, choice of conventions, and structuring of the narrative. As a **crafted construction**, documentaries contain the **bias, perspective, agenda,** and aesthetics of the filmmaker.

02 Discuss the choice of codes, conventions, and techniques to shape reality:
- **Ordering of events**
- **Point of view** created
- **Codes:** what **audio code** choices have been made? How have authorial voiceover or personal voice created meaning? How do **written codes** anchor meaning? What **symbolic code** choices have been made? Consider the **technical codes**; how do they influence meaning?
- Consider how **conventions** such as statistics, re-enactments, archival footage, experts, testimonials, exposition, emotive appeal and voiceover narration are used.
- Consider how **persuasive techniques** such as bandwagon, card stacking, glittering generalities, name calling, oversimplification, stereotyping, common man, emotional appeal, and scapegoating are used to shape meaning.

03
- How does **context** shape the text's content. What historical events have occurred, what is the political climate, what are the social and cultural norms, what technological advancements have impacted the style of the documentary?

04
- **Agenda**: who funded the film and why? What **constraints** are placed on the content due to the institutional context? Is **bias or selective presentation** of information present?

05
- **Audience expectations**: the audience's expectations of the documentary form, their expectations of social and cultural norms, and their preferences can shape the content and structure of a documentary.

Chapter Twelve

Propaganda

- Propaganda: definition and information
- Propaganda: how does it work
- Propaganda techniques
- Agenda setting and propaganda
- Agenda setting theory
- Propaganda and Trump
- How Trump used propaganda
- Propaganda, Trump, and trends
- Propaganda: Germany vs. America
- Triumph of the Will
- Sample questions
- Review

Propaganda

PROPAGANDA
Definition and information

Propaganda is intentional and systematic; it attempts to persuade the audience to accept a posited idea according to a singular vision. Propaganda attempts to influence beliefs, values, and ideologies by using persuasive techniques to drive the message home, often using bias and manipulation.

MANIPULATION OF EMOTIONS: Propaganda uses powerful emotions such as fear to manipulate people's behaviour and ideologies.

EVERYDAY LIFE: Propaganda is all around us, it is in the social media we consume, the advertisements we watch, the news we engage with, the politicians we elect, the corporations we purchase goods from, the religions we engage with; anything purposely designed to influence our behaviour, values or ideas in an overt or subtle manner, is a form of propaganda.

PROPAGANDA TECHNIQUES include:
- testimonials
- card stacking
- common man
- bandwagon
- glittering generalities
- name calling
- transfer
- scapegoating
- stereotyping
- oversimplification
- repetition
- emotional appeal

CRITICAL THINKING allows you to understand the purpose of propaganda:
- Consider countermeasures such as moving outside of your normal echo chamber of information to include a variety of sources, voices, and points of view.
- Increase your media literacy skills. Be aware of propaganda techniques and deconstruct the media message to evaluate its agenda.
- Navigate the media saturated world with a sense of healthy skepticism, be critical of the media you consume. Obtain an objective view by collecting diverse data points to verify information.

AUDIENCE: propaganda is aimed at a specific audience, its intent may be commercial, ideological, or political; its effects can be far-reaching, shaping and directing the course of history.

Propaganda

Where can propaganda be found? A few examples (but not limited to) are below:

1 **Advertisements and marketing** often attempt to manipulate the beliefs of the audience to persuade them of an idea or the benefits of a product. Propaganda techniques such as testimonials, bandwagon, repetition, glittering generalities or emotional appeal are used to influence consumers to engage with a product or idea.

2 **Political propaganda** is used to spread information designed to influence public opinion. The propagandist's message can be relayed via advertisements, cartoons, speeches, social media posts, interviews, debates, rallies, and so forth. Propaganda techniques such as name-calling, card stacking, oversimplification, and transfer are often used to connect to the audience, discredit an opponent, and promote an ideological agenda.

3 **Social media** is an effective vehicle to spread misinformation. Fake news, rumours and conspiracy theories can be relayed and amplified via shares, retweets, retruths, and likes. Division and mistrust occur as social media algorithms reinforce and feed information to people based on their existing likes and interests. Therefore, an echo chamber effect occurs serving to reinforce their existing ideological view of the world.

4 **News media** - Media institutions are shaped by their corporate culture and ownership. All media outlets have an agenda, some align quite visibly to their ownership structure and display clear bias in reporting; thus, their manipulating of events through selection and omission is a form of propaganda as it is designed to serve their ideological agenda.

5 **Education** - in some areas and places in history education has been used as a propaganda tool as textbooks and curriculum material have been chosen to enhance a specific view of history and control the information being taught in schools.

6 **Corporate propaganda** - companies will employ propaganda techniques to improve their corporate image and attempt to mitigate any negative publicity which may come their way.

Propaganda

How does propaganda work?

INTENT

A propagandist's goal is to persuade their intended audience to believe in a cause, product, political view, issue, or align with an ideology.

AUDIENCE

Targets a specific niche audience with the intention of influencing opinions, beliefs, and behaviours.

TECHNIQUES

Uses crafted propaganda techniques to guide the intended audience towards accepting their message.

REPEAT

Rinse and repeat. Repetition is a crucial tool in funnelling information as it reinforces and solidifies the propagandist's message in a consistent manner.

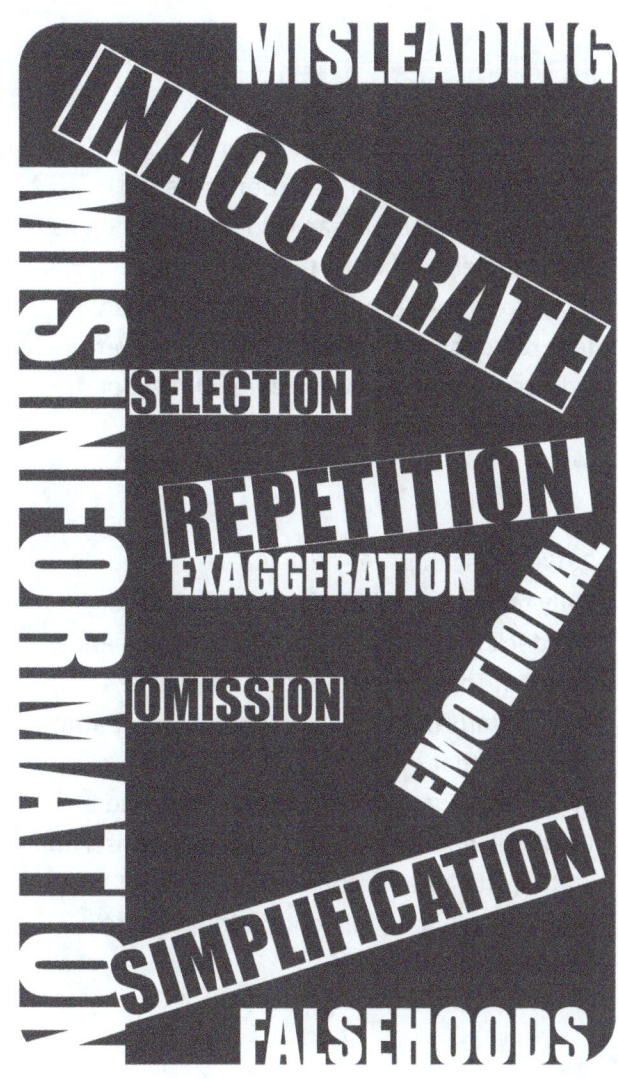

Propaganda

Documentary propaganda techniques used to persuade the audience may include:

1. Bandwagon
Jump on the bandwagon, join in the crowd, the filmmaker attempts to persuade the audience to take the same course of action as everyone else by using the fear of missing out, a basic emotional appeal whereby humans fear rejection and isolation and can therefore sidestep evidence and argument in favour of joining in.

2. Card stacking
Only telling a portion of the truth. Stacking the deck in your favour to influence audience opinion. The user selects and emphasises specific information whilst ignoring or omitting evidence that does not lend weight to their argument. E.g., Donald Trump's response to Covid 19 whereby he ignored the scientists and stated, "It's one person coming in from China, and we have it under control. It's going to be just fine' (Trump, 2020).

3. Glittering generalities
Use of appealing but vague words and images to create a strong emotional response. E.g., Donald Trump's slogan "Make America Great Again" uses words with emotional connotations but that present no specific facts about what exactly constitutes 'great.' The slogan is catchy but in fact says nothing specific.

4. Oversimplification
Presenting a solution in an overly simplistic manner. Donald Trump's oversimplification of building a wall to solve the illegal immigration problem and having the Mexican government pay for it is a prime example of using an oversimplified logical fallacy to hide the flaws in his statement.

5. Common man
The 'plain folks' or common man technique attempts to appeal to the audience by appearing to show a commonsense approach. The language, mannerisms, and clothes worn by the presenter are chosen to reflect a common demeanor and connect with the average person. This connection creates a gateway for the filmmaker to convince the audience to accept their point of view.

Propaganda

6. Transfer
Transfers the positive power and authority of an idea or issue onto something else to make it palatable and acceptable. E.g., through an authority figure or symbol.

7. Emotional appeal
Pathos - appeal to fear, happiness, need to belong and so on. More often, the appeal to fear is used as a scare tactic to persuade audiences to accept an idea.

8. Repetition
Repeating information continually to force others to engage with your agenda.

9. Stereotyping
Using a few traits to represent a group, usually in a negative manner.

10. Testimonial
Individuals share their experiences in a firsthand account, adding authenticity and emotional connection to support the filmmaker's perspective.

11. Scapegoating
Attributing blame to others to distract or avoid personal responsibility. E.g., Rather than accept blame for his inaction and ineptitude over the handling of the Covid crisis, Trump deflected by slurring others, calling the virus the 'Kung-Flu' and the 'foreign virus.'

12. Name calling
Used to create division and fear. The name calling technique is designed to label a group, person, or idea, negatively. Donald Trump employs this propaganda technique with frequency. His cries of 'fake news' are designed to denounce journalists and deflect attention away from real issues.

13. Loaded words
Use of terms which are emotionally charged with an aim to influence the audience by exploiting their vulnerabilities. Words that are 'loaded' or have strong connotations are words like superior, immigrant, pro-life, and freedom. Or, provoking words such as attack, stolen, lies, or stupid. Loaded language contributes to how a group, cause, or idea can be perceived.

Agenda Setting & Propaganda

How do propaganda and agenda setting shape media content?

Propaganda is intentional; its goal is to provoke change, be it in actions or beliefs among an intended audience.

Agenda setting refers to how media institutions can set the agenda regarding what news content the public thinks about by foregrounding certain content, whilst omitting or marginalising other topics through limited coverage.

MEDIA AGENDA

The content that is **selected and omitted** is shaped by institutional ethos, political pressure or alliance, the public's values and ideologies, public relations firms, powerful figures, including those in corporate or government positions.

NEWS PRODUCTION

AGENDA SETTING

- The selection and omission of news sets an agenda and shapes its content. In particular, **framing** of news information means certain content is prioritised, elaborated on, and emphasised thus influencing its perceived importance. What is the lead story? What graphics or captions are selected? What are the connotations of the chosen images and language?
- **Priming** of news content creates a hierarchy of importance as some items are given more time, space, and coverage, implying its significance.
- **Gatekeeping** refers to journalists and editors who shape the news landscape by including or excluding certain content to serve an agenda.
- **Framing, priming, and gatekeeping** shape what issues the public perceive to be of importance.

PROPAGANDA TECHNIQUES

- Bandwagon
- Card stacking
- Glittering generalities
- Oversimplification
- Common man
- Transfer
- Emotional appeal
- Repetition
- Stereotyping
- Scapegoating
- Name calling
- Loaded words
- Testimonial

PUBLIC AGENDA

- What issues do the general public perceive to be important? How did they arrive at this decision? It is important to note that the public can influence the media agenda through social media participation, campaigning, and political pressure.
- The public perceives news content through the lens of their culture, context, demographic factors, previous and current experience, connections with friends, family and colleagues, and through their media exposure.

Agenda Setting Theory

The agenda setting theory (1972) examines the concept of media influence. Posited by Maxwell McCombs and Donald Lewis Shaw, the essence of the theory is that **the media can't tell the audience what to think, but they can tell them what to think about.** This theory posits the notion that the news media has the power to influence by deciding which stories are presented to the public, how often they are shown, how long they are shown for, where they appear, and how the discourse used to surround the topic will set the terms of reference regarding the perceived importance of the issue.

McCombs later evolved the theory to include characteristics that filter and shape how an audience might engage with, and think about, important issues. These include:

1. **Framing:** what news information is selected and what is omitted to 'frame' or compose news items using a coherent narrative and contextual framework. A variety of techniques are used to organise news content by the media and individuals who have a vested interest in the story:
   - **Selection:** prioritising certain issues over others. A news item is selected based on its trigger. Selected stories are built around conflict, winners and losers, and revealing either injustice or irony has become the most common way of framing the news.
   - **Emphasis:** highlighting an issue.
   - **Exclusion:** omitting items from the news agenda.
   - **Elaboration:** expansion of ideas and details that explain an issue in more depth.

2. **Priming:** refers to the time, space, and coverage provided to an issue, making some issues prominent and ignoring or giving minimal coverage to others.

3. **Gatekeeping:** refers to people, such as a news editor, who decide (through selection and omission) the content of media publications. These decisions are based on the values of the news outlet, expectations of the intended audience, deadlines, and policies.

Propaganda and Trump

Donald Trump's Presidency

Agenda - Donald Trump reshaped the Republican party into his own image. He 'set the agenda' for topics and issues of perceived importance to the people he thought would most likely vote for him. Topics such as:

Law and order	Fake news	Make America Great Again	Tax reforms
• secure border • immigration issues • build the wall • race issues	• misinformation • disinformation • e.g., birther myth in relation to Barack Obama supposedly not being born in America	• by creating jobs • creating wealth • returning America to a superpower status	• simplify tax code • delete inheritance tax

Media Agenda: the following few pages contain curated content stated by Donald Trump on social media, at his election rally speeches, and during interviews with various media outlets. Read through his comments and posts as some of them will be used to examine how his rhetoric shaped American politics.

"When Mexico sends its people, they're not sending their best…they're not sending you. They're sending people that have lots of problems, and they're bringing those problems with them. They're bringing drugs. They're bringing crime. They're rapists. And some, I assume, are good people." June 16, 2015, at the announcement rally of his Presidential candidacy (C-SPAN, 2015).

Donald J. Trump ✓
@realDonaldTrump Follow

MAKE AMERICA GREAT AGAIN!

20:30:08 17 March 2016

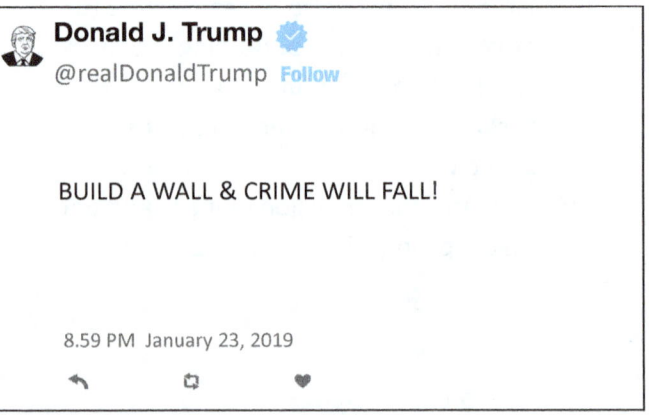

Donald J. Trump ✓
@realDonaldTrump Follow

BUILD A WALL & CRIME WILL FALL!

8.59 PM January 23, 2019

Propaganda and Trump

Donald J. Trump
@realDonaldTrump Follow

The Fake News Media has never been so wrong or so dirty. Purposely incorrect stories and phony sources to meet their agenda of hate. Sad!

6:35:55 AM 23th June 2017
• 19K ♥ • 80K

Donald J. Trump
@realDonaldTrump Follow

The FAKE NEWS media (failing @nytimes, @NBCNews, @ABC, @CBS, @CNN) is not my enemy, it is the enemy of the American People!

4:48:22 PM 17th February 2017
• 44K

Donald J. Trump
@realDonaldTrump Follow

I win an election easily, a great "movement" is verified, and crooked opponents try to belittle our victory with FAKE NEWS. A sorry state!

8:19:23 PM 11th January 2017
• 23K ♥ • 77K

Donald J. Trump
@realDonaldTrump Follow

Some people HATE the fact that I got along well with President Putin of Russia. They would rather go to war than see this. It's called Trump Derangement Syndrome!

7.27.59 AM July 18th, 2018
• 26K

Part 1

Part 2

Donald J. Trump
@realDonaldTrump Follow

...Actually, throughout my life, my two greatest assets have been mental stability and being, like, really smart. Crooked Hillary Clinton also played these cards very hard and, as everyone knows, went down in flames. i went from VERY successful businessman, to top T.V. Star...

7:30:51 AM January 6th, 2018
• 27K

Donald J. Trump
@realDonaldTrump Follow

.......to President of the United States (on my first try). I think that would qualify as not smart, but genius....and a very stable genius at that!

7:30:51 AM January 6th, 2018
• 27K

Propaganda and Trump

Donald J. Trump
@realDonaldTrump Follow

The media has not reported that the National Debt in my first month went down by $12 billion vs. a $200 billion increase in Obama first mo.

8:19:18 AM 25 February 2017

51K

Donald J. Trump
@realDonaldTrump Follow

Funny to hear the Democrats talking about the National Debt when President Obama doubled it in only 8 years!

9:23:14 PM 29 November 2017

28K

Donald J. Trump
@realDonaldTrump Follow

Our Southern Border is under siege. Congress must act now to change our weak and ineffective immigration laws. Must build a Wall. Mexico, which has a massive crime problem, is doing little to help!

8:19:18 AM 4th May 2018

15K 69K

Donald J. Trump
@realDonaldTrump Follow

Why does the Lamestream Fake News Media REFUSE to say that China Virus deaths are down 39%, and that we now have the lowest Fatality (Mortality) Rate in the World. They just can't stand that we are doing so well for our Country!

4:17:46 PM 6th July 2020

38K

Donald J. Trump
@realDonaldTrump Follow

I always treated the Chinese Virus very seriously and have done a very good job from the beginning, including my very early decision to close the "borders" from China - against the wishes of almost all. Many lives were saved. The Fake News narrative is disgraceful & false!

7:46:33 AM 18th March 2020

34K

Donald J. Trump
@realDonaldTrump Follow

Great credit being given for our Coronavirus response, except in the Fake News. They are a disgrace to America!

9:45:17 AM 11th May 2020

27K

Donald J. Trump
@realDonaldTrump Follow

The number of ChinaVirus cases goes up, because of GREAT TESTING, while the number of deaths (mortality rate), goes way down. The Fake News doesn't like telling you that!

12:06:06 PM 25th June 2020

53K

Donald J. Trump
@realDonaldTrump Follow

So now the Fake News @nytimes is tracing the CoronaVirus origins back to Europe, NOT China. This is a first! I wonder what the Failing New York Times got for this one? Are there any NAMED sources? They were recently thrown out of China like dogs, and obviously want back in. Sad!

7:34:58 PM 11th April 2020

39K

Propaganda and Trump

Donald J. Trump
@realDonaldTrump Follow

The News Media in our Country is FAKE and in many cases, totally CORRUPT!

2:06:39 PM 11th December 2019

↺ • 19K   ♥ • 61K

Donald J. Trump
@realDonaldTrump Follow

Now the Fake News Media says I "pressured the Ukrainian President at least 8 times during my telephone call with him." This supposedly comes from a so-called "whistleblower" who they say doesn't even have a first hand account of what was said. More Democrat/Crooked Media con...

8:03:55 PM 22nd December 2019

↺ • 16K   ♥ • 71K

Donald J. Trump
@realDonaldTrump Follow

If it weren't for the never ending Fake News about me, and with all that I have done (more than any other President in the first 2 1/2 years!), I would be leading the "Partners" of the LameStream Media by 20 points. Sorry, but true!

8:19:45 PM 11th September 2019

↺ • 12K   ♥ • 63K

Donald J. Trump
@realDonaldTrump Follow

The Wall is being built and is well under construction. Big impact will be made. Many additional contracts are close to being signed. Far ahead of schedule despite all of the Democrat Obstruction and Fake News!

7:24:07 AM 8th March 2019

↺ • 17K   ♥ • 96K

Donald J. Trump
@realDonaldTrump Follow

The Fake News will knowingly lie and demean in order to make the tremendous success of the Trump Administration, and me, look as bad as possible. They use non-existent sources & write stories that are total fiction. Our Country is doing so well, yet this is a sad day in America!

8:09:03 AM 7th January 2019

↺ • 19K   ♥ • 86K

Donald J. Trump
@realDonaldTrump Follow

The Fake News is doing everything in their power to blame Republicans, Conservatives and me for the division and hatred that has been going on for so long in our Country. Actually, it is their Fake & Dishonest reporting which is causing problems far greater than they understand!

8:12:57 PM 28th October 2018

↺ • 41K   ♥

Donald J. Trump
@realDonaldTrump Follow

Despite the disgusting, illegal and unwarranted Witch Hunt, we have had the most successful first 17 month Administration in U.S. history - by far! Sorry to the Fake News Media and "Haters," but that's the way it is!

9:52:44 AM 17th May 2018

↺ • 26K   ♥

Donald J. Trump
@realDonaldTrump Follow

The Fake News refuses to talk about how Big and how Strong our BASE is. They show Fake Polls just like they report Fake News. Despite only negative reporting, we are doing well - nobody is going to beat us. MAKE AMERICA GREAT AGAIN!

8:48:11 AM 24th December 2017

↺ • 26K   ♥

263

Propaganda and Trump

Donald J. Trump
@realDonaldTrump Follow

These are the things and events that happen when a sacred landslide election victory is so unceremoniously & viciously stripped away from great patriots who have been badly & unfairly treated for so long. Go home with love & in peace. Remember this day forever!

6:01:04 PM 6th January 2021

0   0   Deleted

Donald J. Trump
@realDonaldTrump Follow

Washington is being inundated with people who don't want to see an election victory stolen by emboldened Radical Left Democrats. Our Country has had enough, they won't take it anymore! We hear you (and love you) from the Oval Office. MAKE AMERICA GREAT AGAIN!

5:05:56 PM 5th January 2021

46K

Donald J. Trump
@realDonaldTrump Follow

The 75,000,000 great American Patriots who voted for me, AMERICA FIRST, and MAKE AMERICA GREAT AGAIN, will have a GIANT VOICE long into the future. They will not be disrespected or treated unfairly in any way, shape or form!!!

9:46:38 PM 8th January 2021

90K

Donald J. Trump
@realDonaldTrump Follow

To all of those who have asked, I will not be going to the Inauguration on January 20th.

4:48:22 PM 8th January 2021

79K

Donald J. Trump
@realDonaldTrump Follow

People are not going to stand for having this Election stolen from them by a privately owned Radical Left company, Dominion, and many other reasons!

3:07:56 PM 14th November 2020

66K

Donald J. Trump
@realDonaldTrump Follow

He didn't win the Election. He lost all 6 Swing States, by a lot. They then dumped hundreds of thousands of votes in each one, and got caught. Now Republican politicians have to fight so that their great victory is not stolen. Don't be weak fools!

9:41:03 AM 19th December 2020

17K   96K

Donald J. Trump
@realDonaldTrump Follow

The only thing more RIGGED than the 2020 Presidential Election is the FAKE NEWS SUPPRESSED MEDIA. No matter how big or important the story, if it is even slightly positive for "us", or negative for "them", it will not be reported!

2:54:47 PM 4th December 2020

32K

Donald J. Trump
@realDonaldTrump Follow

I hope the Democrats, and even more importantly, the weak and ineffective RINO section of the Republican Party, are looking at the thousands of people pouring into D.C. They won't stand for a landslide election victory to be stolen. @senatemajldr @JohnCornyn @SenJohnThune

5:12:20 PM 5th January 2021

29K

Propaganda and Trump

 Watch the segment on CNN when Trump claims, "I've been treated very unfairly by this judge. Now, this judge is of Mexican heritage. I'm building a wall, OK? I'm building a wall. I am going to do very well with the Hispanics, the Mexicans..."

 Watch the Fox Business extract where Trump discusses building a border wall to stop illegal immigration. "We will build a great wall along the southern border. And Mexico will pay for the wall. 100%. They don't know it yet, but they are going to pay. On day one we will begin working on an impenetrable, physical, tall, powerful, beautiful southern border wall."

 Consider watching the film *You've Been Trumped* 2023 produced by Journeyman Pictures.

 Watch The Lincoln Project's 2024 presidential campaign advertisement. How does their message and use of persuasive techniques differ to Trump's?

 Watch the *Make America Great For Us Again!* advertisement for the 2024 presidential campaign.

Propaganda and Trump

Agenda setting describes how media content such as news, current affairs, documentaries, and social media create a landscape populated with items of perceived importance that are foregrounded for viewer consumption and shaped to influence the audience's beliefs, values, and ideologies on a given topic. This theory suggests that **the media can't tell the audience what to think but can tell them what to think about** by **foregrounding**, discussing, and repeating issues which set a frame of reference for how the public perceive the issue.

Maxwell McCombs and Donald Shaw, in their 1972 study, looked at how people engaged with political advertising, positing the Agenda Setting function theory which has as its cornerstones, **framing, priming and gatekeeping**. Donald Trump, prior to, and during his term as 45th President of the United States attempted to **set the agenda** regarding topics that would resonate with his base. In particular, Trump played on his audience's conservative ideologies by leaning into issues regarding race, crime, and nationalism. The **agenda setting theory** can be used as a vehicle to examine how Trump's rhetoric shaped the American political and cultural landscape.

Framing (selection): Trump spins his narrative by using **emphasis** whereby he highlights issues of importance to him and his base, and **exclusion**, whereby he **omits information** that does not suit his narrative. For instance, Trump uses the **propaganda technique of repetition** by constantly discussing issues to do with illegal immigration. He **foregrounds** that America needs to be strong on Mexicans crossing the border illegally. To this end Trump employed the **glittering generality** of "build a big, beautiful wall" that would supposedly run the length of the Mexican/American border to prevent illegal immigrants from crossing. Trump claimed that Mexico would pay to build the wall, however, in the true nature of **glittering generalities** the information given by Trump was vague and remained vague throughout his tenure. Trump used **emphasis** to foreground the issue by highlighting its perceived importance, placing immigration high on his agenda, and flooding the media landscape with succinct, digestible soundbites to reinforce his narrative, such as in his January 23, 2019, tweet where he claimed @realDonaldTrump BUILD A WALL AND CRIME WILL FALL.

Trump **excludes** information that does not support his narrative. He uses the **agenda setting** technique of **exclusion** by simply avoiding discussing any point that does not portray him and his policies positively. For instance, during a Presidential Republican debate between Trump and Governor Bush aired on Fox News, the moderator Chris Wallace told Trump, "It has not escaped anybody's notice that you say that the Mexican government is sending criminals, rapists, and drug-dealers across the border. Governor Jeb Bush called those remarks 'extraordinarily ugly'. I'd like you, you're right next to him, talk to him directly and say how you respond to that ... and you have repeatedly said that you have evidence that the Mexican government is doing this but that you have evidence that you have refused or declined to share. Why not use this first Republican Presidential debate to share your proof with the American people" (Time, 2015).Trump does not share any definitive proof, instead he uses the **propaganda technique of name**

Propaganda and Trump

calling by stating, "If it weren't for me you wouldn't even be talking about illegal immigration" as we hear the crowd cheering in the background he continues by stating that "this was not a subject on anybody's mind until I brought it up at my announcement and I said Mexico is sending...except the reporters, because they are a very dishonest lot generally speaking in the world of politics, they didn't cover my statement the way I said it" (Time, 2015).

Trump then goes on to reiterate how the lack of sufficient border security has encouraged "many killings, murder, crime, drugs pouring across the border" and how America needs to build a wall to stop the problem. Trump **excludes** any actual evidence of these events, rather preferring to hype up his audience using emotion rather than facts.

Trump's agenda, prior to and during his presidency was immigration and the economy. He **primed** his audience to see him as a president willing and able to decrease debt, increase wages, and increase employment opportunities by deliberately selecting or **card stacking** information to frame himself in a positive light. For example, a tweet from @realDonaldTrump in 2017 stated that, "national debt fell by 12 million as opposed to 2 million in Obama's first month in presidency." Trump does not contextualise where the money came from to repay the debt, instead claiming credit and **framing** himself as the saviour of the nation.

The Coronavirus hit three years into Trump's presidency. Initially Trump downplayed its severity calling it the "China Virus" using **name calling** as a propaganda tactic to deflect blame from himself and onto the Chinese government. Trump did release an address to the nation in an attempt to showcase his handling of the virus. The video used propaganda techniques of **selection and omission** to showcase his 'efficient' handling of the pandemic whilst **omitting** any coverage that pointed to the delays in reacting to the pandemic which could have saved countless lives. For instance, Trump looked into the camera and stated, "At the very start of the outbreak...we declared a public health emergency and issued the highest level of travel warning on other countries as the virus spread its horrible infection. Taking early and intense action we have seen fewer cases of the virus in the United States then are now present in Europe..." (CNBC, 2020). Trump initially referred to the Coronavirus as a flu, downplaying its severity. On a CNN news report Trump stated, "There's only one person that came into the states with Covid 19, and that we're handling it." Trump's **selection of detail** attempted to show him handling the pandemic masterfully, however, statistics and facts don't lie. Trump delayed mandatory testing and vaccinations, he mocked people who wore masks, and he withdrew America from the World Health Organisation, leading to the unnecessary deaths of 450 000 Americans (Bor et al., 2021).

The agenda setting theory refers to **priming** as the time and space given to a news topic to facilitate its spread. As a tool of propaganda, **repetition** is used by Trump to **prime** his audience by consistently flooding the media landscape with his easily digestible messages. His **agenda is set** through

Propaganda and Trump

priming his audience with phrases such as "build a wall" in reference to his desire to cater to immigration policy, or having his crowds at rallies chant "USA, USA" or "Make America Great Again" to heighten their connected nationalism. Moreover, Trump **primes** his audience by connecting through vehicles of convenience, he was not the first American President to use social media, however, he was the first to do so prolifically. He tweeted more than 57,000 times at his twitter handle @realDonaldTrump and his official @Potus account before both were suspended in January of 2021 due to the claims of Trump inciting violence regarding the Capitol riots and his subsequent re-election loss.

Within the Agenda Setting theory **gatekeeping** refers to people, such as a news editor, who decides on the content of media publications. Even before he was President, Trump railed against media institutions **name calling** them "fake news" and "lame stream media." Trump deployed many sensational sound bites such as claiming some illegal Mexican immigrants to be rapists and drug dealers. Trump avoided traditional **media gatekeepers** by garnering support from right wing outlets such as Fox News, Murdoch press, and the Infowars talk show hosted by Alex Jones. He created a space which operated to disseminate and echo his major ideological issues on race, the environment, and later anti-vaxers when Coronavirus hit. Trump was able to exaggerate and lie, having found a megaphone in these right wing outlets. As journalists from the left tried to investigate Trump's numerous lies, they found themselves drowning in lie after lie after lie. All politicians lie, however, according to Forbes.com Trump told an average of 23.3 lies per day. The Independent.co.uk supports this through their research, finding that Trump told 21 lies per day. By saturating his environment with lies it became difficult to navigate the terrain between facts, opinion, and outright lies. Mainstream media were name-called by Trump, calling them "lame stream media" or "fake news" whenever they attempted to call him out on his lies. The media's role as **gatekeeper,** their attempts to keep him honest, where constrained by Trump who deflected with nasty, and continuous **name calling.** For instance, his tweet @realDonaldTrump 26/3/19 "The Fake News Media has lost tremendous credibility with its corrupt coverage of the illegal Democrat Witch Hunt of your all-time favorite duly elected President, me! T.V. ratings of CNN & MSNBC tanked last night after seeing the Mueller Report statement. @FoxNews up BIG!" Trump is referring to Russian meddling in the 2016 Presidential campaign, particularly in relation to data handed over to Russia regarding which states could swing towards Trump and how this could be moulded to ensure his success. Robert Mueller was tasked with investigating whether Trump colluded with the Russians. His investigation did not totally exonerate Trump but did not implicate him either. However, people close to Trump were either fined or jailed regarding Russian election interference.

Propaganda techniques and agenda setting do impact media content by laying the groundwork for how issues can be perceived by the audience through **priming, selection, and gatekeeping** of information, and by emotionally connecting to the audience through **propaganda techniques such as name calling, glittering generalities, and repetition**. As the agenda setting theory claims, t**he media cannot tell us what to think but they can lay the groundwork for what to think about**, as shown by Donald Trump's tenure as President whereby he used **propaganda techniques such as repetition** to encourage people to think about his agenda of nationalism as well as getting them to question the reliability of media information.

Propaganda

Why is propaganda dangerous?

A propagandist's goal is to give you an easy path to follow, to point you in the direction they want you to take, steering you towards the path of least resistance. As propaganda appeals to a person on an emotional level, not a logical fact-based level, being led by emotions rather than factual evidence can lead to irrational and illogical decision making.

How can we we tackle propaganda?

1. Education: critical literacy and media literacy are the main weapons to counter propaganda techniques. If people are aware of propaganda techniques, they will be less susceptible to manipulation.
2. Fact check: a builder is told to measure twice, cut once; in our media ecosystem we should read once and fact check at least twice by using a variety of reliable, authentic sources.
3. Journalism: support independent reliable journalism. Always question the agenda of the institution producing content and authenticate the source.

The perils of propaganda include its ability to obscure reason, facts and evidence. The propagandist emotionally manipulates people, steering them towards a potentially dangerous outcome.

The Institute of Propaganda Analysis coined seven terms to describe propaganda techniques prevalent during World War Two. Since then, additional techniques have been included to describe how propagandists manipulate their message to connect with their primary audience. The original seven propaganda techniques are name calling, bandwagon, glittering generalities, card stacking, testimonial, transfer, and plain-folks (Institute for Propaganda Analysis, 1938, p iv).

The purpose of the Institute of Propaganda Analysis is clearly stated in its name, it was formed as a non-profit organisation whose aim was primarily to educate American school children and adults about propaganda techniques and their effects. The institute wanted to arm the American public with critical thinking skills to avoid "attempts to persuade them to do something that they might not do if they were given all of the facts." (Institute for Propaganda Analysis, 1938, p iv). Unfortunately, eighty five years later our media saturated landscape has become a hotbed of propaganda, and critical thinking skills are needed more than ever.

How Trump used Propaganda

Propaganda Technique	How Trump used it
1. Name calling	Done to discredit, delegitimise, and create negative associations towards the name called person. The technique diverts attention away from Trump's ineptitude and attempts to implicate others without examining any evidence. • On March 26, 2019, Trump tweeted from his personal account @realDonaldTrump, "The Fake News Media has lost tremendous credibility with its corrupt coverage of the illegal Democrat Witch Hunt of your all time favorite duly elected President, me! T.V. ratings of CNN & MSNBC tanked last night after seeing the Mueller Report statement. @FoxNews up BIG!" (Trump, 2019). This tweet vilifies CNN and MSNBC as news organisations, chastises the Democratic Party for acting within their congressional powers, and favours himself as the one with integrity. • "When Mexico sends its people, they're not sending their best... They're not sending you. They're not sending you. They're sending people that have lots of problems, and they're bringing those problems with them. They're bringing drugs. They're bringing crime. They're rapists. And some, I assume, are good people." June 16, 2015, at the announcement rally of his Presidential Candidacy. Calling Mexicans rapists and drug dealers allows Trump to be a 'saviour' on immigration issues. • Donald Trump repeatedly called Hillary Clinton "Crooked Hillary." The connotation of crooked evokes negative emotions of stealing and cheating, thereby laying the groundwork for him to appeal to audience emotion and ask them to view her in a negative light rather than have them focus on actual policies. • The New York State Attorney General, Letitia James, brought a civil suit for fraud against Donald Trump in 2023. He responded by calling her a 'deranged lunatic' and a 'monster.' • Trump was indicted by Jack Smith, Special Prosecutor, for his alleged theft of classified documents and his involvement in the January 6th 2021 coup attempt. On social media and during interviews Trump has called Smith 'psycho', 'Trump hater', 'deranged', 'thug', 'crackhead' and more.
2. Plain folks or common man	The plain folks approach allows the average common person to see aspects of themselves in the authoritative person. Connections can be made via aspects such as language, clothing, food, entertainment or beliefs. • Through simplistic language in Trump's slogans such as BUILD A WALL & CRIME WILL FALL! and MAKE AMERICA GREAT AGAIN! He connects with 'plain folk' or 'common' people as the language is easily digestible. • Trump's use of the MAGA (Make America Great Again) baseball cap creates an image of him being approachable, a man of the people. • By having every day 'common' people come up on stage with him at a rally, or appear next to him for a photo shoot, suggests that Trump is friendly, open and welcoming.

How Trump used Propaganda

Propaganda Technique	How Trump used it
3. Testimonial	• Citing a testimonial from an authority figure coupled with the transfer propaganda technique allows the reputation of the person giving the testimonial to be used to sanction an idea, cause, belief or person. Authority figures such as Sarah Palin, Tucker Carlson and Sean Hannity are used to endorse Trump's agenda. Celebrities who endorse him such as Kanye West, Dennis Quaid, Roseanne Barr, and Jon Voight lend their testimonial weight to his campaign.
4. Card stacking or selective omission	**Stacking the deck in your favour to influence audience opinion by only telling a small portion of the truth. The user selects and emphasises specific information whilst ignoring or omitting evidence that does not lend weight to their argument.** • Donald Trump's response to Covid 19 whereby he ignored the scientists and stated, "It's one person coming in from China, and we have it under control. It's going to be just fine' (Trump, 2020). His statement card stacks by suggesting that one person carrying the virus will be 'fine.' • Trump told convention delegates in Cleveland on July 21, 2016, as he accepted his Republican nomination for President, "No one knows the system better than me," he said pausing to smile, "which is why I alone can fix it." Let's consider the facts, Trump has filed for corporate bankruptcy six times, and was financed by his father, Fred Trump, his record for managing finances and understanding 'the system' is not good.
5. Bandwagon	**Jump on the bandwagon, join in the crowd, is a technique that attempts to persuade the audience to take the same course of action as everyone else. It uses the fear of missing out, rejection, and isolation to emotionally manipulate the audience to sidestep evidence in favour of joining in.** • Trump's rallies consist of showmanship, he constructs them with a "you don't want to miss out" feeling. His rallies have marching bands and a carnival feel. • Trump consistently claims to be the best. The bandwagon effect is one whereby other people would perceive that Trump has support and feel compelled to join (or investigate why) his actions or intellect are being praised. Tweet Part 1: @realDonaldTrump 6/1/18, "…. actually, throughout my life, my two greatest assets have been mental stability and being, like, really smart. Crooked Hillary Clinton also played these cards very hard and, as everyone knows, went down in flames. i went from VERY successful businessman, to top T.V. Star…" Tweet part 2: @realDonaldTrump 6/1/18 "….to President of the United States (on my first try). I think that would qualify as not smart, but genius….and a very stable genius at that!"

Propaganda and Trump

Propaganda Technique	How Trump used it
6. Repetition	**Repeating information continually to force others to engage with your agenda.** Trump repeats and repeats his contention, without being supported by facts, that Mexicans are streaming over the border, committing crimes and taking jobs away from Americans. His rhetoric plays into his primary audience's base fears of unemployment and displacement by drawing on ideological beliefs about race in relation to xenophobia. Trump stoked a fire regarding racial tensions to further his narrative. Instead of uniting a nation, he divided it. • "Law and order candidate" - repeated numerous times but first heard during his closing speech at the Republican National Convention. • "I alone can fix it." • "Rigged election." • "Stolen election."
7. Scapegoating	**Attributing blame to others to distract or avoid personal responsibility.** • Rather than accept blame for his inaction and ineptitude over the handling of the Covid crisis Trump deflected by slurring others, calling the virus the 'Kung Flu' and the 'foreign virus.'
8. Stereotyping	**Using a few traits to represent a group, usually in a negative manner.** • "I've been treated very unfairly by this judge. Now, this judge is of Mexican heritage. I'm building a wall, OK? I'm building a wall. I am going to do very well with the Hispanics, the Mexicans" (Kertscher,2016). In this quote Trump is making racially charged accusations against the judge to elicit an emotional reaction from his base.
9. Oversimplification	**Presenting a solution in an overly simplistic manner.** Donald Trump's oversimplification of building a wall to solve the illegal immigration problem and having the Mexican government pay for it is a prime example of using an oversimplified logical fallacy to hide the flaws in his statement. • "BUILD A WALL & CRIME WILL FALL!" • "We're going to build a wall, and Mexico's going to pay for it." • "The media has not reported that the National Debt in my first month went down by $12 billion vs. a $200 billion increase in Obama first mo."

Propaganda and Trump

Propaganda Technique	How Trump used it
10. Emotional Appeal	**Pathos - appeal to fear, happiness, need to belong and so on.** More often, the appeal to fear is used as a scare tactic to persuade audiences to accept an idea. • "When Mexico sends its people, they're not sending their best…They're not sending you. They're not sending you. They're sending people that have lots of problems, and they're bringing those problems with us. They're bringing drugs. They're bringing crime. They're rapists. And some, I assume, are good people." June 16, 2015, at the announcement rally of his Presidential Candidacy (C-SPAN, 2015). Trump connects to his base by inciting fear when he suggests that the increase in crime is caused by immigrants. His statements bear no relationship to fact. • Emotional appeals garner audience interest. Consider Trump and his anger at Hillary Clinton and how he used this to provoke his audience into action, chanting "lock her up,' his audience extracted pleasure from his argument.
11. Loaded Words	**Use of terms which are emotionally charged with an aim to influence** the audience by exploiting their vulnerabilities. Words that are 'loaded' or have strong connotations are words like superior, immigrant, pro-life and freedom. Or, provoking words such as attack, stolen, lies, or stupid. Loaded language contributes to how a group, cause, or idea can be perceived.
12. Glittering generalities	**Use of appealing but vague virtue words and images to create a strong emotional response.** These words and images are saturated in positive connotations such as freedom, honesty, great, brave, devoted, caring, intelligent, friendly, justice, peace and so on. People of virtue, who are seen to have a strong moral compass, believe in upholding these ideals. By using virtue words, the propagandist aligns themselves with the word's connotation thus positioning the audience to view the propagandist in favourable terms. • Donald Trump's slogan "Make America Great Again" uses words with emotional connotations that present no specific facts about when America was great or what was great about it. The slogan is catchy, but in fact says nothing specific. • Tweet: @realDonaldTrump 17/3/16 "MAKE AMERICA GREAT AGAIN!" The statement suggests that America was once great, but for whom? Not for minorities, not for women.
13. Transfer	**Transfers the positive power from something like an authority figure or symbol onto an idea or issue to make it palatable and acceptable.** E.g., Trump uses orchestrated rallies to bolster his image as being powerful, sought after, and popular.

PROPAGANDA

Trend of social media use

How do trends affect media consumption?

The evolving media landscape has seen significant changes in how people share, create, and consume media. The rise of social media platforms and their inclusion in the political campaign marketing process during the 2016, 2020 and 2024 American presidential elections has had significant repercussions

The impact of social media trends on media consumption during Donald Trump's presidential campaign include:

- Using social media platforms such as Twitter in the 2016 campaign and Truth Social in the 2024 campaign to **disrupt the delivery of news** originating from traditional media outlets such as newspapers, television, and radio; by cutting out the middle-man no censorship or gatekeeping occurred. The message was delivered to Trump's supporters without mediation. The issue with this is clear, no mediation means no fact-checking. No fact-checking means that people like Trump can spew their unfiltered opinions as if they are fact.

- The **credibility of news** in all forms is now critiqued and challenged due to the scourge of fake news on social media. The rise of fake news and 'alternate facts' arose from Trump as his connection with the truth is limited. His fact-checked count of falsehoods and misleading claims number in the tens of thousands which creates a significant issue as users are finding it harder than ever to know if news content is credible, reliable, and authentic. To authenticate claims use sites such as FactCheck.org, The Washington Post Fact Checker, Reuters Fact Check or AP Fact Check.

- The timeline for traditional news outlets to deliver information is longer as editors, journalists, and media staff check content and verify sources. Social media delivery disrupts this model as it is **immediate, and it instantly disseminates information and disrupts the traditional time based model** of receiving news content. The immediate and real time availability of news content as it is happening is a media trend that **challenges the gatekeeping role of legacy media outlets.** The power associated with traditional media outlets has diminished as Trump's tweets and social media presence allow him to **frame content and set his own news agenda.**

- The **impact of hashtags** on social media allows for topics to trend faster than on legacy media. For instance, Donald Trump's #Stopthesteal promoted baseless claims of election fraud. The content circulated widely due to having a catchy sound bite and being easily consumable.

- Social media has transformed how people consume media by **fragmenting the audience base into segments across many platforms.** For instance, people who get their news source from Truth Social are hearing unfiltered content from Trump. The information is not fact checked and often is designed to connect with emotions rather than being factual. During the lead-up to the 2020 election Trump's social media was littered with claims of the "big lie." He used hashtags such as #RiggedElection! or tweeted "I WON THE ELECTION, BY A LOT," both claims are not supported by evidence.

- **Algorithmic delivery of content** on social media is problematic as it creates an **echo chamber** of ideas that have the potential to polarise people as they are unlikely see content that is not tailored to their existing preferences and value systems. For example, Trump continuously makes the false

Propaganda, Trump and Trends

claim that the 2020 election was rigged, and that voter fraud occurred, circulating this via social media to his pro-Trump base. Despite not having any evidence to show that these statements were true, Trump's base spread the information to engage people with similar beliefs and values thus **weaponising social media and reinforcing their echo chamber of ideas.**

- The **interactive nature of social media** allows for users to re-tweet, share, like, and use hashtags, thus disseminating the content further and ensuring it is spread far and wide. For instance, at 1.8 million retweets "Tonight, @FLOTUS and I tested positive for COVID-19. We will begin our quarantine and recovery process immediately. We will get through this TOGETHER!" the tweet highlights that Trump, and his wife Melania contracted Covid and was a rare personal message that did not contain any insults. Trump's frequently used and circulated hashtags include:
  ➡ #MAGA — Make America Great Again
  ➡ #AmericaFirst in reference to promoting his America First agenda
  ➡ #FakeNewsMedia — an attempt to discredit any authentic or reliable news sources
  ➡ #BuildTheWall — in reference to building a wall between Mexico and America to stop illegal immigration.

- Along with social media has come **the use of bots to artificially inflate the popularity of specific social media posts.** In the 2016 American presidential campaign research claimed that one in five election related tweets originated from a bot not a human. The 2024 campaign has the added assistance of artificial intelligence to enhance the bot's plausibility, making it sound more convincing and harder to detect disinformation. The toxic use of bots and AI to maliciously spread information such as #Crooked Hillary used to suggest that Hillary Clinton, the 2016 Democratic nominee for President was engaged in illegal acts and was therefore untrustworthy, was a baseless claim; however, it had the intended effect of sowing doubt, and in quite a few cases, ensuring people voted for Trump.

- Trump's use of social media has **blurred the lines between news and marketing.** He uses his social media voice to fundraise on platforms like Facebook, Truth Social, and in the past, Twitter. For instance, Trump was convicted of thirty four felony counts in 2024 as he was found guilty of falsifying business records to conceal payments he made to a porn star to prevent her from discussing their affair as he was in the lead up to the 2016 presidential election. Immediately after Trump's conviction was announced his social media presence increased with him claiming that the court case was a 'rigged trial', a 'witch hunt' and he urged people to 'stand with Trump' by donating whatever they could. His social media narrative portrayed him as being a victim and raised fifty million dollars in the 24 hours following his conviction.

- Trump's use of social media allowed him to **bypass the traditional news making cycle** and deliver content directly to his supporters. His controversial and provoking tweets in the 2016 campaign shaped the news cycle. By leveraging social media to divert attention away from issues he did not want his followers to engage with, Trump controlled the narrative with content that suited his **agenda.**

Propaganda: Germany vs America

Propaganda: Nazi Germany 1930s	Propaganda: Florida 2020s
How did Adolf Hitler shape German culture and ideology?	**News headlines showing how Ron DeSantis, Governor of Florida, shaped American culture and ideology.**
1. **Education:** influence education by carefully controlling and approving school curriculum; only allowing textbooks and teachers who supported their ideologies of nationalism and racism. • Teachers needed to support the Nazi party's ideological view, if not, they lost their jobs. • Laws were created aimed at controlling people's ability to access information and education.	• "DeSantis defends banning African American studies course as black leaders call for action" (Atterbury,2023). • "More than 170 books about black historical figures and LGBT themes are under review in Florida schools as part of Ron DeSantis' crackdown on 'woke' literature in classrooms" (Hammer, 2023). • "Deletions from Florida textbooks will weaken history lessons, teacher say"(Brugal,2013). • "Florida Republicans New Bill May Be the Biggest Attack on Academic Freedom Yet" (Thakker, 2023). The bill allows for staff who have tenure to be reviewed 'at any time'.
2. **Book Bans** • May 10, 1933, books considered subversive were brought to massive bonfires where Nazi soldiers ushered students past as they threw the books into the flames. 80 000 books were burned in a symbol of nationalism.	• Floridian schools now require a 'certified media specialist' to approve books. Teachers have been forced to remove books from their classrooms that do not conform, or face criminal charges of up to five years in prison. • "Ron DeSantis' war on woke targets holocaust textbooks" (Murdowanec, 2023).
3. **Ensure no overt or public opposition or criticism**	• "Ron DeSantis is building a state where media criticism of him is no longer allowed" (Otten, 2023).
4. **Women's rights are eroded**	• "Ron DeSantis quietly signs Florida's 6-week abortion ban into law" (Dixon, 2023). • "Florida Will Now Be Ground Zero for the Abortion Wars in 2024" (Stern, 2024).
5. **Gestapo, state police**	• "How Gov. Ron DeSantis deploys state police to enforce political agenda" (Reinhard, 2023). • "DeSantis proposes a new civilian military force in Florida that he would control" (Contorno, 2021).

Propaganda: Germany vs America

Propaganda: Nazi Germany 1930s	Propaganda: Florida 2020s
How did Adolf Hitler shape German culture and ideology?	**News headlines showing how Ron DeSantis, Governor of Florida, shaped American culture and ideology.**
6. Persecuting the gay community	• "No, Florida can't 'kidnap' trans kids under proposed law, but it does affect custody disputes" (Abels, 2023). • "Ron DeSantis Signs 'Right to Discriminate' Law That Could Be Used Against LGBTQ+ Patients" (Ogles, 2023). • DeSantis introduced the "Parental Rights in Education Act" which constrain the instruction on gender and sexuality in schools. Consequently, schools removed books with LGBQTI content to avoid the "Don't Say Gay" bill.
7. Targeting racial minority groups (Jews)	• "DeSantis booed at vigil for Jacksonville shooting victims" (PBS NewsHour, 2023). • "NAACP: Black Folks, Do Not Come to Florida" (Womak, 2023).
8. Creating solidarity • Using visual symbols such as the swastika, flags, slogans, or phrases (Heil Hitler) holding emotionally charged rallies, having parades to create a 'community' or a sense of belonging, thus underpinning the bandwagon technique.	• Merchandise containing the MAGA (Make America Great Again) slogan is used to signal a connection with other Republicans. • Rallies are held with a carnival like atmosphere to reinforce the solidarity of Trump supporters.

A visual depiction of some of the books banned in individual schools and libraries in Florida.

Triumph of the Will

Leni Riefenstahl was commissioned by Hitler through the German **Propaganda Ministry** to make *Triumph of the Will,* a documentary recording the events at the **Nuremberg Rally** held September 4 through to 10th, 1934. Riefenstahl has always stated that her film functioned to record history, it was not propaganda. She claimed its stated function was to **truthfully record the establishment of the Third Reich** as they began their ascent to power. Until her death, Riefenstahl asserted that she was not a propagandist, despite *Triumph of the Will* **functioning as a prime example of Nazi propaganda.** She repeatedly stated that the film was a documentary comprising of actual footage, it was not fiction. Considering the fact that the Nuremberg rallies were held annually from 1933 to 1938 with the **sole purpose of showcasing and reinforcing Nazi power and military strength,** it seems questionable that Riefenstahl was totally unaware of the purpose of the rallies and their influence. However, with or without intent, the film uses **selection and omission, underpinned by propaganda techniques** to deliver its central message highlighting the power of Germany as it is being resurrected by Adolf Hitler after the devastating impact of World War 1. When we consider the choice of film language, coupled with the context of world events, *Triumph of the Will* did **influence attitudes and beliefs** regarding the Nazi movement and Hitler. Through her **aesthetic and technical film choices** Riefenstahl captured the Nuremberg Rally, promoted nationalism, and shaped the **representation** of Adolf Hitler.

Propaganda and agenda setting can shape how an audience perceives their world. **As propaganda is intentional,** with the aim of creating change, we can see how Hitler effectively used propaganda techniques to propel racist, nationalistic, and fascist beliefs and values of the Nazi movement. **Agenda setting** examines media influence looking at how media institutions can set the agenda regarding what news content the public consumes, and therefore thinks about. Nazi Germany of 1934 had Joseph Goebbels as the **Minister of Propaganda,** his function is clearly stated in his title; his job was to control the media and **set the agenda** to ensure German people were surrounded by Nazi approved ideologies. Propaganda techniques, agenda setting, and documentary techniques function to scaffold the delivery of content in *Triumph of the Will,* **framing information and priming** the intended German audience to engage with, and accept Nazi party anti-Semitic, nationalistic values, beliefs and ideologies.

- Year of production: 1934
- Type: German documentary
- Medium: black and white film
- Length: 114 minutes
- Language: German
- Director: Leni Riefenstahl
- Original music: Herbert Windt

Triumph of the Will

A deconstruction of the opening scene of *Triumph of the Will*, using film language including:
- codes
- documentary conventions
- and propaganda techniques employed by Leni Riefenstahl to create a pro-Hitler view of Germany, the Nazi party, and its nationalistic ideology.

An overlap occurs between codes, techniques, and conventions; the most applicable example has been supplied to highlight the film grammar being employed to shape Riefenstahl's message.

Propaganda Techniques

Transfer
A propagandist **uses the prestige and authority** of something that is respected by the intended audience and **'transfers' this respect** to a new object, person or idea. The film's opening scene depicts Hitler as a metaphorical saviour arriving to save the people of Germany. He emerges from the sky as 'God-like', a deity, descending from the clouds in a plane similar to Christ arriving to save his people. The **religious transfer** of feelings is displayed as reverence towards Hitler, and therefore by extension includes his ideas and policies. The **concept of transfer** is heightened by the propagandist's engagement in prayer during political rallies as it sanctions acts deemed as unpalatable.

Glittering generalities
The use of **virtue words** such as 'rebirth' and 'reborn Germany' that **appeal to emotion** are used to frame Hitler's leadership as a revival, suggesting positive connotations without providing any facts or substance to show what Hitler has achieved.

Card stacking
The propagandist **stacks the cards** to emphasise one side of the argument or issue. At the same time the propagandist **omits** facts that may muddy their argument, hence **stacking the cards in their favour**. Hitler's rally stacks the cards in favour of showing him as inspirational, authoritative, and a strong leader. **Selection of content** via low camera angles directs the audience to see Hitler as powerful. Cutaway shots focus on aspects within the crowd such as eager and excited faces, a mother moving her child toward Hitler for his 'blessing' and crowd shots showing adulation and rousing applause. Hitler's speech does not discuss authoritarian control, racism, or hint at any dissent, only unity and power are projected for all to see.

Triumph of the Will

Film codes

Plain folks
As contradictory as it appears Hitler is represented as a **common man** as well as a deity. Riefenstahl employs footage of Hitler as "one of the people" by showing him in a meet and greet scenario during the rally as he mingles with the crowd, thereby creating the connotation of being an ordinary person, a **common man.**

Bandwagon
Conformist behaviour: adopting certain behaviours such as saluting Hitler using the infamous "Sieg Heil" gesture is a **bandwagon propaganda technique** that encouraged people to follow the crowd and embrace a behaviour in order to fit in. The salute was made mandatory in 1933 thereby employing a powerful symbol of obedience and coercing German people to engage with Nazi ideology and unifying them through hate.

Visual motifs
- Stately old, established buildings and statues show historic roots. Moreover, their size and scale radiate culture and history.
- Festooned buildings showing the pageantry, gaiety, and enjoyment of the event.
- Nature: sky, clouds, fire, smoke and mist connect Hitler to the land and people.
- Soldiers marched en-masse showing unity, power, and discipline. Authority, dominance and power shown in the soldiers lining the route as Hitler's cavalcade passes. The unity of the soldiers marching the goose-step in their tens of thousands on such a grand scale depicts strength, order, and national unity.
- The imagery of the iconic swastika and the waving mass of flags created a mighty spectacle; one that projected supremacy.
- Hitler descended from the sky arriving as a suggested saviour or deity. This connotation is reinforced by choir music and the visual metaphor of his descent from the clouds suggesting a heavenly landscape.
- The image of a German mother and her little girl reaching out to give Hitler flowers is used to mediate any suggestion of him being a harsh dictator as he gently accepts the flowers from the innocent child. The **propaganda technique of transfer** is used effectively to humanise and soften Hitler, portraying him as kind and gentle, someone capable of leading with compassion.
- Long shots of the adoring, cheering crowd are used to construct an image of Hitler that suggests he is worshipped and admired. The crowd

Agenda setting: to create a powerful Germany Riefenstahl used visual motifs, selection and omission. For instance, uplifting music, low camera angles on Hitler to create a God like powerful feel, crowds chanting 'Sieg Heil' (hail victory), all show grandness and power through a constructed Nazi ideological lens.

Triumph of the Will

Film codes

are shown cheering in patriotic fervour which promotes the idea that Hitler was liked and loved.
- By having Hitler in **sunlight** rather than shadow, and filming him often using a **low camera angle**, represents him as a strong, courageous leader. The editing techniques employed by Riefenstahl frame Hitler as God-like.

Technical codes
- **Camera movements** create a sense of being connected to the crowd, even when Hitler is still. Riefenstahl employed the use of **tracks** to create motion during Hitler's speeches.
- **Editing** is rhythmic and choreographed creating a propaganda spectacle that showed Hitler as powerful and heroic.
- **Framing**: framed with flags and banners to link the Nazi symbols with the crowd.
- **Close ups** on Hitler are used to connect him to the audience.

Written codes
- What is the connotation of the film's **title**? Whose will? Whose triumph? Is Hitler's will and the Nazi party ideological triumph being **anchored** by the title?

Audio codes
- Nationalistic, rousing **music** creates a patriotic feeling.
- The film begins with a **voiceover** that anchors time and place: "Twenty years since the start of World War" a dissolve delivers the audience to the plane's cockpit showing mist sweeping around it. The innovative use of camera work acts as symbolism for Hitler's representation as being a saviour, someone who could return the German people to power.
- German crowds are shown smiling, happy, and worshipping Hitler, their adoration clear in their gestures as they **chant** "Sieg Heil."

Selection and omission
Triumph of the Will **selectively** used footage that glorified Hitler and the Nazi party. From Hitler's plane descending through the clouds arriving at Nuremberg, to being greeted by cheering crowds, are clear **choices** designed to create support for Nazi ideology. Any references to anti-semitic views or persecution of Jews are **omitted**. In addition, the film preferences large crowds rather than individuals to promote the idea of the collective and being a unified whole.

The conflation of documentary as bearer of truth can be seen via Riefenstahl's use of a clear linear narrative structure. She appropriates some art film aesthetics by selecting visual motifs and camera techniques to manipulate audience reaction. The power of the media and its ability to manipulate its audience is on full display in Triumph of the Will.

Propaganda Essential Content

Sample questions containing propaganda concepts:

1. Discuss how propaganda techniques are used to manipulate their intended audience.
2. Discuss how agenda setting can influence the audience's perception of an issue.
3. Discuss a media trend and how it has impacted media consumption.
4. Analyse how agenda setting influences public opinion on a topic or issue.
5. Discuss the role mainstream media plays in disseminating propaganda.
6. Discuss whether a modern audience is susceptible to media propaganda.

1. Be clear on what propaganda is. Define it. Have around three propaganda techniques you can discuss in detail in relation to a studied text.
2. Be clear on what agenda setting theory is and its associated drop-down list. Discuss the elements of framing, priming, and gatekeeping. Relate these elements to studied media content. What agenda is being pushed? Who benefits from it? Why?
3. Be clear on how propaganda and agenda setting have shaped the chosen media content.

Propaganda | Review

PROPAGANDA - main essential content to discuss:

01
- **Propaganda** is intentional and systematic; it attempts to persuade the audience to accept a posited idea according to a singular vision using persuasive techniques to influence beliefs, values, ideologies, and behaviours.

02
- **How does propaganda work?** Discuss the propagandist's intent, who are they aiming the message at in order to shape values and behaviours? What techniques have been used to guide the audience towards accepting the message? Analyse how repetition of the message has been employed.

03

Propaganda techniques		
• testimonials	• glittering generalities	• oversimplification
• card stacking	• name calling	• repetition
• common man	• transfer	• emotional appeal
• bandwagon	• scapegoating	• assertion
	• stereotyping	• Loaded words

04
- **Agenda setting** refers to how media institutions can set the agenda regarding what news content the public thinks about by foregrounding certain content, whilst omitting or marginalising other topics through limited coverage.

05
- **Agenda setting theory** (1972) posited by **Maxwell McCombs and Donald Shaw,** investigated the influence of the news media and found that **the media can't tell the audience what to think, but they can tell them what to think about**. This theory posits the notion that the news media has the power to influence by deciding which stories are presented to the public. Discuss:
1. **Framing:** what news content is selected and what omitted,
2. **Priming**: how much coverage is given to an issue,
3. **Gatekeeping**: what content is included or omitted by editors based on the values of the institution, the expectations of its audience, and the policies of the outlet.

Index

A

Actualities 13
Aesthetics 65, 66, 67, 68, 70, 71, 72, 83, 90
    Video game aesthetic 86
Agenda setting theory 252, 258, 283
Artificial intelligence 19, 21
    Artificial intelligence reshaping the film industry? 20
Audience 66, 200
    Audience demographics 198, 221
    Audience expectations 93
    Intended audience 197, 221
    Mainstream audience 66, 197, 221
    Niche audience 66, 197, 221
Audio codes 281
Australian New Wave 57
Auteur theory 25, 38, 52
    Andre Bazin 26
    Andrew Sarris 26, 27, 28, 31
    Commodification of the auteur 31
    François Truffaut 25
    Pauline Kael 27, 28, 29
    Pros and cons 30
    Tom Tykwer 35
        Epilog 35, 36, 37
        Run Lola Run 35, 36, 37

B

Bandwagon 271, 280
Bill Nichols 232
Bollywood 51
Book Bans 276
British New Wave 53

C

Card stacking 227, 256, 258, 271, 279
Celluloid film 11
Classical Hollywood 46, 80
Codes 65, 67, 115, 129, 132
    Audio codes 120
    Codes & conventions in Run Lola Run 162
    Symbolic codes 116
    Technical codes 122
    Written Codes 118
Coming of sound 15
Communication theories 197
    Agenda Seting theory applied to The True Cost 212, 213, 214, 215
    Agenda Setting Theory 204, 258, 259, 283
        Maxwell McCombs 283
    Cultivation Theory 206
    Diffusion of Innovation 203
    End of Audience 207
    Fandom Theory 207
    Hypodermic Needle 202
    Reception Theory applied to The True Cost 217, 219, 220
    Reception Theory: Stuart Hall 200, 206, 218
    Reinforcement Theory 203
    Semiotic Theory 205
    Spiral of Silence 205
    Two Step Flow 202
    Uses and Gratification 17, 208
    Uses and Gratifications applied to The True Cost 208, 209, 210, 211
Context 65, 137, 138
    Context shapes content 154
    Cultural context 137, 138
    Historical context 137, 138
    Political context 138
    Production context 93, 139
    Reception context 93, 139, 221
    Run Lola Run context analysis 140, 166
    The Bicycle Thieves context analysis 144
    The True Cost context analysis 147, 148, 149, 150
Conventions 65, 67, 115, 126, 127, 128, 135
    Art film conventions 70, 72

D

David Gauntlett 168, 171, 172
Digital media 169
Distribution and consumption 18
Documentary 223, 229
    Bill Nichols 232
        Expository mode 233
        Observational mode 234
        Participatory mode 235
        Performative mode 237
        Poetic mode 232
        Reflexive mode 236
    Codes and conventions 228
    Codes, conventions & techniques in The True Cost 238, 239, 240, 241, 242, 243, 244, 245, 246, 247
    Documentary conventions 225, 226, 250
    Documentary modes 225
    Persuasion techniques 225, 227, 250
    Subjective vs. objective 224
    The documentary's claim to truth 230, 231
Dogme '95 59
Donald Shaw 266, 283
D.W. Griffith 14

E

Echo chamber 22, 186, 253, 254, 274, 275
Emotional appeal 273
Everything Everywhere All at Once 94, 111

Index

F

Film Aesthetics 65, 67, 70, 71, 73, 90
   Film style 65
   Game aesthetic 83, 86
   Sound as an aesthetic 77
   sound as an aesthetic device 73
Film as art 43, 66
Film Movements 41, 42
   Australian New Wave 57
   Bollywood 51
   British New Wave 53
   Classical Hollywood 46
   Dogme '95 59
   Film as art 43
   Film Movement Timeline 41
   Film Noir 49
   French Impressionism 45
   French New Wave 42, 52, 83
   German Expressionism 47
   Hong Kong New Wave 55
   Italian Neo-Realism 50
   Japanese New Wave 54
   New Hollywood 56
   New Mexican Cinema 58
   Soviet Montage 42, 48
   Surrealism 42, 44
Film Noir 49
Film Style 65, 91
Framing 204, 258, 259, 266, 281, 283
François Truffaut 25
   Cahier du Cinema 25
French Impressionism 45
French New Wave 42, 52

G

Gatekeeping 283
Genre 93, 97
   Horror film 128
German Expressionism 47
Glittering generalities 256, 273, 279

H

Harry Potter and the Philosopher's Stone 103
Hollywood studio system 12
Hong Kong New Wave 55

I

Ideologies 185, 186, 195
   Dominant ideologies 193
Italian Neo-Realism 50

J

Japanese New Wave 54
Jump cuts 83, 84

K

Kinetograph 12
Kinetoscope 11

L

Lumière brothers 13

M

Mainstream audience 66
Manipulation of space 68, 69, 131
Manipulation of time 68, 74, 81, 130
   Flashback 75, 81, 82
   Flash forward 74, 81, 82, 85
   Temporal duration 68, 75, 83
   Temporal frequency 68, 75, 85
   Temporal manipulation
      Simultaneous time 83
      Slow motion 84
      Split screen 83
   Temporal order 68, 82
Maxwell McCombs 212, 259, 266, 283
Media trends 23, 63, 274
Memento 117
Montage 101
Motion Picture Patents Company 12

N

Name calling 270
Narrative 93, 95, 96
Narrative elements 93, 128
   Everything Everywhere All at Once 94
   Narrative structure and elements in The True Cost 242
Narrative structure 68, 93
   Innovative narrative structure 80, 81, 83
   Manipulation of narrative structure 68, 79
   Open-ended narrative 68
Narrative theories 80
   Binary oppositions 108
   Hero's journey 104
   Propp's theory 102
   Syd Field paradigm 110
   Todorov 80, 81
   Todorov's theory 106
New Hollywood 56
New Mexican Cinema 58
Niche audience 17, 18, 43

O

Oversimplification 159, 227, 256, 258, 272

P

Patents war 12
Persistence of vision 11
Personal expression 32, 65, 91
Plain folks 270, 280
Point of view 96, 98, 99, 250
Priming 204, 213, 258, 259, 283
Propaganda 8, 252, 253, 254, 255, 269, 270, 271, 282, 283

Index

Agenda Setting & Propaganda 258, 259
Propaganda and Trump 260, 261, 262, 263, 264, 265, 266, 267, 268, 272, 273
Propaganda: Germany vs. America 276, 277
Propaganda techniques 256, 257
Propaganda, Trump and Trends 274, 275
Triumph of the Will 278, 279, 280, 281

R

Realism 13, 15, 41, 50, 53, 56, 58, 66, 67, 69, 70, 91, 116, 120, 121, 144, 217, 224, 226, 229, 230, 234, 241
Repetition 272
Representations 157
   Challenge stereotypes 173
   David Gauntlett: Representation 168, 170, 172
   How are representations constructed? 157
   Problems with stereotyping 180
   Representations in Run Lola Run 162, 163, 164, 165
   Stuart Hall: Representation Theory 158, 159, 160
   Timeline for Women's Rights 174
Riefenstahl 248, 278, 279, 280, 281
Run Lola Run 35, 36, 37, 64, 70, 71, 72, 73, 74, 75, 76, 77, 78, 79, 80, 81, 82, 83, 84, 85, 86, 87, 88, 89, 99, 101, 107, 109, 136, 140, 142, 143, 156, 162, 163, 164, 165, 166

S

Scapegoating 227, 257, 258, 272
Selection and omission 65, 132, 133, 134, 165, 238, 281
Selective omission 271
Social media impact 18
Social media trends 274
Soviet Montage 42, 48
   Sergei Eisenstein 42, 58
Stereotyping 180, 227, 257, 258, 272
Story elements 93
Streaming services 18
Stuart Hall - Representation theory 158, 160, 181
Stuart Hall's Reception theory 200
Surrealism 42, 44
   Luis Buñuel 42, 58

T

Technicolor 16
Television 17
   Cable television 17
   Digital TV 17
   Video-on-demand 17
Testimonial 226, 257, 258, 271
The Bicycle Thieves 144, 193
The Lego Movie 105
Theme 96, 100
The Story of the Kelly Gang 14, 15
Three Billboards Outside Ebbing, Missouri 123, 124
Todorov 80, 81
Trends 21
   Film trends 22
   Social media trends 274
Triumph of the Will 278, 279, 280, 281

U

Uses and gratification 17

V

Values, attitudes & ideologies 183, 200
   Attitude 184, 195
   Dissemination of values and ideologies 188, 195
   Dominant, emerging & oppositional ideologies 187
   Ideology 184, 185, 195
   Value 184, 185, 195
   Values and attitudes in The Bicycle Thieves 193
   Values and ideologies in Hair Love 189, 190, 191, 192
   Values and Ideologies in Run Lola Run 167
Visual motifs 280

W

Warner Brothers 15
Women's Rights Movements 174
   First Wave 174
   Second Wave 175
   Third Wave 176
   Fourth Wave 177
Written codes 281

Media works

Analysed MEDIA ASSETS

- Cherry, M., Dowing, E., & Smith, B. (Directors). (2019) *Hair Love.* [Film] Sony Pictures Animation. Tykwer, T. (Director). (1998). *Run Lola Run* [Film] X Filme Creative Pool.

- Columbus, C. (Director). (2001) *Harry Potter and the Philosopher's Stone.* [Film] Warner Bros. Pictures.

- De Sica , V. (Director). (1948) *The Bicycle Thieves.* [Film] Produzioni De Sica.

- Docter, P. (Director). (2001) *Monsters Inc.* [Film] Pixar Animation Studios.

- Kwan, D, & Scheinert, D. (Directors). (2022). *Everything Everywhere All at Once* [Film] IAC Films, Gozie AGBO.

- Lord, P. (Director). (2014) *The Lego Movie.* [Film] Warner Animation Group.

- McDonagh, M. (Director). (2018) *Three Billboards Outside Ebbing, Missouri.* [Film] Fox Searchlight Pictures.

- Morgan, A. (Director). (2015) *The True Cost.* [Film] Untold Creative.

- Nolan, C. (Director). (2000) *Memento.* [Film] Summit Entertainment.

- Noun Project. (2021) *Noun Project.* [Icons] https://thenounproject.com/

- Riefenstahl, L. (Director). (1935) *Triumph of the Will.* [Film] Reichsparteitag Film.

- Tykwer, T. (Director). (1992) *Epilog.* [Film] Black Out Films.

- Tykwer, T. (Director). (1998) *Run Lola Run*. [Film] X Creative Filme

- Waititi, T. (Director). (2010) *Boy.* [Film] Whenua Films, Unison Films.

Works Cited

Film History
CHAPTER ONE

Bordwell, D., & Thompson, K. (2010). *Film History: an introduction* (3rd ed.). McGraw Hill Higher Education.

Cook, P. (Ed.). (2007). *The Cinema Book* (3rd ed.). Palgrave MacMillan.

Crosland, A. (Director). (1927). The Jazz Singer [Film]. Warner Bros. Pictures.

Elfassy Bitoun, R. (n.d.). A history of colour: The difficult transition from black and white cinematography. The Artifice. https://the-artifice.com/author/Racheleb

Good, R. (Director), & Benjamin (AI). (2018). Zone Out [Film]. Sci-Fi London 48 Hour Challenge.

Griffith, D. W. (Director). (1915). The Birth of a Nation [Film]. D.W. Griffith Productions.

Jackson, S., & Shirley, G. (n.d.). Restoring the world's first feature. National Film and Sound Archive of Australia. https://www.nfsa.gov.au/latest/story-kelly-gang

Layton, J. (Director & Writer). (n.d.). The dye transfer printing process [Video]. George Eastman Museum. https://www.provideocoalition.com/history-color-film-television/

Lumière, L., & Lumière, A. (Directors). (1895). La sortie des ouvriers de l'usine Lumière [Workers Leaving the Lumière Factory] [Film]. Lumière

Lumière, L., & Lumière, A. (Directors). (1896). L'Arrivée d'un train en gare de La Ciotat [The Arrival of a Train at La Ciotat Station] [Film]. Lumière.

National Museum of Australia. (n.d.). World's first feature film. Defining Moments. https://www.nma.gov.au/defining-moments/resources/world-first-film

Tait, C. (Director). (1906). The Story of the Kelly Gang [Film]. J. & N. Tait, Millard Johnson, & W. A. Gibson

Writers Guild of America. (2023, September 24). WGA and AMPTP reach tentative agreement [Press release].

Auteur Theory
CHAPTER TWO

Astruc, A. (1948, March 30). Du stylo à la caméra et de la caméra au stylo. L'Écran français.

Astruc, A. (1948). The birth of a new avant-garde: La caméra-stylo. L'Écran français.

Bazin, A. (1957). On the politique des auteurs. In J. Hillier (Ed.), Cahiers du Cinéma: The 1950s: Neo-Realism, Hollywood, New Wave (pp. 248-259). Harvard University Press.

Cahiers du Cinéma. (1954). Paris: Éditions de l'Étoile.

Bordwell, D. (2012, June 24). Octave's hop: Andrew Sarris. Observations on Film Art. http://www.davidbordwell.net/blog/2012/06/24/octaves-hop-andrew-sarris/

Eisenstein, S. (1942). The film sense (J. Leyda, Ed.). Harcourt, Brace & World, Inc.

Emerson, J. (2012, June 20). Andrew Sarris, auteurism, and his take on his own legacy. RogerEbert.com. https://www.rogerebert.com/scanners/andrew-sarris-auteurism-and-his-take-on-his-own-legacy

Hodsdon, B. (2017). The elusive auteur: The question of film authorship throughout the age of cinema. McFarland & Company.

Kael, P. (1963). Circles and squares. Film Quarterly, 16(3), 12-26.

Kael, P. (1971). Raising Kane. In The Citizen Kane Book. Bantam Books.

Kael, P. (1971, February 20). Raising Kane—I. The New Yorker. https://www.newyorker.com/magazine/1971/02/20/raising-kane-i

Sarris, A. (1962-1963). Notes on the auteur theory in 1962. Film Culture, (27), 1-8.

Sarris, A. (1968). The American cinema: Directors and directions, 1929-1968. New York, Dutton. https://www.provideocoalition.com/history-color-film-television/

Sims, D. (2018, March 27). Steven Spielberg's Netflix

Works Cited

fears. The Atlantic. https://www.theatlantic.com/entertainment/archive/2018/03/steven-spielbergs-netflix-fears/556550/

Truffaut, F. (1954). Une certaine tendance du cinéma français. Cahiers du Cinéma, 6(31), 15-29.

Tykwer, T. (Director). (1992) *Epilog*. [Film] Black Out Films.

Tykwer, T. (Director). (1998) *Run Lola Run*. [Film] X Creative Filme

Film Movements
CHAPTER THREE

Domenig, R. (2004, June 28). The anticipation of freedom: Art Theatre Guild and Japanese independent cinema. Midnight Eye. http://www.midnighteye.com/features/the-anticipation-of-freedom-art-theatre-guild-and-japanese-independent-cinema/

Dudrah, R. K. (2006). Bollywood: Sociology goes to the movies. SAGE Publications.

Eisenstein, S. (1949). Film form: Essays in film theory. Harcourt, Brace.

Fu, P., & Desser, D. (Eds.). (2002). The cinema of Hong Kong: History, arts, identity. Cambridge University Press.

Hanley, D. (2011, July). The British New Wave and its sources. Offscreen, 15(6). https://offscreen.com/view/british_new_wave

Kearns, M. (n.d.). The Cabinet of Dr. Caligari: Dark relationship with postwar Germany. The Artifice. https://the-artifice.com/the-cabinet-of-dr-caligari-dark-relationship-with-postwar-germany/

Merante, L. (2022). Media analysis: Understanding and applying media theory Y*ear 11*. Media and English Literacy.

Statista. (n.d.). Film industry in India - Statistics & facts. Retrieved September 25, 2024, from https://www.statista.com/topics/2140/film-industry-in-india/

Sterritt, D. (1999). The films of Jean-Luc Godard: Seeing the invisible. Cambridge University Press.

Von Trier, L., & Vinterberg, T. (2014). Dogme '95 manifesto and vow of chastity. In S. MacKenzie (Ed.), Film manifestos and global cinema cultures: A critical

Film Aesthetics
CHAPTER FOUR

Bordwell, D. (1979). The art cinema as a mode of film practice. Film Criticism, 4(1), 56–64.

Tykwer, T. (Director). (1998) *Run Lola Run*. [Film] X Creative Filme

Works Cited

CHAPTER FIVE
How narrative functions in a text

Bordwell, D. (1985). Narration in the fiction film. University of Wisconsin Press.

Borowitz, A., & Borowitz, S. (Writers), & Barnhart, D. (Director). (1990, September 10). The Fresh Prince Project (Season 1, Episode 1) [TV series episode]. In Q. Medina, W. Cosby, & D. Salzman (Executive Producers), The Fresh Prince of Bel-Air. NBC Productions; Quincy Jones Entertainment.

Campbell, J. (2008). The hero with a thousand faces (3rd ed.). New World Library.

Columbus, C. (Director). (2001). Harry Potter and the Philosopher's Stone [Film]. Warner Bros. Pictures.

Coppola, F. F. (Director). (1972). The Godfather [Film]. Paramount Pictures.

Dusi, N. (2005). Film studies, Run Lola Run, remake, videogames, storytelling, narrative variations, adaptation. Cinemascope, 2. http://www.academia.edu/710050/Film_studies_Run_Lola_Run_remake_videogames_storytelling_narrative_variations_adaptation

Eliot, T. S. (n.d.). Little Gidding. Columbia University. http://www.columbia.edu/itc/history/winter/w3206/edit/tseliotlittlegidding.html

Field, S. (1979). Screenplay: The foundations of screenwriting. Dell Publishing.

Kwan, D, & Scheinert, D. (Directors). (2022). *Everything Everywhere All at Once* [Film] IAC Films, Gozie AGBO.

Lord, P., & Miller, C. (Directors). (2014). The Lego Movie [Film]. Warner Bros. Pictures; Village Roadshow Pictures; RatPac-Dune Entertainment; Lego System A/S; Vertigo Entertainment; Lin Pictures.

Merante, L. (2022). Media analysis: Understanding and applying media theory *Year 11*. Media and English Literacy.

Nelmes, J. (Ed.). (2012). Introduction to film studies (5th ed.). Routledge.

Pramaggiore, M., & Wallis, T. (2005). Film: A critical introduction. Laurence King Publishing.

Propp, V. (1968). Morphology of the folktale (L. Scott, Trans.). University of Texas Press. (Original work published 1928)

Todorov, T. (1969). Grammaire du Décaméron [Grammar of the Decameron]. Mouton. (English version: Structural Analysis of Narrative)

Tykwer, T. (Director). (1998). Run Lola Run [Film]. X-Filme Creative Pool; Westdeutscher Rundfunk (WDR); Arte.

Vogler, C. (2007). The writer's journey: Mythic structure for writers (3rd ed.). Michael Wiese Productions.

CHAPTER SIX
Codes, conventions, techniques

Docter, P. (Director). (2001). *Monsters, Inc.* [Film]. Pixar Animation Studios; Walt Disney Pictures.

McDonagh, M. (Director). (2017). Three Billboards Outside Ebbing, Missouri [Film]. Fox Searchlight Pictures; Film4 Productions; Blueprint Pictures.

Merante, L. (2022). Media analysis: Understanding and applying media theory *Year 11*. Media and English Literacy.

Nolan, C. (Director). (2000). *Memento* [Film]. Newmarket Films.

Waititi, T. (Director). (2010). Boy [Film]. Whenua Films; Unison Films; New Zealand Film Commission.

Works Cited

CHAPTER SEVEN
How context affects content

ABC News. (2024, February 21). Plibersek warns clothing industry must turn back on 'fast fashion', as she considers intervention. ABC News. https://www.abc.net.au/news/2024-02-21/plibersek-warns-fast-fashion-considering-clothes-levy/103492154

De Sica, V. (Director). (1948). Ladri di biciclette [The Bicycle Thieves] [Film]. Produzioni De Sica.

Merante, L. (2022). Media analysis: Understanding and applying media theory *Year 11*. Media and English Literacy.

Morgan, A. (Director). (2015). The True Cost [Film]. Untold Creative; Life Is My Movie Entertainment.

Reuters. (2024, March 15). French lawmakers approve bill to apply penalties on fast fashion. Reuters. https://www.reuters.com/sustainability/french-lawmakers-approve-bill-apply-penalties-fast-fashion-2024-03-15/

TEDx Talks. (2023, September 22). The simple solution to fast fashion | Josephine Philips | TEDxLondonWomen [Video]. YouTube. https://www.youtube.com/watch?v=W03Bt0Ou6uo

The Economist. (2018). The true cost of fast fashion [Video]. YouTube. https://www.youtube.com/watch?v=tLfNUD0-8ts

Tykwer, T. (Director). (1998). Run Lola Run [Film]. X-Filme Creative Pool; Westdeutscher Rundfunk (WDR); Arte.

Wolfstreet. (2024). Too Many [Advertisement]. Ads of the World. https://www.adsoftheworld.com/campaigns/too-many

CHAPTER EIGHT
Stereotypes & representations

Always. (2014, June 26). Always #LikeAGirl [Video]. YouTube. https://youtube/joRjb5WOmbM

Blake, Y. (2019, December). For the love of fangirls [Video]. TED Conferences. https://www.ted.com/talks/yve_blake_for_the_love_of_fangirls

Business Insider (2018, January 15). Tarana Burke On How The #MeToo Movement Started And Where It's Headed [Video]. YouTube. https://youtube/u1Rb7TGgsp4

BuzzFeedVideo. (2015, April 10). If Male Athletes Were Asked Questions Aimed at Female Athletes [Video]. YouTube. https://youtube/3aT32m6UH7E

Capalbo, J. (2023, August 14). How much do NFL cheerleaders make? Pro Football Network. https://www.profootballnetwork.com/how-much-do-nfl-cheerleaders-make/

Crenshaw, K. (1989). Demarginalizing the intersection of race and sex: A Black feminist critique of antidiscrimination doctrine, feminist theory and antiracist politics. University of Chicago Legal Forum, 1989(1), 139-167.

CNN Business. (2017, March 7). Why we commissioned Wall St. 'Fearless Girl' [Video]. YouTube. https://youtube/8YZ7nh9ZiS0

Curtin, M. (2018, January 24). Are you on your phone too much? Average person spends this many hours on it every day. Inc. https://www.inc.com/melanie-curtin/are-you-on-your-phone-too-much-average-person-spends-this-many-hours-on-it-every-day.html

Dove. (2023, October 9). The Code | A Dove Film | Dove Self-Esteem Project [Video]. YouTube. https://youtube/reIQAmmpbO8

e.l.f. Beauty. (n.d.). So many dicks. Retrieved July 28, 2024, from https://www.elfbeauty.com/so-many-dicks/

ESPN. (2023, September 26). #1 PLAYER Caitlin Clark RESPONDS To OVERRATED Chants With 42 Points [Video]. YouTube. https://www.youtube.com/watch?v=PfpbavlzdAw

Ford Canada. (2023, March 31). Introducing the Ford Explorer® Men's Only Edition | Ford Canada [Video]. YouTube. https://youtube/ddIwSkXqFU8

Works Cited

Framestore. (2015, January 12). Sport England #ThisGirlCan [Video]. YouTube. https://youtube/dHPwnG4Mfc0

Friedan, B. (1963). The feminine mystique. W. W. Norton & Company.

Gauntlett, D. (2008). Media, gender and identity: An introduction (2nd ed.). Routledge.

Gauntlett, D. (2018). Making is connecting: The social power of creativity, from craft and knitting to digital everything (2nd ed.). Polity Press.

Glenday, J. (2023, December 20). Ad of the Day: Mothers for Democracy gun violence PSA rejects your 'thoughts and prayers'. The Drum. https://www.thedrum.com/news/2023/12/20/ad-the-day-mothers-democracy-gun-violence-psa-rejects-your-thoughts-and-prayers

Hall, S. (1997). Representation: Cultural representations and signifying practices. Sage Publications in association with The Open University. (Original work published 1979)

Karson, K., & Verhovek, J. (2017, July 17). 10 most common words Americans use to describe Trump: Quinnipiac University National Poll. ABC News. https://abcnews.go.com/Politics/10-common-words-americans-describe-trump-poll/story?id=48641706

Lamm, L. (2023, February 10). The Matilda Effect: How women are becoming invisible in science. Lost Women of Science. https://www.lostwomenofscience.org/news/the-matilda-effect-how-women-are-becoming-invisible-in-science

Lauzen, M. M. (2019). It's a man's (celluloid) world: Portrayals of female characters in the top grossing films of 2018. Center for the Study of Women in Television and Film, San Diego State University. https://womenintvfilm.sdsu.edu/wp-content/uploads/2019/02/2018_Its_a_Mans_Celluloid_World_Report.pdf

Marriage Amendment (Definition and Religious Freedoms) Act 2017 (Cth) (Austl.).

Married Women's Property Act 1884 (SA) (Austl.).

Merante, L. (2022). Media analysis: Understanding and applying media theory Year 11. Media and English Literacy.

Nielsen. (2018, July 31). Time flies: U.S. adults now spend nearly half a day interacting with media. https://www.nielsen.com/us/en/insights/article/2018/time-flies-us-adults-now-spend-nearly-half-a-day-interacting-with-media/

Nike. (2019, February 24). Dream Crazier | #JustDoIt [Video]. YouTube. https://youtube/zWfX5jeF6k4

Orange France. (2023, July 18). WoMen's Football / The Bleues' Highlights [Video]. YouTube. https://youtube/X_wLVRYHIS4

Ronaldo, C. [@cristiano]. (n.d.). [Instagram profile]. Instagram. Retrieved April 25, 2024, from https://www.instagram.com/cristiano/

P&G. (2016, April 27). Thank You, Mom - Strong | P&G [Video]. YouTube. https://youtu.be/rdQrwBVRzEg

Tykwer, T. (Director). (1998). Run Lola Run [Film]. X-Filme Creative Pool; Westdeutscher Rundfunk (WDR); Arte.

United Nations. (1995). Beijing declaration and platform for action. Fourth World Conference on Women, 15 September 1995, A/CONF.177/20. https://www.refworld.org/legal/resolution/un/1995/en/73680

U.S. Const. amend. XIX.

Walker, R. (1992). Becoming the third wave. Ms., 2(4), 39-41.

Xu, H., & Li, Y. (2024, February 8). '...Ready for it?': How Taylor is changing modern society. Pursuit. https://pursuit.unimelb.edu.au/articles/ready-for-it-how-taylor-is-changing-modern-society

Zhang, C., Roberson, A., & Shalby, C. (n.d.). 'Racist,' 'ignorant,' 'strong' – The words you used to describe Donald Trump. Los Angeles Times. Retrieved September 25, 2024, from https://www.latimes.com/projects/la-na-pol-trump-words/

Works Cited

CHAPTER NINE
Values, attitudes & ideologies

Cherry, M. A., Downing Jr., E., & Smith, B. W. (Directors). (2019). Hair Love [Animated short film]. Sony Pictures Animation.

De Sica, V. (Director). (1948). Bicycle thieves [Film]. Produzioni De Sica.

Merante, L. (2022). Media analysis: Understanding and applying media theory *Year 11*. Media and English Literacy.

CHAPTER TEN
Audience & communication theories

Blumler, J. G., & Katz, E. (Eds.). (1974). The uses of mass communications: Current perspectives on gratifications research. Sage Publications

Brunsdon, C., & Morley, D. (1999). The Nationwide television studies. Routledge.

Chbosky, S. (Director). (2012). The perks of being a wallflower [Film]. Summit Entertainment; Mr. Mudd.

Eco, U. (1979). A theory of semiotics. Indiana University Press.

Fleming, V. (Director). (1939). Gone with the wind [Film]. Selznick International Pictures; Metro-Goldwyn-Mayer.

Gerbner, G., & Gross, L. (1976). The scary world of TV's heavy viewer. Psychology Today, 10(4), 41-89.

Katz, E. (1957). The two-step flow of communication: An up-to-date report on an hypothesis. Public Opinion Quarterly, 21(1), 61-78

Lull, J. (1980). The social uses of television. Human Communication Research, 6(3), 197-209.

Lull, J. (1990). *Inside family viewing: Ethnographic research on television's audiences*. Routledge.

Merante, L. (2022). *Media Analysis: Understanding and Applying Media Theory Year 11* . Media and English Literacy

Morgan, A. (Director). (2015). *The True Cost* [Film]. Life Is My Movie Entertainment.

Morley, D. (1980). The 'Nationwide' audience: Structure and decoding. British Film Institute.

Noelle-Neumann, E. (1974). The spiral of silence: A theory of public opinion. *Journal of Communication*, 24(2), 43-51

Saussure, F. de. (1983). Course in general linguistics (R. Harris, Trans.). Duckworth. (Original work published 1916)

Works Cited

Documentary techniques
CHAPTER ELEVEN

Aufderheide, P. (2007). Documentary film: A very short introduction. Oxford University Press.

Chanan, M. (2007). The politics of documentary. British Film Institute.

Flaherty, R. J. (Director). (1922). Nanook of the North [Film]. Pathé Exchange.

Morgan, A. (Director). (2015). *The True Cost* [Film]. Life Is My Movie Entertainment.

Niinimäki, K., Peters, G., Dahlbo, H., Roos, S., Lyytimäki, J., Salminen, A., Seppälä, J., & Vähä-Nissi, M. (2020). The environmental price of fast fashion. *Nature Reviews Earth & Environment*, 1(4), 189-200. https://doi.org/10.1038/s43017-020-0039-9

Nichols, B. (2001). Introduction to documentary. Indiana University Press.

Winston, B. (Ed.). (2013). The documentary film book. British Film Institute.

Propaganda
CHAPTER TWELVE

Abels, G. (2023, May 4). No, Florida can't 'kidnap' trans kids under proposed law, but it does affect custody disputes. PolitiFact. https://www.politifact.com/article/2023/may/04/no-florida-cant-kidnap-trans-kids-under-proposed-l/

Atterbury, A. (2023, January 23). DeSantis defends banning African American studies course as Black leaders call for action. Politico. https://www.politico.com/news/2023/01/23/desantis-banning-african-american-studies-00079027

Belvedere, M. (2020, January 22). Trump says he trusts China's Xi on coronavirus and the US has it 'totally under control'. CNBC. https://www.cnbc.com/2020/01/22/trump-on-coronavirus-from-china-we-have-it-totally-under-control.html

Bor, J., Himmelstein, D. U., & Woolhandler, S. (2021, March 5). Trump's policy failures have exacted a heavy toll on public health. Scientific American. https://www.scientificamerican.com/article/trumps-policy-failures-have-exacted-a-heavy-toll-on-public-health1/

Brown, B. (2023). Trump Twitter Archive. https://www.thetrumparchive.com/?searchbox=%22national+debt+%22

Brugal, S. (2023, May 15). Deletions from Florida textbooks will weaken history lessons, teachers say. Miami Herald. https://www.miamiherald.com/news/local/education/article275444901.html

CNN. (2016, June 3). Donald Trump rails against judge's 'Mexican heritage' [Video]. YouTube. https://youtu.be/eKwps5fjjCY

CNBC Television. (2020, March 11). Watch President Donald Trump's address to the nation on coronavirus pandemic [Video]. YouTube. https://www.youtube.com/watch?v=xrPZBTNjX_o

Contorno, S. (2021, December 2). DeSantis proposes a new civilian military force in Florida that he would control. CNN. https://www.cnn.com/2021/12/02/politics/florida-state-guard-desantis/index.html

C-SPAN. (2015, June 16). Donald Trump Presidential Campaign Announcement Full Speech (C-SPAN) [Video]. YouTube. https://www.youtube.com/watch?v=apjNfkysjbM

Dixon, M. (2023, April 14). Ron DeSantis quietly signs

Works Cited

Florida's 6-week abortion ban into law. NBC News. https://www.nbcnews.com/politics/politics-news/ron-desantis-quietly-signs-floridas-6-week-abortion-ban-law-rcna79867

Fox Business. (2015, August 6). Trump: We will build a great wall along the southern border [Video]. YouTube. https://youtu.be/2J9y6s_ukBQ

Hammer, A. (2023, February 14). More than 170 books about black historical figures and LGBT themes are under review in Florida schools - as part of Ron DeSantis' crackdown on 'woke' literature in classrooms. Daily Mail. https://www.dailymail.co.uk/news/article-11748733/More-170-books-black-historical-figures-LGBT-themes-review-Florida-schools.html

Institute for Propaganda Analysis. (1938). Propaganda analysis: Volume I of the publications of the Institute for Propaganda Analysis. Institute for Propaganda Analysis.

Journeyman Pictures. (2020). The film the Trump Organization tried to suppress | You've Been Trumped Too (2020) | Full Film [Video]. YouTube. https://youtu.be/k9RweR9EUSg

Kertscher, T. (2016, June 8). Donald Trump's racial comments about Hispanic judge in Trump University case. PolitiFact. https://www.politifact.com/article/2016/jun/08/donald-trumps-racial-comments-about-judge-trump-un/

Markowitz, D. (2020, May 5). Trump is lying more than ever: Just look at the data. Forbes. https://www.forbes.com/sites/davidmarkowitz/2020/05/05/trump-is-lying-more-than-ever-just-look-at-the-data/

Merante, L. (2022). *Media Analysis: Understanding and Applying Media Theory Year 11*. Media and English Literacy

Murdowanec, N. (2023, May 12). Ron DeSantis' war on woke targets holocaust textbooks. Newsweek. https://www.newsweek.com/ron-desantis-war-woke-targets-holocaust-textbooks-1800493

Ogles, J. (2023, May 13). Ron DeSantis signs 'Right to Discriminate' law that could be used against LGBTQ+ patients. The Advocate. https://www.advocate.com/politics/ron-desantis-discriminate-law-lgbtq

Otten, T. (2023, March 23). Ron DeSantis is building a state where media criticism of him is no longer allowed. The New Republic. https://newrepublic.com/article/171264/ron-desantis-building-state-media-criticism-no-longer-allowed

PBS NewsHour. (2023, August 28). DeSantis booed at vigil for Jacksonville shooting victims. https://www.pbs.org/newshour/politics/desantis-booed-at-vigil-for-jacksonville-shooting-victims

Reinhard, B. (2023, May 5). DeSantis uses state police to enforce his political agenda. The Washington Post. https://www.washingtonpost.com/politics/2023/05/05/desantis-fdle-police-immigration-migrant-flights/

Stern, M. J. (2024, April 1). Florida will now be ground zero for the abortion wars in 2024. Slate. https://slate.com/news-and-politics/2024/04/florida-abortion-ban-constitutional-amendment-2024-desantis.html

The Lincoln Project. (2020, October 20). Security [Video]. YouTube. https://youtu.be/6O61jkz0DDI

The Young Turks. (2015, June 16). Donald Trump's 2016 presidential announcement - The Young Turks [Video]. YouTube. https://youtu.be/xrPZBTNjX_o

Thakker, P. (2023, February 25). Florida Republicans' new bill may be the biggest attack on academic freedom yet. The New Republic. https://newrepublic.com/article/170754/florida-republicans-new-bill-may-biggest-attack-academic-freedom-yet

Trump, D.J. (2022, July 4). Make America Great For Us Again [Video]. YouTube. https://youtu.be/9zwy05u6ncg

Trump, D. J. [@realDonaldTrump]. (2016, March 17).

Works Cited

MAKE AMERICA GREAT AGAIN! [Post]. X.

Trump, D. J. [@realDonaldTrump]. (2017a, February 17). The FAKE NEWS media (failing @nytimes, @NBCNews, @ABC, @CBS, @CNN) is not my enemy, it is the enemy [Post]. X.

Trump, D. J. [@realDonaldTrump]. (2017b, February 25). The media has not reported that the National Debt in my first month went down by $12 billion vs [Post]. X.

Trump, D. J. [@realDonaldTrump]. (2017c, June 23). The Fake News Media has never been so wrong or so dirty. Purposely incorrect stories and phony sources to meet their agenda of hate [Post]. X.

Trump, D. J. [@realDonaldTrump]. (2017d, November 29). Funny to hear the Democrats talking about the National Debt when President Obama doubled it in only 8 years [Post]. X.

Trump, D. J. [@realDonaldTrump]. (2018a, January 6). ....Actually, throughout my life, my two greatest assets have been mental stability and being, like, really smart. Crooked Hillary [Post]. X.

Trump, D. J. [@realDonaldTrump]. (2018b, January 6). ....to President of the United States (on my first try). I think that would qualify as not smart, but [Post]. X.

Trump, D. J. [@realDonaldTrump]. (2018c, May 4). Our Southern Border is under siege. Congress must act now to change our weak and ineffective immigration laws. Must [Post]. X.

Trump, D. J. [@realDonaldTrump]. (2018d, May 17). Despite the disgusting, illegal and unwarranted Witch Hunt, we have had the most successful first 17 month Administration [Post]. X.

Trump, D. J. [@realDonaldTrump]. (2018e, July 18). Some people HATE the fact that I got along well with President Putin of Russia. They would rather go [Post]. X.

Trump, D. J. [@realDonaldTrump]. (2018f, October 28). The Fake News is doing everything in their power to blame Republicans, Conservatives and me for the division [Post]. X.

Trump, D. J. [@realDonaldTrump]. (2018g, December 24). The Fake News refuses to talk about how Big and how Strong our BASE is. They show Fake [Post]. X.

Trump, D. J. [@realDonaldTrump]. (2019a, January 7). The Fake News will knowingly lie and demean in order make the tremendous success of the Trump Administration [Post]. X.

Trump, D. J. [@realDonaldTrump]. (2019b, January 23). BUILD A WALL & CRIME WILL FALL! [Post]. X.

Trump, D. J. [@realDonaldTrump]. (2019c, March 8). The Wall is being built and is well under construction. Big impact will be made. Many additional contracts [Post]. X.

Trump, D. J. [@realDonaldTrump]. (2019d, September 11). If it weren't for the never ending Fake News about me, and with all that I have done... [Post]. X.

Trump, D. J. [@realDonaldTrump]. (2019e, December 11). The News Media in our Country is FAKE and in many cases, totally CORRUPT [Post]. X.

Trump, D. J. [@realDonaldTrump]. (2019f, December 22). Now the Fake News Media says I "pressured the Ukrainian President at least 8 times during my telephone... [Post]. X.

Trump, D. J. [@realDonaldTrump]. (2020a, March 18). I always treated the Chinese Virus very seriously, and have done a very good job from the beginning, including... [Post]. X.

Trump, D. J. [@realDonaldTrump]. (2020b, April 11). So now the Fake News @nytimes is tracing the CoronaVirus origins back to Europe, NOT China. This is... [Post]. X.

Trump, D. J. [@realDonaldTrump]. (2020c, May 11). Great credit being given for our Coronavirus response, except in the Fake News. They are a disgrace to America [Post]. X.

Trump, D. J. [@realDonaldTrump]. (2020d, June 25). The number of ChinaVirus cases goes up, because

Works Cited

of GREAT TESTING, while the number of deaths (mortality [Post]. X.

Trump, D. J. [@realDonaldTrump]. (2020e, July 6). Why does the Lamestream Fake News Media REFUSE to say that China Virus deaths are down 39%, and [Post]. X.

Trump, D. J. [@realDonaldTrump]. (2020f, October 2). Tonight, @FLOTUS and I tested positive for COVID-19. We will begin our quarantine and recovery process immediately. We will [Post]. X.

Trump, D. J. [@realDonaldTrump]. (2020g, November 7). I WON THE ELECTION, BY A LOT! [Post]. X.

Trump, D. J. [@realDonaldTrump]. (2020h, November 14). People are not going to stand for having this Election stolen from them by a privately owned Radical [Post]. X.

Trump, D. J. [@realDonaldTrump]. (2020i, December 4). The only thing more RIGGED than the 2020 Presidential Election is the FAKE NEWS SUPPRESSED MEDIA. No matter [Post]. X.

Trump, D. J. [@realDonaldTrump]. (2020j, December 19). He didn't win the Election. He lost all 6 Swing States, by a lot. They then dumped [Post]. X.

Trump, D. J. [@realDonaldTrump]. (2021a, January 5). Washington is being inundated with people who don't want to see an election victory stolen by emboldened Radical [Post]. X.

Trump, D. J. [@realDonaldTrump]. (2021b, January 5). I hope the Democrats, and even more importantly, the weak and ineffective RINO section of the Republican Party [Post]. X.

Trump, D. J. [@realDonaldTrump]. (2021c, January 6). These are the things and events that happen when a sacred landslide election victory is so unceremoniously & viciously [Post]. X.

Trump, D. J. [@realDonaldTrump]. (2021d, January 8). The 75,000,000 great American Patriots who voted for me, AMERICA FIRST, and MAKE AMERICA GREAT AGAIN, will have [Post]. X.

Trump, D. J. [@realDonaldTrump]. (2021e, January 8). To all of those who have asked, I will not be going to the Inauguration on January 20th [Post]. X.

Time Staff. (2015, August 7). Transcript of the primetime Republican debate. Time. https://time.com/3988276/republican-debate-primetime-transcript-full-text/

Riefenstahl, L. (Director). (1935). Triumph of the will [Film]. Reichsparteitag-Film.

Wolf, B. (2017, April 20). Read this: How Trump defended criticism of judge for being "Mexican." CNN. https://edition.cnn.com/2017/04/20/politics/donald-trump-gonzalo-curiel-jake-tapper-transcript/index.html

Wolf, Z. B. (2017, April 20). Trump's history of anti-Mexican statements. CNN. https://www.cnn.com/2016/08/31/politics/donald-trump-mexico-statements/index.html

Womak, K. (2023, March 30). NAACP: Black folks, do not come to Florida. The Root. https://www.theroot.com/naacp-black-folks-do-not-come-to-florida-1850280303

Books in this series:
AVAILABLE

mediaandenglishliteracy.com

Merante, L. (2022). *Media Analysis: Understanding and Applying Media Theory* **Year 11**. Media and English Literacy

Merante, L. (2024). *Media Analysis: Understanding and Applying Media Theory* **Year 12**. Media and English Literacy

info@mediaandenglishliteracy.com

Merante, L. (2023). *Media Analysis:* **Compendium**. Media and English Literacy

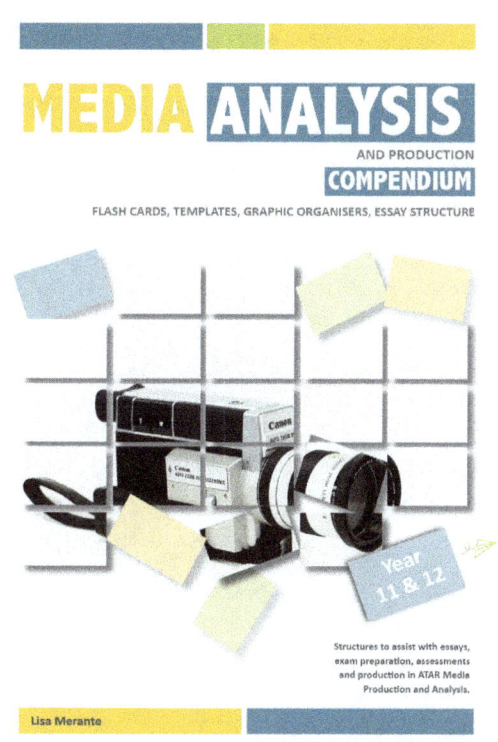

Merante, L. (2023). *Media Journal:* **Production Planning**. Media and English Literacy

www.ingramcontent.com/pod-product-compliance
Lightning Source LLC
Chambersburg PA
CBHW081417300426
44109CB00020BA/2355